FIRST FOOTSTEPS IN
EAST AFRICA

TRAVELLERS AND EXPLORERS

General Editor: Robin Hallett

FIRST FOOTSTEPS
IN
EAST AFRICA

by

SIR RICHARD BURTON

*Edited with an introduction and
additional chapters by*

GORDON WATERFIELD

FREDERICK A. PRAEGER, *Publishers*

NEW YORK · WASHINGTON

BOOKS THAT MATTER

Published in the United States of America
in 1966 by Frederick A. Praeger, Inc.,
Publishers, 111, Fourth Avenue,
New York 3, N.Y.

Library of Congress Catalog
Card Number: 66–14510

Printed in Great Britain

Contents

* New chapters and appendices contributed by Editor, based on official reports, mostly unpublished, and on other sources.

Illustrations

The animals and the *Somali horseman* were drawn by Captain A. G. C. Swayne
and are from his *Seventeen Trips through Somaliland*, Rowland Ward, 1895.

ILLUSTRATIONS

Somali girl, Somali with bow, and A Somali 'gurgi' are from Documents sur l'histoire, la geographie et le commerce de l'Afrique orientale by Juillain, Paris, 1857, (Photo Studios Ltd.). Sailing boat, Hills of the White Ant, The Slave Trade, and Berbera are from the Mansell Collection. Speke's Miraculous Escape from the Somalis is from his What Led to the Discovery of the Nile, Blackwood, 1864.

PLATES

MAPS

vii

Preface

THE INTEREST IN AFRICA has continued to increase since Richard Burton made his pioneer journeys to Harar and Lake Tanganyika only a little over a hundred years ago. There would be no need today for Burton to lament the lack of sales of books on Africa, as he did in a staccato note on the fly-leaf of his own copy of *First Footsteps in East Africa* published in 1856:

> The general reader fears to encounter Africa—squalid subject— want of historical associations—remains centre of want, disease, and death—the monotony of savagery—dullness in hair-breadths escapes which author robs of interest by living to tell his tale.

Burton's adventurous expedition to Harar, which is the main part of his *First Footsteps in East Africa*, was published in 1856, reissued in the memorial edition of his works in 1894 and again in 'Everyman's Library' edition in 1910. In this new edition Burton's story has been enlarged by the inclusion of his own reports to Government following his successful journey to Harar, and of the official reports after the attack on the camp at Berbera when Stroyan was killed while Burton and Speke were severely wounded. This new material from the India Office Library and from the Royal Geographical Society make up Chapters XI and XII and an Appendix. The sworn statements of Somalis and others are given to try to discover what really happened on that confused night of the attack on the camp.

The criticisms of Burton's conduct at Berbera contained in these official reports explain, I believe, his loss of influence with the Royal Geographical Society and supply the reason why the Society ignored Burton and chose Speke to organize the expedition to discover whether the Northern Lake (Lake Victoria Nyanza) was the source of the White Nile—a decision which ended Burton's career as an explorer.

This question was not touched on in previous editions of *First Foot-steps in East Africa*, nor was there any reference to the fact that the famous quarrel between Burton and Speke over the whereabouts of the source of the White Nile had had its beginnings on the Somali Expedition.

This re-issue follows the text of the memorial edition of 1894 which included, though not always entirely accurately, the corrections that Burton made on his own copy of the first edition, which is in the possession of the Royal Anthropological Society in London. It has been possible, therefore, to check the text with Burton's copy and some of his notes, which were omitted, have been included. The re-issue in 'Everyman's Library' followed the published first edition and did not take account of Burton's amendments.

Most of Burton's interesting Preface has been included in the Introduction in order to try to make the sequence of events a little clearer. Burton's four appendices, amounting to one hundred and sixty-one pages of the first edition, have been omitted, except for his short introduction to the Harari language. The only one of the appendices of interest today is 'the diary and observations made by Lieut. Speke when attempting to reach the Wady Nogal', but it is not included because it was severely edited by Burton and the full diary is available in *What Led to the Discovery of the Source of the Nile* by John Hanning Speke; Burton's comments have been included.

Burton had intended to publish another appendix, but the publishers of the first edition refused to issue it and it was lost; only the title was given, 'A brief description of certain peculiar customs noticed in Nubia by Browne and Werne under the name of [in]fibulation'. But as this book was going to press, it was learned that two pages of Burton's appendix, bound by mistake in one copy of the first edition, had been found by Mrs Fawn Brodie of California; she most generously allowed them to be published fot the first time in this edition, although she is herself writing a biography of Burton. (See appendix 2.)

Most of Burton's many notes are entertaining and have been in-cluded, but some have been omitted owing to their great length or to their irrelevance. The briefer notes relating directly to the text have been retained at the bottom of the pages concerned, while others are at the end of the book and are referred to by numbers in the text.

I have kept as much as possible to Burton's spelling which is sometimes inconsistent but clear enough; he often puts capitals to the names of birds and plants, uses Somali terms which are not put in italics, sometimes invents words, uses archaic forms and includes foreign expressions (again not always in italics), because he did not consider that the English language was sufficiently rich; most of these terms can be guessed. Arabic equivalents are omitted. All notes are Burton's, except when there is a suffix, 'Ed.'

Editing this book has given me the pleasure of recalling visits to Zayla, Harar, and Berbera nearly a hundred years after Burton, when I found that the best book to tell me about the country was *First Footsteps in East Africa*. Going from the restrictive life of Aden across the Gulf to Somaliland, I experienced the same excitement and feeling of freedom that Burton had done. The vast herds of elegant antelope, the strange birds and trees, the roar of lion at night were as Burton had described them, and the Somalis were as proud and as entertaining company. Zayla, now isolated between sea and bush, had declined even since Burton's day as a result of the development of the nearby French port of Djibuti and the building of the railway line from there to Addis Ababa; Harar, which was still lovely in its setting of green hills, had lost its mediaeval atmosphere with new Italian buildings, but has now settled down to a more African existence under the Ethiopians; Berbera, since Burton's visit, has been occupied by Egyptians, British, Italians (though very briefly) and is now controlled again by Somalis; some improvement has been made though it has not developed in the way that Burton dreamed it might. 'It was with astonishment,' he wrote, 'that I reflected upon the impolicy of having preferred Aden to this place. . . . It [Berbera] is the meeting place of commerce, has few rivals, and with half the sums lavished in Arabia upon engineer follies of stone and lime, the environs might at this time [1856] have been covered with houses, gardens and trees.' If the British had developed a military base and an oil refinery at Berbera instead of at Aden, it is possible that they would have had less trouble from the Somali Government than they have today in the complicated situation of South Arabia; for one thing the Emperor Menelik would not have been in a position to force our hand and claim Somali territory under the Anglo-Ethiopian Treaty of 1897, which is today the cause of much of the trouble between the British and Somalis.

I wish first of all to thank the officials of the India Office Library in Whitehall for their patience and help—help is certainly needed in view of the complicated and out-of-date indexing system. I also wish to thank for advice and help members of the staff of the Royal Geographical Society, especially Mrs. Middleton; members of the Royal Anthropological Institute and of the Southwark Public Libraries. I am most grateful for information received, to Messrs. Harold Ingrams, I. M. Lewis, B. W. Andrzejewski, D. B. Doe, T. L. Fenton, and Professor Edward Ullendorff. I am also indebted to Mr. Alexander Maitland, who is writing on Speke, for generously letting me make use of unpublished letters from J. H. Speke, to Sir Edward Playfair to whom the letters belong, and to Mr. Quentin Keynes for letting me see part of his extensive collection of Burton manuscripts which include the originals of the reports to Government concerning the Somali attack on the camp at Berbera; I have made use of these reports from the copies in the India Office Library.

GORDON WATERFIELD

Fulham, London,
January, 1966

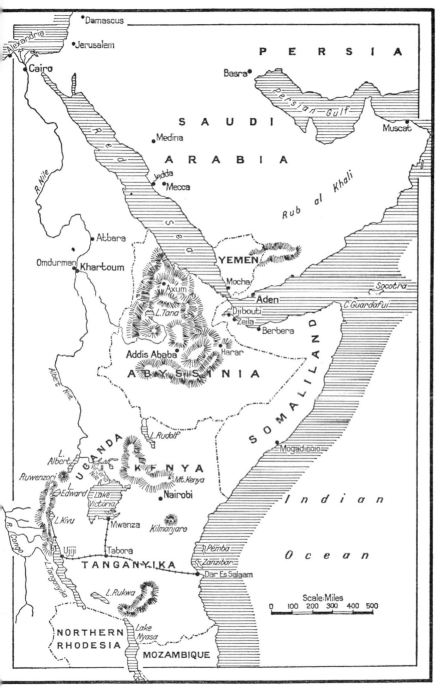

Sketch map of East Africa. The railway from Dar es Salaam to Lake Tanganyika follows very roughly the route taken by Burton and Speke; the line from Tabora to Lake Victoria Nyanza is the route taken by Speke.

Introduction

'THE HUMAN HEAD once struck off does not regrow like the rose,' said British officials in Aden in the autumn of 1854 in an attempt to dissuade Richard Burton from risking his neck by travelling to Harar.[1] No European so far had made the journey because of constant warfare among Somali tribes and the xenophobia of Hararis and their rulers; yet it was a city which had intrigued explorers as much as had Timbuktu, described by Burton as 'ill-famed' because Major Gordon Laing had been murdered in 1826, soon after leaving the town.

At the time that Burton was about to start for Harar, David Livingstone had left Loanda on the west coast of Africa on his great march which brought him eventually to the east coast in 1856; Walter Plowden, the British Consul in Abyssinia, was reporting to the Foreign Office on the rise of Kassai, later to become the Emperor Theodore who killed himself after defeat by Sir Robert Napier at Magdala in 1868. The source of the White Nile was still undiscovered, central Africa not yet fully explored and no one even knew the correct position of Harar.

Burton left Aden for Zayla in October 1854 to collect mules, camels and Somalis for his caravan or *kafilah*. In Zayla the Somali Governor warned him that the road swarmed with brigands, that the Eesa tribe had recently murdered his son, that small-pox was depopulating Harar and that for a foreigner to put himself into the power of the Amir meant certain destruction; but Burton dismissed these warnings as oriental exaggeration, 'one death to a man is a serious thing: a dozen neutralize one another'. He knew that African cities were prisons on a large scale 'into which you enter by your own will, and leave by another's', and that in Harar there was the legend that the ruler would lose his independence once an European had entered the city.

It must be borne in mind [wrote Burton in the preface to *First Footsteps in East Africa*] that the region traversed on this occasion was previously known only by the vague reports of native travellers. All the Abyssinian discoverers had traversed the Dankali and other northern tribes: the land of the Somal was still a *terra incognita*. Harar, moreover, had never been visited, and few are the cities in the world which in the present age, when men hurry about the earth, have not opened their gates to European adventure. The ancient metropolis of a once mighty race, the only permanent settlement in Eastern Africa, the reported seat of Moslem learning, a walled city of stone houses, possessing its independent chief, its peculiar population, its own unknown language, and its own coinage, the emporium of the coffee trade, the headquarters of slavery, the birth-place of the Kat plant, and the great manufactory of cotton-cloths, amply, it appeared, deserved the trouble of exploration.

Burton's journey to Harar followed his pilgrimage to Medina and Mecca in 1853, which had won him European fame. He had been able to convince his fellow pilgrims that he was not a convert but had been born a Muslim, though there were detractors who argued that his disguise must have been penetrated. They repeated a story, which Burton always denied—that he had had to kill a man because, as Stanley Lane-Poole wrote in *the Dictionary of National Biography*, 'he detected him [Burton] performing an operation of nature in a non-oriental fashion'.

For his journey to Harar, Burton again took on the character of a Muslim, but just before entering the city he decided to rely 'upon what has made many a small man great, the good star' and presented himself boldly as an Englishman, though he knew that of all foreigners the English were the most hated, since they were trying to abolish slavery and Harar was one of the main centres of the trade.*

Burton's good star looked after him during that dangerous journey, but deserted him when he was about to set out on his main expedition across Somaliland to Zanzibar, for his camp was attacked by Somalis in Berbera in April 1855. Burton had hoped to continue this expedi-

* Several biographers, including Isabel Burton, have mistakenly stated that Burton entered Harar disguised as a Muslim. This mistake was probably due to the fact that he based his book on his diaries; thus, on the second page Burton wrote: 'It is, therefore, a point of honor with me . . . to utilize my title of Haji by entering the city [Harar], visiting the ruler, and returning in safety, after breaking the guardian spell.' That had been his intention and he did not alter the paragraph when later he changed his mind, and decided to throw off his disguise.

tion into central Africa to look for the source of the White Nile, but four years passed before he was in a position to lead an expedition to discover Lake Tanganyika with John Hanning Speke, who was his surveyor; Speke went north on his own and reached Lake Victoria Nyanza. Then began the famous quarrel between the two men as to the whereabouts of the source of the Nile; though Speke had already come to dislike Burton at the time of the Somali Expedition.

Burton had carried out his three great feats of exploration by the age of thirty-eight—the pilgrimage to Mecca, the trek to Harar, and the discovery of Lake Tanganyika. Afterwards he accomplished many things, but his life as an explorer, which was his ambition, came to an end in 1859, due largely, it is argued here, to the critical reports about him following the disaster to the Somali Expedition in Berbera.

He remained, however, a traveller and a lively writer—one of the most remarkable travellers of all time. During the next thirty years of his life (he died in 1890), he went from one outlandish place to another, noting and writing. An outstanding linguist (he learned twenty-nine languages), a poet, a competent draughtsman, a shrewd observer, an energetic scholar and a prolific writer, Burton published more than forty books based on his experiences or on the material he had collected during his travels in four continents—Asia, Africa, and the two Americas; there were also his many translations including the famous unexpurgated translation of *The Book of the Thousand Nights and a Night*, and of the *Lusiad* by the Portuguese poet, Camoens.

First Footsteps in East Africa is one of the most exciting and entertaining of his books. It contains vivid descriptions of the Somalis and their country, and it is also a story full of adventure, humour, philosophic and religious speculations, acid and amusing comments, and pungent attacks on those in authority. Burton bubbles over with so much strange information that his books are sometimes confusing; in *First Footsteps* he jumps from personal narrative to history and speculation and is sometimes prolix, but he is a natural writer and conveys his own zest and enjoyment in travel.

Character and Views on Sex

To Burton travel provided not only an opportunity of inquiring into the minds and customs of new people but also a means to discover himself—and Burton was indeed stranger than any Somali, Mormon, or Arab Bedouin, though not perhaps as sinister as many

Victorians thought him to be. By his contemporaries Burton was often either extravagantly hated or extravagantly admired; 'what part has death or time in him who rode life's list as a God might ride?', wrote Algernon Swinburne.

There have been many biographies of Richard Burton, but no one has yet written the final story and perhaps no one can. Mr. Alan Moorehead states in his introduction to the re-issue of Burton's *The Lake Regions of Central Africa*:

> He was one of those men in whom nature runs riot; she endows him with not one or two but twenty different talents, all of them far beyond the average, and then witholds the one ingredient that might have brought them to perfection—a sense of balance and direction . . . Burton never entirely went on an expedition to reach a goal; he was also out to explore himself in new surroundings. This is why his books are greater than his journeys and why the man is greater than his career. The mystery of Central Africa died when the country was explored, but Burton lives on as a splendid and provoking enigma.[2]

At every stage of his life Burton puzzled, shocked, and exasperated people, but though he gave them plenty of opportunity to attack him —and, indeed, encouraged them to do so—he could not be thrown down or ignored; he was too talented, hard-working, and original a personality. While an officer in India he lived some of the time in native costume, his head shaven (a wig for social occasions), studying native languages, customs, philosophies, religions, and sex-life. A report he wrote on pederasty in brothels was considered outrageously shocking and, when he buried his favourite fighting-cock near his bungalow, the story spread that it was the body of a child.

He returned to England with a sinister reputation, and it was later said that he had corrupted young Algernon Swinburne. When Richard Monckton Milnes (Lord Houghton) brought together the swarthy traveller and the young poet it was described as 'a piece of calculated corruption'. All three shared an interest in erotic literature and one of the sources of supply from Paris was Frederick Hankey, who shocked the de Goncourt brothers by asserting that he liked to have his books bound with human skin, preferably taken live; Burton, he said, had promised him a skin taken 'sur une négresse vivante'. It was typical of Burton that he should have encouraged Hankey to believe that he would do this. '*Caro* Milnes,' wrote Burton in May 1863 from the barbaric Kingdom of Dahomey, 'I have been here 3 days and am grievously disappointed. Not a man killed, nor a fellow tortured. The canoe floating in blood is a myth of myths. Poor Hankey must still wait for his *peau de femme*.'

Burton had an hypnotic charm which won him many friends and he was a popular visitor at Fryston Hall, the home of Monckton Milnes who described his 'sensitiveness of character and delicacy of perception', his great sense of humour, his varied knowledge and literary attainments, and his 'wonderful endurance of physical hardships'.[3] Burton had such vitality, curiosity, and scholarly fastidiousness that he went to great lengths of discomfort and danger to study the vagaries of men and women, especially their excesses, and he described them with sardonic humour. He found nothing shocking, except the hypocrisy of puritanism, and therefore had the reputation of being a 'dangerous' character with no morals.

This was partly because Burton considered sex to be an important matter for study and, as one of the precursors of Sigmund Freud, he was a disturbing element in Victorian society.* To him the *Arabian Nights' Tales* in their unexpurgated versions were 'a chef-d'œuvre of the highest anthropological and ethnological interest and importance', as he stated in his Foreword to his sixteen-volume edition. In his well-known Terminal Essay he wrote:

> Moslems and Easterns in general study, and intelligently study, the art and mystery of satisfying the physical woman. In my Foreword I have noticed among barbarians the system of 'making men', that is, of teaching lads first arrived at puberty the nice conduct of the instrumentum paratum plantandis civibus; a branch of the knowledge-tree which our modern education grossly neglects, thereby entailing untold miseries upon individuals, families and generations.
>
> The mock virtue, the most immodest modesty of England and of the United States in the nineteenth century, pronounces the subject foul and fulsome: 'Society' sickens at all details; and hence it is said abroad that the English have the finest women in Europe and least know how to use them. Throughout the East such studies are aided by a long series of volumes, many of them written by learned physiologists, by men of social standing, and by religious dignitaries high in office.

In social gatherings Burton was regarded with apprehension by mothers anxious to protect their daughters. 'Strictly dishonourable,' said Burton when asked by a mother what were his intentions. But the

---

* On January 6, 1863, he founded, with others, the Anthropological Society, which in two years increased to five hundred members; he could say in 1865, 'The *Memoirs of the Anthropological Society* now acts the good Samaritan to facts which the publisher and the drawing-room table proudly pass by.'[4]

aristocratic Lady Arundell failed (worse luck for Burton) to prevent her daughter Isabel, from falling in love and marrying him in 1861. Isabel described him as nearly six foot tall, very broad, thin, muscular, black hair, a weather-beaten face, straight Arab features and a determined mouth and chin nearly covered by an enormous black moustache; 'the most remarkable part of his appearance was two large black flashing eyes that pierced you through and through. He had a fierce, proud, melancholy expression and when he smiled, he smiled as though it hurt him, and looked with impatient contempt at things generally.[5] Swinburne wrote of 'the look of unspeakable horror in those eyes which gave him at times an almost unearthly appearance . . . He had the brow of a god and the jaw of a devil.'

His friends, such as Lovett Cameron, the explorer, argued that he was by no means as sinister a figure as he was reported to be, and that his wit and humour were directed against himself rather than against others; 'most of the stories which have circulated to his detriment have arisen from his way of telling anecdotes about himself, and putting his own share in the transaction in the blackest possible light. He knew his friends would understand him and recked nothing of what the rest of the world would think. . . . Under the rugged exterior there was concealed a heart as tender as that of any woman.'[6] His niece, Georgiana Stisted, wrote that he was very brave as a child but that where his affections were concerned his stoicism vanished; he adored his mother 'and one of the earliest stories recorded of him is that he was found rolling on the floor, howling with mingled rage and anguish because some women had carriages to drive in, while for a time his parents had to go on foot'.[7]

'A blaze of light without focus'

Richard Burton was born on March 19, 1821, at Barham House, Herts (though some accounts give his place of birth as Torquay). It was four months before Queen Caroline was prevented by order of George IV from entering Westminster Abbey for the ceremony of coronation. Richard Burton's father, Lieutenant-Colonel Joseph Netterville Burton, ended a distinguished career in the army by refusing an order from the Duke of Wellington to give evidence against Queen Caroline because George IV wanted to obtain a divorce; Colonel Burton had been an officer in Genoa when Queen Caroline had lived there and he considered that she had shown great kindness to the

British officers quartered in the town. As a result of his refusal to give evidence, he was put on half-pay and the family, for reasons of economy, lived most of the time in France and Italy.

Joseph Burton was the son of the Rev. Edward Burton, Rector of Tuam in Galway, who had settled in Ireland from Shap in Westmoreland. 'In mind he was a thorough Irishman,' wrote Joseph's son, Richard; he spent any money he could acquire in wild speculations and on two occasions, after wounding a fellow-officer in a duel, he devotedly nursed him back to health. The Colonel was anxious that his sons Richard and Edward, and his daughter Maria, should succeed in life and was determined that his sons should enter the Church, but he gave them very little suitable education. Richard Burton was very ambitious and he had serious regrets in later life that he had not been brought up in a more orthodox way.

A man who brings up his family abroad [he wrote later with some feeling, about his father], and who lives there for years, must expect to lose all the friends who could be useful to him when he wishes to start them [his children] in life. The conditions of society in England are so complicated, and so artificial, that those who would make their way in the world, especially in public careers, must be broken to it from their earliest day. The future soldiers and statesmen must be prepared by Eton and Cambridge. The more English they are, even to the cut of their hair, the better. In consequence of being brought up abroad, we never thoroughly understood English society, nor did society understand us. And, lastly, it is a *real* advantage to belong to some parish. It is a great thing, when you have won a battle, or explored central Africa, to be welcomed home by some little corner of the Great World, which takes a pride in your exploits, because they reflect honour upon itself. In the contrary condition you are a waif, a stray; you are a blaze of light, without a focus. Nobody outside your own fireside cares.[8]

It is a shrewd, revealing, and a rather sad comment. Throughout his life there was talk of Burton's wildness, bohemianism, and stories of a gipsy background, encouraged by his excessively romantic wife; but at the same time there is no doubt that he was eager to succeed in an ordinary profession, whether military, or as an explorer and writer or in the consular service, but his haphazard and undisciplined upbringing, and the quarrels he had with his good-looking but raffish father, implanted in him a dislike of those in authority. It was not only English society but also official society, that he did not understand and which did not understand him. The Government of India resented his

7

repeated attacks, and made it difficult for him to obtain advancement. During the first half of his life Burton wins sympathy, but during the latter part one cannot but feel sorry for the officials who had to deal with him. 'What a grand man!' wrote the explorer H. M. Stanley. 'One of the real great ones of England he might have been, if he had not been cursed with cynicism.' It was more than cynicism; it was a deep-seated bitterness at his failure to obtain promotion in conventional careers when far less talented men than he succeeded—'a surcharge of spleen' against those who had excited 'his envy, dislike or scorn'.[9] Burton pursued Speke and his theories too relentlessly, drank too much when Consul at Santos in Brazil, and wrote too bitterly about himself and others. Towards the end of his life as Consul in Trieste he was famous as a scholar and traveller, had been made a K.C.M.G., and had received sixteen thousand guineas for his privately printed translation of the *Arabian Nights*. But he was not content. He had, for instance, been famous as a swordsman, yet he felt it necessary to commission a life-size painting of himself in his fencing costume when over sixty—a huge, swarthy, angry-looking man.*

In his own account of the seven ages of man he wrote of the man of fifty, 'whose experience is mostly disappointment with regrets for lost time and vanished opportunities; sixty, when the man begins to die and mourns for his past youth, at seventy when he *ought* to prepare for his long journey and never does'. At the time of his travels in Somaliland he was in his thirties and of that age he wrote more cheerfully—'the *homme fait* in the full warmth and heyday of life'.[10]

Certainly Burton's upbringing accounted for much of his later troubles and Burton's stories of his boyhood, wandering about Europe with his parents is most unusual. In Naples, for instance, he and his brother went round with the cholera carts collecting the dead which were thrown into pits. 'The decay,' he wrote, 'caused a kind of lambent flame, which lit up a mass of human corruption worthy to be described by Dante.'[11] He was too precocious and wayward to settle down at Oxford and he could not bring himself to accept the authority exercised 'by those half-reformed monks calling themselves Fellows'. He considered that the only way he could stop his father sending him into the Church was by having himself sent down from the University, and this he arranged with his usual panache. Later he regretted that he had not studied more; he worked hard at fencing and Arabic. After leaving

* This painting in oil by A. Letchford is in the store-room of the South London Art Gallery; the canvas is over nine feet high and nearly six feet across.

Oxford he studied Hindustani, for he had decided to earn glory as an officer in the service of the East India Company and to help revenge the terrible disaster in Afghanistan when several thousand British and Indian troops and camp-followers died in 1842 on the retreat from Kabul.

INDIA

Burton arrived in Bombay as an Ensign in October 1842 only to learn that the first Afghan War had ended with victory for the British and there was no fighting to be done. He was not attracted by Bombay and as to its society: 'I stood aghast in its presence,' he wrote. 'The rank climate of India, which produces such a marvellous development of vegetation, seems to have a similar effect on the Anglo-Indian individuality. It shot up, as if suddenly relieved of the weight with which society controls it in England.'[12] There were only two things that a young officer could do: either 'cut down a few of the enemy' and shoot big game, or study the people and their languages. He decided to do the second, and threw himself 'with a kind of frenzy' upon a study of languages for twelve hours a day with two *munshis*. He passed first in the interpretership examinations for Hindustani, Gujerati, Mahratta, and Persian, also doing well in a number of other languages, such as Telegu and Multani, an achievement which has not been surpassed by any other young officer.

Appointed regimental interpreter to Sir Charles Napier, conqueror of Sind, he became one of his many admirers, and was indirectly involved in the quarrel between Napier and James Outram ('the Bayard'), which divided western India. Outram accused Napier of excessive ruthlessness in dealing with the rulers of Sind; he was supported by Dr. Buist, Editor of *The Bombay Times*, and by members of the Board of the East India Company. 'Napier did not care a fig', Burton wrote, 'how many enemies he made and his tongue was like a scorpion-sting.' Napier called Buist 'the blatant beast', and referred to members of the Board as 'the twenty-four kings of Leadenhall Street—ephemeral sovereigns'. Burton agreed with his chief's criticisms, and himself attacked the Company for allowing their officers in India to be constantly robbed, and occasionally even murdered, without taking any action: 'An ignoble position for a dominant race ... The rule of the good company was, however, not a rule of honour, but of expediency, and the safety of its officers was little regarded.'

9

Napier liked Burton and sent him to help survey and administer Sind, working for Captain (later General) Walter Scott, nephew of the novelist, to whom Burton dedicated his book *Scinde or the Unhappy Valley*. Napier gave Burton the task of reporting on the brothels of Karachi, since a large garrison of five thousand European and Indian troops was quartered there. Burton disguised as a native, discovered a startling amount of highly scabrous information, such as that the price of boys was double the price of eunuchs and the reasons were given in detail. The report did not shock Napier, and had been intended for his eyes alone, but it was later discovered in the official files at Bombay and was used by Burton's enemies as ammunition against him.

Burton decided to make a systematic study of the Sindis. 'The first difficulty,' he wrote, 'was to pass for an Oriental, and this was as necessary as it was difficult. The European official in India seldom, if ever, sees anything in its real light, so dense is the veil which the fearfulness, the duplicity, the prejudice and the superstitions of the natives hang before his eyes.' There are many stories about the effectiveness of his disguises; how he would pass his commanding officer and even his native friends unrecognized. Burton is probably the inspiration of Kipling's character of Strickland.

In April 1845 he made friends with Mirza Ali Akhbar, who had served Sir Charles Napier with great gallantry and had retired to a bungalow outside Karachi with a friend, Mirza Daud, who was a fine Persian scholar. 'My life became much mixed up with these gentlemen, and my brother officers fell to calling me "the white nigger".' He also had a Persian *munshi* or teacher, Mirza Mohammed Musayn of Shiraz, and with his assistance Burton opened three shops in Karachi, where he used to sit and listen to the gossip, assuming the character of Mirza Abdullah of Bushire, 'a half-Arab, half-Iranian . . . with hair falling upon his shoulders, a long beard, face and hands, arms and feet, stained with a thin coat of henna'.

In this disguise and carrying fine linens, muslins and jewellery he could go anywhere, even into the harems; or 'he played chess with some native friend, or he consorted with the hemp-drinkers and opium-eaters in the *estaminets*, or he visited the Mrs. Gadabouts and Go-betweens who make matches among the Faithful, and gathered from them a precious budget of private history and domestic scandal'. In such ways he brought back valuable intelligence to Napier, and he also carried on his anthropological studies. 'It is impossible,' he wrote,

Drawing by Burton of the Cathedral of Goa.

'to acquire an intimate knowledge of Oriental manners and customs without mixing familiarly with all orders low as well as high.'[13]

Burton worked with great enthusiasm because he was extremely interested in native life, and because he had a passionate ambition to advance his career. 'I found that it took me some years of hard study before I could walk into a bazaar and distinguish the several castes, and know something of them, their manners and customs, religion and superstitions.' He used often to sit by the banks of the Fulaili river, about a mile from the Fort of Hyderabad, in the garden of a purblind old tailor, Mohamed Baksh, and study 'the truly oriental peculiarities' of his ways of thought with its 'regular irregularities of deduction and its strange monotonous one-ideadness . . . The knowledge of one mind is that of a million—after a fashion. I hold by way of general rule, that the Eastern mind is always in extremes; that it ignores what is meant by "golden mean", and that it delights to range in flights limited only by the *ne plus ultra* of Nature herself.'*

By spending several years with various religious teachers he obtained a thorough grounding in the study of Hinduism and Islam, together with some of the variations on the orthodox faiths; 'my experience of eastern faiths became phenomenal and I became a Master-Sufi'. His talent for languages was helped by his extraordinary memory, and at one period he became interested in studying the language of monkeys, who used to sit round him at meals as if in a regimental mess with the bearers waiting on them. He did not, however, cut himself off from regimental life or from European society. 'I had a host of good friends,' he wrote, 'especially Dr. J. J. Steinhaüser, who in after years was to have accompanied me, but for an accident, to Lake Tanganyika, and who afterwards became my collaborator in *The Thousand Nights and a Night*.' If Steinhaüser had been able to accompany Burton and Speke on that fateful journey to Lake Tanganyika the unfortunate quarrel might have been avoided.

For some time in Karachi Burton shared a bungalow with his great friend Dr. Ellerton Stocks, Assistant Surgeon of the Medical Establishment in Bombay, and a distinguished botanist who employed a draughtsman, Walter Abraham. This man worked in the hall of the bungalow and wrote of Burton as he was in 1847:

* Compare T. E. Lawrence: 'Their thoughts were at ease only in extremes. They inhabited superlatives by choice. Sometimes inconsistencies seemed to possess them at once in joint sway; but they never compromised: they pursued the logic of several incompatible opinions to absurd ends, without perceiving the incongruity. . . . Their imaginations were vivid but not creative.' (*Seven Pillars of Wisdom*, ch. 3.)

He was on special duty, which in his case meant to perfect himself for some political duty, by mastering the languages of the country. When I knew him he was master of half a dozen languages, which he wrote and spoke so fluently that a stranger who did not see him and heard him speak would fancy he heard a native . . .

His domestic servants were—a Portuguese, with whom he spoke Portuguese and Goanese, an African, a Persian and a Sindi or Belochee. These spoke their mother tongue to Sir Richard as he was engaged in his studies with *moonshees*, who relieved each other every two hours, from ten to four daily . . .

His habits at home were perfectly Persian or Arabic. His hair was dressed *à la Persian*—long and shaved from the forehead to the top of the head; his eyes, by some means or other he employed, resembled Persian or Arabian; he used the Turkish bath and wore a cowl; and when he went out for a ride he used a wig and goggles . . . Such a jovial companion Sir Richard was, that his bungalow was the resort of the learned men of the place.*

In 1847 Burton contracted cholera and was granted six months' sick leave in Goa, where he laid elaborate but ineffective plans to elope with a beautiful nun, and found plenty of material for a book, *Goa and the Blue Mountains.*

On his return to duty Burton believed that he would at last be able to see active service in the second Sikh War and asked to be appointed interpreter to the army setting out for Multan in May 1848. Though he was the only interpreter with a knowledge of the Multani language, an officer far less qualified than himself was given the post.

This last misfortune broke my heart [he wrote]. I had been seven years in India, working like a horse, volunteering for every bit of service, and qualifying myself for all contingencies. Rheumatic ophalmia, which had almost left me in hopes of marching northwards, came on with redoubled force, and no longer had I any hope of curing it except by a change to Europe. Sick, sorry, and almost in tears of rage, I bade adieu to my friends and comrades in Scinde . . . my career in India had been, in my eyes, a failure, and by no fault of my own; the dwarfish demon called interest had fought against me, and as usual had won the fight.

In fact, the great knowledge he had acquired of native life, customs, philosophy, religions, ways of thought and of language proved of considerable value to him on his later travels.

While in England and Italy Burton wrote a number of books;[14] he

* *The Times*, October 31, 1891.

soon recovered his health, and once more took up fencing and swordsmanship, inventing two new strokes and becoming a Maître d'Armes. It was during this leave that he had his first encounter on the ramparts of Boulogne with Isabel Arundell, then a school-girl who was 'struck with the shaft of destiny' and decided that Burton was going to marry her.

ARABIA

Burton was considering a plan for exploring Arabia which would take three years and he certainly did not want to get married.* He considered it 'an opprobrium to modern adventure' that the eastern and central regions of Arabia were unknown and unmapped, and he wanted to cross from the Red Sea coast of Arabia to Muscat on the Persian Gulf or to do the reverse journey from east to west. He wished to investigate the possibility of exporting Arab horses to India, especially for polo; to discover the lie of the land and to study the races.†

His plan was warmly supported by the Royal Geographical Society; but Sir James Hogg, Chairman of the Court of Directors of the East India Company, considered the expedition too dangerous and only gave permission for Burton to have a year's extension of leave to study Arabic 'in lands where the language is best learned'. It was a great disappointment, but Burton was determined to make the best use possible of that year and decided that there could be no better place for study than the forbidden cities of Mecca and Medina; he also wanted to show 'that Hogg', as Sir Charles Napier called him, 'that what might be perilous to other travellers was safe to me'. Courageous and obstinate, Burton still hoped to be able to carry out his original plans to travel across Arabia, and he reckoned he would be better able to do this as a Muslim who had accomplished the pilgrimage.

Burton left England in April 1853, and in Cairo studied the Muslim faith and behaviour.

* 'So Galton is married and the world has lost a right good traveller,' Burton wrote to Dr. Norton Shaw, Secretary of the Royal Geographical Society. Sir Francis Galton married the daughter of the Dean of Peterborough in 1853, after his travels in Egypt, Syria, the Sudan and West Africa.

† He believed that there were some tribes with physiological differences 'sufficient to warrant our questioning the common origin of the Arab family'. Mr. Bertram Thomas refers to four languages in Arabia which he considered were nearer to the Semitic languages of Ethiopia than to Arabic, and discusses the theory that some of the tribes of North-East Africa and of Southern Arabia had a common origin (see Burton Memorial Lecture by Mr. Bertram Thomas, *The Journal of the Royal Asiatic Society*, 1931).

14

A fortnight [he wrote] was profitably spent in getting into the train of Oriental manners. For what polite Chesterfield says of the difference between a gentleman and his reverse,—namely, that both perform the same offices of life, but each in a several and widely different way—is notably as applicable to the manners of the Eastern as of Western men. Look, for instance, at an Indian Moslem drinking a glass of water. With us the operation is simple enough, but his performance includes no less than five novelties. In the first place, he clutches his tumbler as though it were the throat of a foe; secondly, he ejaculates, 'In the name of Allah the Compassionate, the Merciful!' before wetting his lips; thirdly, he imbibes the contents, swallowing them, not drinking, and ending with a satisfied grunt; fourthly before setting down the cup, he sighs forth, 'Praise be to Allah!'—of which you will understand the full meaning in the Desert; and, fifthly, he replies, 'May Allah make it pleasant to thee!' in answer to his friends polite 'Pleasurably and health!'

He pointed out that in the East it was important to remember to use the right hand, and a chair should not be sat in with comfort; 'your genuine Oriental looks almost as comfortable in one as a sailor upon the back of a high-trotting horse'.[15]

All such things and many others he had to remember. If he had gone on the pilgrimage as a convert to Islam, he would have been excused from making mistakes in the elaborate ritual, but posing as a Muslim born meant that he risked death if discovered. His *Personal Narrative of a Pilgrimage to El-Medinah and Meccah* shows how much he enjoyed this tough and adventurous journey through 'a haggard land infested with wild beasts and wilder men—a region whose very fountains murmur the warning "Drink and away!" ' He loved the open desert and bush country:

> There is a keen enjoyment in mere animal existence. The sharp appetite disposes of the most indigestible food; the sand is softer than a bed of down and the purity of the air suddenly puts to flight a dire cohort of diseases. Here Nature returns to man, however unworthily he has treated her and, believe me, when once your tastes have conformed to the tranquility of such travel, you will suffer real pain in returning to the turmoil of civilization . . . The air of cities will suffocate you, and the careworn and cadaverous countenances of citizens will haunt you like a vision of judgement.'[16]

The pilgrimage, which had not been written about by an European since Burckhardt's journey forty years earlier, earned Burton fame in

View of El Medinah, the burial place of the Prophet. Drawing by Burton.

England and on the Continent, both for the journey itself and for the vividness and precision of his account. He had considered continuing from Mecca across the *Rub al-Khali* or 'Empty Quarter' of Arabia:

> The journey would have been of fifteen or sixteen hundred miles and have occupied at least ten months longer than my leave. The quarrelling of the tribes prevented me from carrying it out. I had arranged with the Beni Harb, the Bedouin tribe, to join them after the pilgrimage like a true Bedouin, but . . . I found it useless to be killed in a petty tribal quarrel, perhaps about a mare, and once I joined them it would have been a point of honour to aid in all their quarrels and raids.

Instead, Burton had become fascinated by Zanzibar; he wrote from Cairo on November 16, 1853, to Dr. Norton Shaw, Secretary of the Royal Geographical Society in London, saying that he wished to lead a scientific expedition there:

> It is one of the headquarters of slavery—the Americans are gently but surely carrying off the commerce of the country—and it has vast resources undeveloped . . . You will ask why I now prefer Zanzibar to Arabia. Because I have now tried both sides of Arabia and can see no practical results. Travelling is a joy there and nothing would delight me more than leave for 3 or 4 years to the Eastern coast (of Arabia).

16

But nothing except more discovery of deserts, valleys and tribes would come of it.[17]

At first Burton stayed at Shepeards Hotel, and then moved to live with Galeazzo Visconti, an Italian revolutionary, and a young man called Sankey who had been travelling in Barbary; he wrote to Shaw that the house was 'a scene of depravity, showing what Cairo can do at a pinch, and beating the Arabian Nights all to chalk—that, too, when the Pasha has positively forbidden fornication'. He also said in this letter of November 1853, that the missionary Dr. J. L. Krapf, who had lived in Ethiopia and was then settled in Mombasa, had just arrived from Zanzibar 'with discoveries about sources of the White Nile, Killamanjaro, and Mts of the Moon which remind one of a de Lunatico. I have not seen him but don't intend to miss the spectacle, especially to pump what really has been done and what remains to be done.'

Burton was intrigued by the stories that Krapf had to tell, and this was probably the beginning of his own determination to discover the source of the White Nile; at the same time he was wary of these stories which came from Arab slave traders and merchants travelling between the Zanzibari coast and Central Africa; we find him referring to the Mountains of the Moon as the 'Lunatic Mountains'.* The source of the White Nile was a problem which had interested and baffled European travellers from the time of Herodotus. In the 1820s the African Association, a predecessor of the Royal Geographical Society, and in the 1830s the Egyptian Government of Mohamed Ali, had supported expeditions to explore the river. The stories from the missionaries of East Africa about huge lakes in the interior of Africa and snow on the mountains, gathered from Arab traders, had once more aroused interest.

THE SOMALI EXPEDITION

An expedition to Zanzibar acquired, therefore, the added importance to Burton that it was a good point of departure for any expedition into Central Africa. He had received information from his friend Ellerton Stocks in Bombay that the Government there would not oppose any plans he might have for another expedition, but that they would do nothing to help. Burton knew that the Royal Geographical Society had

* In 1860 Dr. J. L. Krapf published *Travels and researches and missionary labours during eighteen years residence in Eastern Africa. . . with an appendix respecting the snow-capped mountains of East Africa.*

been trying ever since 1849 to persuade the East India Company to release an officer, or officers, to explore 'the productive resources of the unknown Somali country in East Africa'. In March 1850 Dr. Carter of the Brig *Palinurus* put forward a plan for travelling along the coast to a depth of about eighty miles, using a ship as a base, but nothing came of this because the Royal Geographical Society wanted the interior explored.

In his letter of November to Dr. Norton Shaw, Burton suggested that this plan might be revived and that the expedition should cross the Somali country to Zanzibar. He reminded Shaw that the Bombay Government had a little time previously sanctioned an expedition to the Somali country. 'But Carter [the *Palinurus* doctor], not relishing the chance of losing his cods—that misguided people are in the habit of cutting them off and hanging them as ornaments round their arms—refused to explore the interior.'

On December 15 he wrote again from Cairo, and made it clear that he hoped to be able to pass right across Africa from Zanzibar to the Atlantic:

> Lord Elphinstone* passed through Cairo and I went with him to the Pyramids. I flatter myself that leave will not be witheld and if so I only want your interest to get up something like an expedition to Zanzibar. If time be only allowed me I will pass on to the Atlantic: all (that was) wanted to make my last trip perfect was five or six months more than they gave me.

Burton returned to India at the beginning of 1854 and stayed with his friend James Grant Lumsden, Senior Member of the Bombay Council; there he finished writing his book on the pilgrimage to Mecca and planned the next expedition. He became friends with young Foster Fitzgerald Arbuthnot of the Bombay Civil Service, an enthusiastic student of oriental literature, with whom Burton was later to form the Kamashastra Society.[18]

Burton had been away from India for five years and it might be expected that he would have returned to normal regimental duties, but he had friends in high places, such as Elphinstone and Lumsden, to help him with his plans. He asked permission 'to penetrate via Harar

---

* John Elphinstone, 13th Baron, 1807–60, had been appointed Governor of Bombay in October 1853 and was on his way to India to take up his post. He was a Scottish peer, but was created an English peer in 1859 for his valuable services during the Indian Mutiny. Mountstuart Elphinstone, son of the 11th Baron, 1779–1859, was Governor of Bombay 1819–27.

and Gananah to Zanzibar' accompanied by Lieut. G. E. Herne of the
1st Bombay European Regiment of Fusiliers, 'an officer skilfull in
surveying, photography and mechanics', and Assistant Surgeon J.
Ellerton Stocks. It was decided that the plan had to be approved by the
Court of Directors in London so that he could not start in the spring of
1854 as he had hoped.

In his Preface to *First Footsteps in East Africa* the author describes
the great days of exploration in the early nineteenth century on the
Somali Coast, the Red Sea, Muscat, Socotra, and the mouths of the
rivers of Mesopotamia. When Vice-Admiral Sir Charles Malcolm had
been in charge of the Bombay dockyards, 'the British name rose high
in the Indian, African and Arabian seas. Each vessel had its presents—
guns, pistols and powder, abbas [cloaks], crimson cloth and shawls,
watches, telescopes and similar articles—with a suitable stock of which
every officer visiting the interior on leave was supplied.'

In 1838 Sir Charles Malcolm had been succeeded by Sir Robert
Oliver, who was criticized by Burton in his Preface:

> a strict disciplinarian, a faithful and honest servant of Government, but
> a violent, limited and prejudiced man. About twenty surveys were
> ordered to be discontinued as an inauguratory measure, causing the
> loss of many thousand pounds, independent of such contingencies as the
> *Memnon.*ᐟ An order from Sir Robert Oliver withdrew presents as well
> as instruments: with them disappeared the just idea of our faith and
> greatness as a nation entertained by the maritime races, who formerly
> looked forward to the arrival of our cruizers. Thus the Indian navy was
> crushed by neglect and routine into a mere transport service, remark-
> able for little beyond constant quarrels between sea-lieutenants and
> land-lieutenants, sailor-officers and soldier-officers, their 'passengers'.

It was yet another passage in his book, which earned for Burton the
dislike of the directors of the East India Company.[19]

In May 1854, however, Burton still had support from the Bombay
Government. In anticipation that the reply from London would be
favourable, he was granted free passage to Aden; he was to spend six

* Note by Burton: In A.D. 1838, Lieut. Carless surveyed the seaboard of the Somali
country, from Ras Hafun to Burnt Island; unfortunately, his labours were allowed by Sir
Charles Malcolm's successor to lie five years in the obscurity of MS. Meanwhile, the
steam frigate *Memnon*, Capt. Powell commanding, was lost at Ras Assayr; a Norie's
chart, an antiquated document, with an error of from fifteen to twenty miles, being the
only map of reference on board. Thus the Indian Government, by the dilatoriness and
prejudices of its Superintendent of Marine, sustained an unjustifiable loss of at least
£50,000.

months there to await the reply, and 'to enable him to perfect himself in the Somali language and obtain such preliminary information relative to the country he proposes to explore as the merchants of that place may be able to afford'.[20] It was certainly no good asking British officials in Aden anything about the Somalis and their country. He consulted Arabs, and Somalis, including prostitutes; he pays tribute in his Preface to the 'excellent papers' published by Lieut. Cruttenden on Somaliland and to the *Outline of the Somali Language with Vocabulary* by Lieut. C. P. Rigby, who had been his rival in the study of languages in India, but less successful.

Burton continued his preparations and was eager to leave Aden with its cramped garrison life. He was exasperated, as were many officials, at the timid policy adopted by the Court of Directors of the East India Company in London towards the Arab tribes of the interior. Ever since the capture of Aden at the beginning of 1839 by a British force from India there had been trouble. In November 1839 and in May and July of 1840, a force of about five thousand Arabs had tried unsuccessfully to recapture Aden which had belonged to the Sultan of Lahej. Peace was concluded in May 1843, but incidents continued, the main trouble-centre being the tribes around the Arab fort of Bir Ahmed near Aden. Captain Haines, the Political Resident, had repeatedly asked the authorities in India for permission to destroy the fort. Having at length received official support for his policy from the Government of Bombay he warned the tribesmen of his intention; but when the Court of Directors in London learned of the proposed expedition they countermanded the action 'and Captain Haines had the mortification of knowing that the enemy treated him as an idle boaster who held out threats which he lacked the power to enforce'.[21]

It had been a set-back to British prestige that Captain Stafford B. Haines, R.N., the political Resident in Aden, had been removed from his post at the beginning of 1854 on a charge of embezzlement—'a dark chapter in the history of the Bombay Government'.[22] It was also unfortunate for Burton, since Haines would certainly have given him more help than did subsequent Political Residents. Haines was a remarkable man, and had for fifteen years, since the capture of Aden, controlled the tribes through his excellent intelligence service. He believed in defeating Arabs with their own weapons 'by quietly letting them know you perceive their intentions, before they are prepared to carry them out and that you are prepared to counter their designs'. Haines was put into prison in Bombay on criminal charges and twice acquitted by a jury, but he remained in prison for nearly six years, being released on June 9, 1860. 'But it was too late, and he died on the day week of his release, a signal instance of ingratitude and criminal harshness,' stated Charles Low in his *History of the Indian Navy*. It was a warning to Burton and to others that the East India Company authorities could be vindictive.

When Burton arrived in Aden in the spring of 1854 Brigadier Clarke, Commander-in-Chief of the garrison, had been appointed Acting Political Resident in succession to Captain Haines. He was naïve in his dealings with Arab chiefs, which led to serious trouble later, which prevented Burton receiving the help he needed from the Aden authorities. The Court of Directors were short of funds—the Company was not taken over by the India Office until 1858—and they were hoping to maintain peace by a passive imperialism which in the Aden area meant forbidding any military expedition into the interior. Haines, Burton, and others pointed out that it was extremely difficult in these circumstances to keep the road open to the Yemen. Aden was described as the 'Eye of the Yemen' because of its good port, and the British garrison was dependent for its supplies of fresh vegetables and meat from the Yemen and the interior, and also from Somali ports, especially Berbera; nor was it possible under these conditions to maintain order by taking reprisals on tribes responsible for the murder of British military and naval personnel. In January 1855 an order had to be issued that no Europeans were to go outside the walls of Aden or to land on the Arabian shores from ships.

In his Preface to *First Footsteps in East Africa*, which Burton wrote at the beginning of 1856, he made a vigorous attack on the East India Company's policy. It must have angered his superiors all the more since he had assured them, in seeking the Company's permission to publish the diary of his journey to Harar, 'that all political allusions would carefully be avoided'. It is a strong statement in favour of a forward, rather than a passive policy, and Burton makes clear his wholehearted support for British imperialism in the East.

> For half a generation we have been masters of Aden, filling southern Arabia with our calicoes and rupees—what is the present state of affairs there? We are dared by the Bedouin to come forth from behind our stone walls and fight like men in the plain—British *protégés* are slaughtered within range of our guns—our allies' villages have been burned in sight of Aden—our deserters are welcomed and our fugitive felons protected—our supplies are cut off, and the garrison is reduced

to extreme distress, at the word of a half-naked bandit—the miscreant Bhagi who murdered Captain Mylne in cold blood still roams the hills unpunished,[23] gross insults are the sole acknowledgements of our peaceful overtures—the British flag has been fired upon without return, our cruizers being ordered to act only on the defensive,—our forbearance to attack is universally asserted and believed to arise from mere cowardice. Such is, and such will be, the character of the Arabs!

The Sublime Porte still preserves her possessions in the Tahamah, and the regions conterminous to El-Yemen, by the stringent measures with which Mohammed Ali of Egypt opened the robber-haunted Suez road. Whenever a Turk or a traveller is murdered, a few squadrons of Irregular Cavalry are ordered out; they are not too nice upon the subject of retaliation, and rarely refuse to burn a village or two, or to lay waste the crops near the scene of the outrage.

A civilized people, like ourselves, objects to such measures for many reasons, of which none is more feeble than the fear of perpetuating a blood feud with the Arabs. Our present relations with them are a 'very pretty quarrel', and moreover one which time must strengthen, cannot efface. By a just, wholesome, and unsparing severity we may inspire the Bedouin with fear instead of contempt: the veriest visionary would deride the attempt to animate him with a higher sentiment.

'Peace,' observes a modern sage, 'is the dream of the wise, war is the history of man.' To indulge in such dreams is but questionable wisdom. It was not a 'peace-policy' which gave the Portuguese a seaboard extending from Cape Non to Macao. By no peace policy the Osmanlis of a past age pushed their victorious arms from the deserts of Tartary to Aden, to Delhi, to Algiers, and to the gates of Vienna. It was no peace policy which made the Russians seat themselves upon the shores of the Black, the Baltic, and the Caspian seas: gaining in the space of 150 years, and, despite war, retaining, a territory greater than England and France united. No peace policy enabled the French to absorb region after region in Northern Africa, till the Mediterranean appears doomed to sink into a Gallic lake.

The English of a former generation were celebrated for gaining ground in both hemispheres: their broad lands were not won by a peace policy, which, however, in this our day has on two distinct occasions well nigh lost for them the 'gem of the British Empire'— India. The philanthropist and the political economist may fondly hope, by outcry against 'territorial aggrandizement', by advocating a compact frontier, by abandoning colonies, and by cultivating 'equilibrium', to retain our rank amongst the great nations of the world. Never! The facts of history prove nothing more conclusively than this: a race either progresses or retrogades, either increases or diminishes: the children of Time, like their sire, cannot stand still.

1　Richard Burton in his early thirties at the time of his expedition to
Harar (photograph with the Royal Anthropological Society, London)

2   Burton as 'Hajj Abdullah', pilgrim to Mecca and Medina in 1853,
drawn by himself and published in the first edition of his *Personal
Narrative of a Pilgrimage to El-Medinah and Meccah*

Burton could not avoid being caught up in the politics of Aden and Southern Arabia, but his main concern was the planning of his expedition to Zanzibar. In the early summer he received the sad news that his friend J. Ellerton Stocks had died suddenly of apoplexy while on leave in England. He was relying a great deal on Stocks as a companion; according to a statement in his preface he altered his plans because of Stocks' death: 'No longer hoping to carry out his first project, the writer determined to make the geography and commerce of the Somali country his principal objects.'

Officially, this was the expedition he was due to undertake and the reference is confusing unless one realizes that what Burton really meant by his first, and more important, project was to strike into Central Africa from Zanzibar or Harar to discover the source of the Nile and perhaps cross to the Atlantic. It was a tremendous and imaginative plan, already referred to in his letter to the Governor of Bombay, which had been passed on to London. The Court of Directors of the East India Company replied in a letter of August 23, 1854.

> Lt. Burton proposes to proceed in October from Aden to Berbera: thence to Hurra [Harar] the capital of the Somali country [*sic*], thence south-west to Ganana: thence south-eastwards to Zanzibar. He looks forward, however, to a more important expedition westwards. Respecting this you observe: [i.e. the Governor in Council in Bombay] 'the question of Lt. Burton's ulterior researches in Africa, to which allusion is made in this letter, may be deferred until the results of the expedition to the Somali country can be estimated'.[24]

In spite of this reply he was not disheartened, and in the report he sent to the Government on February 22, 1855, when about to start for Berbera and Zanzibar, he wrote that he hoped that the expedition 'may extend to the Ethiopic Olympus (Kilimanjaro) and settle the question of its eternal snows'. Three days later he sent a letter from Aden to Dr. Norton Shaw: 'My plans (public) are now to march southwards to the Webbe Shebbeli and Ganana; privately and *entre nous* I want to settle the question of Krapf and "eternal snows". There is little doubt that there is an open route through Africa to the Atlantic. I heard of it in Harar and will give the whole account . . .'*

Burton's imaginative projects were circumvented by the Aden

---

* In *First Footsteps in East Africa* he wrote: 'I repeatedly heard at Zayla and at Harar that traders had visited the far West, traversing for seven months a country of pagans wearing golden bracelets, till they reached the Salt Sea, upon which Franks sail in ships.'

authorities. Burton was Napier's disciple and he resembled the older man in his courage, passion for detail and for his lively criticism of those in authority. It was most unfortunate, therefore, that Napier's opponent, Colonel James Outram, should have been appointed Political Agent in Aden at a time when Burton was planning his expedition. Owing to his bad health Colonel Outram only stayed at Aden from July to December 1854, but those five months were critical for the Somali Expedition. 'I had no reason to like him,' wrote Burton; 'in his younger days, thirsting for distinction, Outram was ambitious to explore the Somali country, then considered the most dangerous in Africa, but when I prepared to do so he openly opposed me.'[25] Dr. Buist confirmed this in an editorial in the *Bombay Times* after the disaster to the Somali Expedition.

> Once spending a morning in Aden in August last, Col. Outram, then only a fortnight in office, but basing his views on those of the oldest and most experienced residents on the spot, pointed out to us most emphatically the extreme unwisdom of the so-called Somali Expedition and the tragedy that in some shape or other was almost certain to follow the wild adventure of a set of reckless young men, who, whatever their talents ... did not seem likely to add greatly to our scientific knowledge ... Mr. Burton wrote to us with his usual ability, defending his case in reply to a short editorial, embodying sentiments such as these, and expressing views opposed as much as possible to those we had advanced.*

Outram, summoned as his assistant Robert Lambert Playfair (later General Sir Robert Playfair), who had served with Outram on a mission in Syria from 1848 to 1850, and was made Political assistant. Playfair knew Arabic, and was later made responsible for obtaining all the evidence from Somalis and others who had been concerned with the attack on Burton's camp in April 1855. It will be seen that from the first he was inclined to accept the Somali stories rather than Burton's account.†

---

* The editorial by Dr. Buist was published on Saturday, May 12, 1855, and opened with the sentence: 'The Somali Expedition has come to a more sudden and bloody termination than our worst fears ever apprehended, although we were never void of the most serious alarms.'

† *Richard F. Burton* by Francis Hitchman, 1887, p. 252. After referring to Col. Outram's objections, Mr. Hitchman states: 'Captain Playfair, his Assistant, did all in his power to thwart Burton's views and Dr. Buist, the Editor of the *Bombay Times*, received a hint to "run down" the Somali Expedition—a task in which he was ably assisted by the Chaplain of Aden.'

John Hanning Speke

Lieut. John Hanning Speke had arrived in Aden in September 1854 with three years' furlough from India and wished to go on an expedition to Africa. He was astonished and discomfited to find that Colonel Outram not only refused to help his plans but also prohibited him from going at all, 'as the countries opposite Aden were so extremely dangerous for any foreigners to travel in', and the Somali was 'of such a wild and inhospitable nature that no stranger could possible live amongst them'.*²⁶

While Burton was in Aden details of the first part of his journey as far as Medina had been received by the Royal Geographical Society.

They prove [the Earl of Ellesmere stated in his presidential address on May 22, 1854] that the confidence of our Society has not been thrown away. Lieut. Burton travelled in the disguise of an Afghan pilgrim. His knowledge of the language and habits of his desert companions, and his boldness and sagacity, enabled him to maintain this disguise, the detection of which might have been dangerous, with complete success. A skirmish with Bedouin Arabs was fatal to twelve of the party, and no one, not inured to climate and observant of precautions, could have easily surmounted the difficulties of such a journey.²⁷

He had won fame by his exploit, but it did not prevent many in Aden from being very critical of his plans to explore Somaliland.

The letter of August 23 from the Directors of the East India Company reached Aden in October 1854; they were most careful to avoid any commitment. The expedition was not to be official 'but undertaken by Lieut. Burton as a private traveller, the Government giving no more protection to him than they would to any individual totally unconnected with the service'. There was nothing unusual in these instructions but they were not very sensible or honest, for the Company could not, in fact, avoid responsibility if there were trouble.

Lieutenant Burton [it was also stated] must be positively enjoined not to incur any immoderate risk, in carrying out the objects in view. He should carefully feel his way, and not proceed onwards, unless he

* The British officials of Aden have never liked the Somalis or troubled to discover their character; the author of this introduction heard talk about the treachery and savagery of the Somalis in October 1940 when he was a member of an irregular Somali–Arab force, trained in Aden, which helped in the recapture of Berbera and Somaliland from the Italians. In fact, the Somalis showed good discipline and were as entertaining company as Burton found them to be.

has reasonable grounds for believing that his own life and those of his associates will not be seriously endangered.

The Directors could hardly have expected Burton to go into unexplored country, among tribes described in official documents as 'savages', without endangering his life. Burton would never have left Zayla for Harar if he had been cautious and listened to the warnings of Hajj Ali Sharmakay, the Governor. The letter concluded with the statement that Lieut. Burton appeared 'eminently qualified to conduct such an expedition, which requires not only peculiar attainments, but the combination of energy and perseverance with prudence and discretion'. This was an echo of Lord Ellesmere's praise of Burton to the Royal Geographical Society.

It was not long, however, before the Court of Directors began to dislike Burton almost as much as they disliked Napier, not only because the disaster to the Somali Expedition caused them a great deal of trouble but also because Burton in his reports and his publications attacked the policy of the Court of Directors at every opportunity.

The fact that the Somali Expedition was sponsored by the Royal Geographical Society, had been approved by the Government of India and by the Court of Directors in London, had little effect in changing Outram's view. As a result of his opposition Burton felt obliged to take a decision which proved disastrous. He split up the party and made a series of preliminary surveys of the country in order to obtain information and to prove to the Aden authorities that travelling in Somaliland was feasible, and that he was justified in launching his main expedition to Zanzibar. The result of this delay, however, was to arouse suspicion among the Somali tribes; wild rumours spread rapidly about the intentions of the British Government when it was learned that officers were exploring different parts of Somaliland.

In his book *The Lake Regions of Central Africa*, Burton referred to the kindness and hospitality of Lieut.-Colonel Hamerton, the British Consul in Zanzibar, who helped him prepare for his expedition with John Speke into Central Africa in 1856, 'a well-omened contrast with my inauspicious reception at Aden in 1855, before my departure to explore the Eastern Horn of Africa, when the coldness of some, and the active jealousy of other political authorities, thwarted all my projects, and led to the tragic disaster at Berbera'.[28] Burton gives an account of this opposition and of his change of plans in the preface to *First Footsteps in East Africa*:

26

The voice of society at Aden was loud against the expedition. The rough manners, the fierce looks, and the insolent threats of the Somal* —the effects of our too peaceful rule—had prepossessed the timid colony at the 'Eye of El Yemen' with an idea of extreme danger. The Anglo-Saxon spirit suffers, it has been observed, from confinement with any but wooden walls, and the European degenerates rapidly, as do his bulldogs, his game-cocks, and other pugnaceous animals, in the hot, enervating, and unhealthy climates of the East.

The writer and his comrades were represented to be men deliberately going to their death, and the Somal at Aden were not slow in imitating the example of their rulers. The savages had heard of the costly Shoa Mission,[29] and its camels and 50 mules, and they longed for another rehearsal of the drama: according to them a vast outlay was absolutely necessary, every village must be feasted, every chief propitiated with magnificent presents, and dollars must be dealt out by handfuls. The Political Resident refused to countenance the scheme proposed, and his objection necessitated a further change of plans.

Accordingly, Lieut. Herne was directed to proceed, after the opening of the annual fair season, to Berbera, where no danger was apprehended. It was judged that the residence of this officer upon the coast would produce a friendly feeling on the part of the Somal and, indeed, as afterwards proved to the case, would facilitate the writer's egress from Harar, by terrifying the ruler for the fate of his caravans. Lieut. Herne, who on the 1st of January 1855, was joined by Lieut. Stroyan, resided on the African coast from November 1854 to April 1855;—Lieut. Speke was directed to land at Bunder Garay a small harbour in the 'Arz al-Aman', or 'Land of Safety', as the windward Somal style their country. His aim was to trace the celebrated Wady Nogal, noticing its watershed and other peculiarities, to purchase horses and camels for the future use of the Expedition, and to collect specimens of the reddish earth which, according to the older African travellers, denotes the presence of gold dust.

Meanwhile the author, assuming the disguise of an Arab merchant, prepared to visit the forbidden city of Harar.

To Colonel Outram it was a further outrage that Burton should go in Arab clothes; he argued that it lowered the British in the estimate of the native.

But [wrote Speke] this did not suit Lieut. Burton's plans, who, not wishing to be conspicuous whilst travelling to Harar, determined on going there disguised as an Arab Merchant and thought it better we should appear as his disciples, in accordance with which Herne had al-

* The Somali tribes used to have pitched battles on the high ground of Crater in Aden.

27

ready purchased his dress, and now I bought mine. It was anything but pleasant to feel. I had a huge hot turban, a long close-fitting gown, baggy loose drawers, drawn in at the ankles, sandals on my naked feet, and a silk girdle decorated with pistol and dirk.[30]

Although Lieut. John Speke was six years younger than Burton he had seen a good deal of active service in India under Sir John Campbell. He was physically strong, moody, and quite likeable, but a lack of education made him naïve, over-confident, and very susceptible to 'slights'. The account he gives of his activities in India shows a simple approach to life:

> There are now but few animals to be found in either India, Tibet, or the Himalaya Mountains, specimens of which have not fallen victims to my gun. Of this the paternal hall is an existing testimony ... The commander-in-Chief, Sir William Gomm, observing to what good account I always turned my leave, instead of idling my time away, or running into debt, took great pleasure in encouraging my hobby; and his staff were even heard to say it would be a pity if I did not get leave, as so much good resulted from it.*

In his book *What Led to the Discovery of the Source of the Nile*, published in 1864 and dedicated to Sir James Outram, Speke stated that he had come to Aden with the intention of leading an expedition to find the sources of the Nile, and that as early as 1849 he had planned 'to strike the Nile at its head, and then sail down that river to Egypt'; he referred to the Mountains of the Moon and thought he would find the Nile rising in the snow as did the Ganges in the Himalayas. Burton's account, although written during the quarrel, is more accurate:

> His [Speke's] heart was set on spending two years of his leave in collecting animals north of the line (of the Equator) in Africa. He never thought in any way of the Nile, and he was astonished at *my* views, which he deemed impracticable. He had no qualifications for the excursion he proposed to himself, except that of being a good sportsman. He was ignorant of the native races in Africa, he had brought with him almost £400 worth of cheap and useless guns and revolvers

* Speke appeared modest but was, in fact, exceedingly vain. After he had been on the expedition with Burton to Lake Tanganyika he wrote to his friend Rigby in Zanzibar describing how Burton had urged him to come with him on the expedition: 'I told him [Burton] I would not go again with him if I should be led into such expenses as I was at Berbera, so little did I care about acting second fiddle to him whom I have always thought I could show the way to better than he me.'[31]

. . . which the Africans would have rejected with disdain. He did not know any of the manners and customs of the East.

I saw that he was going to lose his money and his 'leave' and his life. Why should I have cared? I do not know . . . I first took him to Somaliland; then I applied officially for him and thus saved his furlough and his money by putting him on full service. You would now think, to see his conduct, that the case was reversed—that he had taken me, not I him.[32]

Speke was, in fact, both eager and thankful to have permission to join the expedition, but Burton did not at first assign him to any preliminary exploration since he had no surplus funds; the Government of India had only agreed to allocate one thousand pounds for the expedition, and that was to be paid in quarterly instalments. Speke was averse to being left waiting in Aden and he agreed to advance funds from his own private resources 'trusting to Lieut. Burton's promises in the future for being repaid'. He left Aden for the Nogal Valley on October 23, 1854, on an expedition which lasted three months.

Burton sailed from Aden on October 29, 1854, arrived at Harar on January 3, 1855, and on February 9 returned in safety to Aden, 'with the view of purchasing stores and provisions for a second and a longer journey. What unforeseen circumstances cut short the career of the proposed Expedition, the Postscript of the present volume will show.'

Burton as a Muslim at Zayla

The 'Postscript' only consists of twelve pages; the main story of the book covers the three months and ten days that Burton spent in Zayla, and on his travels from there to Harar and back to Berbera. It is a delightfully written and exciting travel adventure in which he also conveys his own pleasure in being with Arabs and Somalis. When delayed in the port of Zayla he led the prayers in the mosque,* and talked tirelessly in his house with Arabs, Somalis, Persians, and Indians; he read them stories from *The Thousand and One Nights*, told fortunes by palmistry or drew out horoscopes.

---

* Ralph E. Drake-Brockman in his book *British Somaliland*, published in 1912, states that the mosque where Burton led the prayers and read the Koran was still standing; the author also knew an old man who had been at Zayla as a boy of fifteen when Burton was there; the old Somali told Mr. Drake-Brockman that not only could Burton read the Koran better than any of the Mullahs but he was also better versed in the teachings of the Prophet of Islam.

It argues 'peculiarity', I own, to enjoy such a life [he wrote]. . . . You will doubtless, dear L,* convict me, by my own sentiments, of being an 'amateur barbarian'! You must, however, remember that I visited Africa fresh from Aden with its dull routine of meaningless parades and tiresome court-martial, where society is broken by ridiculous distinctions of staff men, and regimental men, Madras-men and Bombay-men, 'European' officers and 'black' officers, etc.

Burton's companions in Somaliland enjoyed his company just as he did theirs.

With Orientals [he wrote] you *must* be on extreme terms, as in Hibernia, either an angel of light or, that failing, a goblin damned. In East Africa especially, English phlegm, shyness, or pride, will bar every heart and raise every hand against you, whereas what M. Rochet calls 'a certain *rondeur* of manner is a specific for winning affection'.[33]

The Arabs and Somalis laughed at his bawdy stories, respected his physical powers and reverenced his learning, and the fact that he had done the pilgrimage to Mecca. No one among the Muslims he met considered that Burton was an infidel who had played a trick in doing the pilgrimage, nor did Burton look on it in this light. In such company he was a true Muslim and there are those, such as Dr. Hogarth, who argued that Burton 'professed to be a Moslem up to the day of his death', though his devout and devoted wife persisted in declaring that he had died a Roman Catholic.

When Burton had been removed from his post as British Consul in Damascus, he argued, in a long letter of October 16, 1871, to the Secretary of State for Foreign Affairs, that he had been unjustly dismissed. He said that as soon as he had been appointed to the post in November 1868: 'A rumour was at once spread abroad that the Muslims hated me because I had pilgrimaged to Meccah and that my life would be placed in danger by their fanaticism.' The story had been spread by those who feared that he might be against the Christian missionaries and too much in favour of the Muslims: 'after my pilgrimage to Meccah I had lived for several years in Moslem communities, Arab, African, and Indian still more fanatical than the Syrian.'[34]

It is difficult to know what Burton did believe and, anyway, he considered it was his own affair. In his remarkable poem 'The Kasidah of Haji Abdu el-Yezdi' (two hundred and sixty-eight couplets), and in

* The Hon. James Grant Lumsden, member of the Governing Council of the East India Company in Bombay, to whom the book is dedicated. Every now and again Burton wrote as if addressing him in a letter which helped to enliven his narrative.

3   Burton at the age of forty at the time of his marriage to Isabel
Arundell (watercolour by Louis Desanges, in possession of the
South London Art Gallery, Southwark)

4   Watercolour of John Hanning Speke with a background of Lake Victoria Nyanza, in possession of the Royal Geographical Society, London

his other poems, it is clear that he thought deeply on morality, and man's destiny. Any preference he had was certainly for Islam.*

Burton liked Muslim ways and admired their poetry which he compared very favourably with 'that poverty of invention and puerility of imagination that distinguish the religious rhymsters of Christianity'. He defended the Muslim custom of keeping the women apart: 'Al-Islam seems purposely to have loosened the ties between the sexes in order to strengthen the bonds which connect man with man.' But he was always quick to note the charms of an attractive Somali girl, and he has sympathetic accounts of the two fat Somali women he named Shehrazade and Deenarzade, who came with the expedition to do the cooking.

It was the different types of Somali males who interested him most, for they were to him a new and entertaining people—a combination of African fecklessness and enjoyment in life combined with intelligence, a slim elegance and sometimes a handsome Arab profile. His remarks on the Somali character are sometimes caustic and uncomplimentary, but he was writing of a period of over a hundred years ago when the tribes he contacted were suffering from great poverty and were more than usually disturbed; many of his comments concerned the Eesa and, 'traitorous as an Eesa', was a saying among the inhabitants of Zayla at the time.

On his way from Zayla to Harar he was intrigued and surprised, as many travellers have been, to meet Somalis who had wandered through Arabia, India, and Egypt: 'Many speak with fluency,' he wrote, 'three or four languages and are perfectly acquainted with English manners and customs.' He found, too, that news travelled very fast and that they learned of events in the Crimean War remarkably quickly after they had occurred. His views of the Somali were a great deal more favourable than is generally realized. In his official report to Government he wrote: 'they evince a gentleness of disposition and a docility which offer fair hopes to civilization in this region of barbarism ... people who, in my humble opinion, are capable of being raised high in the scale of humanity. .... Every free-born man holds himself equal to his ruler, and allows no royalties or prerogatives to abridge his birth-right of liberty. Yet I have observed, that with all their passion for

* He was accepted by other Muslims as a genuine Hajji and this was not surprising considering his great knowledge of the written and spoken traditions of al-Islam: but in England there was criticism and Isabel Burton wrote indignantly: 'He never profaned the sanctuaries of Mecca and Medina, and so far from being unpopular with the Moslems, he received almost yearly an invitation to go back with the Hajji' (*Life*, vol. 1, p. 181).

independence, the Somal, when subject to strict rule as at Zayla and Harar, are both apt to discipline and subservient to command.[35] Those who have known Somalis have found that they make good soldiers and officers; they are full of curiosity and travel the world, accepting almost any job without feeling a sense of inferiority, perhaps because they believe that they are superior to everyone else.'

Burton also described them as 'a fierce and turbulent race of Republicans'; but he realized, although he was in their country for only five months, that in spite of the apparent lawlessness, the Somalis had a well-balanced and intricate society, and he noted very wisely:

A partial intermeddling with the quarrels of these people is unwise. Either our intervention should be complete—either we should constitute ourselves sole judges of all disputes, or we should sedulously turn a deaf ear to their complaints . . . Nothing is more dangerous than to influence in any way the savage balance of power between these tribes: by throwing our weight on one side we may do them incalculable mischief. The Somal, like the Arab Bedouin, live in a highly artificial, though an apparently artless, state of political relations; and the imperfect attempt of strangers to interfere would be turned to the worst account by the designing adventurer and the turbulent spirit, who expect to rise by means of anarchy and confusion. Hitherto our partial intervention between the Habr Awal of Berbera and the Habr Girhajis of Zayla has been fraught with evils to them, and consequently to us.[36]

Dr. I. M. Lewis, a modern anthropologist with an intimate knowledge of Somali society, has written that *First Footsteps in East Africa* 'remains the best general description of northern Somali society'. Burton realized the importance that Somalis attached to their forebears and he was careful to find out and write down the genealogies of the various big divisions in the Somali nation.

It is of the first importance [writes Dr. Lewis] to appreciate that a Somali genealogy is not a mere family tree recording the historical descent and connections of a particular individual or group. Whatever its historical significance, in the sphere of politics its importance lies in the fact that it represents the social divisions of people into corporate political groups. By reference to his ancestors, a man's relations with others are defined, and his position in Somali society as a whole determined.[37]

When a Somali delegation visited London in 1955 to have discussions with the Colonial Office, Burton's book of a century before was quoted to show that in his day the Somali country stretched 'to within a few miles of Harar'. It was argued that Britain, which had agreements to protect these tribes, had betrayed them when Somali territory had been handed over under the Anglo-Ethiopian Treaty of 1897. It was also argued that Ethiopia had not, in fact, occupied these grazing lands, and that there had been a second betrayal under the Anglo-Ethiopian Agreement of 1954 when these regions were formally handed over—regions which the Somalis still consider belong to them. The Ethiopians have not this time left the area uncolonized and have moved in police and troops; 'to the present day the people of Shoa retain an inherited dread of the lowland Moslems', wrote Burton. He tells the story of the Somali leader, Mohamed Gragne (Ahmed Ibn Ibrahim Al-Ghazi), who invaded the highlands of Ethiopia, dominating the country for several years and 'is still the subject of many a wild and grisly legend'. The history that Burton recounts is today still a vivid background to the tension between the Muslim Somalis and the Christian Ethiopians.

Burton did not want the Somalis interfered with, but at the same time he considered it very important that the British should set up an Agency in Berbera, and he considered that this could be done without any control of territory inland.

In the first place [he wrote in his Preface], Berbera is the true key of the Red Sea, the centre of East African traffic, and the only safe place for shipping upon the western Erythraean shore, from Suez to Gardafui. Backed by lands capable of cultivation, and by hills covered with pine and other valuable trees, enjoying a comparatively temperate climate, with a regular although thin monsun, this harbour has been coveted by many a foreign conqueror. Circumstances have thrown it, as it were, into our arms and, if we refuse the chance, another and a rival nation will not be so blind.

Secondly, we are bound to protect the lives of British subjects upon this coast. In 1825 the crew of the *Mary Ann* brig was treacherously murdered by the Somal. The consequence of a summary and exemplary punishment* was that in August 1843, when the Honourable East India

* In a note Burton states that the East India Company sent the sloop-of-war *Elphinstone* to blockade the coast; 'when her guns opened fire, the people fled with their wives and children, and the spot where a horseman was killed by a cannon ball is still shown on the plain near the town. Through the intervention of El Hajj Sharmakay[38] [he had been sent with Lieut. Cruttenden from Aden to investigate], the survivors were recovered; the Somal bound themselves to refrain from future attacks upon English vessels, and also to refund by annual instalments the full amount of plundered property … About £6,000 were recovered, and the people were strongly impressed with the fact that we had both the will and the means to keep their plundering propensities within bounds.'

33

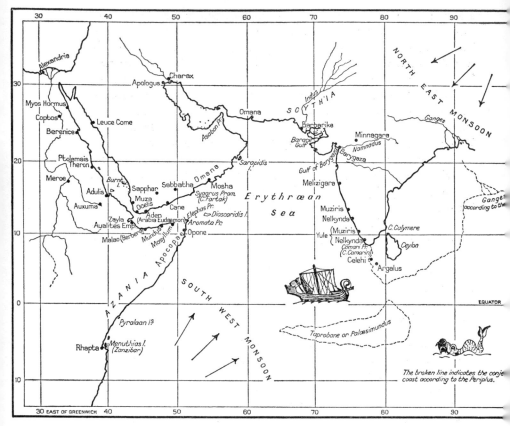

'The Periplus of the Erythraean Sea' was written about A.D. *60 by an anonymous Greek trader living in Egypt. It is the first record there is of ports on the African or Somali Coast where an important entrepôt trade was carried on between India, Egypt, and Rome, and whence frankincense and myrrh were exported from the area of Cape Gardafui for the temples of Egypt, of Rome, and later for the churches of Byzantium.*

Company's war-steamer *Memnon* was stranded at Ras Assayr near Cape Gardafui, no outrage was attempted by the barbarians, upon whose barren shores our seamen remained for months labouring at the wreck.

In 1855 the Somal, having forgotten the old lesson, renewed their practice of pillaging and murdering strangers [that is the attack on Burton's camp at Berbera]. It is evident that this people cannot be trusted without supervision, and equally certain that vessels are liable to be cast ashore in this part of the Red Sea. But a year ago the French

34

steam corvette, *Le Caiman*, was lost within sight of Zayla; the Bedouin Somal, principally Eesa, assembled a fanatic host which was, however, dispersed before blood had been drawn by the exertions of the governor and his guards. It remains for us, therefore, to provide against such contingencies. Were one of the Peninsular and Oriental Company's vessels cast upon this inhospitable shore, in the present state of affairs the lives of the passengers, and the cargo, would be placed in imminent peril.

Burton has been criticized for being over-optimistic about the possibilities of developing the Somali country and the importance of Berbera, which was not occupied by the British until 1884. From his reading of the Periplus of the Erythraean Sea, of writings by Arab travellers and because of the remains he found of a past civilization, perhaps Persian, he knew that the country had been much richer and more densely populated in the past. He noted the great variety of shrubs and trees growing in the wadis and his expedition discovered good drinking water near Berbera.

Burton wanted to advance the British cause and to help Somalis; the development of the hinterland round Berbera would, he believed, be a good beginning. He was an imperialist because he considered it was important to maintain British prestige in the East. He had seen in India the ill effect of the Afghan disaster of 1842, and he had also seen the great benefit the peasants of Sind obtained from the wise administration of Sir Charles Napier. He was in favour of a forward policy as against the negative imperialism of the East India Company. A forward policy was suited to those days of British expansion; whereas today, with British imperialism in retreat, it is a dangerous and embarrassing policy, as Burton would probably have been the first to realize. 'He had,' said the late Sir Arnold Wilson, 'great sympathy with and understanding of the common people, but little sympathy with their rulers.' [39]

Disaster at Berbera and the Quarrel with Speke

An attempt has been made so far in this introduction to give some picture of this extraordinary man, Richard Burton; to show that the Somali Expedition had long been planned by the Royal Geographical Society and that Burton was already considering striking westwards to discover the source of the Nile; and to show the opposition he encountered in Aden and the enmity which his outspokenness was building up for himself in the future. The disaster to the Somali Expedition

D

led to the crystallization of this enmity, though it took some years for this to happen.

The main expedition consisting of forty-two men and twenty-six camels assembled in Berbera on April 7, 1855. Colonel James Outram had left Aden in December and Colonel W. M. Coghlan (later to be General Sir William Coghlan) had taken over as Acting Political Resident with Lieutenant Robert Lambert Playfair as his Assistant. On the night of April 18/19 Burton's camp was attacked by a large force of Somalis; Lieut. Stroyan was killed, Burton and Speke were severely wounded, the camp was plundered, and the expedition had to retreat to Aden. Burton only described this important event briefly in his 'Postscript'; he refuted the charge that he had, as commander of the expedition, failed to take adequate precautions and asked that the project should be revived, 'nothing is required but permission to renew the attempt'.

For about a year and a half reports were exchanged between William Coghlan, promoted Lieut.-Colonel and Political Resident in Aden; the Governor of Bombay (Lord Elphinstone); the Governor-General of India (Lord Dalhousie) and the Board of the East India Company in London. 'The murderous attack,' wrote Burton's friend, Lord Elphinstone, 'must retard, if it does not altogether impede, the progress of discovery in these regions and the establishment of friendly and commercial intercourse with their inhabitants.' [40] It was not, indeed, until thirty years later than an expedition went from Berbera to the Webbe Shebelli and Juba rivers, and it was thirty-seven years before Speke's attempt to reach the Nogal Valley was followed by a successful exploration of the area. [41]

Looking back on these events in the light of Burton's subsequent career it seemed that more information was needed about the planning of the main expedition, about what happened after the disaster at Berbera and about the early relationship between Burton and Speke. The failure of the main expedition was even more significant to Burton's career than was the success of the Harar journey. He naturally gives much more space to the Harar story, and this lack of balance is to some extent corrected by the addition of Chapters XI and XII based on the official reports.

Did Burton show a lack of prudence in allowing his camp at Berbera to be overrun—'an overweening confidence', as Lord Elphinstone described it? There were certainly plenty of reasons why he should have been wary. Had the Somali Elders at Berbera warned the members of the expedition that an attack had been planned on the camp, and was Burton telling the truth when he said that there had been no such warnings? Were the attackers a band of Somali plunderers out for loot, or were they 'nationalists' protecting their country from foreigners who coveted it, as was argued by the Somalis? How far was the disaster the fault of Colonel Outram in putting difficulties in the

*Speke's arrival at the Northern Lake.**

way so that the start was delayed and rumours spread, and how much was it the fault of the British authorities later, in not supplying the help required? The disaster caused the authorities a great deal of trouble and Burton was held responsible.

* This dramatic 'diorama' of Speke catching his first sight of the northern lake, to be called Lake Victoria Nyanza, is on the wall of the East African Section of the Commonwealth Institute in London, where presumably it is intended that visitors should be given accurate information.

Alongside is a printed story of African exploration in which it is stated: 'None had penetrated inland other than slave traders following established routes. It was left to men like John Hanning Speke [pictured here on the shores of Lake Victoria] to reveal to the world something of the great hinterland now known as Kenya, Uganda and Tanganyika.'

Why is Burton's name omitted? There is one reference to him: 'In 1858 Speke and Richard Burton reached Lake Tanganyika', as if Speke were the leader of the Expedition.

When it became known that Burton was severely criticized in official quarters, his enemies felt encouraged to make personal attacks. Colonel C. P. Rigby, the British Consul in Zanzibar, sent home reports criticizing Burton for the way he had treated the Zanzibaris sent with him on the expedition to Lake Tanganyika, and in a private letter to a friend Rigby wrote: 'Speke is a right good, jolly, resolute fellow. Burton is not fit to hold a candle to him and has done nothing in comparison with what Speke has, but Speke is a modest, unassuming man, not very ready with his pen. Burton will blow his trumpet very loud and get all the credit of the discoveries. Speke works. Burton lies on his back all day and picks other people's brains.'[42]

This was, in fact, Burton's great strength. Owing to his knowledge of Arabic he was able to explore the great store-house of Arabic literature and books of travel, and to obtain valuable information from the Arab traders; they gave the information about the great lake to the north. It was Speke's lack of modesty which led him to make inaccurate statements such as the following: 'I am sure that everybody at Zanzibar knows it, that I was the leader and Burton the second of the Expedition [to Lakes Tanganyika and Victoria Nyanza]. Had I not been with him he never could have undergone the journey . . .'[43]

The younger man had borne resentment against Burton ever since they had met in Aden in 1854, but it was only under the stresses and strains of the journey through central Africa that Burton realized this. It was at Unanymebi, or Tabora, on the way back from Lake Tanganyika to Zanzibar that the quarrel began about the source of the White Nile. The two men were on friendly terms when Speke started north from Tabora leaving Burton there to recover from an illness and to plan the journey back. On June 28, 1858, Burton wrote from Unanyembi to the Secretary of the Royal Geographical Society:

> We left the Lake Ujiji [Lake Tanganyika] about a month ago and are now halted at the main depot of Arab trade. Captain Speke has volunteered . . . to visit the Ukerere Lake [Victoria Nyanza] of which Arabs give grand accounts. It lies nearly due north of Unanyembi at a distance of from 12 to 15 marches. Thus we shall be enabled to bring home authentic details of the four great waters which drain Eastern and Central Africa, viz. the Nyassa, the Chawa, the Ujiji Lake, and the Ukerere.*

* M.S. letter in the possession of the R.G.S. Owing to difficulties with the porters they were not able to visit Lake Nyassa, now called Lake Malawi, nor Lake Chilwa or Shirwa, which Burton called the Chawa.

Speke returned, having reached the Lake but not having had time to explore it; he asserted, however, that he had discovered the source of the White Nile. Burton was annoyed that Speke should be so certain without evidence, except hearsay, and Speke was angry that his arguments were questioned. By a stroke of good fortune Speke's guess was correct, though the controversy over the source of the White Nile was not finally settled until H. M. Stanley's journey in 1876 twelve years after Speke's death. On the journey back to Zanzibar from Tabora Burton and Speke decided not to discuss the subject of the source of the White Nile since it aroused too much emotion.

They arrived in Aden on April 16, 1859, and three days later Burton wrote to the Secretary of the Royal Geographical Society to explain that he was going to delay a little longer in Aden after Speke had left:

> Captain Speke, however, will lay before you his map observations and two papers, one a diary of his passage of the Tanganyika Lake between Ujiji and Kasengi, and the other his exploration of the Nyanza Ukerewe or Northern Lake. To this I would respectfully direct the serious attention of the Committee as there are now reasons for believing it to be the source or the principal feeder of the White Nile.

It was a generous letter and gave Speke the benefit of the doubt with regard to his theories about the Nile. It is a great pity that Burton decided to argue against the Nile theory, since he was in fact robbing his own expedition of one of its great achievements.

One would have expected that Sir Roderick Murchison, President of the Royal Geographical Society, and Speke, would have waited until Burton arrived before making any plans for a further expedition, but that is not what happened. On the first day after his return to England, Speke went to see the President of the Society. 'Sir Roderick, I need hardly say,' he wrote, 'at once accepted my views . . . and said to me, "Speke, we must send you there again."'[44] One can guess what were Speke's views   that Burton was ill and unfit to lead another expedition, and that he, Speke, had done all the work. He had returned from Aden on board the warship *Furious* carrying Lord Elgin, late Governor-General of India, and probably learned how unpopular Burton had become. Laurence Oliphant, Secretary to the Governor-General was also on board and apparently encouraged Speke to think that he was a better man than Burton and had been the most important figure both on the Somali and the Central African Expeditions. 'Jack is one of the bravest fellows in the world,' wrote

Burton; 'if he has a fault it is overweening vanity, and being so easily flattered; in good hands he would be the best of men.'

Burton arrived in England on May 21, a fortnight after Speke, but it was already too late. Speke had become the hero and Burton was set aside. 'Sir Roderick Murchison had given Jack the leadership of a new expedition,' wrote Burton; 'my own long-cherished plan of entering Africa through Somaliland, landing at the Arab town Mombas, was dismissed as unworthy of notice.'[45] Judging from his letter from Aden to the Royal Geographical Society, Burton certainly expected his companion to visit the Society, although later he expressed annoyance that he had done this; but the main quarrel was that Speke had exploited the advantage of his earlier arrival to oust Burton.

> Can I feel otherwise than indignant [wrote Burton in *Lake Regions of Africa*], when I find that, after preceding me from Aden to England, with the spontaneous offer on his part of not appearing before the Society that originated the expedition until my return,* he had lost no time in taking measures to secure for himself the right of working the field which I had opened, and that from that day he has placed himself *en evidence* as the *primum mobile* of an Expedition in which he signed himself 'surveyor'.

To a friend Burton wrote with regard to Speke: 'Let him alone; he will be very sorry some day, though that won't mend my case.'†

* 'And the last words Jack ever spoke to me on earth were, "*Good-bye, old fellow; you may be quite sure I shall not go up to the Royal Geographical Society until you come to the fore and we appear together. Make your mind quite easy about that.*"' Burton's account of Speke's statement before leaving Aden in April 1859.[46]

† The day after Speke met his death on September 15, 1864, he was to have debated with Burton the vexed question of the source of the White Nile in one of the committee rooms of the British Association which was meeting in Bath. It would have been the first meeting between the two travellers since they had parted at Aden in April 1859.

In 1863 Speke had published his *Journal of the Discovery of the Source of the Nile*, describing how the river flowed from Lake Victoria Nyanza, as he had argued it did ever since his discovery of the lake on the expedition with Burton. The book was violently attacked by geographers such as M'Queen, who agreed with Burton that nothing had been proved.

It had been hoped that the truth would be established by the 'Nile Duel' between Burton and Speke. On the day before the debate Burton and Speke saw each other at the meeting of the Association but did not converse. Isabel Burton, who is not a very reliable witness, described Speke's face as 'full of sorrow, of yearning and perplexity'; she wrote that he left the hall saying 'I cannot stand this any longer' and that he hoped that he would not return.[47]

That afternoon Speke went out shooting with a cousin in Neston Park near Bath; his gun was discharged into his side as he climbed over a wall, so that he died shortly after-

Why should Sir Roderick Murchison and the members of the Royal Geographical Society have been influenced by Speke, of whom they knew little? Burton had been the favourite son of the Society for over six years, ever since it had supported his expedition to Medina and Mecca in 1852. This exploit and his scholarly account of it, had been followed by his successful journey to Harar, and now he had returned from leading the first successful expedition into central Africa with the discovery of two lakes. Yet the Royal Geographical Society ignored his plan for another expedition. The fact that he was ill at the time was not a sufficient reason.

It is true that the Society presented Burton with its Gold Medal in May 1859, but it could not have done less, and Sir Roderick Murchison remarked on several occasions that Speke deserved it as much. The most reasonable explanation is that the critical official reports on Burton's handling of the Berbera trouble and the hostility expressed by high officials of the East India Company, to a great extent provoked by Burton, had finally made some members of the Society very critical of him.

This was a serious set-back to his career as an explorer and it came at a time when he was in financial difficulties, since his name had been removed from the Indian Army list and he received neither pay nor pension; this followed the taking over of the East India Company by the India Office in 1858. Burton still hoped, however, to be received back into the good graces of the Royal Geographical Society, and he would have been if he could have proved that Speke was wrong in his belief that Lake Victoria Nyanza was the main source of the White Nile.

Burton was therefore very sensitive to any criticism of himself received by the Royal Geographical Society. When his friend Dr. Norton Shaw, the Secretary, showed Burton an unpleasant letter written to the Society by Rigby, from Zanzibar, criticizing him, Burton sent Rigby a long and extremely angry letter:

> You have addressed a virulent attack on me to a quarter in which you had hoped it would prove deeply injurious to me; and this, not in the discharge of any public duty, but for the gratification of a long-standing private pique . . . I shall at all times, in all companies, even in print if it suits me, use the same freedom in discussing your character and conduct that you have presumed to exercise in discussing mine.

---

wards. The verdict at the inquest was that the gun had been fired accidentally. Richard Burton believed that it was suicide. He knew how expert Speke was at handling a gun and he could not believe that it was an accident.

It was not possible to find a sponsor for his further exploration of Africa and he left England to travel in north America and visit the Mormons which resulted in his remarkable book, *The City of the Saints*. 'The explorer,' he wrote prophetically in his *First Footsteps in East Africa*, 'too frequently must rest satisfied with descrying from his Pisgah the promised Land of Knowledge, which another more fortunate is destined to conquer'; but he added: 'failure inspirits a man ... strengthens the mind to fresh exertions, and gives a double value to the prize'.

Burton married, entered the Consular Service, travelled, wrote, and finally near the end of his life as Consul in Trieste produced perhaps his greatest work—his privately printed and unexpurgated translation of the *Arabian Nights'* tales in Sixteen volumes with copious and erudite notes. Considering the prudery of Victorian England and the difficulty he had had in publishing matters of anthropological interest, he was amazed at its success. 'I struggled for forty-seven years,' he said sardonically, at the end of his life. 'I distinguished myself in every way I possibly could. I never had a compliment nor a "Thank you", nor a single farthing. I translated a doubtful book in my old age, and I immediately made sixteen thousand guineas. Now that I know the tastes of England, we need never be without money.'[48]

Burton died in 1890, five years after his edition of the *Arabian Nights* had been published, and his devout Roman Catholic wife, Isabel, burned the notes and manuscripts of which she disapproved.

> Like many geniuses [wrote Professor Sayce, the well-known orientalist], Burton lived before his time and suffered accordingly. His insight enabled him to reach conclusions which conflicted with the orthodox theories of the day; it is not wonderful that there was friction between him and the bureaucrats of red tapeism, or that the reward of his work was to be sent to some remote and insanitary corner of the earth to die. But instead of dying he usually managed to discover new parts and make additions to science in his place of exile.[49]

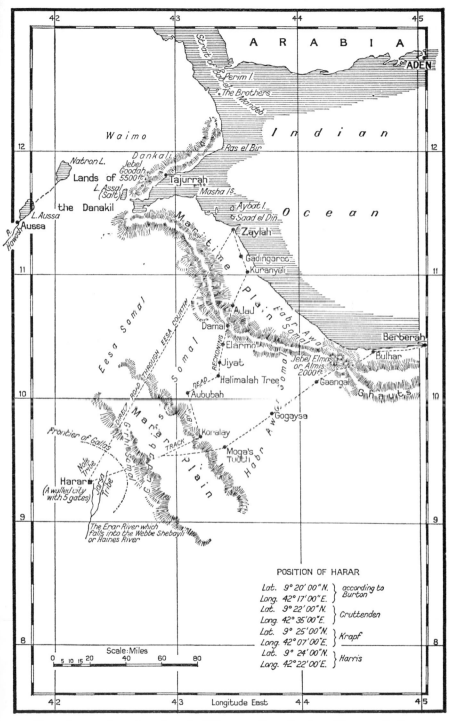

Burton's map (exactly redrawn) of his route from Zayla to Harar to Berbera.

Within the map:

42   43   44   45

A R A B I A
ADEN

Strait of Bab el Mandeb
Perim I.
The Brothers

W a i m o
I n d i a n

12   12
Ras el Bir

D a n k a l i
Natron L.
Jebel
Goodah
5500 ft.
Lands of
Tajurrah
L. Assal
(Salt)
Masha Is.
the Danakil
Aybat I.
Saad el Din
O c e a n
L. Aussa
Aussa
R. Hawash
Zaylah

11   11
Gadingaroo
Kuranyeli

Eesa Somal
Maritime Plain
Tabra Somal Awa

Aluo
Damal
Somal
Elarmo
Berberah
Jiyat
Jebel Elmas
or Almis
2000 ft.
Bulhar
Halimalah Tree
Gaangal
Ghauts

10   10
Aububah
DIRECT ROAD THROUGH EESA COUNTRY
REDKONING
NEAP
Gogaysa
Frontier of Gallas
Nole Tribe
Marar Plain
Koralay
TRACK
Habr Awal Somal
Moga's
Tuuli
Harar
(A walled city
with 5 gates)
Jersi Tribe

9   9
The Erar River which
falls into the Webbe Shebayli
or Haines River

POSITION OF HARAR

Lat. 9° 20' 00" N. } according to
Long. 42° 17' 00" E. } Burton

Lat. 9° 22' 00" N. } Cruttenden
Long. 42° 35' 00" E. }

Lat. 9° 25' 00" N. } Krapf
Long. 42° 07' 00" E. }

8   8
Scale: Miles
0 5 10 15 20   40   60   80

Lat. 9° 24' 00" N. } Harris
Long. 42° 22' 00" E. }

42   43   Longitude East   44   45

I

Departure from Aden

I DOUBT NOT THERE are many who ignore the fact that in Eastern Africa, scarcely three hundred miles distant from Aden, there is a counterpart of ill-famed Timbuctoo in the Far West. The more adventurous Abyssinian travellers, Salt and Stuart, Krapf and Isenberg, Barker and Rochet—not to mention divers Roman Catholic Missioners—attempted Harar, but attempted it in vain. The bigoted ruler and barbarous people threatened death to the Infidel who ventured within their walls; some Negro Merlin having, it is said, read Decline and Fall in the first footsteps of the Frank.* Of all foreigners the English were, of course, the most hated and dreaded; at Harar slavery still holds its headquarters, and the old Dragon well knows what to expect from the hand of St. George. Thus the various travellers who appeared in beaver and black coats became persuaded that the city was inaccessible, and Europeans ceased to trouble themselves about Harar.

It is, therefore, a point of honour with me, dear L.,† to utilize my title of Haji by entering the city, visiting the ruler, and returning in safety, after breaking the guardian spell.

* 'A tradition exists,' says Lieut. Cruttenden, 'amongst the people of Harar, that the prosperity of their city depends upon the exclusion of all travellers not of the Moslem faith, and all Christians are specially interdicted.' These freaks of interdiction are common to African rulers, who on occasions of war, famine, or pestilence, struck with some superstitious fear, close their gates to strangers.

† J. G. Lumsden, see dedication, opposite.

The most auspicious day in the Moslem year for beginning a journey is, doubtless, the 6th of the month Safar, on which, quoth the Prophet, al-Islam emerged from obscurity. Yet even at Aden we could not avail ourselves of this lucky time: our delays and difficulties were a fit prelude for a journey amongst those 'Blameless Ethiopians', with whom no less a personage than august Jove can dine and depart.*

On Sunday, the 29th October, 1854, our manifold impediments were pronounced complete. Friend Steinhauser threw the slipper of blessing at my back, and about 4 p.m. embarking from Maala Bunder, we shook out our 'muslin', and sailed down the fiery harbour. Passing the guard-boat, we delivered our permit; before venturing into the open sea we repeated the Fâtihah-prayer in honour of the Shaykh Majid, inventor of the mariners' compass, and evening saw us dancing on the bright clear tide, whose 'magic waves', however, murmured after another fashion the siren song which charmed the senses of the old Arabian voyagers. †¹

Suddenly every trace of civilization fell from my companions as if it had been a garment. At Aden, shaven and beturbaned, Arab fashion, now they threw off all dress save the loin cloth, and appeared in their dark morocco. Mohammed filled his mouth with a mixture of coarse Surat tobacco and ashes—the latter article intended, like the Anglo-Indian soldier's chili in his arrack, to 'make it bite'. Gulad uncovered his head, a member which in Africa is certainly made to go bare, and buttered himself with an unguent redolent of sheep's tail; and Ismail, the rais or captain of our 'foyst',‡ the *Sahalah*, applied himself to puffing his nicotiana out of a goat's shank-bone. Our crew, consisting of seventy-one men and boys, prepared, as evening fell, a mess of Jowari grain§ and grease, the recipe of which I spare you, and it was dispatched in a style that would have done credit to Kafirs as regards gobbling, bolting, smearing lips, licking fingers, and using ankles as napkins. Then with a light easterly breeze and the ominous cliffs of

* The Abyssinian law of detaining guests—Pedro Covilhaõ, the first Portuguese envoy (A.D. 1499), lived and died a prisoner there—appears to have been the Christian modification of the old Ethiopic rite of sacrificing strangers.

† The curious reader will find in the Herodotus of the Arabs, Al-Masudi's 'Meadows of gold and mines of gems', a strange tale of the blind billows and the singing waves of Berbera and Jofuni (Cape Guardafui, the classical Aromata).

‡ 'Foyst' and 'buss', are the names applied by old travellers to the half-decked vessels of these seas.

§ Holcus Sorghum, the common grain of Africa and Arabia: the Somali call it Hirad; the people of El Yemen, Ta'am.

46

Little Aden still in sight, we spread our mats on deck and prepared to sleep under the moon.*

My companions, however, felt, without perhaps comprehending, the joviality arising from a return to Nature. Every man was forthwith nicknamed, and pitiless was the raillery upon the venerable subjects of long and short, fat and thin. One sang a war-song, another a love-song, a third some song of the sea, whilst the fourth, an Eesa youth, with the villanous expression of face common to his tribe, gave us a rain measure, such as men chant during wet weather. All these effusions were *naïve* and amusing: none, however, could bear English translation without an amount of omission which would change their nature. Each effort of minstrelsy was accompanied by roars of laughter, and led to much manual pleasantry. All swore that they had never spent, intellectually speaking, a more charming *soirée*, and pitied me for being unable to enter thoroughly into the spirit of the dialogue. Truly it is not only the polished European, as was said of a certain travelling notability, that lapses with facility into pristine barbarism.

I will now introduce you to my companions. The managing man is one Mohammed Mahmud,† generally called al-Hammal, or the porter: he is a Havildar, or sergeant in the Aden police, and was entertained for me by Lieut. Dansey, an officer who unfortunately was not 'confirmed' in a political appointment at Aden. The Hammal is a bullnecked, round-headed fellow of lymphatic temperament, with a lampblack skin, regular features, and a pulpy figure—two rarities amongst his countrymen, who compare him to a Banyan. An orphan in early youth, and becoming, to use his own phrase, sick of milk, he ran away from his tribe, the Habr Girhajis, and engaged himself as a coaltrimmer with the slaves on board an Indian war-steamer. After rising in rank to the command of the crew, he became servant and interpreter to travellers, visited distant lands—Egypt and Calcutta—and finally settled as a Faringhi policeman. He cannot read or write, but he has all the knowledge to be acquired by fifteen or twenty years' hard 'knocking about': he can make a long speech, and, although he never prays, a longer prayer; he is an excellent mimic, and delights his auditors by imitations and descriptions of Indian ceremony, Egyptian dancing, Arab vehemence, Persian abuse, European vivacity, and Turkish

* The Somal being a people of less nervous temperament than the Arabs and Indians, do not fear the moonlight.

† The first name is that of the individual, as the Christian name with us, the second is that of the father; in the Somali country, as in India, they are not connected by the Arab 'bin'—son of. (See p. 86 for illustration.—Ed.)

insolence. With prodigious inventiveness, and a habit of perpetual intrigue, acquired in his travels, he might be called a 'knowing' man, but for the truly Somali weakness of showing in his countenance all that passes through his mind. This people can hide nothing: the blank eye, the contracting brow, the opening nostril and the tremulous lip, betray, despite themselves, their innermost thoughts.

The second servant whom I bring before you is Gulad, another policeman at Aden. He is a youth of good family, belonging to the Ismail Arrah, the royal clan of the great Habr Girhajis tribe. His father was a man of property, and his brethren near Berbera, are wealthy Bedouin: yet he ran away from his native country when seven or eight years old, and became a servant in the house of a butter merchant at Mocha. Thence he went to Aden, where he began with private service, and ended his career in the police. He is one of those long, live skeletons, common amongst the Somal: his shoulders are parallel with his ears, his ribs are straight as a mummy's, his face has not an ounce of flesh upon it, and his features suggest the idea of some lank bird: we call him Long Gulad, to which he replies with the Yemen saying 'Length is Honour, even in Wood'. He is brave enough, because he rushes into danger without reflection; his great defects are weakness of body and nervousness of temperament, leading in times of peril to the trembling of hands, the dropping of caps, and the mismanagement of bullets: besides which, he cannot bear hunger, thirst, or cold.

The third is one Abdi Abokr, also of the Habr Girhajis, a personage whom, from his smattering of learning and his prodigious rascality, we call the Mulla 'End of Time'.* He is a man about forty, very old-looking for his age, with small, deep-set cunning eyes, placed close together, a hook nose, a thin beard, a bulging brow, scattered teeth,† and a short scant figure, remarkable only for length of back. His gait is stealthy, like a cat's, and he has a villanous grin. This worthy never prays, and can neither read nor write; but he knows a chapter or two of the Koran, recites audibly a long Ratib or task, morning and evening,‡

* Abdi is an abbreviation of Abdullah; Abokr, a corruption of Abu Bakr. The 'End of Time' alludes to the prophesied corruption of the Moslem priesthood in the last epoch of the world.

† This peculiarity is not uncommon amongst the Somal; it is considered by them a sign of warm temperament.

‡ The Moslem should first recite the Farz prayers, or those ordered in the Koran; secondly, the Sunnat or practice of the Prophet; and, thirdly, the Nafilah or Supererogatory. The Ratib or self-imposed task is the last of all; our Mulla placed it first, because he could chant it upon his mule within hearing the of people.

whence, together with his store of hashed Hadís (tradition), he derives the title of Widad or hedge-priest. His tongue, primed with the satirical sayings of Abn Zayd al-Halali, and Humayd ibn Mansur,* is the terror of men upon whom repartee imposes. His father was a wealthy ship-owner in his day; but, cursed with Abdi and another son, the old man has lost all his property, his children have deserted him, and he now depends entirely upon the charity of the Zayla chief. The 'End of Time' has squandered considerable sums in travelling far and wide from Harar to Cutch; he has managed everywhere to perpetrate some peculiar villany. He is a pleasant companion, and piques himself upon that power of quotation which in the East makes a polite man. If we be disposed to hurry, he insinuates that 'Patience is of Heaven, Haste of Hell'. When roughly addressed, he remarks—

> 'There are cures for the hurts of lead and steel,
> But the wounds of the tongue—they never heal.'

If a grain of rice adhere to our beards, he says, smilingly, 'the gazelle is in the garden'; to which we reply 'we will hunt her with the five'.† Despite these merits, I hesitated to engage him, till assured by the governor of Zayla that he was to be looked upon as a son, and, more-over, that he would bear with him one of those state secrets to an influential chief which in this country are never committed to paper. I found him an admirable buffoon, skilful in filling pipes and smoking them; au reste, an individual of 'many words and little work', in-finite intrigue, cowardice, cupidity, and endowed with a truly evil tongue.

The morning sun rose hot upon us, showing Mayyum and Zubah, the giant staples of the 'Gate under the Pleiades'.‡ Shortly afterwards, we came in sight of the Barr al-'Ajam (barbarian land), as the Somal call their country,§ a low glaring flat of yellow sand, desert and heat-

---

* Two modern poets and wits well known in al-Yemen.

† That is to say, 'we will remove it with the five fingers'. These are euphuisms to avoid speaking broadly and openly of that venerable feature, the beard.

‡ Bab al-Mandab is called as above by Humayd from its astronomical position. Jabal Mayyum is in Africa, Jabal Zubah or Muayyin, celebrated as the last resting-place of a great saint, Shaykh Sa'id, is in Arabia.

§ 'Ajam properly means all nations not Arab. In Egypt and Central Asia it is now con-fined to Persians. On the west of the Red Sea, it is invariably used to denote the Somali country: thence Bruce draws the Greek and Latin name of the coast, Azamia, and De Sacy derives the word 'Ajan', which in our maps is applied to the inner regions of the Eastern Horn. So in Africa, Al-Sham, which probably means Damascus and Syria, is applied to Al-Hijaz.

reeking, tenanted by the Eesa, and a meet habitat for savages. Such to us, at least, appeared the land of Adel.² At midday we descried the Ras al-Bir—Headland of the Well—the promontory which terminates the bold Tajjurrah range, under which lie the sleeping waters of the Maiden's Sea.* During the day we rigged out an awning, and sat in the shade smoking and chatting merrily, for the weather was not much hotter than on English summer seas. Some of the crew tried praying; but prostrations are not easily made on board ship, and Al-Islam, as Umar shrewdly suspected, was not made for a seafaring race. At length the big red sun sank slowly behind the curtain of sky-blue rock, where lies the not yet 'combusted' village of Tajjurrah.† We lay down to rest with the light of day, and had the satisfaction of closing our eyes upon a fair though captious breeze.

On the morning of the 31st October, we entered the Zayla Creek, which gives so much trouble to native craft. We passed, on the right, the low island of Masha, belonging to the 'City of the Slave Merchant' —Tajjurrah—and on the left two similar patches of seagirt sand, called Aybat and Sa'ad al-Din. These places supply Zayla, in the Kharif or hot season,‡ with thousands of gulls' eggs—a great luxury. At noon we sighted our destination. Zayla is the normal African port—a strip of sulphur-yellow sand, with a deep blue dome above, and a foreground of the darkest indigo. The buildings, raised by refraction, rose high, and apparently from the bosom of the deep. After hearing the worst accounts of it, I was pleasantly disappointed by the spectacle of white-washed houses and minarets, peering above a long low line of brown wall, flanked with round towers.

As we slowly threaded the intricate coral reefs of the port, a bark came scudding up to us; it tacked, and the crew proceeded to give news in roaring tones. Friendship between the Amir of Harar and the governor of Zayla had been broken; the road through the Eesa Somal had been closed by the murder of Mas'ud, a favourite slave and adopted son of Sharmakay; all strangers had been expelled the city for some misconduct by the Harar chief; moreover, small-pox was raging there

* Bahr al-Banattin, the Bay of Tajjurrah.

† A certain German missionary, well known in this part of the world, exasperated by the seizure of a few dollars and a claim to the *droit d'aubaine*, advised the authorities of Aden to threaten the 'combustion' of Tajjurrah. The measure would have been equally unjust and unwise. A traveller, even a layman, is bound to put up peacefully with such trifles; and to threaten 'combustion' without being prepared to carry out the threat is the readiest way to secure contempt.

‡ The Kharif in most parts of the Oriental world corresponds with our autumn. In Eastern Africa it invariably signifies the hot season preceding the monsoon rains.

with such violence that the Galla peasantry would allow neither ingress nor egress.* I had the pleasure of reflecting for some time, dear L., upon the amount of responsibility incurred by using the phrase 'I will'; and the only consolation that suggested itself was the stale assurance that 'things at the worst most surely mend'.

No craft larger than a canoe can ride near Zayla. After bumping once or twice against the coral reefs, it was considered advisable for our good ship, the *Sahalah*, to cast anchor. My companions caused me to dress, put me with my pipe and other necessaries into a cock-boat, and, wading through the water, shoved it to shore. Lastly, at Bab al-Sahil, the Seaward or Northern Gate, they proceeded to array themselves in the bravery of clean Tobes and long daggers strapped round the waist; each man also slung his targe to his left arm, and in his right hand grasped lance and javelin. At the gate we were received by a tall black spearman with a 'Ho there! to the governor'; and a crowd of idlers gathered to inspect the strangers. Marshalled by the warder, we traversed the dusty roads — streets they could not be called — of the old Arab town, ran the gauntlet of a gaping mob, and finally entering a mat door, found ourselves in the presence of the governor.

I had met Sharmakay at Aden, where he received from the authorities strong injunctions concerning my personal safety: the character of a Moslem merchant, however, requiring us to appear strangers, an introduction by our master of ceremonies, the Hammal, followed my entrance. Sharmakay was living in an apartment by no means splendid, preferring an Arish or kind of cow-house—as the Anglo-Indian Nabobs do the bungalow 'with mat half hung, The walls of plaster and the floors of dung'—to all his substantial double-storied houses. The ground was wet and comfortless; a part of the reed walls was lined with cots bearing mattresses and silk-covered pillows, a cross between a divan and a couch: the only ornaments were a few weapons, and a

* The circumstances of Mas'ud's murder were truly African. The slave caravans from Abyssinia to Tajjurrah were usually escorted by the Rer Guleni, a clan of the great Eesa tribe, and they monopolized the profits of the road. Summoned to share their gains with their kinsmen generally, they refused, upon which the other clans rose about August 1854, and cut off the road. A large caravan was travelling down in two bodies, each of nearly 300 slaves; the Eesa attacked the first division, carried off the wives and female slaves, whom they sold for ten dollars a head, and savagely mutilated upwards of 100 wretched boys. This event caused the Tajjurrah line to be permanently closed. The Rer Guleni in wrath, at once murdered Mas'ud, a peaceful traveller, because Inna Handun, his Abban or protector, was of the party who had attacked their protégés: they came upon him suddenly as he was purchasing some article, and stabbed him in the back, before he could defend himself.

E

necklace of gaudy beads suspended near the door. I was placed upon the principal seat: on the right were the governor and the Hammal; whilst the lowest portion of the room was occupied by Mohammed Sharmakay, the son and heir. The rest of the company squatted upon chairs, or rather stools, of peculiar construction. Nothing could be duller than this *assemblée*: pipes and coffee are here unknown; and there is nothing in the East to act substitute for them.*

The governor of Zayla, al-Hajj Sharmakay bin Ali Salih, is rather a remarkable man. He is sixteenth, according to his own account, in descent from Ishak al-Hazrami,[3] the saintly founder of the great Girhajis and Awal tribes. His enemies derive him from a less illustrious stock; and the fairness of his complexion favours the report that his grandfather Salih was an Abyssinian slave. Originally the Nacoda or captain of a native craft, he has raised himself, chiefly by British influence, to the chieftainship of his tribe.† As early as May 1825 he received from Captain Bagnold, then our resident at Mocha, a testimonial and a reward, for a severe sword wound in the left arm, received whilst defending the lives of English seamen.‡ He afterwards went to Bombay, where he was treated with consideration; and about fifteen years ago he succeeded the Sayyid Mohammed al-Barr as governor of Zayla and its dependencies, under the Ottoman Pasha in Western Arabia.

The Hajj Sharmakay in his youth was a man of valour: he could not read or write; but he carried in battle four spears, and his sword-cut was recognizable. He is now a man about sixty years old, at least six feet two inches in stature, large-limbed, and raw-boned: his leanness is hidden by long wide robes. He shaves his head and upper lip Sháfe'i-

---

* In Zayla there is not a single coffee-house. The settled Somal care little for the Arab beverage, and the Bedouin's reasons for avoiding it are not bad. 'If we drink coffee once,' say they, 'we shall want it again, and then where are we to get it?' The Abyssinian Christians, probably to distinguish themselves from Moslems, object to coffee as well as to tobacco. The Gallas, on the other hand, eat it: the powdered bean is mixed with butter.

† Not the hereditary chieftainship of the Habr Girhajis, which belongs to a particular clan.

‡ The following is a copy of the document:

'This Testimonial,
together with an Honorary Dress, is presented by the British Resident at Mocha to Nagoda Shurmakey Ally Sumaulley, in token of esteem and regard for his humane and gallant conduct at the Port of Burburra, on the coast of Africa, April 10, 1825, in saving the lives of Captain William Lingard, chief officer of the Brig Mary Anne, when that vessel was attacked and plundered by the natives. The said Nagoda is therefore strongly recommended to the notice and good offices of Europeans in general, but particularly so to all English gentlemen visiting these seas.'

fashion, and his beard is represented by a ragged tuft of red-stained hair on each side of his chin. A visit to Aden and a doctor cost him one eye, and the other is now white with age. His dress is that of an Arab, and he always carries with him a broad-bladed, silver-hilted sword. Despite his years, he is a strong, active, and energetic man, ever looking to the 'main chance'. With one foot in the grave, he meditates nothing but the conquest of Harar and Berbera, which, making him master of the seaboard, would soon extend his power as in days of old even to Abyssinia.[4] To hear his projects, you would fancy them the offspring of a brain in the prime of youth: in order to carry them out he would even assist in suppressing the profitable slave-trade.*

After half an hour's visit I was led by the Hajj through the streets of Zayla,[5] to one of his substantial houses of coralline and mud plastered over with glaring whitewash. The ground floor is a kind of warehouse full of bales and boxes, scales and buyers. A flight of steep steps leads into a long room with shutters to exclude the light, floored with tamped earth, full of 'evening flyers',† and destitute of furniture. Parallel to it are three smaller apartments; and above is a terraced roof, where they who fear not the dew and the land breeze sleep. I found a room duly prepared; the ground was spread with mats, and cushions against the walls denoted the Divan: for me was placed a Kursi or cot, covered with fine Persian rugs and gaudy silk and satin pillows. The Hajj installed us with ceremony, and insisted, despite my remonstrances, upon occupying the floor whilst I sat on the raised seat. After ushering in supper, he considerately remarked that travelling is fatiguing, and left us to sleep.

---

* During my residence at Zayla few slaves were imported, owing to the main road having been closed. In former years the market was abundantly stocked; the numbers annually shipped to Mocha, Hodaydah, Jeddah, and Berbera, varied from 600 to 1,000. The Hajj received as duty one gold 'Kirsh', or about three-fourths of a dollar, per head.

† 'Fid-mer', or the evening flyer, is the Somali name for a bat. These little animals are not disturbed in houses, because they keep off flies and mosquitoes, the plagues of the Somali country. Flies abound in the very jungles wherever cows have been, and settle in swarms upon the traveller. Before the monsoon their bite is painful, especially that of the small green species; and there is a red variety called 'Diksi as', whose venom, according to the people, causes them to vomit. The latter abounds in Gulays and the hill ranges of the Berbera country: it is innocuous during the cold season. The mosquito bites bring on, according to the same authority, deadly fevers: the superstition probably arises from the fact that mosquitoes and fevers become formidable about the same time.

[In other words, the Somali realized the connection between the mosquito and fever long before it was known in Europe at the end of the nineteenth century. That quinine was the treatment for malaria had been known since about A.D. 1700, but the part played by the mosquito was not known until two centuries later.—Ed.]

The well-known sounds of Al-Islam returned from memory. Again the melodius chant of the Muezzin—no evening bell can compare with it for solemnity and beauty—and in the neighbouring mosque, the loudly-intoned Amin and Allaho Akbar—far superior to any organ—rang in my ear. The evening gun of camp was represented by the Nakyarah, or kettle-drum, sounded about 7 p.m. at the southern gate; and at ten a second drumming warned the paterfamilias that it was time for home, and thieves, and lovers—that it was the hour for bastinado. Nightfall was ushered in by the song, the dance, and the marriage festival—here no permission is required for 'native music in the lines'—and muffled figures flitted mysteriously through the dark alleys.

.   .   .   .   .

After a peep through the open window, I fell asleep, feeling once more at home.

Somali girl.

II

Life in Zayla

I WILL NOT WEARY you, dear L., with descriptions of twenty-six quiet, similar, uninteresting days—days of sleep, and pipes, and coffee —spent at Zayla, whilst a route was traced out, guides were propitiated, camels were bought, mules sent for, and all the wearisome preliminaries of African travel were gone through. But a *journée* in the Somali country may be a novelty to you: its events shall be succinctly depicted.

With earliest dawn we arise, thankful to escape from mosquitoes and close air. We repair to the terrace where devotions are supposed to be performed, and busy ourselves in watching our neighbours. Two in particular engage my attention: sisters by different mothers. The daughter of an Indian woman is a young person of fast propensities— her chocolate-coloured skin, long hair, and parrot-like profile* are much admired by the *élegants* of Zayla; and she coquettes by combing, dancing, singing, and slapping the slave-girls, whenever an adorer may

---

* This style of profile—highly oval, with the chin and brow receding—is very conspicuous in Eastern Africa, where the face, slightly prognathous, projects below the nose.

be looking. We sober-minded men, seeing her, quote the well-known lines—

Sans justice a king is a cloud without rain;
Sans goodness a sage is a field without grain;
Sans manners a youth is a horse taking rein;
Sans lore an old man is a waterless plain;
And bread without salt is a woman sans shame.

The other is a matron of Abyssinian descent, as her skin, scarcely darker than a gipsy's, her long and bright blue fillet, and her gaudily-fringed dress, denote. She tattoos her face: a livid line extends from her front hair to the tip of her nose; between her eyebrows is an ornament resembling a *fleur-de-lis*, and various beauty-spots adorn the corners of her mouth and the flats of her countenance. She passes her day superintending the slave-girls, and weaving mats,* the worsted work of this part of the world. We soon made acquaintance, as far as an exchange of salaams. I regret, however, to say that there was some scandal about my charming neighbour; and that more than once she was detected making signals to distant persons with her hands.

At 6 a.m. we descend to breakfast, which usually consists of sour grain cakes and roast mutton—at this hour a fine trial of health and cleanly living. A napkin is passed under my chin, as if I were a small child, and a sound scolding is administered when appetite appears deficient. Visitors are always asked to join us: we squat on the uncarpeted floor, round a circular stool, eat hard, and never stop to drink. The appetite of Africa astonishes us; we dispose of six ounces here for every one in Arabia—probably the effect of sweet water, after the briny produce of the 'Eye of Yemen'. We conclude this early breakfast with coffee and pipes, and generally return, after it, to the work of sleep.

Then, provided with some sanctified Arabic book, I prepare for the reception of visitors. They come in by dozens—no man having apparently any business to occupy him—doff their slippers at the door, enter wrapped up in their Tobes or togas,[1] and deposit their spears, point-upwards, in the corner; those who have swords—the mark of respectability in Eastern Africa—place them at their feet. They shake the full hand (I was reproved for offering the fingers only); and when

---

* Mats are the staple manufacture in Eastern, as in many parts of Western Africa. The material is sometimes Daum or other palm: there are, however, many plants in more common use; they are made of every variety in shape and colour, and are dyed red, black, and yellow—madder from Tajjurrah and alum being the matter principally used.

politely disposed, the inferior wraps his fist in the hem of his garment. They have nothing corresponding with the European idea of manners; they degrade all ceremony by the epithet Shughl al-banat, or 'girls' work', and pique themselves upon downrightness of manner—a favourite mask, by-the-by, for savage cunning to assume. But they are equally free from affectation, shyness, and vulgarity; and, after all, no manners are preferable to bad manners.

Sometimes we are visited at this hour by Mohammed Sharmakay, eldest son of the old governor. He is in age about thirty, a fine tall figure, slender but well knit, beardless and of light complexion, with large eyes, and a length of neck which a lady might covet. His only detracting feature is a slight projection of the oral region, that unmistakable proof of African blood. His movements have the grace of strength and suppleness: he is a good jumper, runs well, throws the spear admirably, and is a tolerable shot. Having received a liberal education at Mocha, he is held a learned man by his fellow-countrymen. Like his father he despises presents, looking higher; with some trouble I persuaded him to accept a common map of Asia, and a revolver. His chief interest was concentrated in books: he borrowed my Abu Kasim to copy,* and was never tired of talking about the religious sciences: he had weakened his eyes by hard reading, and a couple of blisters were sufficient to win his gratitude. Mohammed is now the eldest son; he appears determined to keep up the family name, having already married ten wives: the issue however, two infant sons, were murdered by the Eesa Bedouin. Whenever he meets his father in the morning, he kisses his hand, and receives a salute upon the forehead. He aspires to the government of Zayla, and looks forward more reasonably than the Hajj to the day when the possession of Berbera will pour gold into his coffers. He shows none of his father's 'softness': he advocates the bastinado, and, to keep his people at a distance, he has married an Arab wife, who allows no adult to enter the doors. The Somal, Spaniard-like, remark, 'He is one of ourselves, though a little richer'; but when times change and luck returns, they are not unlikely to find themselves mistaken.

Amongst other visitors, we have the Amir al-Bahr, or Port Captain, and the Nakib al-Askar (*Commandant de place*), Mohammed Umar al-Hamumi. This is one of those Hadramaut adventurers so common in all the countries bordering upon Arabia: they are the Swiss of the East,

---

* Abu Kasim of Gaza, a well-known commentator upon Abu Shuja'a of Isfahan, who wrote a textbook of the Shafe'i school.

a people equally brave and hardy, frugal and faithful, as long as pay is regular. Feared by the soft Indians and Africans for their hardness and determination, the common proverb concerning them is, 'If you meet a viper and a Hadrami, spare the viper.' Natives of a poor and rugged region, they wander far and wide, preferring every country to their own; and it is generally said that the sun rises not upon a land that does not contain a man from Hadramaut.* This commander of an army of forty men† often read out to us from the Kitab al-Anwar (the Book of Lights) the tale of Abu Jahl, that Judas of al-Islam made ridiculous. Sometimes comes the Sayyid Mohammed al-Barr, a stout personage, formerly governor of Zayla, and still highly respected by the people on account of his pure pedigree. With him is the Fakih Adan, a *savan* of ignoble origin.[2] When they appear the conversation becomes intensely intellectual: sometimes we dispute religion, sometimes politics, at others history and other humanities. Yet, it is not easy to talk history with a people who confound Miriam and Mary, or politics to those whose only idea of a king is a robber on a large scale, or religion to men

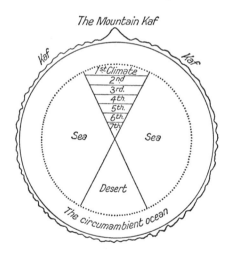

The Mountain Kaf

* It is related that a Hadrami, flying from his fellow-countrymen, reached a town upon the confines of China. He was about to take refuge in a mosque, but entering, he stumbled over the threshold. 'Ya Amud al-Din'—'O Pillar of the Faith!' exclaimed a voice from the darkness, calling upon the patron saint of Hadramaut to save a Moslem from falling. 'May the Pillar of the Faith break thy head!' exclaimed the unpatriotic traveller, at once rising to resume his vain peregrinations.

† Mercenaries from Mocha, Hadramaut, and Bir Hamid, near Aden: they are armed with matchlock, sword, and dagger; and each receives from the governor a monthly stipend of two dollars and a half.

who measure excellence by forbidden meats, or geography to those who represent the earth in this guise. Yet, though few of our ideas are in common, there are many words; the verbosity of these anti-Laconic Oriental dialects* renders at least half the subject intelligible to the most opposite thinkers. When the society is wholly Somal, I write Arabic, copy some useful book, or extract from it, as Bentley advised, what is fit to quote. When Arabs are present, I usually read out a tale from *The Thousand and One Nights*, that wonderful work, so often translated, so much turned over, and so little understood at home. The most familiar of books in England, next to the Bible, it is one of the least known, the reason being that about one-fifth is utterly unfit for translation; and the most sanguine Orientalist would not dare to render literally more than three-quarters of the remainder. Consequently, the reader loses the contrast—the very essence of the book—between its brilliancy and dullness, its moral putrefaction, and such pearls as—

> Cast the seed of good works on the least fit soil,
> Good is never wasted, however it may be laid out.

And in a page or two after such divine sentiment, the ladies of Baghdad sit in the porter's lap, and indulge in a facetiousness which would have killed Pietro Aretino before his time.[3][†]

Often I am visited by the Topchi-Bashi, or master of the ordnance half a dozen honey-combed guns—a wild fellow, Bashi Buzuk in the Hijaz and commandant of artillery at Zayla. He shaves my head on Fridays, and on other days tells me wild stories about his service in the Holy Land; how Kurdi Usman slew his son-in-law, Ibn Rumi, and how Turkchih Bilmaz would have murdered Mohammed Ali in his bed. Sometimes the room is filled with Arabs, Sayyids, merchants, and others settled in the place: I saw nothing amongst them to justify the oft-quoted saw, 'Koraysh pride and Zayla's boastfulness.' More generally the assembly is one of the Somal, who talk in their own tongue, laugh, yell, stretch their legs, and lie like cattle upon the floor,

---

* The reason why Europeans fail to explain their thoughts to Orientals generally is that they transfer the Laconism of Western to Eastern tongues. We for instance say, 'Fetch the book I gave you last night.' This in Hindustani, to choose a well-known tongue, must be smothered with words thus, 'What book was by me given to you yesterday by night, that book bringing to me, come!'

† Pietro Aretino, 1492–1556, was a painter, but was better known for his obscene and satirical verses which made him feared by the Kings, Queens, and Princes of Europe; he retired to Venice, where he lived very comfortably on presents received from those who wished to keep in favour. He is said to have died of suffocation from laughing too much.—Ed.

smoking the common Hukkah, which stands in the centre, industriously cleaning their teeth with sticks, and eating snuff like Swedes. Meanwhile, I occupy the Kursi or couch, sometimes muttering from a book to excite respect, or reading aloud for general information, or telling fortunes by palmistry, or drawing out a horoscope.

It argues 'peculiarity', I own, to enjoy such a life. In the first place there is no woman's society: al-Islam seems purposely to have loosened the ties between the sexes in order to strengthen the bonds which connect man and man.* Secondly, your house is by no means your castle. You must open your doors to your friend at all hours; if when inside it suits him to sing, sing he will; and until you learn solitude in a crowd, or the art of concentration, you are apt to become *ennuyé* and irritable. You must abandon your prejudices, and for a time cast off all European prepossessions in favour of Indian politeness, Persian polish, Arab courtesy, or Turkish dignity. 'They are as free as Nature e'er made man'; and he who objects to having his head shaved in public, to seeing his friends combing their locks in his sitting-room, to having his property unceremoniously handled, or to being addressed familiarly by a perfect stranger, had better avoid Somaliland.

You will doubtless, dear L., convict me, by my own sentiments, of being an 'amateur barbarian'. You must, however, remember that I visited Africa fresh from Aden, with its dull routine of meaningless parades and tiresome courts-martial, where society is broken by ridiculous distinctions of staff-men and regimental-men, Madras-men and Bombay-men, 'European' officers, and 'black' officers; where literature is confined to acquiring the art of explaining yourself in the jargons of half-naked savages; where the business of life is comprised in ignoble official squabbles, dislikes, disapprobations, and 'references to superior authority'; where social intercourse is crushed by 'gup', gossip, and the scandal of small colonial circles; where—pleasant predicament for those who really love women's society!—it is scarcely possible to address fair dame, preserving at the same time her reputation and your own, and if seen with her twice, all 'camp' will swear it is an 'affair': where, briefly, the march of mind is at a dead halt, and the march of matter is in double-quick time to the hospital or sick-quarters. Then the fatal struggle for Name, and the painful necessity of doing the most

* This is one of the stock complaints against the Moslem scheme. Yet is it not practically the case with ourselves? In European society, the best are generally those who prefer the companionship of their own sex; the 'ladies' man' and the woman who avoids women are rarely choice specimens.

with the smallest materials for a reputation! In Europe there are a thousand grades of celebrity, from statesmanship to taxidermy; all, therefore, co-exist without rivalry. Whereas, in these small colonies, there is but one fame, and as that leads directly to rupees and rank, no man willingly accords it to his neighbour. And, finally, such semi-civilized life abounds in a weary ceremoniousness. It is highly improper to smoke outside your bungalow. You shall pay your visits at 11 a.m., when the glass stands at 120°. You shall be generally shunned if you omit your waistcoat, no matter what the weather be. And if you venture to object to these Median laws—as I am now doing—you elicit a chorus of disapproval, and acquire some evil name.

About 11 a.m., when the fresh water arrives from the Hissi or wells, the Hajj sends us dinner, mutton stews of exceeding greasiness, boiled rice, maize cakes, sometimes fish, and generally curds or milk. We all sit round a primitive form of the Round Table, and I doubt that King Arthur's knights ever proved doughtier trenchermen than do my companions. We then rise to pipes and coffee, after which, excluding visitors, my attendants apply themselves to a siesta, I to my journal and studies.

At 2 p.m. there is a loud clamour at the door: if it be not opened in time, we are asked if we have a Nazarene inside. Enters a crowd of visitors, anxious to pass the afternoon. We proceed with a copy of the forenoon till the sun declines, when it is time to escape the flies, to repair to the terrace for fresh air, or to dress for a walk. Generally our direction is through the town eastwards, to a plain of dilapidated graves and salt sand, peopled only by land-crabs. At the extremity near the sea is a little mosque of wattle-work: we sit there under the shade, and play a rude form of draughts, called Shantarah, or at Shahh, a modification of the former. More often, eschewing these effeminacies, we shoot at a mark, throw the javelin, leap, or engage in some gymnastic exercise. The favourite Somali weapons are the spear, dagger, and war-club; the bow and poisoned arrows are peculiar to the servile class, who know 'the dreadful art, to taint with deadly drugs the barbed dart'; and the people despise, at the same time that they fear firearms, declaring them to be cowardly weapons* with which the poltroon can slay the bravest.

---

* The same objection against 'villanous saltpetre' was made by ourselves in times of old: the French knights called gunpowder the Grave of Honour. This is natural enough, the bravest weapon being generally the shortest—that which places a man hand to hand with his opponent. Some of the Kafir tribes have discontinued throwing the Assegai, and

The Somali spear is a form of the Cape Assegai. A long, thin, pliant, and knotty shaft of the Dibi, Diktab, and Makari trees, is dried, polished, and greased with rancid butter: it is generally of a dull yellow colour, and sometimes bound, as in Arabia, with brass wire for ornament. Care is applied to make the rod straight, or the missile flies crooked; it is garnished with an iron button at the head, and a long, thin, tapering head of coarse bad iron, made at Berbera and other places by the Tomal. The length of the shaft may be four feet eight inches; the blade varies from twenty to twenty-six inches, and the whole weapon is about seven feet long. Some polish the entire spear-head, others only its socket or ferrule; commonly, however, it is all blackened by heating it to redness, and rubbing it with cow's horn. In the towns, one of these weapons is carried; on a journey and in battle two, as amongst the Tíbús—a small javelin for throwing and a large spear reserved for the thrust. Some warriors, especially amongst the Eesa, prefer a coarse heavy lance, which never leaves the hand. The Somali spear is held in various ways: generally the thumb and forefinger grasp the third nearest to the head, and the shaft resting upon the palm is made to quiver. In action, the javelin is rarely thrown at a greater distance than six or seven feet, and the heavier weapon is used for 'jobbing'. Stripped to his waist, the thrower runs forward with all the action of a Kafir, whilst the attacked bounds about and crouches to receive it upon the round targe, which it cannot pierce. He then returns the compliment, at the same time endeavouring to break the weapon thrown at him by jumping and stamping upon it. The harmless missiles being exhausted, both combatants draw their daggers, grapple with the left hand, and with the right dig hard and swift at each other's necks and shoulders. When matters come to this point the duel is soon decided, and the victor, howling his slogan, pushes away from his front the dying enemy, and rushes off to find another opponent. A puerile weapon during the day when a steady man can easily avoid it, the spear is terrible in night attacks or in the 'bush', whence it can be hurled unseen. For practice we plant a pair of slippers upright in the ground, at the distance of twelve yards, and a skilful spearman hits the mark once in every three throws.

The Somali dagger is an iron blade about eighteen inches long by two in breadth, pointed and sharp at both edges. The handle is of

---

enter battle wielding it as a pike. Usually, also, the shorter the weapon is, the more fatal are the conflicts in which it is employed. The old French 'Briquet', the Afghan 'Charay', and the Goorkha 'Kukkri', exemplify this fact in the history of arms.

buffalo or other horn, with a double scoop to fit the grasp; and at the hilt is a conical ornament of zinc. It is worn strapped round the waist by a thong sewed to the sheath, and long enough to encircle the body twice: the point is to the right, and the handle projects on the left. When in town, the Somal wear their daggers under the Tobe: in battle, the strap is girt over the cloth to prevent the latter being lost. They always stab from above: this is as it should be, a thrust with a short weapon 'underhand' may be stopped, if the adversary have strength enough to hold the stabber's forearm. The thrust is parried with the shield, and the wound is rarely mortal except in the back: from the great length of the blade, the least movement of the man attacked causes it to fall upon the shoulder-blade.

The 'Budd', or Somali club, resembles the Kafir 'Tonga'. It is a knobstick about a cubit long, made of some hard wood: the head is rounded on the inside, and the outside is cut to an edge. In quarrels it is considered a harmless weapon, and is often thrown at the opponent and wielded viciously enough where the spear point would carefully be directed at the buckler. The Gashan or shield is a round targe about eighteen inches in diameter; some of the Bedouin make it much larger. Rhinoceros' skin being rare, the usual material is common bull's hide, or, preferably, that of the Oryx, called by the Arabs, Wa'al, and by the Somal, Da'id. These shields are prettily cut, and are always protected when new with a covering of canvas. The boss in the centre easily turns a spear, and the strongest throw has very little effect even upon the thinnest portion. When not used, the Gashan is slung upon the left forearm: during battle, the handle, which is in the middle, is grasped by the left hand, and held out at a distance from the body.

We are sometimes joined in our exercises by the Arab mercenaries, who are far more skilful than the Somal. The latter are unacquainted with the sword, and cannot defend themselves against it with the targe; they know little of dagger practice, and were beaten at their own weapon, the javelin, by the children of Bir Hamid. Though unable to jump for the honour of the turban, I soon acquired the reputation of being the strongest man in Zayla: this is perhaps the easiest way of winning respect from a barbarous people, who honour body, and degrade mind to mere cunning.

When tired of exercise we proceed round the walls to the Ashurbara or Southern Gate. Here boys play at 'hockey' with sticks and stones energetically as in England: they are fine manly specimens of the race, but noisy and impudent, like all young savages. At two years of age they hold out their right hand for sweetmeats, and if refused become insolent. The citizens amuse themselves with the ball, at which they play roughly as Scotch linkers: they are divided into two parties, bachelors and married men; accidents often occur, and no player wears any but the scantiest clothing, otherwise he would retire from the conflict in rags. The victors sing and dance about the town for hours, brandishing their spears, shouting their slogans, boasting of ideal victories—the Abyssinian Donfatu, or war vaunt—and advancing in death-triumph with frantic gestures: a battle won would be celebrated with less circumstance in Europe. This is the effect of no occupation— the *primum mobile* of the Indian prince's kite-flying and all the puerilities of the pompous East.

We usually find an encampment of Bedouin outside the gate. Their tents are worse than any gipsy's, low, smoky, and of the rudest construction. These people are a spectacle of savageness. Their huge heads of shock hair, dyed red and dripping with butter, are garnished with a Firin, or long three-pronged comb, a stick, which acts as scratcher when the owner does not wish to grease his fingers, and sometimes with the ominous ostrich feather, showing that the wearer has 'killed his man'; a soiled and ragged cotton cloth covers their shoulders, and a similar article is wrapped round their loins. All wear coarse sandals, and appear in the bravery of targe, spear, and dagger. Some of the women would be pretty did they not resemble the men in their scowling, Satanic expression of countenance: they are decidedly *en deshabille*, but a black skin always appears a garb. The cantonment is surrounded by asses, camels, and a troop of native Flibbertigibbets, who dance and jump in astonishment whenever they see me: 'The white man! the white man!' they shriek; 'run away, run away, or we shall be eaten!'* On one occasion, however, my *amour propre* was decidedly flattered by the attentions of a small black girl, apparently four or five years old, who followed me through the streets ejaculating 'Wa Wanaksan!'— 'O fine!' The Bedouin, despite their fierce scowls, appear good-natured; the women flock out of the huts to stare and laugh, the men to look and wonder. I happened once to remark, 'Lo, we come forth to look at them and they look at us; we gaze at their complexion and they gaze at ours!' A Bedouin who understood Arabic translated this speech to the others, and it excited great merriment. In the mining counties of civilized England, where the 'genial brickbat' is thrown at

* I often regretted having neglected the precaution of a bottle of walnut-juice—a white colour is decidedly too conspicuous in this part of the East.

the passing stranger, or in enlightened Scotland, where hair a few inches too long or a pair of mustachioes justifies 'mobbing', it would have been impossible for me to have mingled as I did with these wild people.

We must return before suns:t, when the gates are locked and the keys are carried to the Hajj, a vain precaution, when a donkey could clear half a dozen places in the town wall. The call to evening prayers sounds as we enter: none of my companions prays, but all when asked reply in the phrase which an Englishman hates, 'Inshallah Bukra'—'if Allah please, tomorrow!'—and they have the decency not to appear in public at the hours of devotion. The Somal, like most Africans, are of a somewhat irreverent turn of mind.* When reproached with gambling, and asked why they persist in the forbidden pleasure, they simply answer, 'Because we like.' One night, encamped among the Eesa, I was disturbed by a female voice indulging in the loudest lamentations: an elderly lady, it appears, was suffering from tooth-ache, and the refrain of her groans was, 'O Allah, may thy teeth ache like mine! O Allah, may thy gums be sore as mine are!'

A well-known and characteristic tale is told of the Gerad Hirsi, now chief of the Berteri tribe. Once meeting a party of unarmed pilgrims, he asked them why they had left their weapons at home: they replied in the usual phrase, 'Nahnu mutawakkilin'—'we are trusters (in Allah)'. That evening, having feasted them hospitably, the chief returned hurriedly to the hut, declaring that his soothsayer ordered him at once to sacrifice a pilgrim, and begging the horror-struck auditors to choose the victim. They cast lots and gave over one of their number: the Jirad placed him in another hut, dyed his dagger with sheep's blood, and returned to say that he must have a second life. The unhappy pilgrims rose *en masse*, and fled so wildly that the chief, with all the cavalry of the desert, found difficulty in recovering them. He dismissed

---

* Equally irreverent are the Kafirs of the Cape. They have proved themselves good men in wit as well as in war; yet, like the old Greenlanders and some of the Burmese tribes, they are apparently unable to believe in the existence of the Supreme. A favourite question to the missionaries was this, 'Is your God white or black?' If the European, startled by the question, hesitated for a moment, they would leave him with open signs of disgust at having been made the victims of a hoax.

The assertion generally passes current that the idea of an Omnipotent Being is familiar to all people, even the most barbarous. My limited experience argues the contrary. Savages begin with fetishism and demon-worship, they proceed to physiolatry (the religion of the Vedas) and Sabaeism: the deity is the last and highest pinnacle of the spiritual temple, not placed there except by a comparatively civilized race of high development, which leads them to study and speculate upon cosmical and psychical themes. This progression is admirably wrought out in Professor Max Müller's *Rig Veda Sanhita*.

them with liberal presents, and not a few jibes about their 'trustfulness' in Allah. The wilder Bedouin will inquire where Allah is to be found: when asked the object of the question, they reply, 'If the Eesa could but catch him, they would spear him upon the spot—who but he lays waste their homes and kills their cattle and wives?' Yet, conjoined to this truly savage incapability of conceiving the idea of a Supreme Being, they believe in the most ridiculous exaggerations: many will not affront a common pilgrim, for fear of being killed by a glance or a word.

Our supper, also provided by the hospitable Hajj, is the counterpart of the midday dinner. After it we repair to the roof, to enjoy the prospect of the far Tajjurrah hills and the white moonbeams sleeping upon the nearer sea. The evening star hangs like a diamond upon the still horizon: around the moon a pink zone of light mist, shading off into turquoise blue, and a delicate green like chrysopraz, invests the heavens with a peculiar charm. The scene is truly suggestive: behind us, purpling in the night-air and silvered by the radiance from above, lie the wolds and mountains tenanted by the fiercest of savages; their shadowy mysterious forms exciting vague alarms in the traveller's breast. Sweet as the harp of David, the night-breeze and the music of the water come up from the sea: but the ripple and the rustling sound alternate with the hyena's laugh, the jackal's cry, and the wild dog's lengthened howl.

Or, the weather becoming cold, we remain below, and Mohammed Umar returns to read out more 'Book of Lights', or some pathetic ode. I will quote in free translation the following production of the celebrated poet Abd al-Rahman al-Burai, as a perfect specimen of melancholy Arab imagery:

> No exile is the exile to the latter end of earth,
> The exile is the exile to the coffin and the tomb!

> He hath claims on the dwellers in the places of their birth
> Whoso wandereth the world, for he lacketh him a home.

> Then blamer, blame me not, were my heart within their breast,
> The sigh would take the place of thy laughter and thy scorn.

> Let me weep for the sin that debars my soul of rest,
> The tear may yet avail,—all in vain I may not mourn!*

* The Moslem corpse is partly sentient in the tomb, reminding the reader of Tennyson:
I thought the dead had peace, but it is not so;
To have no peace in the grave, is that not sad?

66

Woe! woe to thee, Flesh!—with a purer spirit, now
The death-day were a hope, and the judgment-hour a joy!

One morn I woke in pain, with a pallor on my brow,
As though the dreaded Angel was descending to destroy:

They brought to me a leech, saying, 'Heal him lest he die!'
On that day, by Allah, were his drugs a poor deceit!

They stripped me and bathed me, and closed the glazing eye,
And dispersed unto prayers, and to haggle for my sheet.

The prayers without a bow* they prayed over me that day,
Brought nigh to me the bier, and disposèd me within.

Four bear upon their shoulders this tenement of clay,
Friend and kinsman in procession bore the dust of friend and kin.

They threw upon me mould of the tomb, and went their way—
A guest, 'twould seem, had flitted from the dwellings of the tribe!

My gold and my treasures each a share they bore away,
Without thanks, without praise, with a jest and with a jibe.

My gold and my treasures each a share they bore away,
On me they left the weight!—with me they left the sin!

That night within the grave without hoard or child I lay,
No spouse, no friend were there, no comrade and no kin.

The wife of my youth soon another husband found—
A stranger sat at home on the hearthstone of my sire.

My son became a slave, though not purchasèd nor bound,
The hireling of a stranger, who begrudged him his hire.

Such, alas, is human life! such the horror of his death!
Man grows like a grass, like a god he sees no end.

Be wise, then, ere too late, brother! praise with every breath
The Hand that can chastise, the Arm that can defend:

And bless thou the Prophet, the averter of our ills,
While the lightning flasheth bright o'er the ocean and the hills.

At this hour my companions become imaginative and superstitious.
One Salimayn, a black slave from the Sawahil,† now secretary to the

---

* The prayers for the dead have no Ruka'at, or bow, as in other orisons.
† The general Moslem name for the African coast from the Somali seaboard southwards
to the Mozambique, inhabited by Negroid races.

Hajj, reads our fortunes in the rosary. The 'fal',[4] as it is called, acts a prominent part in Somali life. Some men are celebrated for accuracy of prediction; and in times of danger, when the human mind is ever open to the 'fooleries of faith', perpetual reference is made to their art. The worldly-wise Salimayn, I observed, never sent away a questioner with an ill-omened reply, but he also regularly insisted upon the efficacy of sacrifice and almsgiving, which, as they would assuredly be neglected, afforded him an excuse in case of accident. Then we had a recital of the tales common to Africa, and perhaps to all the world. In modern France, as in ancient Italy, 'versipelles' become wolves and hide themselves in the woods: in Persia they change themselves into bears, and in Bornou and Shoa assume the shapes of lions, hyenas, and leopards. The origin of this metamorphic superstition is easily traceable like man's fetishism or demonology, to his fears; a Bedouin, for instance, becomes dreadful by the reputation of sorcery: bears and hyenas are equally terrible; and the two objects of horror are easily connected. Curious to say, individuals having this power were pointed out to me, and people pretended to discover it in their countenances: at Zayla I was shown a Bedouin, by name, Farih Badaun, who notably became a hyena at times, for the purpose of tasting human blood. About forty years ago, three brothers, Kayna, Fardayna, and Sollan, were killed on Gulays near Berbera for the crime of metamorphosis. The charge is usually substantiated either by the bestial tail remaining appended to a part of the human shape which the owner has forgotten to rub against the magic tree, or by some peculiar wound which the beast received and the man retained. Kindred to this superstition is the belief that many of the Bedouin have learned the languages of birds and beasts. Another widely-diffused fancy is that of the Aksar,* which in this pastoral land becomes a kind of wood: wonderful tales are told of battered milk-pails which, by means of some peg accidently cut in the jungle, have been found full of silver, or have acquired the qualities of cornucopiæ. It is supposed that a red heifer always breaks her fast upon the wonderful plant, consequently much time and trouble have been expended by the Somal in watching the morning proceedings of red heifers. At other times we hear fearful tales of old women who, like the Jigar Khwar of Persia, feed upon man's liver; they are fond of destroying young children; even adults are not ashamed of defending themselves with talismans. In this country the crone is called Bida'a or Kumayyo, words signifying a witch: the worst is she that destroys her

* Our Elixir, a corruption of the Arabic Al-Iksir.

own progeny. No wound is visible in this vampire's victim: generally he names his witch, and his friends beat her to death unless she heal him: many are thus martyred; and in Somaliland scant notice is taken of such a peccadillo as murdering an old woman.[5] The sex indeed has by no means a good name: here, as elsewhere, those who degrade it are the first to abuse it for degradation. At Zayla almost all quarrels are connected with women; the old bewitch in one way, the young in another, and both are equally maligned. 'Wit in a woman,' exclaims one man, 'is a habit of running away in a dromedary.' 'Allah,' declares another, 'made woman of a crooked rib; he who would straighten her, breaketh her.' Perhaps, however, by these generalisms of abuse the sex gains: they prevent personal and individual details; and no society of French gentlemen avoids mentioning in public the name of a woman more scrupulously than do the misogynist Moslems.

After a conversazione of two hours my visitors depart, and we lose no time—for we must rise at cock-crow—in spreading our mats round the common room. You would admire the Somali pillow, a dwarf pedestal of carved wood, with a curve upon which the greasy poll and its elaborate *frisure* repose. Like the Abyssinian article, it resembles the head-rest of ancient Egypt in all points, except that it is not worked with Typhons and other horrors to drive away dreadful dreams. Sometimes the sound of the kettledrum, the song, and the clapping of hands, summon us at a later hour than usual to a dance. The performance is complicated, and, as usual with the trivialities easily learned in early youth, it is uncommonly difficult to a stranger. Each dance has its own song and measure, and, contrary to the custom of al-Islam, the sexes perform together. They begin by clapping the hands and stamping where they stand; to this succeed advancing, retiring, wheeling about, jumping about, and the other peculiarities of the Jim Crow school. The principal measures are those of Ugadayn and Batar; these are again divided and subdivided. I fancy that the description of Dileho, Jibwhayn, and Hobala would be as entertaining and instructive to you, dear L., as Polka, Gavotte, and Mazurka would be to a Somali.

On Friday—our Sunday—a drunken crier goes about the town, threatening the bastinado to all who neglect their five prayers. At half-past eleven a kettle-drum sounds a summons to the Jami or Cathedral. It is an old barn rudely plastered with whitewash; posts or columns of artless masonry support the low roof, and the smallness of the windows, or rather air-holes, renders its dreary length unpleasantly hot.

69

There is no pulpit; the only ornament is a rude representation of the Meccan Mosque, nailed like a pot-house print to the wall; and the sole articles of furniture are ragged mats and old boxes containing tattered chapters of the Koran in greasy bindings. I enter with a servant carrying

a prayer carpet, encounter the stare of 300 pairs of eyes, belonging to parallel rows of squatters, recite the customary two-bow prayer in honour of the mosque, placing sword and rosary before me, and then, taking up a Koran, read the Cow Chapter (No. 18) loud and twangingly. At the Zohr or midday hour, the Muezzin inside the mosque, standing before the Khatib, or preacher, repeats the call to prayer, which the congregation, sitting upon their shins and feet, intone after him. This ended, all present stand up, and recite every man for himself a two-bow prayer of Sunnat or Example, concluding with the blessing on the Prophet and the Salaam over each shoulder to all brother Believers. The Khatib then ascends his hole in the wall, which serves for pulpit, and thence addresses us with 'The peace be upon you, and the mercy of Allah, and his bene-

Somali with bow.

diction'; to which we respond through the Muezzin, 'And upon you be peace, and Allah's mercy!' After sundry other religious formulas and their replies, concluding with a second call to prayer, our preacher rises, and in a voice with which Sir Hudibras was wont 'to blaspheme custard through the nose,' preaches Al-Wa'az, or the advice sermon. He sits down for a few minutes, and then, rising again, recites Al-Na'at, or the Praise of the Prophet and his Companions. These are the two heads into which the Moslem discourse is divided; unfortunately, however, there is no application. Our preacher, who is also Kazi or Judge, makes several blunders in his Arabic, and he reads his sermons, a thing never done in al-Islam, except by the *modicè docti*. The discourse over, our clerk, who is, if possible, worse than the curate, repeats the form of call termed al-Ikamah: then entering the Mihrab, or niche, he recites the two-bow Friday litany, with, and in front of, the congregation. I remarked no peculiarity in the style of praying, except that all followed the practice of the Shafe'is in al-Yemen—raising the hands for a moment, instead of letting them depend along the thighs, between the Ruka'at or bow and the Sujdah or prostration. This public prayer concluded, many people leave the mosque; a few remain for more prolonged devotions.

There is a queer kind of family likeness between this scene and that of a village church in some quiet nook of rural England. Old Sharmakay, the squire, attended by his son, takes his place close to the pulpit, and although the *Honoratioren* have no padded and cushioned pews, they comport themselves very much as if they had. Recognitions of the most distant description are allowed before the service commences: looking around is strictly forbidden during prayers; but all do not regard the prohibition, especially when a new moustache enters. Leaving the church, men shake hands, stand for a moment to exchange friendly gossip, or address a few words to the preacher, and then walk home to dinner. There are many salient points of difference. No bonnets appear in public: the squire, after prayers, gives alms to the poor, and departs escorted by two dozen matchlockmen, who perseveringly fire their shotted guns. So in the last century the Highland piper played before the laird every Sunday on his way to kirk, which he circled three times performing the family march which implied defiance to all the enemies of the clan. In Ireland at the early part of the century gentlemen went to church with a brace of bull dogs or a brass blunderbuss, the article to clear a staircase.*

---

* The last two sentences were added by Burton on his own copy.

Somali 'gurgi' huts.

III

Excursions near Zayla

WE DETERMINED ON THE 9th of November to visit the island of
Saad el Din, the larger of the two patches of ground which lie about
two miles north of the town. Reaching our destination, after an hour's
lively sail, we passed through a thick belt of underwood tenanted by
swarms of midges, with a damp chill air crying fever, and a fetor of
decayed vegetation smelling death. To this succeeded a barren flat of
silt and sand, white with salt and ragged with salsolaceous stubble,
reeking with heat, and covered with old vegetation. Here, says local
tradition, was the ancient site of Zayla, built by Arabs from al-
Yemen. The legend runs that when Saad el Din was besieged and
slain by David, king of Æthiopia, the wells dried up and the island
sank. Something doubtless occurred which rendered a removal
advisable: the sons of the Moslem hero fled to Ahmad bin al-Ashraf,
Prince of Sana'a, offering their allegiance if he would build fortifications
for them and aid them against the Christians of Abyssinia. The consequence was a walled circuit upon the present site of Zayla; of its old
locality almost may be said *'perière ruinae'*.

During my stay with Sharmakay I made many inquiries about
historical works, and the Kazi, Mohammed Khatib, a Harar man of the
Hawiyah tribe, was at last persuaded to send his Daftar, or office papers

for my inspection. They formed a kind of parish register of births, deaths, marriages, divorces, and manumissions. From them it appeared that in A.H. 1081 (A.D. 1670–1) the Shanabila Sayyids were Kazis of Zayla and retained the office for 138 years. It passed two generations ago into the hands of Mohammed Musa, a Hawiyah, and the present Kazi is his nephew.

The origin of Zayla, or as it is locally called, 'Audal', is lost in the fogs of Phœnician fable. The Avalites of the Periplus and Pliny, it was in earliest ages dependent upon the kingdom of Axum. About the seventh century, when the Southern Arabs penetrated into the heart of Abyssinia,[1] it became the great factory of the eastern coast, and rose to its height of splendour. Taki al-Din Makrizi includes, under the name of Zayla, a territory of forty-three days' march by forty and divides it into seven great provinces, speaking about fifty languages, and ruled by Amirs, subject to the Hati (Hatze) of Abyssinia.

In the fourteenth century it became celebrated by its wars with the kings of Abyssinia: sustaining severe defeats the Moslems retired upon their harbour, which after an obstinate defence fell into the hands of the Christians. The land was laid waste, the mosques were converted into churches, and the Abyssinians returned to their mountains laden with booty. About A.D. 1400, Saad el Din, the heroic prince of Zayla, was besieged in his city by the Hatze David the Second: slain by a spear-thrust, he left his people powerless in the hands of their enemies, till his sons, Sabr al-Din, Ali, Mansur, and Jamal al-Din retrieved the cause of al-Islam.

Ibn Batutah, a voyager of the fourteenth century, thus describes the place: 'I then went from Aden by sea, and after four days came to the city of Zayla. This is a settlement of the Berbers,* a people of Sudan, of the Shafi'a sect. Their country is a desert of two months' extent; the first part is termed Zayla, the last Makdashu. The greatest number of the inhabitants, however, are of the Rafizah sect.† Their food is mostly camels' flesh and fish.‡ The stench of the country is extreme, as is also its filth, from the stink of the fish and the blood of camels which are slaughtered in its streets.'

---

* The affinity between the Somal and the Berbers of Northern Africa, and their descent from Cana'an, son of Ham, has been learnedly advanced and refuted by several Moslem authors. The theory appears to have arisen from a mistake; Berbera, the great emporium of the Somali country, being confounded with the Berbers of Nubia.

† Probably Za'idi from El-Yemen. At present the people of Zayla are all orthodox Sunnites.

‡ Fish, as will be seen in these pages, is no longer a favourite article of diet.

73

About A.D. 1500 the Turks conquered al-Yemen, and the lawless Janissaries, 'who lived upon the very bowels of commerce', drove the peaceable Arab merchants to the opposite shore. The trade of India, flying from the same enemy, took refuge in Adel, amongst its partners.*

The Turks of Arabia, though they were blind to the cause, were sensible to the great influx of wealth into the opposite kingdoms. They took possession, therefore, of Zayla, which they made a den of thieves, established there what they called a custom-house,² and, by means of that post and galleys cruising in the narrow straits of Bab al-Mandab, they laid the Indian trade to Adel under heavy contributions that might indemnify them for the great desertion their violence and injustice had occasioned in Arabia.

This step threatened the very existence both of Adel and Abyssinia; and considering the vigorous government of the one, and the weak politics and prejudices of the other, it is more than probable that the Turks would have subdued both, had they not in India, their chief object, met the Portuguese strongly established.

Bartema, travelling in A.D. 1503, treats in his 15th chapter of 'Zayla in Æthiopia and the great fruitlessness thereof, and of certain strange beasts seen there'.

'In this city is great frequentation of merchandise, as in a most famous mart. There is marvellous abundance of gold and iron, and an innumerable number of black slaves sold for small prices; these are taken in war by the Mahomedans out of Æthiopia, of the kingdom of Presbyter Johannes, or Preciosus Johannes, which some also call the king of Jacobins or Abyssins, being a Christian; and are carried away from thence into Persia, Arabia Felix, Babylonia of Nilus or Alcair, and Meccah. In this city justice and good laws are observed. . . . It hath an innumerable multitude of merchants; the walls are greatly decayed, and the haven rude and despicable. The King or Sultan of the city is a Mahomedan, and entertaineth in wages a great multitude of footmen and horsemen. They are greatly given to war, and wear only one loose single vesture: they are of dark ash colour, inclining to black.'³

In July 1516 Zayla, described as then the 'great market of those parts', was taken, and the town burned by a Portuguese armament, under Lopez Suarez Alberguiera, and Berbera would have shared the

---

*Hence the origin of the trade between Africa and Cutch, which continues uninterrupted to the present time. Adel, Arabia, and India, as Bruce remarks, were three partners in one trade, who mutually exported their produce to Europe, Asia, and Africa, at that time the whole known world.

74

same fate had not the fleet been dispersed by storms. When the Turks were compelled to retire from Southern Arabia, it became subject to the Prince of Sana'a, who gave it in perpetuity to the family of a Sana'ani merchant. The kingdom of al-Yemen falling into decay, Zayla passed under the authority of the Sherif of Mocha, who, though receiving no part of the revenue, had yet the power of displacing the Governor. By him it was farmed out to the Hajj Sharmakay, who paid annually to Sayyid Mohammed al-Barr, at Mocha, the sum of 750 crowns, and reserved all that he could collect above that sum for himself. In A.D. 1848 Zayla was taken from the family Al-Barr, and farmed out to Sharmakay by the Turkish Governor of Mocha and Hodaydah.

The extant remains at Saad el Din are principally those of water-courses, rude lines of coralline, stretching across the plain towards wells, now lost,* and diminutive tanks, made apparently to collect rain-water. One of these latter is a work of some art—a long sunken vault, with a pointed arch projecting a few feet above the surface of the ground; outside, it is of rough stone, the interior is carefully coated with fine lime, and from the roof long stalactites depend. Near it is a cemetery: the graves are, for the most part, provided with large slabs of close black basalt, planted in the ground edgeways, and in the shape of a small oblong. The material was most probably brought from the mountains near Tajjurrah: at another part of the island I found it in the shape of a gigantic mill-stone, half imbedded in the loose sand. Near the cemetery we observed a mound of rough stones surrounding an upright pole; this is the tomb of Shaykh Saad el Din, formerly the hero, now the favourite patron saint of Zayla—still popularly vene-rated, as was proved by the remains of votive banquets, broken bones, dried garbage, and stones blackened by the fire.

After wandering through the island, which contained not a human being save a party of Somal boatmen cutting firewood for Aden, and having massacred a number of large fishing hawks and small sea-birds, to astonish the natives our companions, we returned to the landing-place. Here an awning had been spread; the goat destined for our dinner—I have long since conquered all dislike, dear L., to seeing dinner perambulating—had been boiled and disposed in hunches upon small mountains of rice, and jars of sweet water stood in the air to cool.

* The people have a tradition that a well of sweet water exists unseen in some part of the island. When Saad el Din was besieged in Zayla by the Hatzi David, the host of al-Islam suffered severely for the want of the fresh element.

After feeding, regardless of Quartana* and her weird sisterhood, we all lay down for siesta in the light sea-breeze. Our slumbers were heavy, as the Zayla people say is ever the case at Saad el Din, and the sun had declined low ere we awoke. The tide was out, and we waded a quarter of a mile to the boat, amongst giant crabs who showed grisly claws, sharp coralline, and sea-weed so thick as to become almost a mat. You must believe me when I tell you that in the shallower parts the sun was painfully hot, even to my well-tried feet. We picked up a few specimens of fine sponge, and coral, white and red, which, if collected, might be valuable to Zayla, and, our picnic concluded, we returned home.

On the 14th November we left the town to meet a caravan of the Danakil, and to visit the tomb of the great saint Abu Zarbay. The former approached in a straggling line of asses, and about fifty camels laden with cows' hides, ivories, and one Abyssinian slave-girl. The men were wild as ourang-outangs, and the women fit only to flog cattle: their animals were small, meagre-looking, and loosely made; the asses of the Bedouin, however, are far superior to those of Zayla, and the camels are, comparatively speaking, well bred.[4] In a few minutes the beasts were unloaded, the Gurgis or wigwams pitched, and all was prepared for repose. A caravan so extensive being an unusual event— small parties carrying only grain come in once or twice a week—the citizens abandoned even their favourite game of ball, with an eye to speculation. We stood at 'Government House', over the Ashurbara Gate, to see the Bedouin, and we quizzed (as Town men might denounce a tie or scoff at a boot) the huge round shields and the uncouth spears of these provincials. Presently they entered the streets, where we witnessed their frantic dance in presence of the Hajj [Sharmakay] and other authorities. This is the wild men's way of expressing their satisfaction that Fate has enabled them to convoy the caravan through all the dangers of the desert.

The Shaykh Ibrahim Abu Zarbay lies under a whitewashed dome close to the Ashurbara Gate of Zayla: an inscription cut in wood over the doorway informs us that the building dates from A.H. 1155= A.D. 1741–2. It is now dilapidated, the lintel is falling in, the walls are decaying, and the cupola, which is rudely built, with primitive gradients—each step supported as in Kashmír and other parts of India, by wooden beams—threatens the heads of the pious. The building is divided into two compartments, forming a Mosque and a Mazar or

* Quartan ague or fever.—Ed.

place of pious visitation: in the latter are five tombs, the two largest covered with common chintz stuff of glaring colours. Ibrahim was one of the forty-four Hadrami saints who landed at Berbera, sat in solemn conclave upon Auliya Kumbo or Holy Hill, and thence dispersed far and wide for the purpose of propagandism. He travelled to Harar about A.D. 1430,* converted many to al-Islam, and left there an honoured memory. His name is immortalized in al-Yemen by the introduction of Kât.5

Tired of the town, I persuaded the Hajj to send me with an escort to the Hissi or well. At daybreak I set out with four Arab matchlock-men, and taking a direction nearly due west, waded and walked over an alluvial plain flooded by every high tide. On our way we passed lines of donkeys and camels carrying water-skins from the town; they were under guard like ourselves, and the sturdy dames that drove them indulged in many a loud joke at our expense. After walking about four miles we arrived at what is called the 'Takhushshah—the sandy bed of a torrent nearly a mile broad,† covered with a thin coat of caked mud: in the centre is a line of pits from three to four feet deep, with turbid water at the bottom. Around them were several frame-works of four upright sticks connected by horizontal bars, and on these were stretched goats' skins, forming the cattle trough of the Somali country. About the well stood troops of camels, whose Eesa proprietors scowled fiercely at us, and stalked over the plain with their long, heavy spears: for protection against these people, the citizens have erected a kind of round tower, with a ladder for a staircase. Near it are some large tamarisks and the wild henna of the Somali country, which supplies a sweet-smelling flower, but is valueless as a dye. A thick hedge of thorn-trees surrounds the only cultivated ground near Zayla: as Ibn Sa'id declared in old times, 'the people have no gardens, and know nothing of fruits'. The variety and the luxuriance of growth, however, prove that industry is the sole desideratum. I remarked the castor-plant—no one knows its name or nature‡—the Rayhan or Basil, the Kadi, a species of aloe, whose strongly-scented flowers the Arabs of El-

* In the same year (A.D. 1429–30) the Shaykh al-Shazil, buried under a dome at Mocha, introduced coffee into Arabia.

† This is probably the 'River of Zayla', alluded to by Ibn Sa'id [or Ibn Sa'd] and others. Like all similar features in the low country, it is a mere surface drain.

‡ In the upper country I found a large variety growing wild in the fiumaras. The Bedouin named it Buamado, but ignored its virtues.

[Burton described fiumaras as 'a hill water-course, which rolls a torrent after rain, and is either partially or wholly dry during the drought season'. (Introduction to *Personal Narrative of a Pilgrimage to El-Medinah and Meccah*, 1855.)—Ed.]

77

Yemen are fond of wearing in their turbans. Of vegetables, there were cucumbers, egg-plants, and the edible hibiscus; the only fruit was a small kind of water-melon.

After enjoying a walk through the garden and a bath at the well, I started, gun in hand, towards the jungly plain that stretches towards the sea. It abounds in hares, and in a large description of spur-fowl; the beautiful little sand antelope, scarcely bigger than an English rabbit, bounded over the bushes, its thin legs being scarcely perceptible during the spring. I was afraid to fire with ball, the place being full of Bedouin huts, herds, and dogs, and the vicinity of man made the animals too wild for small shot. In revenge, I did considerable havoc amongst the spur-fowl, who proved equally good for sport and the pot, besides knocking over a number of old crows, whose gall the Arab soldiers wanted for collyrium [eye-lotion].* Beyond us lay Warabalay or Hyænas' hill†: we did not visit it, as all its tenants had been driven away by the migration of the Nomads.

Returning, we breakfasted in the garden, and rain coming on, we walked out to enjoy the Oriental luxury of a wetting. Ali Iskandar, an old Arab mercenary, afforded us infinite amusement: a little opium made him half crazy, when his sarcastic pleasantries never ceased. We then brought out the guns, and being joined by the other escort, proceeded to a trial of skill. The Arabs planted a bone about 200 paces from us—a long distance for a people who seldom fire beyond fifty yards; moreover, the wind blew the flash strongly in their faces. Some shot two or three dozen times wide of the mark and were derided accordingly: one man hit the bone; he at once stopped practice, as the wise in such matters will do, and shook hands with all the party. He afterwards

* The Somal hold the destruction of the 'Turka' next in the religious merit to that of the snake. They have a tradition that the crow, originally white, became black for his sins. When the Prophet and Abubekr were concealed in the cave, the pigeon hid there from their pursuers: the crow, on the contrary, sat screaming 'ghar! ghar!' (the cave! the cave!) upon which Mohammed ordered him into eternal mourning, and ever to repeat the traitorous words.

There are several species of crows in this part of Africa. Besides the large-beaked bird of the Harar Hills, I found the common European variety, with, however, the breast feathers white tipped in small semicircles as far as the abdomen. The little 'king crow' of India is common: its bright-red eye and purplish plume render it a conspicuous object as it perches upon the tall camel's back or clings to waving plants.

† This animal swarms throughout the Somali country, prowls about the camps all night, dogs travellers, and devours everything he can find, at times pulling down children and camels, and when violently pressed by hunger, men. The Somal declare the Waraba to be a hermaphrodite; so the ancients supposed the hyæna to be of both sexes—an error arising from the peculiar appearance of an orifice situated near two glands which secret an unctuous fluid.

78

showed that his success on this occasion had been accidental; but he was a staunch old sportsman, remarkable, as the Arab Bedouin generally are, for his skill and perseverance in stalking. Having no rifle, I remained a spectator. My revolvers excited abundant attention, though none would be persuaded to touch them. The largest, which, fitted with a stock, became an excellent carbine, was at once named Abu Sittah (the Father of Six) and the Shaytan or Devil: the pocket pistol became the Malunah or Accursed, and the distance to which it carried ball made every man wonder. The Arabs had antiquated match-locks, mostly worn away to paper thinness at the mouth: as usual they fired with the right elbow raised to the level of the ear, and the left hand grasping the barrel, where with us the breech would be. Hassan Turki had one of those fine old Shishkhanah rifles formerly made at Damascus and Sana'a: it carried a two-ounce ball with perfect correctness, but was so badly mounted in its block-butt, shaped like a Dutch cheese, that it always required a rest.

On our return home we met a party of Eesa girls, who derided my colour and doubted the fact of my being a Moslem. The Arabs declared me to be a Shaykh of Shaykhs, and translated to the prettiest of the party an impromptu proposal of marriage. She showed but little coyness, and stated her price to be an Audulli or necklace,* a couple of Tobes—she asked one too many—a few handfuls of beads,† and a small present for her papa. She promised, naïvely enough, to call next day and inspect the goods: the publicity of the town did not deter her, but the shamefacedness of my two companions prevented our meeting again. Arrived at Zayla after a sunny walk, the Arab escort loaded their guns, formed a line for me to pass along, fired a salute, and entered to coffee and sweetmeats.

On the 24th of November I had an opportunity of seeing what a

* Men wear for ornament round the neck a bright red leather thong, upon which are strung in front two square bits of true or imitation amber or honey stone: this 'Makkawi', however, is seldom seen amongst the Bedouin. The Audulli or woman's necklace is a more elaborate affair of amber, glass beads, generally coloured, and coral: every matron who can afford it possesses at least one of these ornaments. Both sexes carry round the necks or hang above the right elbow, a talisman against danger and disease, either in a silver box or more generally sewn up in a small case of red morocco. The Bedouin are fond of attaching a tooth-stick to the neck thong.

† Beads are useful in the Somali country as presents, and to pay for trifling purchases: like tobacco they serve for small change. The kind preferred by women and children is the 'binnur', large and small white porcelain: the others are the red, white, green, and spotted twisted beads, round and oblong. Before entering a district the traveller should ascertain what may be the especial variety. Some kind are greedily sought for in one place, and in another rejected with disdain.

79

timid people are these Somal of the towns, who, as has been well remarked, are, like the settled Arabs, the worst specimens of their race. Three Eesa Bedouin appeared before the southern gate, slaughtered a cow, buried its head, and sent for permission to visit one of their number who had been imprisoned by the Hajj for the murder of his son Mas'ud. The place was at once thrown into confusion, the gates were locked, and the walls manned with Arab matchlock-men: my three followers armed themselves, and I was summoned to the fray. Some declared that the Bedouin were 'doing'*₊the town; others that they were the van of a giant host coming to ravish, sack, and slay: it turned out that these Bedouin had preceded their comrades, who were bringing in, as the price of blood,⁶ an Abyssinian slave, seven camels, seven cows, a white mule, and a small black mare. The prisoner was visited by his brother, who volunteered to share his confinement, and the meeting was described as most pathetic: partly from mental organization and partly from the peculiarities of society the only real tie acknowledged by these people is that which connects male kinsmen. The Hajj, after speaking big, had the weakness to let the murderer depart alive; this measure like peace-policy in general, is the best and surest way to encourage bloodshed and mutilation. But a few months before, an Eesa Bedouin enticed out of the gate a boy about fifteen, and slaughtered him for the sake of wearing the feather. His relations were directed to receive the Diyat or blood fine, and the wretch was allowed to depart unhurt—a silly clemency!

You must not suppose, dear L., that I yielded myself willingly to the weary necessity of a month at Zayla. But how explain to you the obstacle thrown in our way by African indolence, petty intrigue, and interminable suspicion? Four months before leaving Aden I had taken the precaution of meeting the Hajj, requesting him to select for us an Abban,† or protector, and to provide camels and mules; two months

* The Somali word 'Fäl' properly means 'to do'; 'to bewitch', is its secondary sense.

† The Abban or protector of the Somali country is the Mogasa of the Gallas, the Akh of Al-Hijaz, the Ghafir of the Sinaitic Peninsula, and the Rabi'a of Eastern Arabia. It must be observed however, that the word denotes the protégé as well as the protector; in the latter sense it is the polite address to a Somali, as Ya Abbanah, O Protectress, would be to his wife.

The Abban acts at once as broker, escort, agent, and interpreter, and the institution may be considered the earliest form of transit dues. In all sales he receives a certain percentage, his food and lodging are provided at the expense of his employer, and he not unfrequently exacts small presents for his kindred. In return he is bound to arrange all differences, and even to fight the battles of his client against his fellow-countrymen. Should an Abban be slain, his tribe is bound to take up the cause and to make good the before starting I had advanced to him the money required in a country where nothing can be done without a whole or partial prepayment. The protector was to be procured anywhere, the cattle at Tajjurrah, scarcely a day's sail from Zayla: when I arrived nothing was forthcoming. I at once begged the governor to exert himself; he politely promised to start a messenger that hour, and he delayed doing so for ten days. An easterly wind set in and gave the crew an excuse for wasting another fortnight. Travellers are an irritable genus: I stormed and fretted at the delays, to show earnestness of purpose. All the effect was a paroxysm of talking. The Hajj and his son treated me, like a spoilt child, to a double allowance of food and milk: they warned me that the small-pox was depopulating Harar, that the road swarmed with brigands, and that the Amir or prince was certain destruction—I contented myself with determining that both were true Oriental hyperbolists, and fell into more frequent fits of passion. The old man could not comprehend my secret. 'If the English,' he privately remarked, 'wish to take Harar, let them send me 500 soldiers; if not, I can give all information concerning it.' When convinced of my determination to travel, he applied his mind to calculating the benefit which might be derived from the event, and, as the following pages will show, he was not without success.

Towards the end of November, four camels were procured, an Abban was engaged, we hired two women cooks and a fourth servant; my baggage was reformed, the cloth and tobacco being sewn up in matting, and made to fit the camels' sides*, sandals were cut out for walking, letters were written, messages of dreary length—too important to be set down in black and white—were solemnly entrusted to us, palavers were held, and affairs began to wear the semblance of departure. The Hajj strongly recommended us to one of the principal

* The Somal use as camel saddles the mats which compose their huts; these lying loose upon the animal's back, cause, by slipping backwards and forwards, the loss of many a precious hour, and in wet weather become half a load. The more civilized make up of canvas or 'gunny bags' stuffed with hay and provided with cross bars, a rude pack saddle, which is admirably calculated to gall the animal's back.

losses of their protégé. Al-Ta'abanah, the office, being one of 'name', the eastern synonym for our honour, as well as of lucre, causes frequent quarrels, which become exceedingly rancorous.

According to the laws of the country, the Abban is master of the life and property of his client. The traveller's success will depend mainly upon his selection: if inferior in rank, the protector can neither forward nor defend him; if timid, he will impede advance; and if avaricious, he will, by means of his relatives, effectually stop the journey by absorbing the means of prosecuting it.

families of the Gudabirsi tribe, who would pass us on to their brother-in-law Adan, the Gerad or prince of the Girhi; and he, in due time, to his kinsman the Amir of Harar. The chain was commenced by placing us under the protection of one Raghi, a petty Eesa chief of the Mummasan clan. By the good aid of the Hajj and our sweetmeats, he was persuaded, for the moderate consideration of ten Tobes,* to accompany us to the frontier of his clan, distant about fifty miles, to introduce us to the Gudabirsi, and to provide us with three men as servants, and a suitable escort, a score or so, in dangerous places. He began with us in an extravagant manner, declaring that nothing but 'name' induced him to undertake the perilous task; that he had left his flocks and herds at a season of uncommon risk, and that all his relations must receive a certain honorarium. But having paid at least three pounds for a few days of his society, we declined such liberality, and my companions, I believe, declared that it would be 'next time': on all such occasions I make a point of leaving the room, since for one thing given, at least five are promised on oath. Raghi warned us seriously to prepare for dangers and disasters, and this seemed to be the general opinion of Zayla, whose timid citizens determined that we were tired of our lives. The cold had driven the Nomads from the hills to the warm maritime plains,† we should therefore traverse a populous region; and, as the End of Time aptly observed, 'Man eats you up, the Desert does not.' Moreover this year the Ayyal Nuh Ismail, a clan of the Habr Awal tribe, is 'out', and has been successful against the Eesa, who generally are the better men. They sweep the country in Kaum or Commandos, numbering from twenty to two hundred troopers, armed with assegai, dagger, and shield, and carrying a water-skin and dried meat for a three days' ride, sufficient to scour the length of the low land. The honest fellows are not so anxious to plunder as to ennoble themselves by taking life: every man hangs to his saddle bow an ostrich‡ feather—

* He received four cloths of Cutch canvas, and six others of coarse American sheeting. At Zayla these articles are double the Aden value, which would be about thirteen rupees or twenty-six shillings; in the bush the price is quadrupled. Before leaving us the Abban received at least double the original hire. Besides small presents of cloth, dates, tobacco, and rice to his friends, he had six cubits of Sa'uda Wilayati or English indigo-dyed calico for women's fillets, and two of Sa'uda Kashshi, a Cutch imitation, a Shukkah or half Tobe for his daughter, and a sheep for himself, together with a large bundle of tobacco.

† When the pastures are exhausted and the monsún sets in, the Bedouin return to their cool mountains; like the Iliyat of Persia, they have their regular Kishlakh and Yaylakh.

‡ Amongst the old Egyptians the ostrich feather was the symbol of truth. The Somal call it 'Bal', the Arabs 'Rish'; it is universally used here as the sign and symbol of victory. Generally the white feather only is stuck in the hair; the Eesa are not particular in using black when they can procure no other. All the clans wear it in the back hair, but each has

emblem of truth—and the moment his javelin has drawn blood, he sticks it into his tufty poll with as much satisfaction as we feel when attaching a medal to our shell-jackets. It is by no means necessary to slay the foe in fair combat: Spartan-like, treachery is preferred to stand-up fighting; and you may measure their ideas of honour, by the fact that women are murdered in cold blood, as by the Amazulus [Zulus], with the hope that the unborn child may prove a male. The hero carries home the trophy of his prowess,* and his wife, springing from her tent, utters a long shrill scream of joy, a preliminary to boasting of her man's valour, and bitterly taunting the other possessors of noirs fainéants: the derided ladies abuse their lords with peculiar virulence, and the lords fall into paroxysms of envy, hatred, and malice. During my short stay at Zayla six or seven murders were committed close to the walls: the Abban brought news, a few hours before our departure, that two Eesas had been slaughtered by the Habr Awal. The Eesa and Dankali also have a blood feud, which causes perpetual loss of life. But a short time ago six men of these two tribes were travelling together, when suddenly the last but one received from the hindermost a deadly spear-thrust in the back. The wounded man had the presence of mind to plunge his dagger in the side of the wayfarer who preceded him, thus dying as the people say, in company. One of these events throws the country into confusion, for the vendetta is rancorous and bloody, as in ancient Germany or in modern Corsica. Our Abban enlarged upon the unpleasant necessity of travelling all night towards the hills, and lying perdu during the day. The most dangerous times are dawn and evening-tide: the troopers spare their horses during the heat, and themselves during the dew-fall. Whenever, in the desert—where, says the proverb, all men are enemies—you sight a fellow-creature from afar, you wave the right arm violently up and down, shouting, 'War Joga! War Joga!'—stand still! stand still! If they halt, you send

---

* This is an ancient practice in Asia as well as in Africa. The Egyptian temples show heaps of trophies placed before the monarchs as eyes or heads were presented in Persia. Thus in 1 Sam. xviii. 25, David brings the spoils of 200 Philistines, and shows them in full tale to the king, that he might be the king's son-in-law. Any work upon the subject of Abyssinia (Bruce, book 7, chap. 8), or the late Afghan war, will prove that the custom of mutilation, opposed as it is both to Christianity and to al-Islam, is still practised in the case of hated enemies and infidels.

---

its own rules; some make it a standard decoration, others discard it after the first few days. The learned have an aversion to the custom, stigmatizing it as pagan and idolatrous; the vulgar look upon it as the highest mark of honour.

a parliamentary to within speaking distance. Should they advance,* you fire, taking especial care not to miss; when two saddles are emptied the rest are sure to decamp.

I had given the Abban orders to be in readiness—my patience being thoroughly exhausted—on Sunday, the 26th of November, and determined to walk the whole way, rather than waste another day waiting for cattle. As the case had become hopeless, a vessel was descried standing straight from Tajjurrah, and, suddenly as could happen in the *Arabian Nights*, four fine mules, saddled and bridled, Abyssinian fashion, appeared at the door.†

* When attacking cattle, the plundering party endeavour with shouts and noise to disperse the herds, whilst the assailed huddle them together, and attempt to face the danger in parties.

† For the cheapest I paid twenty-three, for the dearest twenty-six dollars, besides a Riyal upon each, under the names of custom dues and carriage. The Hajj had doubtless exaggerated the price, but all were good animals, and the traveller has no right to complain, except when he pays dear for a bad article.

The Sand antelope—Dik Dik.

IV

The Somal, their Origin, and Peculiarities

BEFORE LEAVING ZAYLA, I must not neglect a short description of its inhabitants, and the remarkable Somal races around it.

Eastern Africa, like Arabia, presents a population composed of three markedly distinct races.

1. The Aborigines, such as the Negroes, the Bushmen, Hottentots, and other races, having such physiological peculiarities as the steatopyge*, the tablier, and other developments described, in 1815, by the great Cuvier.

2. The almost pure Caucasian of the northern regions, west of Egypt: their immigration comes within the range of comparatively modern history.

3. The half-castes in Eastern Africa are represented principally by the Abyssinians, Gallas, Somal, Sawahili, Hamitic, and Kafirs. The first-named people derive their descent from Menelek, son of Solomon by the Queen of Sheba: it is evident from their features and figures—too well known to require description—that they are descended from Semitic as well as Negrotic (Nigro-Hamitic) progenitors. About the origin of the Gallas there is a diversity of opinion. Some declare them to be Meccan Arabs, who settled on the western coast of the Red Sea at a remote epoch: according to the Abyssinians, however, and there is little to find fault with in their theory, the Gallas are descended from a princess of their nation, who was given in marriage to a slave from the country south of Gurague. She bare seven sons, who became mighty robbers and founders of tribes: their progenitors obtained the name of Gallas, after the river Gala, in Gurague, where they gained a decisive victory over their kinsmen the Abyssins. A variety of ethnologic and physiological reasons—into which space and subject prevent my entering—argue the Kafirs of the Cape to be a northern people,

* Protuberance of the buttocks.—Ed.

Mohammed Mahmud, Sergeant in the Aden Police, called al-Hammal, or 'the porter'.

pushed southwards by some, to us, as yet, unknown cause. The origin of the Somal is a matter of modern history.

'Barbarah' (Berbera),[1] according to the Kamus [an Arabic dictionary], is 'a well known town in El Maghrib, and a race located between El Zanj—Zanzibar and the Negrotic coast—and El Habash [Abyssinia]: they are descended from the Himyar chiefs Sanhàj

86

(Sinhagia) and Sumámah, and they arrived at the epoch of the conquest of Africa by the king Afríkús (Scipio Africanus?).' A few details upon the subjects of mutilation and excision[2] prove these to have been the progenitors of the Somal, who are nothing but a slice of the great Galla nation Islamized and Semiticized by repeated immigrations from Arabia. In the Kamus we also read that Samal is the name of the father of a tribe, so called because he *thrust out* (*samala*) his brother's eye.

The Shaykh Jami, a celebrated genealogist, informed me that in A.H. 666[*] = A.D. 1266–7, the Sayyid Yusuf al-Baghdadi visited the port of Siyaro near Berbera, then occupied by an infidel magician, who passed through mountains by the power of his gramarye: the saint summoned to his aid Mohammed bin Yunis al-Siddiki, of Bayt al-Fakih in Arabia, and by their united prayers a hill closed upon the pagan. Deformed by fable, the foundation of the tale is fact: the numerous descendants of the holy men still pay an annual fine, by way of blood-money to the family of the infidel chief. The last and most important Arab immigration took place about fifteen generations or 450 years ago, when the Sharif Ishak bin Ahmad,[†] left his native country Hadramaut, and, with forty-four saints, before mentioned, landed on Makhar—the windward coast extending from Karam Harbour to Cape Guardafui. At the town of Met [or Mait], near Burnt Island, where his tomb still exists, he became the father of all the gentle blood and the only certain descent in the Somali country: by Magaden, a free woman, he had Jirhajis, Awal, and Arab; and by a slave or slaves, Jailah, Sambur, and Rambad. Hence the great clans, Habr Jirhajis and Awal, who prefer the matronymic—Habr signifying a mother—since, according to their dictum, no man knows who may be his sire. These increased and multiplied by connection and affiliation to such an extent that about A.D. 1500 they drove their progenitors, the Galla, from Berbera, and gradually encroached upon them, till they entrenched themselves in the Highlands of Harar.

The old and pagan genealogies still known to the Somal, are Dirr, Aydur, Darud, and, according to some, Hawiyah. Dirr and Aydur, of whom nothing is certainly known but the name, are the progenitors of the northern Somal, the Eesa, Gudabirsi, Ishak, and Bursuk tribes. Darud Jabarti bin Ismail bin Akil (or Ukayl) is supposed by his

* A.H. = after the Hejira, the departure of the Prophet Mohammed with his followers from Mecca to Medina in A.D. 622, which is the beginning of the Mohammedan era.—Ed.

† According to others he was the son of Abdullah. The written genealogies of the Somal were, it is said, stolen by the Sherifs of al Yemen, who feared to leave with the wild people documents that prove the nobility of their descent.

descendants to have been a noble Arab from Al-Hijaz, who, obliged to flee his country, was wrecked on the north-east coast of Africa, where he married a daughter of the Hawiyah tribe: rival races declare him to have been a Galla slave, who, stealing the Prophet's slippers, was dismissed with the words, Inná-*tarad*-ná-hu (verily we have rejected him): hence his name Tarud or Darud, the Rejected. The etymological part of the story is, doubtless, fabulous; it expresses however, the popular belief that the founder of the eastward or windward tribes, now extending over the seaboard from Bundir Jadid to Ras Hafun, and southward from the sea to the Webbes,* was a man of ignoble origin. The children of Darud are now divided into two great bodies: 'Harti' is the family name of the Dulbahanta, Ogadayn, Warsangali, and Mijjarthayn, who call themselves sons of Harti bin Kombo bin Kabl Ullah bin Darud: the other Darud tribes not included under that appellation are the Girhi, Berteri, Marayhan, and Bahabr Ali. The Hawiyah are doubtless of ancient and pagan origin; they call all Somal except themselves Hashiyah, and thus claim to be equivalent to the rest of the nation. Some attempt, as usual, to establish a holy origin, deriving themselves like the Shaykhash from the Caliph Abu Bakr: the antiquity, and consequently the pagan origin of the Hawiyah are proved by its present widely scattered state; it is a powerful tribe in the Mijjarthayn country, and yet is found in the hills of Harar.

The Somal, therefore, by their own traditions, as well as their strongly-marked physical peculiarities, their customs, and their geographical position, may be determined to be a half-caste tribe, an offshoot of the great Galla race, approximated, like the originally Negro-Egyptian, to the Caucasian type by a steady influx of pure Asiatic blood.

In personal appearance the race is not unprepossessing. The crinal hair is hard and wiry, growing, like that of a half-caste West Indian, in stiff ringlets which sprout in tufts from the scalp, and, attaining a moderate length, which they rarely surpass, hang down. A few elders, savans, and the wealthy, who can afford the luxury of a turban, shave the head. More generally, each filament is duly picked out with the comb or a wooden scratcher like a knitting-needle, and the mass made to resemble a child's 'pudding', an old bob-wig, a mop, a counsellor's peruke, or an old-fashioned coachman's wig—there are a hundred ways of dressing the head. The Bedouin, true specimens of the 'greasy African race', wear locks dripping with rancid butter, and accuse their

* The two rivers Shebayli or Shebelli and Juba.—Ed.

88

citizen brethren of being more like birds than men. The colouring matter of the hair, naturally a bluish-black, is removed by a mixture of quicklime and water, or in the desert by a *lessive* of ashes: this makes it a dull yellowish-white, which is converted into red permanently by henna, temporarily by ochreish earth kneaded with water. The ridiculous Somali peruke of crimsoned sheepskin—almost as barbarous an article as the Welsh—is apparently a foreign invention: I rarely saw one in the low country, although the hill tribes about Harar sometimes wear a black or white 'scratch-wig'. The head is rather long than round, and generally of the amiable variety, it is gracefully put on the shoulders, belongs equally to Africa and Arabia, and would be exceedingly weak but for the beauty of the brow. As far as the mouth, the face, with the exception of high cheek-bones, is good; the contour of the forehead ennobles it; the eyes are large and well-formed, and the upper features are frequently handsome and expressive. The jaw, however, is almost invariably prognathous and African; the broad, turned-out lips betray approximation to the Negro; and the chin projects to the detriment of the facial angle. The beard is represented by a few tufts; it is rare to see anything equal to even the Arab development: the long and ample eyebrows admired by the people are uncommon, and the mustachios are short and thin, often twisted outwards in two dwarf curls. The mouth is coarse as well as thick-lipped; the teeth rarely project as in the Negro, but they are not good: the habit of perpetually chewing coarse Surat tobacco stains them,* the gums become black and mottled, and the use of ashes with the quid discolours the lips. The skin, amongst the tribes inhabiting the hot regions, is smooth, black, and glossy; as the altitude increases it becomes lighter, and about Harar it is generally of a *café au lait* colour. The Bedouin are fond of raising beauty marks in the shape of ghastly seams, and the thickness of the epidermis favours the size of these *stigmates*. The male figure is tall and somewhat ungainly. In only one instance I observed an approach to the steatopyge, making the shape to resemble the letter S; but the shoulders are high, the trunk is straight, the thighs fall off, the shin bones bow slightly forwards, and the feet, like the hands, are coarse, large, and flat. Yet with their hair, of a light straw colour, decked with the light waving feather, and their coal-black complexions set off by that most graceful of garments the clean white Tobe, the contrasts are decidedly effective.

* Few Somal except the citizens smoke, on account of the expense; all, however, use the Takhzinah or quid.

89

In mind the Somal are peculiar as in body. They are a people of most susceptible character, and withal uncommonly hard to please. They dislike the Arabs, fear and abhor the Turks, have a horror of Franks, and despise all other Asiatics who with them come under the general name of Hindí (Indians). The latter are abused on all occasions for cowardice, and a want of generosity, which has given rise to the following piquant epigram:

> Ask not thy want from the Hindi:
> Impossible to find liberality in the Hindi!
> Had there been one liberal man in Al-Hind,
> Allah had raised up a prophet in Al-Hind!

They have all the levity and instability of the Negro character; light-minded as the Abyssinians—described by Gobat* as constant in nothing but inconstancy—soft, merry, and affectionate souls, they pass without any apparent transition into a state of fury, when they are capable of terrible atrocities. At Aden they appear happier than in their native country. There I have often seen a man clapping his hands and dancing, child-like, alone to relieve the exuberance of his spirits: here they become as the Mongols and other pastoral people, a melancholy race, who will sit for hours upon a bank gazing at the moon, or croning some old ditty under the trees. This state is doubtless increased by the perpetual presence of danger and the uncertainty of life, which make them think of other things than dancing and singing. Much learning seems to make them mad; like the half-crazy Fakíhs of the Sahara in Northern Africa, the Widad, or priest, is generally unfitted for the affairs of this world, and the Hafiz or Koran-reciter, is almost idiotic.

As regards courage, they are no exception to the generality of savage races. They have none of the recklessness standing in lieu of creed which characterizes the civilized man. In their great battles a score is considered a heavy loss; usually they will run after the fall of half a dozen: amongst a Kraal full of braves who boast a hundred murders, not a single maimed or wounded man will be seen, whereas in an Arabian camp half the male population will bear the marks of lead and steel. The bravest will shirk fighting if he has forgotten his shield: the sight of a lion and the sound of a gun elicit screams of terror, and their Kaum or forays much resemble the style of tactics

---

* Samuel Gobat, Roman Catholic missionary who travelled in Ethiopia in the 1830's; he wrote *Journal of Three Years Residence in Abyssinia*, New York, Dodd; 1850.—Ed.

rendered obsolete by the Great Turenne, when the tactician's chief aim was not to fall in with his enemy.[3] Yet they are by no means deficient in the wily valour of wild men: two or three will murder a sleeper bravely enough; and when the passions of rival tribes, between whom there has been a blood feud for ages, are violently excited, they will use with asperity the dagger and spear. Their massacres are fearful. In February 1847 a small sept, the Ayyal Yunis, being expelled from Berbera, settled at the roadstead of Bulhar, where a few merchants, principally Indian and Arab, joined them. The men were in the habit of leaving their women and children, sick and aged, at the encampment inland, whilst, descending to the beach, they carried on their trade. One day, as they were thus employed, unsuspicious of danger, a foraging party of about 2,500 Eesas attacked the camp: men, women, and children were indiscriminately put to the spear, and the plunderers returned to their villages in safety, laden with an immense amount of booty. At present, a man armed with a revolver would be a terror to the country; the day, however, will come when the matchlock will supersede the assegai, and then the harmless spearman in his strong mountains will become, like the Arab, a formidable foe.

Travelling among the Bedouin, I found them kind and hospitable. A pinch of snuff or a handful of tobacco sufficed to win every heart, and a few yards of coarse cotton cloth supplied all our wants. I was petted like a child, forced to drink milk and to eat mutton; girls were offered to me in marriage; the people begged me to settle amongst them, to head their predatory expeditions, free them from lions, and kill their elephants; and often a man has exclaimed in pitying accents, 'What hath brought thee, delicate as thou art, to sit with us on the cowhide in this cold under a tree?' Of course they were beggars, princes and paupers, lairds and loons, being all equally unfortunate; the Arabs have named the country Bilad Wa Issi—the 'Land of Give me Something'—but their wants were easily satisfied, and the open hand always made a friend.

The Somal hold mainly to the Shafe'i school of al-Islam: their principal peculiarity is that of not reciting prayers over the dead even in the towns. The marriage ceremony is simple: the price of the bride and the feast being duly arranged, the formula is recited by some priest or pilgrim. I have often been requested to officiate on these occasions, and the End of Time has done it by irreverently reciting the Fatihah over the happy pair.* The Somal, as usual among the heterogeneous

* Equivalent to reading out the Church Catechism at an English wedding.

mass amalgamated by Al-Islam, have a diversity of superstitions attesting their pagan origin. Such, for instance, are their oaths by stones, their reverence of cairns and holy trees, and their ordeals of fire and water—the Bolungo of Western Africa. A man accused of murder or theft walks down a trench full of live charcoal and about a spear's length, or he draws out of the flames a smith's anvil heated to redness: some prefer picking four or five cowries from a large pot full of boiling water. The member used is at once rolled up in the intestines of a sheep and not inspected for a whole day. They have traditionary seers called Tawuli, like the Greegreemen of Western Africa, who, by inspecting the fat and bones of slaughtered cattle, 'do medicine', predict rains, battles, and diseases of animals. This class is of both sexes: they never pray or bathe, and are therefore considered always impure; thus, being feared, they are greatly respected by the vulgar. Their predictions are delivered in a rude rhyme, often put for importance into the mouth of some deceased seer. During the three months called Rajalo the Koran is not read over graves, and no marriage ever takes place. The reason of this peculiarity is stated to be imitation of their ancestor Ishak, who happened not to contract a matrimonial alliance at such epoch: it is, however, a manifest remnant of the pagan's auspicious and inauspicious months. Thus they sacrifice she-camels in the month Sabuh, and keep holy with feasts and bonfires the Dubshid or New Year's Day. At certain unlucky periods when the moon is in ill-omened asterisms* those who die are placed in bundles of matting upon a tree, the idea being that if buried a loss would result to the tribe.

Though superstitious, the Somal are not bigoted like the Arabs, with the exception of those who, wishing to become learned, visit al Yemen or al-Hijaz, and catch the complaint. Nominal Mohammedans, al-Islam hangs so lightly upon them, that apparently they care little for making it binding upon others.

The Somali language is no longer unknown to Europe. It is strange that a dialect which has no written character should so abound in poetry and eloquence.⁴ There are thousands of songs, some local, others general, upon all conceivable subjects, such as camel loading, drawing water, and elephant hunting; every man of education knows a variety of them. The rhyme is imperfect, being generally formed by the syllable 'ay' (pronounced as in our word 'hay'), which gives the verse a monotonous regularity; but, assisted by a tolerably regular allitera-

* Small groups of stars.—Ed.

tion and cadence, it can never be mistaken for prose, even without the song which invariably accompanies it. The country teems with 'poets, poetasters, poetitos, poetaccios': every man has his recognized position in literature as accurately defined as though he had been reviewed in a century of magazines—the fine ear of this people* causing them to take the greatest pleasure in harmonious sounds and poetical expressions, whereas a false quantity or a prosaic phrase excite their violent indignation. Many of these compositions are so idiomatic that Arabs settled for years amongst the Somal cannot understand them though perfectly acquainted with the conversational style. Every chief in the country must have a panegyric to be sung by his clan, and the great patronize light literature by keeping a poet. The amatory is of course the favourite theme: sometimes it appears in dialogue, the rudest form, we are told, of the Drama. The subjects are frequently pastoral: the lover for instance invites his mistress to walk with him towards the well in Lahelo, the Arcadia of the land; he compares her legs to the tall straight Libi tree, and imprecates the direst curses on her head if she refuse to drink with him the milk of his favourite camel. There are a few celebrated ethical compositions, in which the father lavishes upon his son all the treasures of Somali good advice, long as the somniferous sermons of Mentor to the insipid son of Ulysses. Sometimes a black Tyrtæus breaks into a wild lament for the loss of warriors or territory; he taunts the clan with cowardice, reminds them of their slain kindred, better men than themselves, whose spirits cannot rest unavenged in their gory graves, and urges a furious onslaught upon the exulting victor.

And now, dear L., I will attempt to gratify your just curiosity concerning *the* sex in Eastern Africa.

The Somali matron is distinguished—externally—from the maiden by a fillet of blue network or indigo-dyed cotton, which, covering the head and containing the hair, hangs down to the neck. Virgins wear their locks long, parted in the middle, and plaited in a multitude of hard thin pigails: on certain festivals they twine flowers and plaster the head like Kafir women, with a red ochre—the *coiffure* has the merit of originality. With massive rounded features, large flat craniums, long big eyes, broad brows, heavy chins, rich brown complexions, and round faces, they greatly resemble the stony beauties of Egypt—the models of the land ere Persia, Greece, and Rome reformed the profile

* It is proved by the facility with which they pick up languages, Western as well as Eastern, by mere ear and memory.

and bleached the skin. They are of the Venus Kallipyga* order of beauty: the feature is scarcely ever seen amongst young girls, but after the first child it becomes remarkable to a stranger. The Arabs have not failed to make it a matter of jibe.

> ' 'Tis a wonderful fact that your hips swell
> Like boiled rice or a skin blown out,'

sings a satirical Yemeni: the Somal retort by comparing the lank haunches of their neighbours to those of tadpoles or young frogs. One of their peculiar charms is a soft, low, and plaintive voice, derived from their African progenitors. Always an excellent thing in woman, here it has an undefinable charm. I have often lain awake for hours listening to the conversation of the Bedouin girls, whose accents sounded in my ears rather like music than mere utterance.

In muscular strength and endurance the women of the Somal are far superior to their lords: at home they are engaged all day in domestic affairs, and tending the cattle; on journeys their manifold duties are to load and drive the camels, to look after the ropes, and if, necessary, to make them; to pitch the hut, to bring water and firewood, and to cook. Both sexes are equally temperate from necessity; the mead and the millet-beer, so common among the Abyssinians and the Danakil, are entirely unknown to the Somal of the plains. As regard their morals, I regret to say that the traveller does not find them in the golden state which Teetotal doctrines lead him to expect. After much wandering, we are almost tempted to believe the bad doctrine that morality is a matter of geography; that nations and races have, like individuals, a pet vice, and that by restraining one you only exasperate another. As a general rule Somali women prefer *amourettes* with strangers, following the well-known Arab proverb, 'The new comer filleth the eye.' In cases of scandal, the woman's tribe revenges its honour upon the man. Should a wife disappear with a fellow-clansman, and her husband accord divorce, no penal measures are taken, but she suffers in reputation, and her female friends do not spare her. Generally, the Somali women are of cold temperament, the result of artificial as well as natural causes:[5] like the Kafirs, they are very prolific, but peculiarly bad mothers, neither loved nor respected by their children. The fair sex lasts longer in Eastern Africa than in India and Arabia: at thirty, however, charms are on the wane, and when old age comes on they are no exceptions to the hideous decrepitude of the East.

* More usual spelling Callipygian, beauty of buttocks; the Callipygian Venus was a famous Greek statue.—Ed.

94

The Somal, when they can afford it, marry between the ages of fifteen and twenty. Connections between tribes are common, and entitle the stranger to immunity from the blood-feud: men of family refuse, however, to ally themselves with the servile castes. Contrary to the Arab custom, none of these people will marry cousins; at the same time a man will give his daughter to his uncle, and take to wife, like the Jews and Gallas, a brother's relict. Some clans, the Habr Yunis for instance, refuse maidens of the same or even of a consanguineous family. This is probably a political device to preserve nationality and provide against a common enemy. The bride, as usual in the East, is rarely consulted, but frequent *tête-à-têtes* at the well and in the bush when tending cattle effectually obviate this inconvenience: her relatives settle the marriage portion, which varies from a cloth and a bead necklace to fifty sheep or thirty dollars, and dowries are unknown. In the towns marriage ceremonies are celebrated with feasting and music. On first entering the nuptial hut, the bridegroom draws forth his horsewhip and inflicts memorable chastisement upon the fair person of his bride, with the view of taming any lurking propensity to shrewishness.* This is carrying out with a will the Arab proverb, 'the slave girl from her capture, the wife from her wedding.'[6]

During the space of a week the spouse remains with his espoused, scarcely ever venturing out of the hut; his friends avoid him, and no lesser event than a plundering party or dollars to gain, would justify any intrusion. If the correctness of the wife be doubted, the husband on the morning after marriage digs a hole before his door and veils it with matting, or he rends the skirt of his Tobe, or he tears open some new nut-covering: this disgraces the woman's family. Polygamy is indispensable in a country where children are the principal wealth.† The chiefs, arrived at manhood, immediately marry four wives: they divorce the old and unfruitful, and, as amongst the Kafirs, allow themselves an unlimited number in peculiar cases, especially when many of the sons have fallen. Daughters, as usual in Oriental countries, do not 'count' as part of the family: they are, however, utilized by the father, who disposes of them to those who can increase his wealth and importance. Divorce is exceedingly common, for the men are liable to sudden fits of disgust. There is little ceremony in contracting marriage

* So the old Muscovites, we are told, always began married life with a sound flogging.

† I would not advise polygamy amongst highly civilized races, where the sexes are nearly equal, and where reproduction becomes a minor duty. Monogamy is the growth of civilization: a plurality of wives is the natural condition of man in thinly-populated countries, where he who has the largest family is the greatest benefactor of his kind.

with any but maidens. I have heard a man propose after half an hour's acquaintance, and the fair one's reply was generally the question direct concerning 'settlements'. Old men frequently marry young girls, but then the portion is high and the *ménage à trois* common.

The Somal know none of the exaggerated and chivalrous ideas by which passion becomes refined affection amongst the Arab Bedouin and the sons of civilization, nor did I ever hear of an African abandoning the spear and the sex to become a Darwaysh. Their 'Hudhudu', however, reminds the traveller of the Abyssinian 'eye-love', the Afghan's 'Namzad-bazi', and the Semite's 'Ishkuzri', which for want of a better expression we translate 'Platonic love'. This meeting of the sexes, however, is allowed in Africa by male relatives; in Arabia and Central Asia it provokes their direst indignation. Curious to say, throughout the Somali country, kissing is entirely unknown.

Children are carried on their mothers' backs or laid sprawling upon the ground for the first two years: they are circumcized at the age of seven or eight, provided with a small spear, and allowed to run about naked till the age of puberty. They learn by conversation, not books, eat as much as they can beg, borrow, and steal, and grow up healthy, strong, and well proportioned according to their race.

As in al-Islam generally, so here, a man cannot make a will. The property of the deceased is divided amongst his children—the daughters receiving a small portion, if any, of it. When a man dies without issue, his goods and chattels are seized upon by his nearest male relatives; one of them generally marries the widow, or she is sent back to her family. Relicts, as a rule receive no legacies.

You will have remarked, dear L., that the people of Zayla are by no means industrious. They depend for support upon the Desert: the Bedouin becomes the Nazil or guest of the townsmen, and he is bound to receive a little tobacco, a few beads, a bit of coarse cotton cloth, or, on great occasions, a penny looking-glass and a cheap German razor, in return for his slaves, ivories, hides, gums, milk, and grain. Any violation of the tie is severely punished by the Governor, and it can be dissolved only by the formula of triple divorce: of course the wild men are hopelessly cheated, and their citizen brethren live in plenty and indolence. After the early breakfast, the male portion of the community leave their houses on business, that is to say, to chat, visit, and *flaner* about the streets and mosques. They return to dinner and the siesta, after which they issue forth again, and do not come home till night. Friday is always an idle day, festivals are frequent, and there is no work during weddings and mournings. The women begin after dawn to plait mats and superintend the slaves, who are sprinkling the house with water, grinding grain for breakfast, cooking, and breaking up firewood; to judge, however, from the amount of chatting and laughter, there appears to be far less work than play.

In these small places it is easy to observe the mechanism of a government which, *en grand*, becomes that of Delhi, Teheran, and Constantinople. The Governor farms the place from the Porte; he may do what he pleases as long as he pays his rent with punctuality and provides presents and *douceurs* for the Pasha of Mocha. He punishes the petty offences of theft, quarrels, and arson by fines, the bastinado, the stocks, or confinement in an Arish or thatch-hut: the latter is a severe penalty, as the prisoner must provide himself with food. In cases of murder, he either refers to Mocha or he carries out the Kisas—*lex talionis*—by delivering the slayer to the relatives of the slain. The Kazi has the administration of the Shariat or religious law: he cannot, however, pronounce sentence without the Governor's permission; and generally his powers are confined to questions of divorce, alimony, manumission, the wound mulct, and similar cases which come within Koranic jurisdiction. Thus the religious code is ancillary and often opposed to 'al-Jabr'—'the tyranny'—the popular designation of what we call Civil Law. Yet is al-Jabr, despite its name, generally preferred by the worldly wise. The Governor contents himself with a moderate bribe, the Kazi is insatiable: the former may possibly allow you to escape unplundered, the latter assuredly will not. This I believe to be the history of religious jurisdiction in most parts of the world.

Lesser Koodoo.

V

From Zayla to the Hills

Two ROUTES CONNECT Zayla with Harar; the south-western or direct line numbers ten long or twenty short stages:* the first eight through the Eesa country, and the last two among the Nole Gallas, who own the rule of 'Waday', a Makad or chief of Christian persuasion. The Hajj objected to this way, on account of his recent blood-feud with the Rer Guleni. He preferred for me the more winding road which passes south, along the coast, through the Eesa Bedouin dependent upon Zayla, to the nearest hills, and thence strikes south-westwards among the Gudabirsi and Girhi Somal, who extend within sight of Harar. I cannot but suspect that in selecting this route the good

* By this route the Mukattib or courier travels on foot from Zayla to Harar in five days at the most. The Somal reckon their journeys by the Gadi or march, the Arab 'Hamlah', which varies from four to five hours. They begin before dawn and halt at about 11 a.m. the time of the morning meal. When a second march is made they load at 3 p.m. and advance till dark; thus fifteen miles would be the average of fast travelling. In places of danger they will cover twenty-six or twenty-seven miles of ground without halting to eat or rest: nothing less, however, than regard for 'dear life' can engender such activity. Generally two or three hours' work per diem is considered sufficient; and, where provisions abound, halts are long and frequent.

Sharmakay served another purpose besides my safety. Petty feuds between the chiefs had long 'closed the path', and perhaps the Somal were not unwilling that British cloth and tobacco should re-open it.

Early in the morning of the 27th of November, 1854, the mules and all the paraphernalia of travel stood ready at the door. The five camels were forced to kneel, growling angrily the while, by repeated jerks at the halter: their forelegs were duly tied or stood upon till they had shifted themselves into a comfortable position, and their noses were held down by the bystanders whenever, grasshopper-like, they attempted to spring up. Whilst spreading the saddle-mats, our women, to charm away remembrance of chafed hump and bruised sides, sang with vigour the 'Song of Travel':

> O caravan-men, we deceive ye not, we have laden the camels!
> Old women on the journey are kenned by their sleeping!
> (O camel) can'st sniff the cock-boat and the sea?
> Allah guard thee from the Mikahil and their Midgans!*

As they arose from squat it was always necessary to adjust their little mountains of small packages by violently 'heaving up' one side—an operation never failing to elicit a vicious grunt, a curve of the neck, and an attempt to bite. One camel was especially savage; it is said that on his return to Zayla, he broke a Bedouin girl's neck. Another, a diminutive but hardy little brute of Dankali breed, conducted himself so uproariously that he at once obtained the name of Al-Harami, or the Ruffian.

About 3 p.m., accompanied by the Hajj, his amiable son Mohammed, and a party of Arab matchlock-men, who escorted me as a token of especial respect, I issued from the Ashurbara Gate, through the usual staring crowds, and took the way of the wilderness. After half a mile march, we exchanged affectionate adieus, received much prudent advice about keeping watch and ward at night, recited the Fatihah with upraised palms, and with many promises to write frequently and to meet soon, shook hands and parted. The soldiers gave me a last volley, to which I replied with the 'Father of Six' [his revolver].

You see, dear L., how travelling maketh man *banal*. It is the natural consequence of being forced to find in every corner where Fate drops you for a month, a 'friend of the soul' and a 'moon-faced beauty'. With Orientals generally you *must* be on extreme terms, as in Hibernia,

---

* The Mikahil is a clan of the Habr Awal tribe living near Berbera, and celebrated for their bloodthirsty and butchering propensities. Many of the Midgan or serviles (a term explained in Chap. II, [note 2]) are domesticated amongst them.

either an angel of light or, that failing, a goblin damned. In East Africa especially, English phlegm, shyness, or pride, will bar every heart and raise every hand against you,* whereas what M. Rochet calls 'a certain *rondeur* of manner' is a specific for winning affection. You should walk up to your man, clasp his fist, pat his back, speak some unintelligible words to him—if, as is the plan of prudence, you ignore the language—laugh a loud guffaw, sit by his side, and begin pipes and coffee. He then proceeds to utilize you, to beg in one country for your interest, and in another for your tobacco. You gently but decidedly thrust that subject out of the way, and choose what is most interesting to yourself. As might be expected, he will at times revert to his own concerns; your superior obstinacy will oppose effectual passive resistance to all such efforts; by degrees the episodes diminish in frequency and duration: at last they cease altogether. The man is now your own.

You will bear in mind, if you please, that I am a Moslem merchant, a character not to be confounded with the notable individuals seen on 'Change. Mercator in the East is a compound of tradesman, divine and T. G. Usually of gentle birth, he is everywhere welcomed and respected; and he bears in his mind and manner that, if Allah please, he may become prime minister a month after he has sold you a yard of cloth. Commerce appears to be an accident, not an essential, with him; yet he is by no means deficient in acumen. He is a grave and reverend signior, with rosary in hand and Koran on lip, is generally a pilgrim, talks at dreary length about Holy Places, writes a pretty hand, has read and can recite much poetry, is master of his religion, demeans himself with respectability, is perfect in all points of ceremony and politeness, and feels equally at home whether sultan or slave sit upon his counter. He has a wife and children in his own country, where he intends to spend the remnant of his days; but 'the world is uncertain'—'Fate descends, and man's eye seeth it not'—'the earth is a charnel house': briefly his many wise old saws give him a kind of theoretical consciousness that his bones may moulder in other places than his fatherland.

To describe my little caravan. Foremost struts Raghi, our Eesa guide, in all the bravery of Abbanship. He is bare-headed and clothed in Tobe and slippers: a long, heavy, horn-hilted dagger is strapped round his waist, outside his dress; in his right hand he grasps a ponderous wire-bound spear, which he uses as a staff, and the left forearm supports a round targe of battered hide. Being a man of education, he

* So the Abyssinian chief informed M. Krapf, that he loved the French, but could not endure us—simply the effect of manner.

bears on one shoulder a Musalla or prayer carpet of tanned leather, the article used throughout the Somali country: slung over the other is a Wesi or wicker bottle containing water for religious ablution. He is accompanied by some men who carry a little stock of town goods and drive a camel colt, which by-the-by they manage to lose before midnight.

My other attendants must now be introduced to you, as they are to be for the next two months companions of our journey.

First in the list are the fair Samaweda Yusuf, and Aybla Farih, buxom dames about thirty years old, who presently secured the classical nicknames of Shehrazade, and Deenarzade. They look each like three average women rolled into one, and emphatically belong to that race for which the article of feminine attire called, I believe, a 'bustle' would be quite superfluous. Wonderful, truly, is their endurance of fatigue! During the march they carry pipe and tobacco, lead and flog the camels, adjust the burdens, and will never be induced to ride, in sickness or in health. At the halt they unload the cattle, dispose the parcels in a semicircle, pitch over them the Gurgi or mat tent, cook our food, boil tea and coffee, and make themselves generally useful. They bivouack outside our abode, modesty not permitting the sexes to mingle, and in the severest cold wear no clothing but a head fillet and an old Tobe. They have curious soft voices, which contrast agreeably with the harsh organs of the males. At first they were ashamed to see me; but that feeling soon wore off, and presently they enlivened the way with pleasantries far more naïve than refined. To relieve their greatest fatigue, nothing seems necessary but the 'Jogsi':* they lie at full length, prone, stand upon each other's backs trampling and kneading with the toes, and rise like giants much refreshed. Always attendant upon these dames is Yusuf, a Zayla lad, who, being one-eyed, was pitilessly named by my companions, the 'Kalendar'; he prays frequently, is strict in his morals, and has conceived, like Mrs. Brownrigg, so exalted an idea of discipline, that, but for our influence, he certainly would have beaten the two female 'prentices to death. They hate him therefore, and he knows it.

Immediately behind Raghi and his party walk Shehrazade and Deenarzade, the former leading the head camel, the latter using my

---

* This delicate operation is called by the Arabs, Da'asah (whence the 'Doseh' ceremony at Cairo). It is used over most parts of the Eastern World as a remedy for sickness and fatigue, and is generally preferred to Takbis or Dugmo, the common style of shampooing, which, say many Easterns, loosens the skin.

chibúk stick as a staff. She has been at Aden, and sorely suspects me; her little black eyes never meet mine; and frequently, with affected confusion, she turns her sable cheek the clean contrary way. Strung together by their tails, and soundly beaten when disposed to lag, the five camels pace steadily along under their burdens—bales of Wilayati or American sheeting, Duwwarah or Cutch canvas, with indigo-dyed stuff slung along the animals' sides, and neatly sewn up in a case of matting to keep off dust and rain—a cow's hide, which serves as a couch, covering the whole. They carry a load of 'Mushakkar' (bad Mocha dates) for the Somal, with a parcel of better quality for ourselves, and a half hundredweight of coarse Surat tobacco;* besides which we have a box of beads, and another of trinkets, mosaic-gold earrings, necklaces, watches and similar nick-nacks. Our private provisions are represented by about 300 lb. of rice—here the traveller's staff of life—a large pot full of 'Kawurmah',† dates, salt,‡ clarified butter, tea, coffee, sugar, a box of biscuits in case of famine, 'Halwá' or Arab sweetmeats to be used when driving hard bargains, and a little turmeric for seasoning. A simple *batterie de cuisine*, and sundry skins full of potable water,§ dangle from chance rope-ends: and last but not the least important, is a heavy box of ammunition sufficient for a three months' sporting tour.[1] In the rear of the caravan trudges a Bedouin woman driving a donkey—the proper 'tail' in these regions, where camels start if followed by a horse or mule. An ill-fated sheep, a parting present from the Hajj, races and frisks about the Kafilah. It became so tame that the Somal received an order not to 'cut' it; one day, however, I found myself dining, and that pet lamb was the *menu*.

* The Somal, from habit, enjoy no other variety; they even showed disgust at my Latakia. Tobacco is grown in some places by the Gudabirsi and other tribes; but it is rare and bad. Without this article it would be impossible to progress in East Africa; every man asks for a handful, and many will not return milk for what they expect to receive as a gift.

† Flesh boiled in large slices, sun-dried, broken to pieces and fried in ghi.

‡ The Bahr Assal or Salt Lake, near Tajjurrah, annually sends into the interior thousands of little matted parcels containing this necessary. Inland, the Bedouin will rub a piece upon the tongue before eating, or pass about a lump; at Harar a donkey load is the price of a slave; and the Abyssinians say of a *millionaire*, 'he eateth salt'.

§ The element found upon the maritime plain is salt or brackish. There is nothing concerning which the African traveller should be so particular as water; bitter with nitre, and full of organic matter, it causes all those dysenteric diseases which have made research in this part of the world a Upas tree to the discoverer. Pocket filters are inv luable. The water of wells should be boiled and passed through charcoal; and even then it might be mixed to a good purpose with a few drops of proof spirit. The Somal generally carry their stores in large wickerwork pails. I preferred skins, as more portable and less likely to taint the water.

By the side of the camels ride my three attendants, the pink of Somali fashion. Their frizzled wigs are radiant with grease; their Tobes are splendidly white, with borders dazzlingly red; their new shields are covered with canvas cloth; and their two spears, poised over the right shoulder, are freshly scraped, oiled, blackened, and polished. They have added my spare rifle and guns to the camel-load; such weapons are well enough at Aden, in Somaliland men would deride the outlandish tool! I told them that in my country women use bows and arrows, moreover that lancers are generally considered a corps of non-combatants; in vain! they adhered as strongly—so mighty a thing is prejudice—to their partiality for bows, arrows, and lances. Their horsemanship is peculiar, they balance themselves upon little Abyssinian saddles, extending the leg and raising the heel in the Louis Quinze style of equitation, and the stirrup is an iron ring admitting only the big toe. I follow them mounting a fine white mule, which with its gaudily *galonné* Arab pad and wrapper cloth, has a certain dignity of look; a double-barrelled gun lies across my lap; and a rude pair of holsters, the work of Hasan Turki, contains my Colt's six-shooters.

Marching in this order, which was to serve as a model, we travelled due south along the coast, over a hard, stoneless, and alluvial plain, here dry, there muddy (where the tide reaches), across boggy creeks, broad water-courses, and warty flats of black mould powdered with nitrous salt, and bristling with the salsolaceous vegetation familiar to the Arab voyager. Such is the general formation of the plain between the mountains and the sea, whose breadth, in a direct line, may measure from forty-five to forty-eight miles. Near the first zone of hills, or sub-Ghauts, it produces a thicker vegetation; thorns and acacias of different kinds appear in clumps; and ground broken with ridges and ravines announces the junction. After the monsún this plain is covered with rich grass. At other seasons it affords but a scanty supply of 'aqueous matter' resembling bilge-water. The land belongs to the Mummasan clan of the Eesa: how these 'Kurrah-jog' or 'sun-dwellers', as the Bedouin are called by the burgher Somal, can exist here in summer, is a mystery. My arms were peeled even in the month of December; and my companions, panting with the heat, like the Atlantes of Herodotus, poured forth reproaches upon the rising sun. The townspeople, when forced to hurry across it in the hotter season, cover themselves during the day with Tobes wetted every half hour in sea water; yet they are sometimes killed by the fatal thirst which the Samún engenders. Even the Bedouin are now longing for rain; a few weeks' drought destroys half their herds.

Early in the afternoon our Abban and a woman halted for a few minutes, performed their ablutions, and prayed with a certain display: satisfied apparently, with the result, they never repeated the exercise. About sunset we passed, on the right, clumps of trees overgrowing a water called 'Warabod', the Hyena's Well; this is the first Marhalah or halting-place usually made by travellers to the interior. Hence there is a direct path leading south-south-west, by six short marches, to the hills. Our Abban, however, was determined that we should not so easily escape his kraal. Half an hour afterwards we passed by the second station, 'Hangagarri', a well near the sea: frequent lights twinkling through the darkening air informed us that we were in the midst of the Eesa. At 8 p.m., we reached 'Gagab', the third Marhalah, where the camels, casting themselves upon the ground, imperatively demanded a halt. Raghi was urgent for an advance, declaring that already he could sight the watch-fires of his Rer or tribe: but the animals carried the point against him. They were presently unloaded and turned out to graze, and the lariats of the mules, who are addicted to running away, were fastened to stones for want of pegs. Then lighting a fire, we sat down to a homely supper of dates.

The air was fresh and clear, and the night breeze was delicious after the steamy breath of day. The weary confinement of walls made the splendid expanse a luxury to the sight, whilst the tumbling of the surf upon the near shore, and the music of the jackal, predisposed to sweet sleep. We now felt that at length the die was cast. Placing my pistols by my side, with my rifle-butt for a pillow, and its barrel as a bed-fellow, I sought repose with none of that apprehension which even the most stout-hearted traveller knows before the start. It is the difference between fancy and reality, between anxiety and certainty: to men gifted with any imaginative powers the anticipation must ever be worse than the event. Thus it happens, that he who feels a thrill of fear before engaging in a peril, exchanges it for a throb of exultation when he finds himself hand to hand with the danger.

The 'End of Time' volunteered to keep watch that night. When the early dawn glimmered he aroused us, and blew up the smouldering fire, whilst our women proceeded to load the camels. We pursued our way over hard alluvial soil to sand, and thence passed into a growth of stiff yellow grass not unlike a stubble in English September. Day broke upon a Somali Arcadia, whose sole flaws were salt water and Samun.

Whistling shepherds* carried in their arms the younglings of the herds, or, spear in hand, drove to pasture long regular lines of camels, that waved their vulture-like heads, and arched their necks to bite in play their neighbours' faces, humps, and hind thighs. They were led by a patriarch, to whose throat hung a Kor or wooden bell, the preventative for straggling: and most of them were followed (for winter is the breeding season) by colts in every stage of infancy. Patches of sheep, with snowy skins, and jetty faces, flecked the yellow plain;† and herds of goats resembling deer were driven by hide-clad children to the bush. Women, in similar attire, accompanied them, some chewing the inner bark of trees, others spinning yarn of a white creeper called Sagsug for ropes and tent mats. The boys carried shepherds' crooks, and bore their watering pails, foolscap fashion, upon their heads. Sometimes they led the ram, around whose neck a cord of white leather was bound for luck; at other times they frisked with the dog, an animal by no means contemptible in the eyes of the Bedouin. As they advanced, the graceful little sand antelopes bounded away over the bushes; and above them, soaring high in the cloudless skies, were flights of vultures and huge percnopters, unerring indicators of man's habitation in Somaliland.

A network of paths showed that we were approaching a populous place; and presently men swarmed forth from their hive-shaped tents, testifying their satisfaction at our arrival, the hostile Habr Awal having threatened to 'eat them up'. We rode cautiously, as is customary, amongst the yeaning she-camels, who are injured by a sudden start, and about 8 a.m. arrived at our guide's kraal, the fourth station, called 'Gudingaras', or the low place where the Garas tree grows. The encampment lay south-east (165°) of, and about twenty miles from, Zayla.

Raghi disappeared, and the Bedouin flocked out to gaze upon us as we approached the kraal. Meanwhile Shehrazade and Deenarzade fetched tent-sticks from the village, disposed our luggage so as to form a wall, rigged out a wigwam, spread our beds in the shade, and called

---

* Arabs hate 'al-Sifr' or whistling, which they hold to be the chit-chat of the Jinns. Some say that the musician's mouth is not to be purified for forty days; others that Satan, touching a man's person, causes him to produce the offensive sound. The Hijazis objected to Burckhardt that he could not help talking to devils, and walking about the room like an unquiet spirit. The Somali has no such prejudice. Like the Kafir of the Cape, he passes his day whistling to his flocks and herds; moreover, he makes signals by changing the note, and is skilful in imitating the song of birds.

† This sheep, originally from central Asia, may show some old connection between Persians and Somal. [Note added by Burton to his own copy.—Ed.]

aloud for sweet and sour milk. I heard frequently muttered by the red-headed spearmen the ominous term 'Faranj';* and although there was no danger, it was deemed advisable to make an impression without delay. Presently they began to deride our weapons: the Hammal requested them to put up one of their shields as a mark; they laughed aloud but shirked compliance. At last a large brown, bare-necked vulture settled on the ground at twenty paces' distance. The Somal hate the 'Gurgur', because he kills the dying and devours the dead on the battle-field: a bullet put through the bird's body caused a cry of wonder, and some ran after the lead as it span whistling over the ridge. Then loading with swan shot which these Bedouin had never seen, I knocked over a second vulture flying. Fresh screams followed the marvellous feat; the women exclaimed, 'Lo! he bringeth down the birds from heaven'; and one old man, putting his forefinger in his mouth, praised Allah and prayed to be defended from such a calamity. The effect was such that I determined always to carry a barrel loaded with shot as the best answer for all who might object to 'Faranj'.

We spent our day in the hut after the normal manner, with a crowd of woolly-headed Bedouin squatting perseveringly opposite our quarters, spear in hand, with eyes fixed upon every gesture. Before noon the door-mat was let down—a precaution also adopted whenever box or package was opened—we drank milk and ate rice with 'a kitchen' of Kawurmah. About mid-day the crowd retired to sleep; my companions followed their example, and I took the opportunity of sketching and jotting down notes.† Early in the afternoon the Bedouin returned, and resumed their mute form of pleading for tobacco: each man, as he received a handful, rose slowly from his hams and went his way. The senior who disliked the gun was importunate for a charm to cure his sick camel: having obtained it, he blessed us in a set speech, which lasted at least half an hour, and concluded with spitting upon the whole party for good luck.‡ It is always well to encourage these Nestors; they are regarded with the greatest reverence by the tribes,

---

* They apply this term to all but themselves; an Indian trader who had travelled to Harar, complained to me that he had always been called a Frank by the Bedouin in consequence of his wearing Shalwar, or drawers.

† Generally it is not dangerous to write before these Bedouin as they only suspect account-keeping, and none but the educated recognizes a sketch. The traveller, however, must be on his guard: in the remotest villages he will meet Somal who have returned to savage life after visiting the sea-board, Arabia, and possibly India or Egypt.

‡ I have often observed this ceremony performed upon a new turban or other article of attire; possibly it may be intended as a mark of contempt, assumed to blind the evil eye.

who believe that 'old experience doth attain, to something like prophetic strain'; and they can either do great good or cause much petty annoyance.

In the evening I took my gun, and, accompanied by the End of Time, went out to search for venison: the plain, however, was full of men and cattle, and its wilder denizens had migrated. During our walk we visited the tomb of an Eesa brave. It was about ten feet long, heaped up with granite pebbles, bits of black basalt, and stones of calcareous lime: two upright slabs denoted the position of the head and feet, and upon these hung the deceased's milk-pails, much the worse for sun and wind. Round the grave was a thin fence of thorns: opposite the single narrow entrance were three blocks of stone planted in line, and showing the number of enemies slain by the brave. Beyond these trophies, a thorn roofing, supported by four bare poles, served to shade the relatives, when they meet to sit, feast, weep, and pray.

The Bedouin funerals and tombs are equally simple. They have no favourite cemeteries as in Sind and other Moslem and pastoral lands: men are buried where they die, and the rarity of the graves scattered about the country excited my astonishment. The corpse is soon interred. These people, like most barbarians, have a horror of death and all that reminds them of it: on several occasions I have been begged to throw away a hut-stick, that had been used to dig a grave. The bier is a rude framework of poles bound with ropes of hide. Some tie up the body and plant it in a sitting posture, to save themselves the trouble of excavating deep: this perhaps may account for the circular tombs seen in many parts of the country. Usually the corpse is thrust into a long hole, covered with wood and matting, and heaped over with earth and thorns, half-protected by an oval mass of loose stones, and abandoned to the jackals and hyenas.

We halted a day at Gudingaras, wishing to see the migration of a tribe. Before dawn, on the 30th November, the Somali Stentor proclaimed from the ridge-top, 'Fetch your camels!—Load your goods!— We march!' About 8 a.m. we started in the rear. The spectacle was novel to me. Some 150 spearmen, assisted by their families, were driving before them divisions which, in total, might amount to 200 cows, 7,000 camels, and 11,000 or 12,000 sheep and goats. Only three wore the Bal or feather, which denotes the brave; several, however, had the other decoration—an ivory armlet.* Assisted by the boys, whose heads were shaved in a cristated fashion truly ridiculous, and

* In the south this denotes the elephant-slayer.

large pariah dogs with bushy tails, they drove the beasts and carried the colts, belaboured runaway calves, and held up the hind legs of struggling sheep. The sick, of whom there were many—dysentery being at the time prevalent—were carried upon camels with their legs protruding in front from under the hide-cover. Many of the dromedaries showed the Habr Awal brand:* laden with hutting materials and domestic furniture, they were led by the maidens: the matrons followed, bearing their progeny upon their backs, bundled in the shoulder-lappets of cloth or hide. The smaller girls, who, in addition to the boys' crest, wore a circlet of curly hair round the head, carried the weakling lambs and kids, or aided their mammas in transporting the baby. Apparently in great fear of the 'All' or Commando, the Bedouin anxiously inquired if I had my 'fire' with me, and begged us to take the post of honour—the van. As our little party pricked forward, the camels started in alarm, and we were surprised to find that this tribe did not know the difference between horses and mules. Whenever the boys lost time in sport or quarrel, they were threatened by their fathers with the jaws of that ogre, the white stranger; and the women exclaimed, as they saw us approach, 'Here comes the old man who knows knowledge!'

Having skirted the sea for two hours, I rode off with the 'End of Time' to inspect the Dihh Silil,† a fiumara which runs from the western hills north-eastwards to the sea. Its course is marked by a long line of graceful tamarisks, whose vivid green looked doubly bright set off by tawny stubble and amethyst-blue sky. These freshets are the Edens of Adel. The banks are charmingly wooded with acacias of many varieties, some thorned like the fabled Zakkum, others parachute-shaped, and planted in impenetrable thickets: huge white creepers, snake-shaped, enclasp giant trees, or connect with their cordage the higher boughs, or depend like cables from the lower branches to the ground. Luxuriant parasites abound: here they form domes of flashing green, there they surround with verdure decayed trunks, and not unfrequently cluster into sylvan bowers, under which—grateful sight!—appears succulent grass. From the thinner thorns the bell-shaped nests of the Loxia depend, waving in the breeze, and the wood resounds with the cries of bright-winged choristers. The torrent-beds are of the clearest and finest white sand, glittering with gold-coloured mica, and varied

* It is sufficient for a Bedouin to look at the general appearance of an animal; he at once recognizes the breed. Each clan, however, in this part of Eastern Africa has its own mark.

† I saw these Dihhs [or fiumaras] only in the dry season; at times the torrent must be violent, cutting ten or twelve feet deep into the plain.

with nodules of clear and milky quartz, red porphyry, and granites of many hues. Sometimes the centre is occupied by an islet of torn trees and stones rolled in heaps, supporting a clump of thick jujube or tall acacia, whilst the lower parts of the beds are overgrown with long lines of lively green colocynth. Here are usually the wells, surrounded by heaps of thorns, from which the leaves have been browsed off, and dwarf sticks that support the water-hide. When the flocks and herds are absent, troops of gazelles may be seen daintily pacing the yielding surface; snake trails streak the sand, and at night the fiercer kind of animals, lions, leopards, and elephants, take their turn. In Somaliland the well is no place of social meeting; no man lingers to chat near it, no woman visits it, and the traveller fears to pitch hut where torrents descend, and where enemies, human and bestial, meet.

We sat under a tree watching the tribe defile across the water-course: then remounting, after a ride of two miles, we reached a ground called Kuranyali, upon which the wigwams of the Nomads were already rising. The parched and treeless stubble lies about eight miles from and 145° S.E. of Gudingaras; both places are supplied by Angagarri, a well near the sea, which is so distant that cattle, to return before nightfall, must start early in the morning.

My attendants had pitched the Gurgi or hut: the Hammal and Long Gulad were, however, sulky on account of my absence, and the Kalendar appeared disposed to be mutinous. The End of Time, who never lost an opportunity to make mischief, whispered in my ear, 'Despise thy wife, thy son, and thy slave, or they despise thee!' The old saw was not wanted, however, to procure for them a sound scolding. Nothing is worse for the Eastern traveller than the habit of 'sending to Coventry': it does away with all manner of discipline.

We halted that day at Kuranyali, preparing water and milk for two long marches over the desert to the hills. Being near the shore, the air was cloudy, although men prayed for a shower in vain: about midday the pleasant sea-breeze fanned our cheeks, and the plain was thronged with tall pillars of white sand.

The heat forbade egress, and our wigwam was crowded with hungry visitors. Raghi, urged thereto by his tribe, became importunate, now for tobacco, then for rice, now for dates, then for provisions in general. No wonder that the Prophet made his Paradise for the Poor a mere place of eating and drinking. The half-famished Bedouin, Somal or Arab, think of nothing beyond the stomach—their dreams know no higher vision of bliss than mere repletion. A single article of diet, milk or flesh, palling upon man's palate, they will greedily suck the stones of eaten dates: yet Abyssinian-like, they are squeamish and fastidious as regards food. They despise the excellent fish with which Nature has so plentifully stocked their seas. 'Speak not to me with that mouth which eateth fish!' is a favourite insult amongst the Bedouin. If you touch a bird or a fowl of any description, you will be despised even by the starving beggar. You must not eat marrow or the flesh about the sheep's thigh-bone, especially when travelling, and the kidneys are called a woman's dish. None but the Northern Somal will touch the hares which abound in the country, and many refuse the sand antelope and other kinds of game, not asserting that the meat is unlawful, but simply alleging a disgust. Those who chew coffee berries are careful not to place an even number in their mouths, and camel's milk is never heated, for fear of bewitching the animal.* The Somali, however, differs in one point from his kinsman the Arab: the latter prides himself upon his temperance; the former, like the North American Indian, measures manhood by appetite. A 'Son of the Somal' is taught, as soon as his teeth are cut, to devour two pounds of the toughest mutton, and ask for more: if his powers of deglutition fail, he is derided as degenerate.

On the next day (Friday, December 1st) we informed the Abban that we intended starting early in the afternoon, and therefore warned him to hold himself and his escort, together with the water and milk necessary for our march, in readiness. He promised compliance and disappeared. About 3 p.m. the Bedouin, armed as usual with spear and shield, began to gather round the hut, and—nothing in this country can be done without that terrible 'palaver!'—the speechifying presently commenced. Raghi, in a lengthy harangue hoped that the tribe would afford us all necessary supplies and assist us in the arduous undertaking. His words elicited no hear, hear! there was an evident unwillingness on the part of the wild men to let us, or rather our cloth and tobacco, depart. One remarked, with surly emphasis, that he had 'seen no good and eaten no Bori† from that caravan, why should he aid it?' When we asked the applauding hearers what they had done for us, they rejoined by inquiring whose the land was? Another smitten by the fair Shehrazade's bulky charms, had proposed matrimony, and offered as dowry a milch camel: she 'temporized', not daring to return a positive refusal,

* This supersition may have arisen from the peculiarity that the camel's milk, however fresh, if placed upon the fire, breaks like some cow's milk.

† 'Bori' in Southern Arabia popularly means a water-pipe: here it is used for tobacco.

and the suitor betrayed a certain Hibernian *velléité* to consider consent an unimportant part of the ceremony. The mules had been sent to the well, with orders to return before noon: at 4 p.m. they were not visible. I then left the hut, and, sitting on a cow's-hide in the sun, ordered my men to begin loading, despite the remonstrances of the Abban and the interference of about fifty Bedouin. As we persisted, they waxed surlier, and declared all which was ours became theirs, to whom the land belonged: we did not deny the claim, but simply threatened sorcery-death, by wild beasts and foraging parties, to their 'camels, children, and women'. This brought them to their senses, the usual effect of such threats; and presently arose the senior who had spat upon us for luck's sake. With his toothless jaws he mumbled a vehement speech, and warned the tribe that it was not good to detain such strangers: they lent ready ears to the words of Nestor, saying, 'Let us obey him, he is near his end!' The mules arrived, but when I looked for the escort, none was forthcoming. At Zayla it was agreed that twenty men should protect us across the desert, which is the very passage of plunder; now, however, five or six paupers offered to accompany us for a few miles. We politely declined troubling them, but insisted upon the attendance of our Abban and three of his kindred: as some of the Bedouin still opposed us, our aged friend once more arose, and by copious abuse finally silenced them. We took leave of him with many thanks and handfuls of tobacco, in return for which he blessed us with fervour. Then, mounting our mules, we set out, followed for at least a mile by a long tail of howling boys, who, ignorant of clothing, except a string of white beads round the neck, but armed with dwarf spears, bows, and arrows, showed all the impudence of baboons. They derided the End of Time's equitation till I feared a scene; sailor-like, he prided himself upon graceful horsemanship, and the imps were touching his tenderest point.

Hitherto, for the Abban's convenience, we had skirted the sea, far out of the direct road: now we were to strike south-westwards into the interior. At 6 p.m. we started across a 'Goban'* which eternal summer gilds with a dull ochreish yellow, towards a thin blue strip of hill on the far horizon. The Somal have no superstitious dread of night and its horrors, like Arabs and Abyssinians: our Abban, however, showed a

---

* 'Goban' is the low maritime plain lying below the 'Bor' or Ghauts, and opposed to Ogú, the table-land above. 'Ban' is an elevated grassy prairie, where few trees grow; 'Dir', a small jungle, called Haija by the Arabs; and Khain is a forest or thick bush. 'Bor', is a mountain, rock, or hill: a stony precipice is called 'Jar', and the high clay banks of a ravine 'Gebi'.

wholesome mundane fear of plundering parties, scorpions, and snakes.[2] I had been careful to fasten round my ankles the twists of black wool called by the Arabs Za'al,* and universally used in al Yemen: a stock of garlic and opium, here held to be specifics, fortified the courage of the party, whose fears were not wholly ideal, for, in the course of the night, Shehrazade nearly trod upon a viper.

At first the plain was a network of holes, the habitations of the Jir Ad,† a field rat with ruddy back and white belly, the Mullah or Parson, a smooth-skinned lizard, and the Dabagalla, a ground squirrel with a brilliant and glossy coat. As it became dark arose a cheerful moon, exciting the howlings of the hyenas, the barkings of their attendant jackals, and the chattered oaths of the Hidinhitu bird [red plover]. Dotted here and there over the misty landscape, appeared dark clumps of a tree called 'Kullan', a thorn with an edible berry not unlike the jujube, and banks of silvery mist veiled the far horizon from the sight.

We marched rapidly and in silence, stopping every quarter of an hour to raise the camels' loads as they slipped on one side. I had now an opportunity of seeing how feeble a race is the Somali.[3] My companions on the line of march wondered at my being able to carry a gun; they could scarcely support, even whilst riding, the weight of their spears, and preferred sitting upon them to spare their shoulders. At times they were obliged to walk because the saddles cut them, then they remounted because their legs were tired; briefly, an English boy of fourteen would have shown more bottom than the sturdiest. This cannot arise from poor diet, for the citizens, who live generously, are yet weaker than the Bedouin; it is a peculiarity of race. When fatigued they become reckless and impatient of thirst: on this occasion, though want of water stared us in the face, one skin of the three was allowed to fall upon the road and burst, and the contents of the second was drunk before we halted.

At 11 p.m., after marching twelve miles in direct line, we bivouacked upon the plain. The night breeze from the hills had set in, and my attendants chattered with cold: Long Gulad in particular became stiff as a mummy. Raghi was clamorous against a fire, which might betray

---

* These are tightened in case of accident, and act as superior ligatures. I should, however, advise every traveller in these regions to provide himself with a pneumatic pump, and not to place his trust in Za'al, garlic, or opium.

† The grey rat is called by the Somal 'Baradublay': in Eastern Africa it is a minor plague, as in India and Arabia, where, neglecting to sleep in boots, I have sometimes been lamed for a week by their venomous bites.

our whereabouts in the 'Bush Inn'. But after such a march the pipe was a necessity, and the point was carried against him.

After a sound sleep under the moon, we rose at 5 a.m. and loaded the camels. It was a raw morning. A large nimbus rising from the east obscured the sun, the line of blue sea was raised like a ridge by refraction, and the hills, towards which we were journeying, now showed distinct falls and folds. Troops of Dera or gazelles, herding like goats, stood, stared at us, turned their white tails, faced away, broke into a long trot, and bounded over the plain as we approached. A few ostriches appeared, but they were too shy even for bullet. At 8 p.m. we crossed one of the numerous drains which intersect this desert— 'Biya Hablod', or the Girls' Water, a fiumara running from south-west to east and north-east. Although dry, it abounded in the Marar, a tree bearing yellowish red berries full of viscous juice like green gum— edible but not nice—and the brighter vegetation showed that water was near the surface. About two hours afterwards, as the sun became oppressive, we unloaded in a water-course, called by my companions Adad or the Acacia Gum:* the distance was about twenty-five miles, and the direction S.W. 225° of Kuranyali.

We spread our couches of cowhide in the midst of a green mass of tamarisk under a tall Kud tree, a bright-leaved thorn, with balls of golden gum clinging to its boughs, dry berries scattered in its shade, and armies of ants marching to and from its trunk. All slept upon the soft white sand, with arms under their hands, for our spoor across the desert was now unmistakable. At midday, rice was boiled for us by the indefatigable women, and at 3 p.m. we resumed our march towards the hills, which had exchanged their shadowy blue for a coat of pronounced brown. Journeying onwards, we reached the Barragid fiumara, and presently exchanged the plain for rolling ground covered with the remains of an extinct race, and probably alluded to by Al-Makrizi when he records that the Moslems of Adel had erected, throughout the country, a vast number of mosques and oratories for Friday and festival prayers. Places of worship appeared in the shape of parallelograms, unhewed stones piled upon the ground, with a semicicular niche in the direction of Meccah. The tombs, different from the heaped form now in fashion, closely resembled the older erections in the island of Saad el Din, near Zayla—oblong slabs planted deep in the soil. We also observed hollow rings of rough blocks, circles measuring

---

* Several Acacias afford gums, which the Bedouin eat greedily to strengthen themselves. The town's people declare that the food produces nothing but flatulence.

about a cubit in diameter: I had not time to excavate them and the End of Time could only inform me that they belonged to the 'Awwalin', or olden inhabitants.

At 7 p.m., as evening was closing in, we came upon the fresh trail of a large Habr Awal cavalcade. The celebrated footprint seen by Robinson Crusoe affected him not more powerfully than did this 'daaseh' my companions. The voice of song suddenly became mute. The women drove the camels hurriedly, and all huddled together, except Raghi, who kept well to the front ready for a run. Whistling with anger, I asked my attendants what had slain them: the End of Time, in a hollow voice, replied, 'Verily, O pilgrim, whoso seeth the track, seeth the foe!' and he quoted in tones of terror those dreary lines—

'Man is but a handful of dust,
And life is a violent storm.'

We certainly were a small party to contend against 200 horsemen— nine men and two women: moreover all except the Hammal and Long Gulad would infallibly have fled at the first charge.

Presently we sighted the trails of sheep and goats, showing the proximity of a village: their freshness was ascertained by my companions after an eager scrutiny in the moon's bright beams. About half an hour afterwards, rough ravines with sharp and thorny descents warned us that we had exchanged the dangerous plain for a place of safety where horsemen rarely venture. Raghi, not admiring the 'open', hurried us onward, in hope of reaching some kraal. At 8 p.m., however, seeing the poor women lamed with thorns, and the camels casting themselves upon the ground, I resolved to halt. Despite all objections, we lighted a fire, finished our store of bad milk—the water had long ago been exhausted—and lay down in the cold, clear air, covering ourselves with hides and holding our weapons.

At 6 a.m. we resumed our ride over rough stony ground, the thorns tearing our feet and naked legs, and the camels slipping over the rounded waste of drift pebbles. The Bedouin, with ears applied to the earth, listened for a village, but heard none. Suddenly we saw two strangers, and presently we came upon an Eesa kraal. It was situated in a deep ravine, called Damal, backed by a broad and hollow fiumara at the foot of the hills, running from west to east, and surrounded by lofty trees, upon which brown kites, black vultures, and percnopters like flakes of snow were mewing. We had marched over a winding path about eleven miles from, and in a south-west direction (205°) of,

Adad. Painful thoughts suggested themselves: in consequence of wandering southwards, only six had been taken off thirty stages by the labours of seven days.

As usual in Eastern Africa, we did not enter the kraal uninvited, but unloosed and pitched the wigwam under a tree outside. Presently the elders appeared bringing, with soft speeches, sweet water, new milk, fat sheep and goats, for which they demanded a Tobe of Cutch canvas. We passed with them a quiet luxurious day of coffee and pipes, fresh cream and roasted mutton: after the plain-heats we enjoyed the cool breeze of the hills, the cloudy sky, and the verdure of the glades, made doubly green by comparison with the parched stubbles below.

The Eesa, here mixed with the Gudabirsi, have little power: we found them poor and proportionally importunate. The men, wild-looking as open mouths, staring eyes, and tangled hair could make them, gazed with extreme eagerness upon my scarlet blanket: for very shame they did not beg it, but the inviting texture was pulled and fingered by the greasy multitude. We closed the hut whenever a valuable was produced, but eager eyes peeped through every cranny, till the End of Time ejaculated 'Praised be Allah!' and quoted the Arab saying, 'Show not the Somali thy door, and if he find it, block it up!' The women and children were clad in chocolate-coloured hides, fringed at the tops to gratify them I shot a few hawks, and was rewarded with loud exclamations—'Allah preserve thy hand!'—'May thy skill never fail thee before the foe!' A crone seeing me smoke, inquired if the fire did not burn; I handed my pipe, which nearly choked her, and she ran away from a steaming kettle, thinking it a weapon. As my companions observed, there was not a 'Miskal of sense in a Maund of heads': yet the people looked upon my sun-burnt skin with a favour they denied to the 'lime-white face'.

I was anxious to proceed in the afternoon, but Raghi had arrived at the frontier of his tribe: he had blood to settle amongst the Gudabirsi, and without a protector he could not enter their lands. At night we slept armed on account of the lions that infest the hills, and our huts were surrounded with a thorn fence—a precaution here first adopted, and never afterwards neglected. Early on the morning of the 14th of December heavy clouds rolled down from the mountains, and a Scotch mist deepened into a shower: our new Abban had not arrived, and the hut-mats, saturated with rain, had become too heavy for the camels to carry.

In the forenoon the Eesa kraal, loading their asses, set out towards the plain. This migration presented no new features, except that several sick and decrepid were barbarously left behind, for lions and hyenas to devour.* To deceive 'warhawks' who might be on the look-out, the migrators set fire to logs of wood and masses of sheep's earth, which, even in rain, will smoke and smoulder for weeks.

About midday arrived the two Gudabirsi who intended escorting us to the village of our Abbans. The elder, Rirash, was a black-skinned, wild-looking fellow, with a shock head of hair and a deep scowl which belied his good temper and warm heart: the other was a dun-faced youth betrothed to Raghi's daughter. They both belonged to the Mahadasan clan, and commenced operations by an obstinate attempt to lead us far out of our way eastwards. The pretext was the defenceless state of their flocks and herds, the real reason an itching for cloth and tobacco. We resisted manfully this time, nerved by the memory of wasted days, and, despite their declarations of Absi,† we determined upon making westward for the hills.

At 2 p.m. the caravan started along the fiumara course in rear of the deserted kraal, and after an hour's ascent Rirash informed us that a well was near. The Hammal and I, taking two water-skins, urged our mules over stones and thorny ground: presently we arrived at a rocky ravine, where, surrounded by brambles, rude walls, and tough frame works, lay the wells—three or four holes sunk ten feet deep in the limestone. Whilst we bathed in the sulphureous spring, which at once discoloured my silver ring, Rirash, baling up the water in his shield, filled the bags and bound them to the saddles. In haste we rejoined the caravan, which we found about sunset, halted by the vain fears of the guides. The ridge upon which they stood was a mass of old mosques and graves, showing that in former days a thick population tenanted these hills: from the summit appeared distant herds of kine and white flocks scattered like patches of mountain quartz.‡ Riding in advance, we traversed the stony ridge, fell into another ravine, and soon saw signs of human life. A shepherd descried us from afar and ran away reckless of property: causing the End of Time to roll his head with dignity, and to ejaculate, 'Of a truth said the Prophet of Allah, "fear is divided".' Presently we fell in with a village, from which the people rushed out, some exclaiming, 'Lo! let us look at the kings!' others, 'Come, see the

* This barbarous practice is generally carried out in cases of small-pox where contagion is feared.
† Fear—danger; it is a word which haunts the traveller in Somaliland.
‡ See map, p. 131, and note 2, p. 299.

white man, he is governor of Zayla!' I objected to such dignity, principally on account of its price: my companions, however, were inexorable; they would be Salatin—kings—and my colour was against claims to low degree. This fairness, and the Arab dress, made me at different times the ruler of Aden, the chief of Zayla, the Hajj's son, a boy, an old woman, a man painted white, a warrior in silver armour, a merchant, a pilgrim, a hedgepriest, Ahmad the Indian, a Turk, an Egyptian, a Frenchman, a Banyan, a shariff, and lastly a Calamity sent down from heaven to weary out the lives of the Somal: every kraal had some conjecture of its own, and each fresh theory was received by my companions with roars of laughter.

As the Gudabirsi pursued us with shouts for tobacco and cries of wonder, I dispersed them with a gun-shot: the women and children fled precipitately from the horrid sound, and the men, covering their heads with their shields, threw themselves face foremost upon the ground. Pursuing the fiumara course, we passed a number of kraals, whose inhabitants were equally vociferous: out of one came a Zayla man, who informed us that the Gudabirsi Abbans, to whom we bore Sharmakay's letter of introduction, were encamped within three days' march. It was reported, however, that a quarrel had broken out between them and the Gerad Adan, their brother-in-law; no pleasant news!—in Africa, under such circumstances, it is customary for friends to detain, and for foes to oppose, the traveller. We rode stoutly on, till the air darkened and the moon tipped the distant hill peaks with a dim mysterious light. I then called a halt: we unloaded on the banks of the Darkaynlay fiumara, so called from a tree which contains a fiery milk, fenced ourselves in—taking care to avoid being trampled upon by startled camels during our sleep, by securing them in a separate but neighbouring inclosure—spread our couches, ate our frugal suppers, and lost no time in falling asleep. We had travelled five hours that day, but the path was winding, and our progress in a straight line was at most eight miles.

And now, dear L., being about to quit the land of the Eesa, I will sketch the tribe.

The Eesa, probably the most powerful branch of the Somali nation, extends northwards to the Wayma family of the Dankali; southwards to the Gudabirsi, and midway between Zayla and Berbera; eastwards it is bounded by the sea, and westwards by the Gallas around Harar. It derives itself from Dirr and Aydur, without, however, knowing aught beyond the ancestral names, and is twitted with paganism by its enemies. This tribe, said to number 100,000 shields, is divided into numerous clans:⁴ these again split up into minor septs which plunder, and sometimes murder, one another in time of peace.

A fierce and turbulent race of republicans, the Eesa own nominal allegiance to a Ugaz or chief residing in the Hadagali hills. He is generally called 'Roblay'—Prince Rainy—the name or rather title being one of good omen, for a drought here, like a dinner in Europe, justifies the change of a dynasty. Every kraal has its Oddai (shaykh or head man), after whose name the settlement, as in Sind and other pastoral lands, is called. He is obeyed only when his orders suit the taste of King Demos, is always superior to his fellows in wealth of cattle, sometimes in talent and eloquence, and in deliberations he is assisted by the Wail or Akil—the Pítzo-council of Southern Africa— elders obeyed on account of their age. Despite, however, this apparatus of rule, the Bedouin have lost none of the characteristics recorded in the Periplus: they are still 'uncivilized and under no restraint'. Every free-born man holds himself equal to his ruler, and allows no royalties or prerogatives to abridge his birthright of liberty. Yet I have observed, that with all their passion for independence, the Somal, when subject to strict rule as at Zayla and Harar, are both apt to discipline and sub-servient to command.

In character, the Eesa are childish and docile, cunning, and deficient in judgment, kind and fickle, good-humoured and irascible, warm-hearted, and infamous for cruelty and treachery. Even the protector will slay his *protégé*, and citizens married to Eesa girls send their wives to buy goats and sheep from, but will not trust themselves amongst, their connections. 'Traitorous as an Eesa,' is a proverb at Zayla, where the people tell you that these Bedouin with the left hand offer a bowl of milk, and stab with the right. 'Conscience', I may observe, does not exist in Eastern Africa, and 'Repentance' expresses regret for missed opportunities of mortal crime. Robbery constitutes an honourable man: murder—the more atrocious the midnight crime the better— makes the hero. Honour consists in taking human life: hyena-like, the Bedouin cannot be trusted where blood may be shed. Glory is the having done all manner of harm. Yet the Eesa have their good points: they are not noted liars, and will rarely perjure themselves: they look down upon petty pilfering without violence, and they are generous and hospitable compared with the other Somal. Personally, I had no reason to complain of them. They were importunate beggars, but a pinch of snuff or a handful of tobacco always made us friends: they begged me to settle amongst them, they offered me sundry wives and

—the Somali Bedouin, unlike the Arab, readily affiliates strangers to his tribe—they declared that after a few days' residence, I should become one of themselves.

In appearance, the Eesa are distinguished from other Somal by blackness, ugliness of feature, and premature baldness of the temples; they also shave, or rather scrape off with their daggers, the hair high up the nape of the neck. The locks are dyed dun, frizzled, and greased; the Widads, or learned men, remove them, and none but paupers leave them in their natural state; the mustachioes are clipped close, the straggling whisker is carefully plucked, and the pile—erroneously considered impure—is removed either by vellication, or by passing the limbs through the fire. The eyes of the Bedouin, also, are less prominent than those of the citizens: the brow projects in pent-house fashion, and the organ, exposed to bright light, and accustomed to gaze at distant objects, acquires more concentration and power. I have seen amongst them handsome profiles, and some of the girls have fine figures with piquant, if not pretty, features.

Flocks and herds form the true wealth of the Eesa. According to them, sheep and goats are of silver, and the cow of gold: they compare camels to the rock, and believe, like most Moslems, the horse to have been created from the wind. Their diet depends upon the season. In hot weather, when forage and milk dry up, the flocks are slaughtered, and supply excellent mutton; during the monsun, men become fat, by drinking all day long the produce of their cattle. In the latter article of diet, the Eesa are delicate and curious: they prefer cow's milk, then the goat's, and lastly the ewe's, which the Arab loves best: the first is drunk fresh, and the two latter clotted, whilst the camel's is slightly soured. The townspeople use camel's milk medicinally: according to the Bedouin, he who lives on this beverage, and eats the meat for forty-four consecutive days, acquires the animal's strength. It has perhaps less 'body' than any other milk, and is deliciously sweet shortly after foaling: presently it loses flavour, and nothing can be more nauseous than the produce of an old camel. The Somal have a name for cream— 'Laban'—but they make no use of the article, churning it with the rest of the milk. They have no buffaloes, they shudder at the Tartar idea of mare's-milk, like the Arabs they hold the name Labban ['Milkseller'] a disgrace, and they make it a point of honour not to draw supplies from their cattle during the day.

The life led by these wild people is necessarily monotonous. They rest but little—from 11 p.m. till dawn—and never sleep in the bush for fear of plundering parties. Few begin the day with prayer as Moslems should: for the most part they apply themselves to counting and milking their cattle. The animals, all of which have names, come when called to the pail, and supply the family with a morning meal. Then the warriors, grasping their spears, and sometimes the young women armed only with staves, drive their herds to pasture: the matrons and children spinning or rope-making, tend the flocks, and the kraal is abandoned to the very young, the old, and the sick. The herdsmen wander about, watching the cattle and tasting nothing but the pure element or a pinch of coarse tobacco. Sometimes they play at Shahh, Shantarah, and other games, of which they are passionately fond: with a board formed of lines traced in the sand, and bits of dry wood or camel's earth acting pieces, they spend hour after hour, every looker-on vociferating his opinion, and catching at the men, till apparently the two players are those least interested in the game. Or, to drive off sleep, they sit whistling to their flocks, or they perform upon the Florimo, a reed pipe generally made at Harar, which has a plaintive sound uncommonly pleasing. In the evening the kraal again resounds with lowing and bleating: the camel's milk is all drunk, the cow's and goat's reserved for butter and ghi, which the women prepare; the numbers are once more counted, and the animals are carefully penned up for the night. This simple life is varied by an occasional birth and marriage, dance and foray, disease and murder. Their maladies are few and simple;[5] death generally comes by the spear, and the Bedouin is naturally long-lived. I have seen Macrobians hale and strong, preserving their powers and faculties in spite of eighty and ninety years.

The Klip Springer, or Alakud.

Rock rabbits, or coneys.

VI

From the Zayla Hills to the Marar Prairie

I HAVE NOW, DEAR L., quitted the maritime plain or first zone, to enter the Ghauts, that threshold of the Æthiopian highlands, which, beginning at Tajjurrah, sweeps in semicircle round the bay of Zayla, and falls about Berbera into the range of mountains which fringes the bold Somali coast. This chain has been inhabited, within History's memory, by three distinct races—the Gallas, the ancient Moslems of Adel, and by the modern Somal. As usual, however, in the East, it has no general vernacular name.*

The aspects of these Ghauts is picturesque. The primitive base consists of micaceous granite, with veins of porphyry and dykes of the purest white quartz: above lie strata of sandstone and lime, here dun, there yellow, or of a dull grey, often curiously contorted and washed clear of vegetable soil by the heavy monsun. On these heights, which are mostly conoid with rounded tops, joined by ridges and saddlebacks, various kinds of Acacia cast a pallid and sickly green, like the olive tree upon the hills of Provence. They are barren in the cold season, and the Nomads migrate to the plains: when the monsun covers

* Every hill and peak ravine and valley, will be known by some striking epithet: as Borad, the White Hill; Libahlya, the Lions' Mountain; and so forth. Comprehensive names are not adapted to social wants of uncivilized men.

them with rich pastures, the people revisit their deserted kraals. The kloofs or ravines are the most remarkable features of this country: in some places the sides rise perpendicularly, like gigantic walls, the breadth varying from one hundred yards to half a mile; in others cliffs and scars, sapped at their foundations, encumber the bed, and not unfrequently a broad band of white sand stretches between two fringes of emerald green, delightful to look upon after the bare and ghastly basalt of Southern Arabia. The Jujube grows to a height already betraying signs of African luxuriance: through its foliage flit birds, gaudy-coloured as kingfishers, of vivid red, yellow, and changing-green. I remarked a long-tailed jay called Gobiyan or Fat, russet-hued ringdoves, the modest honey-bird, corn quails, canary-coloured finches, sparrows gay as those of Surinam, humming-birds with a plume of metallic lustre, and especially a white-eyed kind of maina, called by the Somal, Shimbir Load, or the cow-bird. The Armo-creeper, with large fleshy leaves, pale green, red, or crimson, and clusters of bright berries like purple grapes, forms a conspicuous ornament in the valleys. There is a great variety of the Cactus tribe, some growing to the height of thirty and thirty-five feet: of these one was particularly pointed out to me. The vulgar Somal call it Guraato, the more learned Shajarat al-Zakkum: it is the mandrake of these regions, and the round excrescences upon the summits of its fleshy arms are supposed to resemble men's heads and faces.

On Tuesday, the 5th December, we arose at 6 a.m., after a night so dewy that our clothes were drenched, and we began to ascend the Wady Darkaynlay, which winds from east to south. After an hour's march appeared a small cairn of rough stones, called Siyaro, or Mazar, to which each person, in token of honour, added his quotum. The Abban opined that Auliya or holy men had sat there, but the End of Time more sagaciously conjectured that it was the site of some Galla idol or superstitious rite. Presently we came upon the hills of the White Ant, a characteristic feature in this part of Africa. Here the land has the appearance of a Turkish cemetery on a grand scale: there it seems like a city in ruins: in some places the pillars are truncated into a resemblance to bee-hives, in others they cluster together, suggesting the idea of a portico: whilst many of them, veiled by trees, and overrun with gay creepers, look like the remains of sylvan altars. Generally the hills are conical, and vary in height from four to twelve feet: they are counted by hundreds, and the Somal account for the number by declaring that the insects abandon their home when dry, and com-

Hills of the White Ant.

mence building another. The older erections are worn away, by wind and rain, to a thin tapering spire, and are frequently hollowed out and arched beneath by rats and ground squirrels. The substance, fine yellow mud, glued by the secretions of the ant, is hard to break: it is pierced sieve-like, by a net-work of tiny shafts. I saw these hills for the first time in the Wady Darkaynlay: in the interior they are larger and longer than near the maritime regions.

We travelled up the fiumara in a southerly direction till 8 a.m., when the guides led us away from the bed. They anticipated meeting Gudabirsis: pallid with fear, they also trembled with cold and hunger. Anxious consultations were held. One man, Ali—surnamed 'Doso', because he did nothing but eat, drink, and stand over the fire—determined to leave us: as, however, he had received a tobe for pay, we put a veto upon that proceeding. After a march of two hours, over ground so winding that we had not covered more than three miles, our guides halted under a tree, near a deserted kraal, at a place called al-Armo, the 'Armo-creeper water', or more facetiously Dabadaláshay: from Damal it bore S.W. 190°. One of our Bedouin, mounting a mule, rode forward to gather intelligence, and bring back a skin full of water. I asked the End of Time what they expected to hear: he replied with the proverb 'News liveth!' The Somal Bedouin have a passion for knowing how the world wags. In some of the more desert regions the whole population will follow the wanderer. No traveller ever passes a kraal without planting spear in the ground, and demanding answers to a lengthened string of queries: rather than miss intelligence he will inquire of a woman. Thus it is that news flies through the country. Among the wild Gudabirsi the Russian war was a topic of interest, and at Harar I heard of a violent storm which had damaged the shipping in Bombay Harbour, but a few weeks after the event.

The Bedouin returned with an empty skin but a full budget. I will offer you, dear L., a specimen of the 'palaver' which is supposed to prove the aphorism that all barbarians are orators. Demosthenes leisurely dismounts, advances, stands for a moment cross-legged—the favourite posture in this region—supporting each hand with a spear planted in the ground: thence he slips to squat, looks around, ejects saliva, shifts his quid to behind his ear, places his weapons before him, takes up a bit of stick, and traces lines which he carefully smooths away—it being ill-omened to mark the earth. The listeners sit gravely in a semicircle upon their heels, with their spears, from whose bright heads flashes a ring of troubled light, planted upright, and look steadfastly on his countenance over the upper edges of their shields, with eyes apparently planted, like those of the Blemmyes, in their breasts. When the moment for delivery is come, the head man inquires, 'What is the news?' The informant would communicate the important fact that he has been to the well: he proceeds as follows, noting emphasis by raising his voice, at times about six notes, and often violently striking at the ground in front.

'It is good news, if Allah please!'

'Wa Sidda!'—Even so! respond the listeners, intoning or rather groaning the response.

'I mounted mule this morning.'

'Even so!'

'I departed from ye riding.'

'Even so!'

'*There!*' (with a scream and pointing out the direction with a stick).

'Even so!'

'*There* I went.'

'Even so!'

'I threaded the wood.'

'Even so!'

'I traversed the sands.'

'Even so!'

'I feared nothing.'

'Even so!'

'At last I came upon cattle tracks.'

'Hoo! hoo!! hoo!!!' (An ominous pause follows this exclamation of astonishment.)

'They were fresh.'

'Even so!'

'So were the earths.'

'Even so!'

'I distinguished the feet of women.'

'Even so!'

'But there were no camels.'

'Even so!'

'At last I saw sticks'—

'Even so!'

'Stones'—

'Even so!'

'Water'—

'Even so!'

'A well!!!'

Then follows the palaver, wherein, as occasionally happens further West, he distinguishes himself who can rivet the attention of the audience for at least an hour without saying anything in particular. The advantage of *their* circumlocution, however, is that by considering a subject in every possible light and phase as regards its cause and effect, antecedents, actualities, and consequences, they are prepared for any emergency which, without the palaver, might come upon them unawares.

Although the thermometer showed summer heat, the air was cloudy and raw blasts poured down from the mountains. At half past 3 p.m. our camels were lazily loaded, and we followed the course of the fiumara, which runs to the W. and S.W. After half an hour's progress, we arrived at the gully in which are the wells, and the guides halted because they descried half a dozen youths and boys bathing and washing their Tobes. All, cattle as well as men, were sadly thirsty: many of us had been chewing pebbles during the morning, yet, afraid of demands for tobacco, the Bedouin would have pursued the march without water had I not forced them to halt. We found three holes in the sand; one was dry, a second foul, and the third contained a scanty supply of the pure element from twenty to twenty-five feet below the surface. A youth stood in the water and filled a wicker-pail, which he tossed to a companion perched against the side half way up: the latter in his turn hove it to a third, who, catching it at the brink, threw the contents, by this time half wasted, into the skin cattle trough. We halted about half an hour to refresh man and beast, and then resumed our way up the Wady, quitting it where a short cut avoids the frequent windings of the bed. This operation saved but little time; the ground was stony, the rough ascents fatigued the camels, and our legs and feet were lacerated by the spear-like thorns. Here, the ground was overgrown with aloes, sometimes six feet high with pink and 'pale Pomona green' leaves, bending in the line of beauty towards the ground, graceful in form as the capitals of Corinthian columns, and crowned with gay-coloured bells, but barbarously supplied with woody thorns and strong serrated edges. There the Hig, an aloetic plant with a point so hard and sharp that horses cannot cross ground where it grows, stood in bunches like the largest and stiffest of rushes. Senna sprang spontaneously on the banks, and the gigantic Ushr or Asclepias shed its bloom upon the stones and pebbles of the bed. My attendants occupied themselves with gathering the edible pod of an Acacia called Kura, whilst I observed the view. Frequent ant-hills gave an appearance of habitation to a desert still covered with the mosques and tombs of old Adel; and the shape of the country had gradually changed, basins and broad slopes now replacing the thickly crowded conoid peaks of the lower regions.

As the sun sank towards the west, Long Gulad complained bitterly of the raw breeze from the hills. We passed many villages, distinguished by the barking of dogs and the bleating of flocks, on their way to the field: the unhappy Raghi, however, who had now become our *protégé*, would neither venture into a settlement, nor bivouac amongst the lions. He hurried us forwards till we arrived at a hollow called Gud, 'the Hole', which supplied us with the protection of a deserted kraal, where our camels, half-starved and knocked-up by an eight miles' march, were speedily unloaded. Whilst pitching the tent, we were visited by some Gudabirsi, who attempted to seize our Abban, alleging that he owed them a cow. We replied doughtily, that he was under our sandals: as they continued to speak in a high tone, a pistol was discharged over their heads, after which they cringed like dogs. A blazing fire, a warm supper, dry beds, broad jests, and funny stories, soon restored the flagging spirits of our party. Towards night the moon dispersed the thick mists which, gathering into clouds, threatened rain, and the cold sensibly diminished: there was little dew, and we should have slept comfortably had not our hungry mules hobbled as they were, hopped about the kraal and fought till dawn.

On the 6th December, we arose late to avoid the cold morning air, and at 7 a.m. set out over rough ground, hoping to ascend the Ghauts that day. After creeping about two miles, the camels unable to proceed, threw themselves upon the earth, and we unwillingly called a halt at Jiyaf, a basin below the Dobo fiumara. Here, white flocks dotting the hills, and the scavengers of the air warned us that we were in the vicinity of villages. Our wigwam was soon full of fair-faced Gudabirsi, mostly Loajira or cow-herd boys, who, according to the custom of their class, wore their Tobes bound scarf-like round their necks. They begged us to visit their village, and offered a heifer for each lion shot on Mount Libahlay: unhappily we could not afford time. These youths were followed by men and women bringing milk, sheep, and goats, for which, grass being rare, they asked exorbitant prices—eighteen cubits of Cutch canvas for a lamb, and two of blue cotton for a bottle of ghi. Amongst them was the first really pretty face seen by me in the Somali country. The head was well formed, and gracefully placed upon a long thin neck and narrow shoulders; the hair, brow, and nose were unexceptionable, there was an arch look in the eyes of jet and pearl, and a suspicion of African protuberance about the lips, which gave the countenance an exceeding *naïveté*. Her skin was a warm, rich nutbrown, an especial charm in these regions, and her movements had that grace which suggests perfect symmetry of limb. The poor girl's costume, a coif for the back hair, a cloth imperfectly covering the bosom, and a petticoat of hides, made no great mystery of forms: equally rude were her ornaments; an armlet and pewter earrings, the work of some blacksmith, a necklace of white porcelain beads, and sundry talismans in cases of tarnished and blackened leather. As a tribute to her prettiness I gave her some cloth, tobacco, and a bit of salt, which was rapidly becoming valuable: her husband stood by, and, although the preference was marked, he displayed neither anger nor jealousy. She showed her gratitude by bringing us milk, and by assisting us to start next morning. In the evening we hired three fresh camels* to carry our goods up the ascent, and killed some antelopes which, in a stew, were not contemptible. The End of Time insisted upon firing a gun to frighten away the lions, who make night hideous with their growls, but never put in an appearance.

The morning cold greatly increased, and we did not start till 8 a.m. After half an hour's march up the bed of a fiumara, leading apparently to a *cul de sac* of lofty rocks in the hills, we quitted it for a rude zig-zag winding along its left side, amongst bushes, thorn trees, and huge rocks. The walls of the opposite bank were strikingly perpendicular; in some places stratified, in others solid and polished by the course of stream and cascade. The principal material was a granite, so coarse, that the composing mica, quartz, and felspar separated into detached pieces as large as a man's thumb; micaceous grit, which glittered in the sunbeams, and various sandstones, abounded. The road caused us some trouble; the camels' loads were always slipping from their mats; I found it necessary to dismount from my mule, and, sitting down, we were stung by the large black ants which infest these hills.†

About half way up, we passed two cairns, and added to them our mite like good Somal. After two hours of hard work the summit of this primitive pass was attained, and sixty minutes more saw us on the plateau above the hills—the second zone of East Africa. Behind us lay the plains, of which we vainly sought a view: the broken ground at the foot of the mountains is broad, and mists veiled the reeking expanse of the low country. The plateau in front of us was a wide extent of rolling ground, rising slightly towards the west; its colour was brown with a threadbare coat of verdure, and at the bottom of each rugged slope ran a stony water-course trending from south-west to north-east. The

---

* For these we paid twenty-four cubits of canvas, and two of blue cotton; equivalent to about three shillings.

† The natives call them Jana; they are about three-fourths of an inch long, and armed with stings that prick like thorns and burn violently for a few minutes.

mass of tangled aloes, ragged thorn, and prim-looking poison trees,* must once have been populous; tombs and houses of the early Moslems covered with ruins the hills and ridges.

About noon, we arrived at a spot called the Kafir's Grave. It is a square enceinte of rude stones about one hundred yards each side; and legends say that one Misr, a Galla chief, when dying, ordered the place to be filled seven times with she-camels destined for his Ahan or funeral feast. This is the fourth stage upon the direct road from Zayla to Harar: we had wasted ten days, and the want of grass and water made us anxious about our animals. The camels could scarcely walk, and my mule's spine rose high beneath the Arab pad: such are the effects of Jilál,† the worst of travelling seasons in Eastern Africa.

At 1 p.m. we unloaded under a sycamore tree, called, after a Galla chieftain, 'Halimalah', and giving its name to the surrounding valley. This ancient of the forest is more than half decayed, several huge limbs lie stretched upon the ground, whence, for reverence, no one removes them: upon the trunk, or rather trunks, for it bifurcates, are marks deeply cut by a former race, and Time has hollowed in the larger stem an arbour capable of containing half a dozen men. This holy tree was, according to the Somal, a place of prayer for the infidel, and its ancient honours are not departed. Here, probably to commemorate the west-ward progress of the tribe, the Gudabirsi Ugaz or chief has the white canvas turban bound about his brows, and hence rides forth to witness the equestrian games in the Harawwah Valley. As everyone who passes by, visits the Halimalah tree, foraging parties of the Northern Eesa and the Jibril Abokr (a clan of the Habr Awal) frequently meet, and the traveller wends his way in fear and trembling.

The thermometer showed an altitude of 3,350 feet: under the tree's cool shade, the climate reminded me of Southern Italy in winter. I found a butter-cup, and heard a wood-pecker tapping on the hollow trunk, a reminiscence of English glades. The Abban and his men urged an advance in the afternoon. But my health had suffered from the bad water of the coast, and the camels were faint with fatigue: we therefore dismissed the hired beasts, carried our property into a deserted kraal, and, lighting a fire, prepared to 'make all snug' for the night. The Bedouin, chattering with cold, stood closer to the comfortable blaze

* This is the celebrated Wǎbá, which produces the Somali Wǎbáyo, a poison applied to darts and arrows.[1]
† Jílál is the dry season from December to April. The country then becomes Abar (in Arabic, Jahr), a place of famine: the Nomads migrate to the low plains, where pasture is procurable. Some reckon as a fifth season, Kalíl, or the heats between Jílál and the monsun.

than ever did pater-familias in England: they smoked their faces, toasted their hands, broiled their backs with intense enjoyment, and waved their legs to and fro through the flame to singe away the pile, which at this season grows long. The End of Time, who was surly, compared them to demons, and quoted the Arab's saying: 'Allah never bless smooth man, or hairy woman!'

On the 8th of December, at 8 a.m., we travelled slowly up the Halimalah Valley, whose clayey surface glistened with mica and quartz pebbles from the hills. All the trees are thorny except the Sycamore and the Asclepias. The Gub, or Jujube, grows luxuriantly in thickets: its dried wood is used by women to fumigate their hair: the Kedi, a tree like the porcupine—all spikes—supplies the Bedouin with hatchet-handles. I was shown the Abol with its edible gum, and a kind of Acacia, here called Galol. Its bark dyes cloth a dull red, and the thorn issues from a bulb which, when young and soft, is eaten by the Somal, when old it becomes woody, and hard as a nut. At 9 a.m. we crossed the Lesser Abbaso, a fiumara with high banks of stiff clay and filled with large rolled stones: issuing from it, we traversed a thorny path over ascending ground between higher hills, and covered with large boulders and step-like layers of grit. Here appeared several Gudabirsi tombs, heaps of stones or pebbles, surrounded by a fence of thorns, or an enceinte of loose blocks: in the latter, slabs are used to make such houses as children would build in play, to denote the number of establishments left by the deceased. The new grave is known by the conical milk-pails surmounting the stick at the head of the corpse, upon the neighbouring tree is thrown the mat which bore the dead man to his last home, and hard by are the blackened stones upon which his funeral feast was cooked. At 11 a.m. we reached the Greater Abbaso, a fiumara about 100 yards wide, fringed with lovely verdure and full of the antelope called Gurnuk: its watershed was, as usual in this region, from west and south-west to east and north-east. About noon we halted, having travelled eight miles from the Holy Tree.

At half past three reloading we followed the course of the Abbaso Valley, the most beautiful spot we had yet seen. The presence of mankind, however, was denoted by the cut branches of thorn encumbering the bed: we remarked too, the tracks of lions pursued by hunters, and the frequent streaks of serpents, sometimes five inches in diameter. Towards evening our party closed up in fear, thinking that they saw spears glancing through the trees: I treated their alarm lightly, but the next day proved that it was not wholly imaginary. At sunset we met a shepherd who swore upon the stone* to bring us milk in exchange for tobacco, and presently, after a five miles' march, we halted in a deserted kraal on the left bank of a fiumara. Clouds gathered black upon the hill tops, and a comfortless blast, threatening rain, warned us not to delay pitching the Gurgi. A large fire was lighted, and several guns were

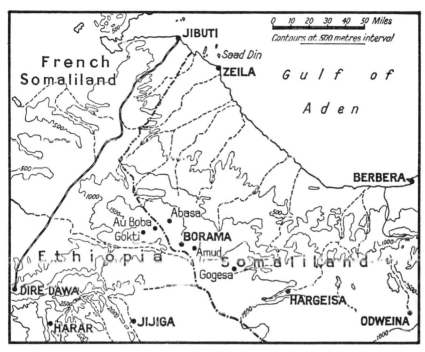

Besides the old settlements of Au Boba, Abasa, Gokti, Amud and Gogesa referred to by Richard Burton, there are fifteen others in the same area marked on the map entitled 'The Ruined Towns of Somaliland', which were visited and described by Mr. A. T. Curle.[2]

discharged to frighten away the lions that infest this place. Twice during the night our camels started up and rushed round their thorn ring in alarm.

* This great oath suggests the litholatry of the Arabs, derived from the Abyssinian and Galla Sabæans; it is regarded by the Eesa and Gudabirsi Bedouin as even more binding than the popular religious adjurations. When a suspected person denies his guilt, the judge places a stone before him saying 'Tabo!' (feel!); the liar will seldom dare to touch it. Sometimes a Somali will take up a stone and say 'Dagáhá', (it is a stone), he may then generally be believed.

Late in the morning of Saturday, the 9th December, I set out accompanied by Rirash and the End of Time, to visit some ruins a little way distant from the direct road. After an hour's ride we turned away from the Abbaso Fiumara and entered a basin among the hills distant about sixteen miles from the Holy Tree. This is the site of Darbiyah Kola—Kola's Fort—so called from its Galla queen. It is said that this city and its neighbour Aububah fought like certain cats in Kilkenny till both were 'eaten up': the Gudabirsi fix the event at the period when their forefathers still inhabited Bulhar on the coast—about 300 years ago. If the date be correct, the substantial ruins have fought a stern fight with time. Remnants of houses cumber the soil, and the carefully built wells are filled with rubbish: the palace was pointed out to me with its walls of stone and clay intersected by layers of wood work. The mosque is a large roofless building containing twelve square pillars of rude masonry, and the Mihrab, or prayer niche, is denoted by a circular arch of tolerable construction. But the voice of the Muezzin is hushed for ever, and creepers now twine round the ruined fane. The scene was still and dreary as the grave; for a mile and a half in length all was ruins—ruins—ruins.

Leaving this dead city, we rode towards the south-west between two rugged hills of which the loftiest summit is called Wanauli. As usual they are rich in thorns: the tall 'Wadi' affords a gum useful to cloth-dyers, and the leaves of the lofty Wumba are considered, after the Daum-palm, the best material for mats. On the ground appeared the blue flowers of the 'Man' or 'Himbah', a shrub resembling a potato: it bears a gay yellow apple full of brown seeds which is not eaten by the Somal. My companions made me taste some of the Karir berries, which in colour and flavour resemble red currants: the leaves are used as a dressing to ulcers. Topping the ridge we stood for a few minutes to observe the view before us. Beneath our feet lay a long grassy plain—the sight must have gladdened the hearts of our starving mules!—and for the first time in Africa horses appeared grazing free amongst the bushes. A little further off lay the Aylonda valley studded with graves, and dark with verdure. Beyond it stretched the Wady Harawwah, a long gloomy hollow in the general level. The background was a bold sweep of blue hill, the second gradient of the Harar line, and on its summit closing the western horizon lay a golden streak—the Marar Prairie. Already I felt at the end of my journey.

About noon, reaching a kraal, whence but that morning our Gudabirsi Abbans had driven off their kine, we sat under a tree and with a pistol reported arrival. Presently the elders came out and welcomed their old acquaintance the End of Time as a distinguished guest. He eagerly inquired about the reported quarrel between the Abbans and their brother-in-law the Gerad Adan. When assured that it was the offspring of Somali imagination, he rolled his head, and with dignity remarked, 'What man shutteth to us, that Allah openeth!' We complimented each other gravely upon the purity of our intentions—amongst Moslems a condition of success—and not despising second causes, lost no time in sending a horseman for the Abbans. Presently some warriors came out and inquired if we were of the Caravan that was travelling last evening up a valley with laden camels. On our answering in the affirmative, they laughingly declared that a commando of twelve horsemen had followed us with the intention of a sham-attack. This is favourite sport with the Bedouin. When however the traveller shows fright, the feint is apt to turn out a fact. On one occasion a party of Arab merchants, not understanding the 'fun of the thing', shot two Somal: the tribe had the justice to acquit the strangers, mulcting them, however, a few yards of cloth for the families of the deceased. In reply I fired a pistol unexpectedly over the heads of my new hosts, and improved the occasion of their terror by deprecating any practical facetiousness in future.

We passed the day under a tree: the camels escorted by my two attendants, and the women, did not arrive till sunset, having occupied about eight hours in marching as many miles. Fearing lions, we pitched inside the kraal, despite crying children, scolding wives, cattle rushing about, barking dogs, flies and ticks, filth and confinement. I will now attempt a description of a village in Eastern Africa.

The Rer or Kraal is a line of scattered huts on plains where thorns are rare, beasts of prey scarce, and raids not expected. In the hills it is surrounded by a strong fence to prevent cattle straying: this, when danger induces caution, is doubled and trebled. Yet the lion will sometimes break through it, and the leopard clears it, prey in mouth, with a bound. The abattis has usually four entrances which are choked up with heaps of bushes at night. The interior space is partitioned off by dwarf hedges into rings, which contain and separate the different species of cattle. Sometimes there is an outer compartment adjoining the exterior fence, set apart for the camels; usually they are placed in the centre of the kraal. Horses being most valuable are side-lined and tethered close to the owner's hut, and rude bowers of brush and fire wood protect the weaklings of the flocks from the heat of the sun and the inclement night breeze.

At intervals around and inside the outer abattis are built the Gurgi or wigwams—hemispheric huts like old bee-hives about five feet high by six in diameter: they are even smaller in the warm regions, but they increase in size as the elevation of the country renders climate less genial. The material is a framework of 'Digo', or sticks bent and hardened in the fire: to build the hut, these are planted in the ground, tied together with cords, and covered with mats of two different kinds: the Aus composed of small bundles of grass neatly joined, is hard and smooth; the Kibid has a long pile and is used as couch as well as roof. The single entrance in front is provided with one of these articles which serves as a curtain; hides are spread upon the top during the monsun, and little heaps of earth are sometimes raised outside to keep out wind and rain. (See p. 72.)

The furniture is simple as the building. Three stones and a hole form the fireplace, near which sleep the children, kids and lambs: there being no chimney, the interior is black with soot. The cow-skin couches are suspended during the day, like arms and other articles which suffer from rats and white ants, by loops of cords to the sides. The principal ornaments are basket-work bottles, gaily adorned with beads, cowries, and stained leather. Pottery being here unknown, the Bedouin twist the fibres of the root into various shapes, and make them water-tight with the powdered bark of another tree. The Han is a large wicker-work bucket, mounted in a framework of sticks, and used to contain water on journeys. The Guraf (a word derived from the Arabic 'Ghurfah') is a conical-shaped vessel, used to bale out the contents of a well. The Del, or milk-pail, is shaped like two cones joined at the base by lateral thongs, the upper and smaller half acting as cup and cover. And finally the Wesi, or water bottle, contains the traveller's store for drinking and religious ablution.

When the kraal is to be removed, the huts and furniture are placed upon the camels, and the hedges and earth are sometimes set on fire, to purify the place and deceive enemies. Throughout the country black circles of cinders or thorn diversify the hill sides, and show an extensive population. Travellers always seek deserted kraals for security of encampment. As they swarm with vermin by night and flies by day, I frequently made strong objections to these favourite localities: the utmost conceded to me was a fresh enclosure added by a smaller hedge to the outside abattis of the more populous cow-kraals.

On the 10th December we halted: the bad water, the noonday sun of 107°, and the cold mornings—51° being the average—had seriously affected my health. All the population flocked to see me, darkening the hut with nodding wigs and staring faces: and—Gudabirsi are polite knaves—apologized for the intrusion. Men, women, and children appeared in crowds, bringing milk and ghi, meat and water, several of the elders remembered having seen me at Berbera,* and the blear-eyed maidens, who were in no wise shy, insisted upon admiring the white stranger.

Feeling somewhat restored by repose, I started the next day, 'with a tail on' to inspect the ruins of Aububah. After a rough ride over stony ground we arrived at a grassy hollow, near a line of hills, and dismounted to visit the Shaykh Aububah's remains. He rests under a little conical dome of brick, clay, and wood, similar in construction to that of Zayla: it is falling to pieces, and the adjoining mosque, long roofless, is overgrown with trees, that rustle melancholy sounds in the light joyous breeze. Creeping in by a dwarf door or rather hole, my Gudabirsi guides showed me a bright object forming the key of the arch: as it shone they suspected silver, and the End of Time whispered a sacrilegious plan for purloining it. Inside the vault were three graves apparently empty, and upon the dark sunken floor lay several rounded stones, resembling cannon balls, and used as weights by the more civilized Somal. Thence we proceeded to the battle-field, a broad sheet of sandstone, apparently dinted by the hoofs of mules and horses: on this ground, which, according to my guides, was in olden days soft and yielding, took place the great action between Aububah and Darbiyah Kola. A second mosque was found with walls in tolerable repair, but, like the rest of the place, roofless. Long Gulad ascended the broken staircase of a small square minaret, and delivered a most ignorant and Bedouin-like Azan or call to prayer. Passing by the shells of houses, we concluded our morning's work with a visit to the large graveyard. Apparently it did not contain the bones of Moslems: long lines of stones pointed westward, and one tomb was covered with a coating of hard mortar, in whose sculptured edge my benighted friends detected magical inscriptions. I heard of another city called Ahammad in the neighbouring hills, but did not visit it. These are all remains of Galla settlements, which the ignorance and exaggeration of the Somal fill with 'writings' and splendid edifices.

* Some years ago a French lady landed at Berbera: her white face, according to the End of Time, made every man hate his wife, and every wife hate herself. I know not who the fair dame was: her charms and black silk dress, however, have made a lasting impression upon the Somali heart; from the coast to Harar she is still remembered with rapture.

Returning home we found that our Gudabirsi Bedouin had at length obeyed the summons. The six sons of a noted chief, Ali Addah or White Ali, by three different mothers, Beuh, Igah, Khayri, Nur, Ismail, and Yunis, all advanced towards me as I dismounted, gave the hand of friendship, and welcomed me to their homes. With the exception of the first-named, a hard-featured man at least forty years old, the brothers were good-looking youths, with clear brown skins, regular features, and graceful figures. They entered the Gurgi when invited, but refused to eat, saying, that they came for honour not for food. The Hajj Sharmakay's introductory letter was read aloud to their extreme delight, and at their solicitation, I perused it a second and a third time; then having dismissed, with sundry small presents, the two Abbans Raghi and Rirash, I wrote a flattering account of them to the Hajj, and entrusted it to certain citizens who were returning in caravan Zaylawards, after a commercial tour in the interior.

Before they departed, there was a feast after the Homeric fashion. A sheep was 'cut', disembowelled, dismembered, tossed into one of our huge cauldrons, and devoured within the hour: the almost live food was washed down with huge draughts of milk. The feasters resembled Wordsworth's cows, 'forty feeding like one': in the left hand they held the meat to their teeth, and cut off the slice in possession with long daggers perilously close, were their noses longer and their mouths less obtrusive. During the dinner I escaped from the place of flies, and retired to a favourite tree. Here the End of Time seeing me still in pain, insisted upon trying a Somali medicine. He cut two pieces of dry wood, scooped a hole in the shorter, and sharpened the longer, applied point to socket, which he sprinkled with a little sand, placed his foot upon the 'female stick', and rubbed the other between his palms till smoke and char appeared. He then cauterized my stomach vigorously in six different places, quoting a tradition, 'the End of Physic is Fire'.

On Tuesday the 12th December, I vainly requested the two sons of White Ali, who had constituted themselves our guides, to mount their horses: they feared to fatigue the valuable animals at a season when grass is rare and dry. I was disappointed by seeing the boasted 'Faras' of the Somal, in the shape of ponies hardly thirteen hands high. The head is pretty, the eyes are well opened, and the ears are small; the form also is good, but the original Arab breed has degenerated in the new climate. They are soft, docile, and—like all other animals in this part of the world—timid: the habit of climbing rocks makes them sure-footed, and they show the remains of blood when forced to fatigue.

The Gudabirsi will seldom sell these horses, the great safeguard against their conterminous tribes, the Eesa and Girhi, who are all infantry: a village seldom contains more than six or eight, and the lowest value would be ten cows or twenty Tobes. Careful of his beast when at rest, the Somali Bedouin in the saddle is rough and cruel: whatever beauty the animal may possess in youth, completely disappears before the fifth year, and few are without spavin, or sprained back-sinews. In some parts of the country,* 'to ride violently to your hut two or three times before finally dismounting, is considered a great compliment, and the same ceremony is observed on leaving. Springing into the saddle (if he has one), with the aid of his spear, the Somali cavalier first endeavours to infuse a little spirit into his half-starved hack by persuading him to accomplish a few plunges and capers: then, his heels raining a hurricane of blows against the animal's ribs, and occasionally using his spear-point as a spur, away he gallops, and after a short circuit, in which he endeavours to show himself to the best advantage, returns to his starting point at full speed, when the heavy Arab bit brings up the blown horse with a shock that half breaks his jaw and fills his mouth with blood. The affection of the true Arab for his horse is proverbial: the cruelty of the Somali to his, may I think be considered equally so.' The Bedouin practise horse-racing, and run for bets, which are contested with ardour: on solemn occasions, they have rude equestrian games, in which they display themselves and their animals. The Gudabirsi, and indeed most of the Somal, sit loosely upon their horses. Their saddle is a demipique, a high-backed wooden frame, like the Egyptian fellah's: two light splinters leave a clear space for the spine, and the tree is tightly bound with wet thongs: a sheepskin shabracque is loosely spread over it, and the dwarf iron stirrup admits only the big toe, as these people fear a stirrup which, if the horse fall, would entangle the foot. Their bits are cruelly severe; a solid iron ring, as in the Arab bridle embracing the lower jaw takes the place of a curb chain. Some of the head-stalls, made at Berbera are prettily made of cut leather and bright steel ornaments like diminutive quoits. The whip is a hard hide handle, plated with zinc, and armed with a single short broad thong.

With the two sons of White Ali and the End of Time, at 8 a.m., on the 12th December, I rode forward, leaving the jaded camels in charge of my companions and the women. We crossed the plain in a south-

* Particularly amongst the windward tribes visited by Lieut. Cruttenden, from whom I borrow this description.

westerly direction, and after traversing rolling ground, we came to a ridge, which commanded an extensive view. Behind lay the Wanauli Hills, already purple in the distance. On our left was a mass of cones, each dignified by its own name; no one, it is said, can ascend them, which probably means that it would be a fatiguing walk. Here are the visitation-places of three celebrated saints, Amud, Sau, and Shaykh Sharlagamadi, or the 'Hidden from Evil'. To the north-west I was shown some blue peaks tenanted by the Eesa Somal. In front, backed by the dark hills of Harar, lay the Harawwah valley. The breadth is about fifteen miles: it runs from south-west to north-east, between the Highlands of the Girhi and the rolling ground of the Gudabirsi Somal, as far, it is said, as the Dankali country. Of old this luxuriant waste belonged to the former tribe; about twelve years ago it was taken from them by the Gudabirsi, who carried off at the same time thirty cows, forty camels, and between three and four hundred sheep and goats.

Large herds tended by spearmen and grazing about the bush, warned us that we were approaching the kraal in which the sons of White Ali were camped; at half past 10 a.m., after riding eight miles, we reached the place which occupies the lower slope of the Northern Hills that enclose the Harawwah valley. We spread our hides under a tree, and were soon surrounded by Bedouin, who brought milk, sun-dried beef, ghi and honey in one of the painted wooden bowls exported from Cutch. After breakfast, at which the End of Time distinguished himself by dipping his meat into honey, we went out gun in hand towards the bush. It swarmed with sand-antelope and Gurnuk: the ground-squirrels haunted every ant-hill, hoopoos and spur-fowls paced among the thickets, in the trees we heard the frequent cry of the Gobiyan and the bird facetiously termed from its cry 'Dobo-dogon-guswen', and the bright-coloured eagle, the Abodi or Bakiyyah,* lay on wing high in the cloudless air. When tired of killing we returned to our cow-hides, and sat in conversation with the Bedouin. They boasted of the skill with which they used the shield, and seemed not to understand the efficiency of a sword-parry: to illustrate the novel idea I gave a stick to the best man, provided myself in the same way, and allowed him to cut at me. After repeated failures he received a sounding blow upon the least bony portion of his person: the crowd laughed long and loud, and the pretending 'knight-at-arms' retired in confusion.

* This beautiful bird, with a black and crimson plume, and wings lined with silver, soars high and seldom descends except at night: its shyness prevented my shooting a specimen.[3]

Darkness fell, but no caravan appeared: it had been delayed by a runaway mule—perhaps by the desire to restrain my vagrant propensities—and did not arrive till midnight. My hosts cleared a Gurgi for our reception, brought us milk, and extended their hospitality to the full limits of even savage complaisance.

Expecting to march on the 13th December soon after dawn, I summoned Beuh and his brethren to the hut, reminding him that the Hajj had promised me an escort without delay to the village of the Gerad Adan. To my instances they replied that, although they were most anxious to oblige, the arrival of Mudah the eldest son rendered a consultation necessary; and retiring to the woods, sat in palaver from 8 a.m. to past noon. At last they came to a resolution which could not be shaken. They would not trust one of their number in the Gerad's country; a horseman, however, should carry a letter inviting the Girhi chief to visit his brothers-in-law. I was assured that Adan would not drink water before mounting to meet us: but, fear is reciprocal, there was evidently bad blood between them, and already a knowledge of Somali customs caused me to suspect the result of our mission. However, a letter was written reminding the Gerad of 'the word spoken under the tree', and containing in case of recusance, a threat to cut off the salt well at which his cows are periodically driven to drink. Then came the bargain for safe conduct. After much haggling, especially on the part of the handsome Igah, they agreed to receive twenty Tobes, three bundles of tobacco, and fourteen cubits of indigo-dyed cotton. In addition to this I offered as a bribe one of my handsome Abyssinian shirts with a fine silk fringe, made at Aden, to be received by the man Beuh on the day of entering the Gerad's village.

I arose early in the next morning, having been promised by the Abbans grand sport in the Harawwah valley. The Somal had already divided the elephants' spoils: they were to claim the hero's feather, I was to receive two-thirds of the ivory—nothing remained to be done but the killing. After sundry pretences and prayers for delay, Beuh saddled his hack, the Hammal mounted one mule, a stout-hearted Bedouin called Fahi took a second, and we started to find the herds. The End of Time lagged in the rear: the reflection that a mule cannot outrun an elephant, made him look so ineffably miserable, that I sent him back to the kraal. 'Dost thou believe me to be a coward, O Pilgrim?' thereupon exclaimed the Mullah, waxing bold in the very joy of his heart. 'Of a truth I do!' was my reply. Nothing abashed, he hammered his mule with heel, and departed ejaculating, 'What hath man but a single life? and he who throweth it away, what is he but a fool?' Then we advanced with cocked guns, Beuh singing, Boanerges-like, the Song of the Elephant.

In the Somali country, as amongst the Kafirs, after murdering a man or boy, the death of an elephant is considered *the* act of heroism: most tribes wear for it the hair-feather and the ivory bracelet. Some hunters, like the Bushmen of the Cape, kill the Titan of the forests with barbed darts carrying Waba-poison. The general way of hunting resembles that of the Abyssinian Agageers described by Bruce. One man mounts a white pony, and galloping before the elephant, induces him, as he readily does—firearms being unknown—to charge and 'chivy'. The rider directs his course along, and close to, some bush, where a comrade is concealed; and the latter, as the animal passes at speed, cuts the back sinew of the hind leg, where in the human subject the tendon Achilles would be, with a sharp broad and heavy knife. This wound at first occasions little inconvenience: presently the elephant, fancying, it is supposed, that a thorn has stuck in his foot, stamps violently, and rubs the scratch till the sinew is fairly divided. The animal, thus disabled, is left to perish wretchedly of hunger and thirst: the tail, as amongst the Kafirs, is cut off to serve as trophy, and the ivories are removed when loosened by decomposition. In this part of Africa the elephant is never tamed.

For six hours we rode the breadth of the Harawwah Valley: it was covered with wild vegetation, and surface-drains, that carry off the surplus of the hills enclosing it. In some places the torrent beds had cut twenty feet into the soil. The banks were fringed with milk-bush and Asclepias, the Armo-creeper, a variety of thorns, and especially the yellow-berried Jujube: here numberless birds followed bright-winged butterflies, and the 'Shaykhs of the Blind', as the people call the black fly, settled in swarms upon our hands and faces as we rode by. The higher ground was overgrown with a kind of cactus, which here becomes a tree, forming shady avenues. Its quadrangular fleshy branches of emerald green, sometimes forty feet high, support upon their summits large round bunches of a bright crimson berry: when the plantation is close, domes of extreme beauty appear scattered over the surface of the country. This 'Hassadin' abounds in burning milk, and the Somal look downwards when passing under its branches: the elephant is said to love it, and in many places the trees were torn to pieces by hungry trunks. The nearest approaches to game were the last year's earths; likely places, however, shady trees and green thorns near water, were by no means uncommon. When we reached the valley's southern wall, Beuh informed us that we might ride all day, if we pleased, with the same result. At Zayla I had been informed that elephants are 'thick as sand' in Harawwah: even the Gudabirsi, when at a distance, declared that they fed there like sheep, and, after our failure, swore that they had killed thirty but last year. The animals were probably in the high Harirah Valley, and would be driven downwards by the cold at a later period: some future Gordon Cumming may therefore succeed where the Hajj Abdullah notably failed.*

On the 15th December I persuaded the valiant Beuh, with his two brothers and his bluff cousin Fahi, to cross the valley with us. After recovering a mule which had strayed five miles back to the well, and composing sundry quarrels between Shehrazade, whose swains had detained her from camel-loading, and the Kalendar whose one eye flashed with indignation at her conduct, we set out in a southerly direction. An hour's march brought us to an open space surrounded by thin thorn forest: in the centre is an ancient grave, about which are performed the equestrian games when the turban of the Ugaz has been bound under the Holy Tree. Shepherds issued from the bush to stare at us as we passed, and stretched forth the hand for 'Bori': the maidens tripped forwards exclaiming, 'Come, girls, let us look at this prodigy!' and they never withheld an answer if civilly addressed. Many of them were grown up, and not a few were old maids, the result of the tribe's isolation; for here, as in Somaliland generally, the union of cousins is abhorred. The ground of the valley is a stiff clay, sprinkled with pebbles of primitive formation: the hills are mere rocks, and the torrent banks with strata of small stones, showed a water-mark varying from ten to fifteen feet in height: in these fiumaras we saw frequent traces of the Adler-game, deer, and hog. At 1 p.m. our camels and mules were watered at wells in a broad wady called Jannah-Gaban or the Little Garden; its course, I was told, lies northwards through the Harawwah Valley to the Odla and Waruf, two depressions, in the Wayma country near Tajjurrah. About half an hour afterwards we arrived at a deserted sheepfold distant six miles from our last station. After unloading we repaired to a neighbouring well, and found the water so hard that it raised lumps like nettle stings in the bather's skin. The only remedy for the evil is an unguent of oil or butter, a

* Burton (Hajj Abdullah) arrived in India to serve in the army at much the same time as did Gordon Cumming, who retired after a few years and in 1850 published *Five Years of a Hunter's Life in the Far Interior of South Africa*, John Murray, 1850.—Ed.

precaution which should never be neglected by the African traveller. At first the sensation of grease annoys, after a few days it is forgotten, and at last the 'pat of butter' is expected as pleasantly as the pipe or the cup of coffee. It prevents the skin from chaps and sores, obviates the evil effects of heat, cold, and wet, and neutralizes the Proteus-like malaria poison. The Somal never fail to anoint themselves when they can afford ghi, and the Bedouin is at the summit of his bliss, when sitting in the blazing sun, or—heat acts upon these people as upon serpents—with his back opposite a roaring fire, he is being smeared, rubbed, and kneaded by a companion.

My guides, fearing lions and hyenas, would pass the night inside a foul sheepfold: I was not without difficulty persuaded to join them. At eight next morning we set out through an uninteresting thorn-bush towards one of those Têtes or isolated hills which form admirable bench-marks in the Somali country. 'Koralay', a term corresponding with our Saddle-back, exactly describes its shape: pommel and crupper, in the shape of two huge granite boulders, were all complete, and between them was a depression for a seat. As day advanced the temperature changed from 50° to a maximum of 121°. After marching about five miles, we halted in a broad water-course called Gallajab, the 'Plentiful Water': there we bathed, and dined on an excellent camel which had broken its leg by falling from a bank.

Resuming our march at 5 p.m., we travelled over ascending ground which must be most fertile after rain: formerly it belonged to the Girhi, and the Gudabirsi boasted loudly of their conquest. After an hour's march we reached the base of Koralay, upon whose lower slopes appeared a pair of the antelopes called Alakud: they are tame, easily shot, and eagerly eaten by the Bedouin. Another hour of slow travelling brought us to a broad fiumara with high banks of stiff clay thickly wooded and showing a water-mark eighteen feet above the sand. The guides named these wells Agjogsi, probably a generic term signifying that water is standing close by. Crossing the fiumara we ascended a hill, and found upon the summit a large kraal alive with heads of kine. The inhabitants flocked out to stare at us and the women uttered cries of wonder. I advanced towards the prettiest, and fired my rifle by way of salute over her head. The people delighted exclaimed, Mod! Mod!—'Honour to thee!'—and we replied with shouts of Kulliban—'May heaven aid ye!' At 5 p.m., after five miles' march, the camels were unloaded in a deserted kraal whose high fence denoted danger of wild beasts. The cowherds bade us beware of lions: but a day before a girl had been dragged out of her hut, and Moslem burial could be given to only one of her legs. A Bedouin named Uddao, whom we hired as mule-keeper, was ordered to spend the night singing, and, as is customary with Somali watchmen, to address and answer himself dialogue-wise with a different voice, in order to persuade thieves that several men are on the alert. He was a spectacle of wildness as he sat before the blazing fire—his joy by day, his companion and protector in the shades, the only step made by him in advance of his brethren the Cynocephali. [Dog-faced baboons.]

We were detained four days at Agjogsi by the non-appearance of the Gerad Adan: this delay gave me an opportunity of ascending to the summit of Koralay, the Saddleback, which lay about a mile north of our encampment. As we threaded the rocks and hollows of the side we came upon dens strewed with cows' bones, and proving by a fresh taint that the tenants had lately quitted them. In this country the lion is seldom seen unless surprised asleep in his lair of thicket: during my journey, although at times the roaring was heard all night, I saw but one. The people have a superstition that the king of beasts will not attack a single traveller, because such a person, they say, slew the mother of all the lions: except in darkness or during violent storms, which excite the fiercer carnivors, he is a timid animal, much less feared by the people than the angry and agile leopard. Unable to run with rapidity when pressed by hunger, he pursues a party of travellers as stealthily as a cat, and arrived within distance, springs, strikes down the hindermost, and carries him away to the bush.

From the summit of Koralay, we had a fair view of the surrounding country. At least forty kraals, many of them deserted, lay within the range of sight. On all sides except the north-west and south-east was a mass of sombre rock and granite hill: the course of the valleys between the several ranges was denoted by a lively green, and the plains scattered in patches over the landscape shone with dull yellow, the effect of clay and stubble, whilst a light mist encased the prospect in a circlet of blue and silver. Here the End of Time conceived the jocose idea of crowning me king of the country. With loud cries of Buh! Buh! Buh! he showered leaves of a gum tree and a little water from a prayer bottle over my head, and then with all solemnity bound on the turban. It is perhaps fortunate that this facetiousness was not witnessed: a crowd of Bedouin assembled below the hill, suspecting as usual some magical practices, and had they known the truth, our journey might have ended abruptly. Descending, I found porcupines' quills in abundance,* and shot a rock pigeon called Elal-jog—the 'Dweller at wells'. At the foot a 'Baune' or Hyrax Abyssinicus, resembling the Coney of Palestine, was observed at its favourite pastime of sunning itself upon the rocks.

On the evening of the 20th December the mounted messenger returned, after a six hours' hard ride, bringing back unopened the letter addressed by me to the Gerad, and a private message from their sister to the sons of White Ali, advising them not to advance. Ensued terrible palavers. It appeared that the Gerad was upon the point of mounting horse, when his subjects swore him to remain and settle a dispute with the Amir of Harar. Our Abbans, however, withdrew their hired camels, positively refused to accompany us, and Beuh privily informed the End of Time that I had acquired through the land the evil reputation of killing everything, from an elephant to a bird in the air. One of the younger brethren, indeed, declared that we were the forerunners of good, and if the Gerad harmed a hair of our heads, he would slaughter every Girhi under the sun. We had, however, learned properly to appreciate such vaunts, and the End of Time drily answered that their sayings were honey but their doings myrrh. Being a low-caste and a shameless tribe, they did not reply to our reproaches. At last, a manœuvre was successful: Beuh and his brethren, who squatted like sulky children in different places, were dismissed with thanks—we proposed placing ourselves under the safeguard of Gerad Hirsi, the Berteri chief. This would have thrown the protection-price, originally intended for their brother-in-law, into the hands of a rival, and had the effect of altering their resolve. Presently we were visited by two Widad or hedge-priests, Ao Samattar and Ao Nur, both half-witted fellows, but active and kind-hearted. The former wore a dirty turban, the latter a Zabid cap, a wicker-work calotte, composed of the palm leaf's mid-rib: they carried dressed goatskins, as prayer carpets, over their right shoulders dangled huge wooden ink bottles with Lauh or wooden tablets for writing talismans,† and from the left hung a greasy bag, containing a tattered copy of the Koran and a small MS. of prayers. They read tolerably, but did not understand Arabic, and I presented them with cheap Bombay lithographs of the Holy Book. The number of these idlers increased as we approached Harar, the Alma Mater of

---

* The Somal call it Hiddik or Anukub; the quills are used as head scratchers, and are exported to Aden for sale.

† These charms are washed off and drunk by the people: an economical proceeding where paper is scarce.

Somaliland: the people seldom listen to their advice, but on this occasion Ao Samattar succeeded in persuading the valiant Beuh that the danger was visionary. Soon afterwards rode up to our kraal three cavaliers, who proved to be sons of Adam, the future Ugaz of the Gudabirsi tribe: this chief had fully recognized the benefits of re-opening to commerce a highway closed by their petty feuds, and sent to say that, in consequence of his esteem for the Hajj Sharmakay, if the sons of White Ali feared to escort us, he in person would do the deed. Thereupon Beuh became a 'Gesi' or hero, as the End of Time ironically called him: he sent back his brethren with their horses and camels, and valorously prepared to act as our escort. I tauntingly asked him what he now thought of the danger. For all reply he repeated the words, which the Bedouin—who, like the Arabs, have a holy horror of towns —had been dinning daily into my ears, 'They will spoil that white skin of thine at Harar!'

At 3 p.m., on the 21st December, we started in a westerly direction through a gap in the hills, and presently turned to the south-west, over rapidly rising ground, thickly inhabited, and covered with flocks and herds. About 5 p.m., after marching two miles, we raised our wigwam outside a populous kraal, a sheep was provided by the hospitality of Ao Samattar, and we sat deep into the night enjoying a genial blaze.

Early the next morning we had hoped to advance: water, however, was wanting, and a small caravan was slowly gathering; these details delayed us till 4 p.m. Our line lay westward, over rising ground, to-wards a conspicuous conical hill called Konti. Nothing could be worse for camels than the rough ridges at the foot of the mountain, full of thickets, cut by deep fiumaras, and abounding in dangerous water-courses: the burdens slipped now backwards then forwards, sometimes the load was almost dragged off by thorns, and at last we were obliged to leave one animal to follow slowly in the rear. After creeping on two miles, we bivouacked in a deserted cow-kraal—*sub dio*, as it was warm under the hills. That evening our party was increased by a Gudabirsi maiden in search of a husband: she was surlily received by Shehra-zade and Deenarzade, but we insisted upon her being fed, and super-intended the operation. Her style of eating was peculiar; she licked up the rice from the hollow of her hand. Next morning she was carried away in our absence, greatly against her will, by some kinsmen who had followed her.

And now, bidding adieu to the Gudabirsi, I will briefly sketch the tribe.

The Gudabirsi, or Gudabursi, derive themselves from Dirr and Aydur, thus claiming affinity with the Eesa; others declare their tribe to be an offshoot from the Bahgoba clan of the Habr Awal, originally settled near Jabal Almis, and Bulhar, on the sea-shore. The Somal unhesitatingly stigmatize them as a bastard and ignoble race: a noted genealogist once informed me, that they were little better than Midgans or serviles. Their ancestors' mother, it is said, could not name the father of her child: some proposed to slay it, others advocated its preservation, saying, 'Perhaps we shall increase by it.' Hence the name of the tribe.*

The Gudabirsi are such inveterate liars that I could fix them no number between 3,000 and 10,000. They own the rough and rolling ground diversified with thorny hill and grassy vale, above the first or seaward range of mountains; and they have extended their lands by conquest towards Harar, being now bounded in that direction by the Marar Prairie. As usual, they are subdivided into a multitude of clans.[4]

In appearance the Gudabirsi are decidedly superior to their limitrophes the Eesa. I have seen handsome faces amongst the men as well as the women. Some approach closely to the Caucasian type: one old man, with olive-coloured skin, bald brow, and white hair curling round his temples, and occiput, exactly resembled an Anglo-Indian veteran. Generally, however, the prognathous mouth betrays an African origin, and chewing tobacco mixed with ashes stains the teeth, blackens the gums, and mottles the lips. The complexion is the Abyssinian *Café au lait*, contrasting strongly with the sooty skins of the coast; and the hair, plentifully anointed with rancid butter, hangs from the head in lank corkscrews the colour of a Russian pointer's coat. The figure is rather squat, but broad and well set.

The Gudabirsi are as turbulent and unmanageable, though not so bloodthirsty, as the Eesa. Their late chief, Ugaz Roblay of the Bayt Samattar sept, left children who could not hold their own: the turban was at once claimed by a rival branch, the Rer Abdillah, and a civil war ensued. The lovers of legitimacy will rejoice to hear that when I left the country, Galla, son of the former Prince Rainy, was likely to come to his own again.

The stranger's life is comparatively safe amongst this tribe: as long as he feeds and fees them, he may even walk about unarmed. They are, however, liars even amongst the Somal, Bobadils amongst boasters,

* 'Birsan', in Somali, meaning to increase.

inveterate thieves, and importunate beggars. The smooth-spoken fellows seldom betray emotion except when cloth or tobacco is concerned; 'dissimulation is as natural to them as breathing', and I have called one of their chiefs a 'dog' without exciting his indignation.

The commerce of these wild regions is at present in a depressed state; were the roads safe, traffic with the coast would be considerable. The profit on hides, for instance, at Aden, would be at least cent. per cent.: the way, however, is dangerous, and detention is frequent, consequently the gain will not remunerate for risk and loss of time. No operation can be undertaken in a hurry, consequently demand cannot readily be supplied. What Laing applies to Western, may be repeated of Eastern Africa: 'the endeavour to accelerate an undertaking is almost certain to occasion its failure'. Nowhere is patience more wanted, in order to perform perfect work.

The wealth of the Gudabirsi consists principally in cattle, peltries, hides, gums, and ghi. The asses are dun-coloured, small, and weak; the camels large, loose, and lazy; the cows are pretty animals, with small humps, long horns resembling the Damara cattle, and in the grazing season with plump, well-rounded limbs; there is also a bigger breed, not unlike that of Tuscany. The standard is the Tobe of coarse canvas; worth about three shillings at Aden, here it doubles in value. The price of a good camel varies from six to eight cloths; one Tobe buys a two-year-old heifer, three, a cow between three and four years old. A ewe costs half a cloth: the goat, although the flesh is according to the Somal nutritive, whilst 'mutton is disease', is a little cheaper than the sheep. Hides and peltries are usually collected at and exported from Harar; on the coast they are rubbed over with salt, and in this state carried to Aden. Cows' skins fetch a quarter of a dollar, or about one shilling in cloth, and two dollars are the extreme price for the Kurjah or score of goats' skins. The people of the interior have a rude way of tanning; they macerate the hide, dress, and stain it of a deep calf-skin colour with the bark of a tree called Jirmah, and lastly the leather is softened with the hand. The principal gum is the Adad or Acacia Arabica: foreign merchants purchase it for about half a dollar per Farasilah of twenty pounds: cow's and sheep's butter may fetch a dollar's worth of cloth for the measure of thirty-two pounds. This great article of commerce is good and pure in the country, whereas at Berbera, the Habr Awal adulterate it, previous to exportation, with melted sheeps' tails.

The principal wants of the country which we have traversed are coarse cotton cloth, Surat tobacco, beads, and indigo-dyed stuffs for women's coifs. The people would also be grateful for any improvement in their breed of horses, and when at Aden I thought of taking with me some old Arab stallions as presents to chiefs. Fortunately the project fell to the ground: a strange horse of unusual size and beauty, in these regions, would be stolen at the end of the first march.

The Oryx Head.

VII

From the Marar Prairie to Harar

EARLY ON THE 23RD DECEMBER assembled the caravan, which we were destined to escort across the Marar Prairie. Upon this neutral ground the Esa, Berteri, and Habr Awal meet to rob and plunder unhappy travellers. The Somal shuddered at the sight of a wayfarer, who rushed into our encampment *in cuerpo*,* having barely run away with his life. Not that our caravan carried much to lose—a few hides and pots of clarified butter, to be exchanged for the Holcus grain of the Girhi cultivators—still the smallest contributions are thankfully received by these plunderers. Our material consisted of four or five half-starved camels, about fifty donkeys with ears cropped as a mark, and their eternal accompaniments in Somaliland, old women. The latter seemed to be selected for age, hideousness, and strength: all day they bore their babes smothered in hides upon their backs, and they carried heavy burdens apparently without fatigue. Amongst them was a Bedouin widow, known by her 'Wer', a strip of the inner bark of a tree tied round the greasy fillet.† We were accompanied by three

* Naked.

† It is worn for a year, during which modest women will not marry. Some tribes confine the symbol to widowhood, others extend it to all male relations; a strip of white cotton, or even a white fillet, instead of the usual blue cloth, is used by the more civilized.

149

Widads, provided with all the instruments of their craft, and uncommonly tiresome companions. They recited Koran *à tort et à travers:* at every moment they proposed Fatihahs, the name of Allah was perpetually upon their lips, and they discussed questions of divinity, like Gil Blas and his friends, with a violence bordering upon frenzy. One of them was celebrated for his skill in the 'Fal', or Omens: he was constantly consulted by my companions, and informed them that we had nought to fear except from wild beasts. The prediction was a good hit: I must own, however, that it was not communicated to me before fulfilment.

At half past 6 a.m., we began our march over rough and rising ground, a network of thorns and water-courses, and presently entered a stony gap between two ranges of hills. On our right was a conical peak, bearing the remains of buildings upon its summit. Here, said Abtidon, a wild Gudabirsi hired to look after our mules, rests the venerable Shaykh Samawai. Of old, a number of wells existed in the gaps between the hills: these have disappeared with those who drank of them.

Presently we entered the Barr or Prairie of Marar, one of the long strips of plain which diversify the Somali country. Its breadth, bounded on the east by the rolling ground over which we had passed, on the west by Gurays, a range of cones offshooting from the highlands of Harar, is about twenty-seven miles, the general course is north and south: in the former direction, it belongs to the Eesa: in the latter may be seen the peaks of Kadau and Madir, the property of the Habr Awal tribes; and along these ranges it extends, I was told, towards Ogadayn. The surface of the plain is gently rolling ground: the black earth, filled with the holes of small beasts, would be most productive, and the outer coat is an expanse of tall, waving, sunburnt grass, so unbroken, that from a distance it resembles the nap of yellow velvet. In the frequent Wadys, which carry off the surplus rain of the hills, scrub and thorn trees grow in dense thickets, and the grass is temptingly green. Yet the land lies fallow: water and fuel are scarce at a distance from the hills, and the wildest Bedouin dare not front the danger of foraging parties, the fatal heats of day, and the killing colds of night. On the edges of the plain, however, are frequent vestiges of deserted kraals.

About midday, we crossed a depression in the centre, where Acacias supplied us with gum for luncheon, and sheltered flocks of antelope. I endeavoured to shoot the white-tailed Sig, and the large dun Oryx; but the *brouhaha* of the caravan prevented execution. Shortly afterwards we came upon patches of holcus, which had grown wild, from seeds scattered by travellers. This was the first sight of grain that gladdened my eyes since I left Bombay: the grave of the First Murderer never knew a Triptolemus,* and Zayla is a barren flat of sand. My companions eagerly devoured the pith of this African 'sweet cane', despite its ill reputation for causing fever. I followed their example, and found it almost as good as bad sugar. The Bedouin loaded their spare asses with the bitter gourd, called Ubbah; externally it resembles the water melon, and becomes, when shaped, dried, and smoked, the wickerwork of the Somal, and the pottery of more civilized people.

Towards evening, as the setting sun sank slowly behind the distant western hills, the colour of the Prairie changed from glaring yellow to a golden hue, mantled with a purple flush inexpressibly lovely. The animals of the waste began to appear. Shy lynxes and jackals fattened by many sheeps' tails,† warned my companions that fierce beasts were nigh, ominous anecdotes were whispered, and I was told that a caravan had lately lost nine asses by lions. As night came on, the Bedouin Kafilah, being lightly loaded, preceded us, and our tired camels lagged far behind. We were riding in rear to prevent straggling, when suddenly my mule, the hindermost, pricked his ears uneasily, and attempted to turn his head. Looking backwards, I distinguished the form of a large animal following us with quick and stealthy strides. My companions would not fire, thinking it was a man: at last a rifle-ball, pinging through the air—the moon was too young for correct shooting—put to flight a huge lion. The terror excited by this sort of an adventure was comical to look upon: the valiant Beuh, who, according to himself, had made his *preuves* in a score of foughten fields, threw his arms in the air, wildly shouting Libah! Libah!!—the lion! the lion!! —and nothing else was talked of that evening.

The ghostly western hills seemed to recede as we advanced over the endless rolling plain. Presently the ground became broken and stony, the mules stumbled in deep holes, and the camels could scarcely crawl along. As we advanced, our Widads, who poor devils! had been 'roasted' by the women all day on account of their poverty, began to recite the Koran with might, in gratitude for having escaped many

* Cain is said to repose under Jabal Shamsan at Aden—an appropriate sepulchre.

† In the Somali country, as in Kafirland, the Duwao or jackal is peculiarly bold and fierce. Disdaining garbage, he carries off lambs and kids, and fastens upon a favourite *friandise*, the sheep's tail: the victim runs away in terror, and unless the jackal be driven off by dogs, leaves a delicate piece of fat behind it.

perils. Night deepening, our attention was rivetted by a strange spectacle; a broad sheet of bright blaze, reminding me of Hanno's fiery river,* swept apparently down a hill, and, according to my companions, threatened the whole prairie. These accidents are common: a huntsman burns a tree for honey, or cooks his food in the dry grass, the wind rises and the flames spread far and wide. On this occasion no accident occurred; the hills, however, smoked like a Solfatara for two days.

About 9 p.m. we heard voices, and I was told to discharge my rifle lest the kraal be closed to us; in due time we reached a long, low, dark line of sixty or seventy huts, disposed in a circle, so as to form a fence, with a few bushes—thorns being hereabouts rare—in the gaps between the abodes. The people, a mixture of Girhi and Gudabirsi Bedouin, swarmed out to gratify their curiosity, but we were in no humour for long conversations. Our luggage was speedily disposed in a heap near the kraal, the mules and camels were tethered for the night, then, supperless and shivering with cold, we crept under our mats and fell asleep. That day we had ridden nearly fifteen hours; our halting place lay about thirty miles from, and 240° south-west of, Koralay.

After another delay, and a second vain message to the Gerad Adan, about noon appeared that dignitary's sixth wife, sister to the valiant Beuh. Her arrival disconcerted my companions, who were too proud to be protected by a woman. 'Dahabo', however, relieved their anxiety by informing us that the Gerad had sent his eldest son Shirwa, as escort. This princess was a gipsy-looking dame, coarsely-dressed, about thirty years old, with a gay leer, a jaunty demeanour, and the reputation of being 'fast'; she showed little shamefacedness when I saluted her, and received with noisy joy the appropriate present of a new and handsome Tobe. About 4 p.m. returned our second messenger, bearing with him a reproving message from the Gerad, for not visiting him without delay; in token of sincerity, he forwarded his baton, a knobstick about two feet long, painted in rings of Cutch colours, red, black, and yellow alternately, and garnished on the summit with a ball of similar material.

At dawn on the 26th December, mounted upon a little pony, came Shirwa, heir presumptive to the Gerad Adan's knobstick. His father had sent him to us three days before, but he feared the Gudabirsi as much as the Gudabirsi feared him, and he probably hung about our

---

* The well-known Carthaginian navigator who sailed along the West coast of Africa in the fifth century B.C.; the phenomenon of the 'fiery river' was later discovered to be due to a series of bush fires along the Gambia river.—Ed.

camp till certain that it was safe to enter. We received him politely, and he in acknowledgment positively declared that Beuh should not return before eating honey in his cottage. Our Abban's heroism now became infectious. Even the End of Time, whose hot valour had long since fallen below zero, was inspired by the occasion, and recited, as usual with him in places and at times of extreme safety, the Arabs' warrior lines—

> I have crossed the steed since my eyes saw light,
> I have fronted death till he feared my sight,
> And the cleaving of helm and the riving of mail
> Were the dreams of my youth—are my manhood's delight.

As we had finished loading, a mule's bridle was missed. Shirwa ordered instant restitution to his father's stranger, on the ground that all the property now belonged to the Gerad; and we, by no means idle, fiercely threatened to bewitch the kraal. The article was presently found laid by, on a hedge. This was the first and last case of theft which occurred to us in the Somali country;—I have travelled through most civilized lands, and have lost more.

At 8 a.m. we marched towards the north-west, along the southern base of the Gurays hills, and soon arrived at the skirt of the prairie, where a well-trodden path warned us that we were about to quit the desert. After advancing six miles in line we turned to the right, and recited a Fatihah over a heap of rough stones, where, shadowed by venerable trees, lie the remains of the great Shaykh Abd al-Malik. A little beyond this spot, rises suddenly from the plain a mass of castellated rock, the subject of many a wild superstition. Caravans always encamp beneath it, as whoso sleeps upon the summit loses his senses to evil spirits. At some future day Harar will be destroyed, and 'Jannah Siri' will become a flourishing town. We ascended it, and found no life but hawks, coneys, an owl, and a graceful species of black eagle; there were many traces of buildings, walls, ruined houses, and wells, whilst the sides and summit were tufted with venerable sycamores. This act was an imprudence; the Bedouin at once declared that we were 'prospecting' for a fort, and the evil report preceded us to Harar.

After a mile's march from Jannah Siri, we crossed a ridge of rising ground, and suddenly, as though by magic, the scene shifted.

Before us lay a little Alp; the second step of the Æthiopian Highland. Around were high and jagged hills, their sides black with the Saj* and

* The Arabs apply this term to teak.

Somali pine,* and their upper brows veiled with a thin growth of cactus. Beneath was a deep valley, in the midst of which ran a serpentine of shining waters, the gladdest spectacle we had yet witnessed: further in front, masses of hill rose abruptly from shady valleys, encircled on the far horizon by a straight blue line of ground, resembling a distant sea. Behind us glared the desert: we had now reached the outskirts of civilization, where man, abandoning his flocks and herds, settles, cultivates, and attends to the comforts of life.

The fields are either terraces upon the hill slopes or the sides of valleys, divided by flowery hedges with lanes between, not unlike those of rustic England; and on a nearer approach the daisy, the thistle, and the sweet briar pleasantly affected my European eyes. The villages are no longer movable: the Kraal and wigwam are replaced by the Gambisa or bell-shaped hut of Middle Africa, circular cottages of holcus wattle, covered with coarse dab and surmounted by a stiff, conical, thatch roof, above which appears the central supporting post, crowned with a gourd or ostrich egg. A strong abattis of thorns protects these settlements, which stud the hills in all directions: near most of them are clumps of tall trees, to the southern sides of which are hung, like birdcages, long cylinders of matting, the hives of these regions. Yellow crops of holcus rewarded the peasant's toil: in some places the long stems tied in bunches below the ears as piled muskets, stood ready for the reaper; in others, the barer ground showed that the task was done. The boys sat perched upon reed platforms in the trees, and with loud shouts drove away thieving birds, whilst their fathers cut the crop with diminutive sickles, or thrashed heaps of straw with rude flails, or winnowed grain by tossing it with a flat wooden shovel against the wind. The women husked the pineapple-formed heads in mortars composed of a hollowed trunk,† smeared the threshing floor with cow-dung and water to defend it from insects, piled the holcus heads into neat yellow heaps, spanned and crossed by streaks of various colours, brick-red and brownish-purple,‡ and stacked the Karbi or straw, which was surrounded like the grain with thorn, as a defence against the wild hog.

* The Dayyib of the Somal, and the Sinaubar of the Arabs; its line of growth is hereabouts an altitude of 5,000 feet.

† Equally simple are the other implements. The plough, which in Eastern Africa has passed the limits of Egypt, is still the crooked tree of all primitive people, drawn by oxen; and the hoe is a wooden blade inserted into a knobbed handle.

‡ It is afterwards stored in deep dry holes, which are carefully covered to keep out rats and insects; thus the grain is preserved undamaged for three or four years. Like the Matamores, or underground caves of Berbers, and the grain stores of Leghorn; cachettes or siloes of Algerines. When opened the grain must be eaten quickly.

All seemed to consider it a labour of love: the harvest-home song sounded pleasantly to our ears, and, contrasting with the silent desert, the hum of man's habitation was music.

Descending the steep slope, we reposed, after a seven miles' march, on the banks of a bright rivulet, which bisects the Kobbo or valley: it runs according to my guides, from the north towards Ogadayn, and the direction is significant—about Harar I found neither hill nor stream trending from east to west. The people of the Kutti* flocked out to gaze upon us: they were unarmed, and did not, like the Bedouin, receive us with cries of 'Bori'. During the halt, we bathed in the waters, upon whose banks were a multitude of huge Mantidæ, pink and tender green. Returning to the camels, I shot a kind of crow, afterwards frequently seen. It is about three times the size of our English bird, of a bluish-black with a snow-white poll, and a beak of unnatural proportions: the quantity of lead which it carried off surprised me. A number of Widads assembled to greet us, and some Habr Awal, who were returning with a caravan, gave us the salaam, and called my people cousins. 'Verily,' remarked the Hammal, 'amongst friends we cut one another's throats; amongst enemies we become sons of uncles!'

At 3 p.m. we pursued our way over rising ground, dotted with granite blocks fantastically piled, and everywhere in sight of fields and villages and flowing water. A furious wind was blowing, and the End of Time quoted the Somali proverb, 'heat hurts, but cold kills': the camels were so fatigued, and the air became so raw, that after an hour and a half's march we planted our wigwams near a village distant about seven miles from the Gurays Hills. Till late at night we were kept awake by the crazy Widads: Ao Samattar had proposed the casuistical question, 'Is it lawful to pray upon a mountain when a plain is at hand?' Some took the pro, others the contra, and the wordy battle raged with uncommon fury.

On Wednesday morning at half past seven we started down hill towards 'Wilensi', a small table-mountain, at the foot of which we expected to find the Gerad Adan awaiting us in one of his many houses, crossed a fertile valley, and ascended another steep slope by a bad and stony road. Passing the home of Shirwa, who vainly offered hospitality, we toiled onwards, and after a mile and a half's march, which occupied at least two hours, our wayworn beasts arrived at the Gerad's village. On inquiry, it proved that the chief, who was engaged in selecting two horses and two hundred cows, the price of blood claimed

* This word is applied to the cultivated districts, the granaries of Somaliland.

by the Amir of Harar, for the murder of a citizen, had that day removed to Sagharrah, another settlement.

As we entered the long straggling village of Wilensi, our party was divided by the Gerad's two wives. The Hammal, the Kalendar, Shehrazade and Deenarzade, remained with Beuh and his sister in her Gurgi, whilst Long Gulad, the End of Time, and I were conducted to the cottage of the Gerad's prettiest wife, Sudiyah. She was a tall woman, with a light complexion, handsomely dressed in a large Harar Tobe, with silver earrings, and the kind of necklace called Jilbah or Kardas.* The Geradah (princess) at once ordered our hides to be spread in a comfortable part of the hut, and then supplied us with food—boiled beef, pumpkin, and Jowari cakes. During the short time spent in that Gambisa, I had an opportunity, dear L., of seeing the manners and customs of the settled Somal.

The interior of the cottage is simple. Entering the door, a single plank with pins for hinges fitted into sockets above and below the lintel—in fact, as artless a contrivance as ever seen in Spain or Corsica —you find a space, divided by dwarf walls of wattle and dab into three compartments, for the men, women, and cattle. The horses and cows, tethered at night on the left of the door, fill the cottage with the where-withal to pass many a *nuit blanche*: the wives lie on the right, near a large fireplace of stones and raised clay, and the males occupy the most comfortable part, opposite to and farthest from the entrance. The thatched ceiling shines jetty with smoke, which when intolerable is allowed to escape by a diminutive window: this seldom happens, for smoke, like grease and dirt, keeping man warm, is enjoyed by savages. Equally simply is the furniture: the stem of a tree, with branches hacked into pegs, supports the shields, the assegais are planted against the wall, and divers bits of wood, projecting from the sides and the central roof-tree of the cottage, are hung with clothes and other articles that attract white ants. Gourds smoked inside, and coffee cups of coarse black Harar pottery, with deep wooden platters, and prettily carved spoons of the same material, compose the household supellex. The inmates are the Geradah and her baby, Siddik, a Galla serf, the slave girls and sundry Somal: thus we hear at all times three languages† spoken within the walls.

Long before dawn the good wife rises, wakens her handmaidens, lights the fire, and prepares for the Afur or morning meal. The quern

---

* It is a string of little silver bells and other ornaments made by the Arabs at Berbera.
† Harari, Somali, and Galla, besides Arabic, and other more civilized dialects.

is here unknown. A flat, smooth, oval slab, weighing about fifteen pounds, and a stone roller six inches in diameter, worked with both hands, and the weight of the body kneeling ungracefully upon it on 'all fours', are used to triturate the holcus grain. At times water must be sprinkled over the meal, until a finely powdered paste is ready for the oven: thus several hours' labour is required to prepare a few pounds of bread. About 6 a.m. there appears a substantial breakfast of roast beef and mutton, with scones of Jowari grain, the whole drenched in broth. Of the men few perform any ablutions, but all use the tooth stick before sitting down to eat. After the meal some squat in the sun, others transact business, and drive their cattle to the bush till 11 a.m., the dinner hour. There is no variety in the repasts, which are always flesh and holcus: these people despise fowls, and consider vegetables food for cattle. During the day there is no privacy; men, women, and children enter in crowds, and will not be driven away by the Geradah, who inquires screamingly if they come to stare at a baboon. My kettle especially excites their surprise; some opine that it is an ostrich, others, a serpent: Sudiyah, however, soon discovered its use, and begged irresistibly for the unique article. Throughout the day her slave girls are busied in grinding, cooking, and quarrelling with dissonant voices: the men have little occupation beyond chewing tobacco, chatting, and having their wigs frizzled by a professional coiffeur. In the evening the horses and cattle return home to be milked and stabled: this operation concluded, all apply themselves to supper with a will. They sleep but little, and sit deep into the night trimming the fire, and conversing merrily over their cups of Farshu or millet beer.* I tried this mixture several times, and found it detestable: the taste is sour, and it flies directly to the head, in consequence of being mixed with some poisonous bark. It is served up in gourd bottles upon a basket of holcus heads, and strained through a pledget of cotton fixed across the narrow mouth, into cups of the same primitive material: the drinkers sit around their liquor, and their hilarity argues its intoxicating properties. In the morning they arise with headaches and heavy eyes; but these symptoms, which we, an industrious race, deprecate, are not disliked by the Somal—they promote sleep and give something to occupy the vacant mind. I usually slumber through the noise except when Ambar, a half caste Somali, returning from a trip to Harar, astounds

---

* In the Eastern World this well-known fermentation is generally called 'Buzah', whence the old German word 'büsen' and our 'booze'. The addition of a dose of garlic converts it into an emetic.

us with his *contes bleus*, or wild Abtidon howls forth some lay like this:—

I

'Tis joyesse all in Eesa's home!
  The fatted oxen bleed,
And slave girls range the pails of milk,
  And strain the golden mead.

II

'Tis joyesse all in Eesa's home!
  This day the Chieftain's pride
Shall join the song, the dance, the feast,
  And bear away a bride.

III

'He cometh not!' the father cried,
  Smiting with spear the wall;
'And yet he sent the ghostly man,
  Yestre'en before the fall!'

IV

'He cometh not!' the mother said,
  A tear stood in her eye;
'He cometh not, I dread, I dread,
  And yet I know not why.'

V

'He cometh not!' the maiden thought,
  Yet in her glance was light,
Soft as the flash in summer's eve
  Where sky and earth unite.

VI

The virgins, deck'd with tress and flower,
  Danced in the purple shade,
And not a soul, perchance, but wished
  Herself the chosen maid.

VII

The guests in groups sat gathering
  Where sunbeams warmed the air,
Some laughed the feasters' laugh, and some
  Wore the bent brow of care.

158

VIII

' 'Tis he!—'tis he! '—all anxious peer,
Towards the distant lea;
A courser feebly nears the throng—
Ah! 'tis his steed they see.

IX

The grief cry bursts from every lip,
Fear sits on every brow,
There's blood upon the courser's flank!—
Blood on the saddle bow!

X

' 'Tis he!—'tis he! '—all arm and run
Towards the Marar Plain,
Where a dark horseman rides the waste
With dust-cloud for a train.

XI

The horseman reins his foam-fleckt steed,
Leans on his broken spear,
Wipes his damp brow, and faint begins
To tell a tale of fear.

XII

'Where is my son?'—'Go seek him there,
Far on the Marar Plain,
Where vultures and hyenas hold
Their orgies o'er the slain.

XIII

'We took our arms, we saddled horse,
We rode the East countrie,
And drove the flocks and harried herds
Betwixt the hills and sea.

XIV

'We drove the flock across the hill,
The herd across the wold—
The poorest spearboy had returned
That day, a man of gold.

XV

'But Awal's children mann'd the vale
Where sweet the Arman flowers,
Their archers from each bush and tree
Rained shafts in venomed showers.

XVI

'Full fifty warriors bold and true
Fell as becomes the brave;
And whom the arrow spared, the spear
Reaped for the ravening grave.

XVII

'Friend of my youth! shall I remain
When ye are gone before?'
He drew the wood from out his side,
And loosed the crimson gore.

XVIII

Falling, he raised his broken spear.
Thrice wav'd it o'er his head,
Thrice raised the warrior's cry 'revenge!'—
His soul was with the dead.

XIX

Now, one by one, the wounded braves
Homeward were seen to wend,
Each holding on his saddle bow
A dead or dying friend.

XX

Two galliards bore the Eesa's son,
The corpse was stark and bare—
Low moaned the maid, the mother smote
Her breast in mute despair.

XXI

The father bent him o'er the dead,
The wounds were all before;
Again his brow, in sorrow clad,
The garb of gladness wore.

XXII

'Ho! sit ye down nor mourn for me,
Unto the guests he cried;
'My son a warrior's life hath lived
A warrior's death hath died.

XXIII

'His wedding and his funeral feast
Are one, so Fate hath said;
Death bore him from the brides of earth
The brides of Heaven to wed.'

XXIV

They drew their knives, they sat them down,
    And fed as warriors feed;
The flesh of sheep and beeves they ate,
    And quaffed the golden mead.

XXV

And Eesa sat between the prayers
    Until the fall of day,
When rose the guests and grasped their spears,
    And each man went his way.

XXVI

But in the morn arose the cry,
    For mortal spirit flown;
The father's mighty heart had burst
    With woe he might not own.

XXVII

On the high crest of yonder hill,
    They buried sire and son,
Grant, Allah! grant them Paradise—
    Gentles, my task is done!

Immediately after our arrival at Wilensi we sent Yusuf Dera, the Gerad's second son to summon his father. I had to compose many disputes between the Hammal and the End of Time: the latter was swelling with importance; he was now accredited ambassador from the Hajj to the Girhi chief, consequently he aimed at commanding the Caravan. We then made preparations for departure, in case of the Gerad being unable to escort us. Shehrazade and Deenarzade, hearing that the small-pox raged at Harar, and fearing for their charms, begged hard to be left behind: the Kalendar was directed, despite his manly objections, to remain in charge of these dainty dames. The valiant Beuh was dressed in the grand Tobe promised to him; as no consideration would induce him towards the city, he was dismissed with small presents, and an old Girhi Bedouin, generally known as Sa'id Wal, or Mad Sa'id, was chosen as our escort. Camels being unable to travel over these rough mountain paths, our weary brutes were placed for rest and pasture under the surveillance of Shirwa: and not wishing the trouble and delay of hiring asses, the only transport in this country, certain more-over that our goods were safer here than nearer Harar, we selected the most necessary objects, and packed them in a pair of small leathern saddlebags which could be carried by a single mule.

All these dispositions duly made, at 10 a.m. on the 29th December we mounted our animals, and, guided by Mad Sa'id, trotted round the northern side of the Wilensi table-mountain down a lane fenced with fragrant dog roses. Then began the descent of a steep rocky hill, the wall of a woody chasm, through whose gloomy depths the shrunken stream of a large Fiumara wound like a thread of silver. The path would be safe to nought less surefooted than a mule: we rode slowly over rolling stones, steps of micaceous grit, and through thorny bush for about half an hour. In the plain below appeared a village of the Gerad's Midgans, who came out to see us pass, and followed the strangers to some distance. One happening to say, 'Of what use is his gun?—before he could fetch fire, I should put this arrow through him!' I discharged a barrel over their heads, and derided the con-vulsions of terror caused by the unexpected sound.

Passing onwards we entered a continuation of the Wady Harirah. It is a long valley choked with dense vegetation, through which mean-dered a line of water brightly gilt by the sun's rays: my Somal remarked that were the elephants now infesting it destroyed, rice, the favourite luxury, might be grown upon its banks in abundance. Our road lay under clumps of shady trees, over rocky water-courses, through avenues of tall cactus, and down *tranchées* worn by man eight and ten feet below stiff banks of rich red clay. On every side appeared deep clefts, ravines, and earth cracks, all, at this season, dry. The unarmed cultivators thronged from the frequent settlements to stare, and my Somal, being no longer in their own country, laid aside for guns their ridiculous spears. On the way passing Ao Samattar's village, the worthy fellow made us halt whilst he went to fetch a large bowl of sour milk. About noon the fresh western breeze obscured the fierce sun with clouds, and we watered our mules in a mountain stream which crossed our path thrice within as many hundred yards. After six miles' ride reaching the valley's head, we began the descent of a rugged pass by a rough and rocky path. The scenery around us was remarkable. The hill sides were well wooded, and black with pine: their summits were bared of earth by the heavy monsun which spreads the valleys with rich soil; in many places the beds of waterfalls shone like sheets of metal upon the black rock; villages surrounded by fields and fences studded the country, and the distance was a mass of purple peak and blue table in long vanishing succession. Ascending the valley's opposite wall, we found the remains of primæval forests—little glades which had es-caped the axe—they resounded with the cries of pintados [guinea-fowl] and cynocephali.* Had the yellow crops of Holcus been wheat, I might have fancied myself once more riding in the pleasant neighbourhood of Tuscan Sienna.

At 4 p.m., after accomplishing fifteen miles on rough ground, we sighted Sagharrah, a snug high-fenced village of eight or nine huts nestling against a hillside with trees above, and below a fertile grain-valley. Presently Mad Sa'id pointed out to us the Gerad Adan, who, attended by a little party, was returning homewards: we fired our guns as a salute, he however hurried on to receive us with due ceremony in his cottage. Dismounting at the door we shook hands with him, were led through the idle mob into a smoky closet contrived against the inside wall, and were regaled with wheaten bread steeped in honey and rancid butter. The host left us to eat, and soon afterwards returned: I looked with attention at a man upon whom so much then depended.

Adan bin Kaushan was in appearance a strong wiry Bedouin— before obtaining from me a turban he wore his bushy hair dyed dun— about forty-five years old, at least six feet high, with decided features, a tricky smile, and an uncertain eye. In character he proved to be one of those cunning idiots so peculiarly difficult to deal with. Ambitious and wild with greed of gain, he was withal so fickle that his head appeared ever changing its contents; he could not sit quiet for half an hour, and this physical restlessness was an outward sign of the uneasy inner man. Though reputed brave, his treachery has won him a permanent ill fame. Some years ago he betrothed a daughter to the eldest son of Gerad Hirsi of the Berteri tribe, and then, contrary to the Somali laws of honour, married her to Mohammed Wa'iz of the Jibril Abokr. This led to a feud, in which the disappointed suitor was slain. Adan was celebrated for polygamy even in Eastern Africa: by means of his five sons and dozen daughters, he has succeeded in making extensive connections,† and his sister, the Gisti‡ Fâtimah, was married to Abubakr, father of the present Amir. Yet the Gerad would walk into a crocodile's mouth as willingly as within the walls of Harar. His main reason for receiving us politely was an ephemeral fancy for building a fort, to control the country's trade, and rival or overawe the city. Still he did not neglect the main chance: whatever he saw he asked for;

* The Somal will not kill these plundering brutes, like the Western Africans believing them to be enchanted men.

† Some years ago Adan plundered one of Sharmakay's caravans: repenting the action, he offered in marriage a daughter, who, however died before nuptials.

‡ Gisti is a 'princess' in Harari, equivalent to the Somali Geradah.

and after receiving a sword, a Koran, a turban, an Arab waistcoat of gaudy satin, about seventy Tobes, and a similar proportion of indigo-dyed stuff, he privily complained to me that the Hammal had given him but twelve cloths. A list of his wants will best explain the man. He begged me to bring him from Berbera a silver-hilted sword and some soap, 1,000 dollars, two sets of silver bracelets, twenty guns with powder and shot, snuff, a scarlet cloth coat embroidered with gold, some poison that would not fail, and any other little article of luxury which might be supposed to suit him. In return he was to present us with horses, mules, slaves, ivory, and other valuables: he forgot, however, to do so before we departed.

The Gerad Adan was powerful, being the head of a tribe of cultivators, not split up, like the Bedouin, into independent clans, and he thus exercises a direct influence upon the conterminous races.[1] The Girhi or 'Giraffes' inhabiting these hills are, like most of the other settled Somal, a derivation from Darud, and descended from Kombo. Despite the unmerciful persecutions of the Gallas, they gradually migrated westwards from Makhar, their original nest, now number 5,000 shields, possess about 180 villages, and are accounted the power paramount. Though friendly with the Habr Awal, the Girhi seldom descend, unless compelled by want of pasture, into the plains.

The other inhabitants of these hills are the Gallas and the Somali clans of Berteri, Bursuk, Shaykhash, Hawiyah, Usbayhan, Marayhan, and Abaskul.

The Gallas about Harar are divided into four several clans, separating as usual into a multitude of septs. The Alo extend westwards from the city; the Nole inhabit the land to the east and north-east, about two days' journey between the Eesa Somal, and Harar: on the south, are situated the Babuli and the Jarsa at Wilensi, Sagharrah, and Kondura—places described in these pages.

The Berteri, who occupy the Gurays Range, south of, and limitrophe to the Gallas, and thence extend eastward to the Jigjiga hills, are estimated at 3,000 shields. Of Darud origin, they own allegiance to the Gerad Hirsi, and were, when I visited the country, on bad terms with the Girhi. The chief's family has, for several generations, been connected with the Amirs of Harar, and the caravan's route to and from Berbera lying through his country, makes him a useful friend and a dangerous foe. About the Gerad Hirsi different reports were rife: some described him as cruel, violent and avaricious; others spoke of him as a godly and a prayerful person: all, however, agreed that he *had* sowed wild oats. In token of repentance, he was fond of feeding Widads, and the Shaykh Jami of Harar was a frequent guest at his kraal.

The Bursuk number about 5,000 shields, own no chief, and in 1854 were at war with the Girhi, the Berteri, and especially the Gallas. In this country, the feuds differ from those of the plains: the hill men fight for three days, as the End of Time phrased it, and make peace for three days. The maritime clans are not so abrupt in their changes; moreover they claim blood-money, a thing here unknown. The Shaykhash, or 'Reverend' as the term means, are the only Somal of the mountains not derived from Dir and Darud. Claiming descent from the Caliph Abu Bakr, they assert that ten generations ago, one Ao Khutab bin Fakih Umar crossed over from al-Hijaz, and settled in Eastern Africa with his six sons, Umar the greater, Umar the less, two Abdillahs, Ahmad, and lastly Siddik. This priestly tribe is dispersed, like that of Levi, amongst its brethren, and has spread from Efat to Ogadayn. Its principal sub-families are, Ao Umar, the elder, and Bah Dumma, the junior, branch.

The Hawiyah has been noticed in a previous chapter. Of the Usbayhan I saw but few individuals: they informed me that their tribe numbered forty villages, and about 1,000 shields; that they had no chief of their own race, but owned the rule of the Girhi and Berteri Gerads. Their principal clans are the Rer Yusuf, Rer Sa'id, Rer Alwkr and Yusuf Liyo.

In the Eastern Horn of Africa, and at Ogadayn, the Marahayn is a powerful tribe, here it is unconsequential, and affiliated to the Girhi. The Abaskul also lies scattered over the Harar hills, and owns the Gerad Adan as its chief. This tribe numbers fourteen villages, and between 400 and 500 shields, and is divided into the Rer Yusuf, the Jibrailah, and the Warra Dig: the latter clan is said to be of Galla extraction.

On the morning after my arrival at Sagharrah I felt too ill to rise, and was treated with unaffected kindness by all the establishment. The Gerad sent to Harar for millet beer, Ao Samattar went to the gardens in search of Kat, the sons Yusuf Dera and a Dwarf* insisted upon firing me with such ardour, that no refusal could avail: and Khayrah the wife, with her daughters, two tall dark, smiling, and well-favoured girls of thirteen and fifteen, sacrificed a sheep as my Fida, or Expiatory offering. Even the Galla Christians, who flocked to see the stranger, wept for the evil fate which had brought him so far from his

---

* The only specimen of stunted humanity seen by me in the Somali country. He was about eighteen years old, and looked ten.

fatherland, to die under a tree. Nothing indeed, would have been easier than such operation: all required was the turning face to the wall, for four or five days. But to expire of an ignoble colic!—the thing was not to be thought of, and a firm resolution to live on sometimes, methinks, effects its object.

On the 1st January, 1855, feeling stronger, I clothed myself in my Arab best, and asked a palaver with the Gerad. We retired to a safe place behind the village, where I read with pomposity the Hajj Sharmakay's letter. The chief appeared much pleased by our having preferred his country to that of the Eesa: he at once opened the subject of the new fort, and informed me that I was the builder, as his eldest daughter had just dreamed that the stranger would settle in the land. Having discussed the project to the Gerad's satisfaction, we brought out the guns and shot a few birds for the benefit of the vulgar. Whilst engaged in the occupation, appeared a party of five strangers, and three mules with ornamented Morocco saddles, bridles, bells, and brass neck ornaments, after the fashion of Harar. Two of these men, Haji Umar and Nur Ambar, were citizens; the others, Ali Hasan, Husayn Araleh, and Haji Mohammed, were Somal of the Habr Awal tribe, high in the Amir's confidence. They had been sent to settle with Adan the weighty matter of Blood-money. After sitting with us almost half an hour, during which they exchanged grave salutations with my attendants, inspected our asses with portentous countenances, and asked me a few questions concerning my business in those parts, they went privily to the Gerad, told him that the Arab was not one who bought and sold, that he had no design but to spy out the wealth of the land, and that the whole party should be sent prisoners in their hands to Harar. The chief curtly replied that we were his friends, and bade them, 'throw far those words'. Disappointed in their designs, they started late in the afternoon, driving off their 200 cows, and falsely promising to present our salaams to the Amir.

It became evident that some decided step must be taken. The Gerad confessed fear of his Harari kinsman, and owned that he had lost all his villages in the immediate neighbourhood of the city. I asked him point-blank to escort us: he as frankly replied that it was impossible. The request was lowered—we begged him to accompany us as far as the frontier: he professed inability to do so, but promised to send his eldest son, Shirwa.*

* In his account to the Royal Geographical Society Burton said: 'We remained six days under the roof of the Gerad Adan, one of the most treacherous and dangerous Chiefs

Nothing then remained, dear L., but *payer d'audace*, and, throwing all forethought to the dogs, to rely upon what has made many a small man great, the good star. I addressed my companions in a set speech, advising a mount without delay. They suggested a letter to the Amir, requesting permission to enter his city: this device was rejected for two reasons. In the first place, had a refusal been returned, our journey was cut short, and our labours stultified. Secondly, the End of Time had whispered that my two companions were plotting to prevent the letter reaching its destination. He had charged his own sin upon their shoulders: the Hammal and Long Gulad were incapable of such treachery. But our hedge-priest was thoroughly terrified; 'a coward body after a'', his face brightened when ordered to remain with the Gerad at Sagharrah, and though openly taunted with poltroonery, he had not the decency to object. My companions were then informed that hitherto our acts had been those of old women, not soldiers, and that something savouring of manliness must be done before we could return. They saw my determination to start alone, if necessary, and to do them justice, they at once arose. This was the more courageous in them, as alarmists had done their worst: but a day before, some travelling Somali had advised them, as they valued dear life, not to accompany that Turk to Harar. Once in the saddle, they shook off sad thoughts, declaring that if they were slain, I should pay their blood-money, and if they escaped, that their reward was in my hands. When in some danger, the Hammal especially behaved with a sturdiness which produced the most beneficial results. Yet they were true Easterns. Wearied by delay at Harar, I employed myself in meditating flight; they drily declared that after-wit serves no good purpose: whilst I considered the possibility of escape, they looked only at the prospect of being dragged back with pinioned arms by the Amir's guard. Such is generally the effect of the vulgar Moslem's blind fatalism.

I then wrote an English letter* from the Political Agent at Aden to

* At first I thought of writing it in Arabic; but having no seal, a *sine quá non* in an Eastern letter, and reflecting upon the consequences of detection or even suspicion, it appeared more politic to come boldly as a European.

[Burton in the report he read to the R.G.S. stated: 'As I approached the city [Harar] men turned out of their villages to ask if that was the Turk who was going to his death? The question made me resolve to appear before the Amir in my own character, an Englishman.' (*Journal of the Royal Geographical Society*, Vol. 25, 1855).—Ed.]

in this land of treachery and danger. My Somali attendants saw with horror that preparations were being made to enter the city of evil fame. They attempted by all means in their power to deter me from the attempt, but the unfortunates little knew the persistency of a Haji.' (*Journal of the Royal Geographical Society*, Vol. 25, 1855, read June 11, 1855.)—Ed.

the Amir of Harar, proposing to deliver it in person, and throw off my disguise. Two reasons influenced me in adopting this 'neck or nothing' plan. All the races amongst whom my travels lay, hold him nidering who hides his origin in places of danger; and secondly, my white face had converted me into a Turk, a nation more hated and suspected than any Europeans, without our *prestige*. Before leaving Sagharrah, I entrusted to the End of Time a few lines addressed to Lieut. Herne at Berbera, directing him how to act in case of necessity. Our baggage was again decimated: the greater part was left with Adan, and an ass carried only what was absolutely necessary,—a change of clothes, a book or two, a few biscuits, ammunition, and a little tobacco. My Girhi escort consisted of Shirwa, the Bedouin Abtidon, and Mad Sa'id mounted on the End of Time's mule.

At 10 a.m. on the 2nd January, all the villagers assembled, and recited the Fatihah, consoling us with the information that we were dead men. By the worst of footpaths, we ascended the tough and stony hill behind Sagharrah, through bush and burn and over ridges of rock. At the summit was a village, where Shirwa halted, declaring that he dared not advance: a swordsman, however, was sent on to guard us through the Galla Pass. After an hour's ride, we reached the foot of a tall Table-mountain called Kondura, where our road, a goat-path rough with rocks or fallen trees, and here and there arched over with giant creepers, was reduced to a narrow ledge, with a forest above and a forest below. I could not but admire the beauty of this Valombrosa, which reminded me of scenes whilome enjoyed in fair Touraine. High up on our left rose the perpendicular walls of the misty hill, fringed with tufted pine, and on the right the shrub-clad folds fell into a deep valley. The cool wind whistled and sunbeams like golden shafts darted through tall shady trees—'bearded with moss, and in garments green'—the ground was clothed with dank grass, and around the trunks grew thistles, daisies, and blue flowers which, at a distance, might well pass for violets.

Presently we were summarily stopped by half a dozen Gallas attending upon one Rabah, the Chief who owns the Pass.* This is the African style of toll-raking: the 'pike' appears in the form of a plump spearmen, and the gate is a pair of lances thrown across the road. Not without trouble, for they feared to depart from the *mos majorum*, we persuaded them that the ass carried no merchandise. Then rounding

* It belongs, I was informed, to two clans of Gallas, who year by year in turn monopolize the profits.

Kondura's northern flank, we entered the Amir's territory: about thirty miles distant, and separated by a series of blue valleys, lay a dark speck upon a tawny sheet of stubble—Harar.

Having paused for a moment to savour success, we began the descent. The ground was a slippery black soil—mist ever settles upon Kondura—and frequent springs oozing from the rock formed beds of black mire. A few huge Birbisa trees, the remnant of a forest still thick around the mountain's neck, marked out the road: they were branchy from stem to stern, and many had a girth of from twenty to twenty-five feet.*

After an hour's ride amongst thistles, whose flowers of a bright red-like worsted were not less than a child's head, we watered our mules at a rill below the slope. Then remounting, we urged over hill and dale, where Galla peasants were threshing and storing their grain with loud songs of joy: they were easily distinguished by their African features, mere caricatures of the Somal, whose type has been Arabized by repeated immigrations from al Yemen and Hadramaut. Late in the afternoon, having gained ten miles in a straight direction, we passed through a hedge of plantains, defending the windward side of Gafra, a village of Midgans who collect the Gerad Adan's grain. They shouted delight on recognizing their old friend, Mad Sa'id, led us to an empty Gambisa, swept and cleaned it, lighted a fire, turned our mules into a field to graze, and went forth to seek food. Their hospitable thoughts, however, were marred by the two citizens of Harar, who privately threatened them with the Amir's wrath, if they dared to feed that Turk.

As evening drew on, came a message from our enemies, the Habr Awal, who offered, if we would wait till sunrise, to enter the city in our train. The Gerad Adan had counselled me not to provoke these men; so, contrary to the advice of my two companions, I returned a polite answer, purporting that we would expect them till eight o'clock the next morning.

At 7 a.m., on the 3rd January, we heard that the treacherous Habr Awal had driven away their cows shortly after midnight. Seeing their hostile intentions, I left my journal, sketches, and other books in charge of an old Midgan, with directions that they should be forwarded to the Gerad Adan, and determined to carry nothing but our arms and a few presents for the Amir. We saddled our mules, mounted, and rode hurriedly along the edge of a picturesque chasm of tender pink granite, here and there obscured by luxuriant vegetation. In the centre, fringed

* Of this tree are made the substantial doors, the basins and the porringers of Harar.

169

with bright banks a shallow rill, called Doghlah, now brawls in tiny cascades, then whirls through huge boulders towards the Erar river. Presently, descending by a ladder of rock scarcely safe even for mules, we followed the course of the burn, and emerging into the valley beneath, we pricked forward rapidly, for day was wearing on, and we did not wish the Habr Awal to precede us.

About noon we crossed the Erar river. The bed is about one hundred yards broad, and a thin sheet of clear, cool, and sweet water covered with crystal the great part of the sand. According to my guides, its course, like that of the hills, is southerly towards the Webbe of Ogadayn:* none, however, could satisfy my curiosity concerning the course of the only perennial stream which exists between Harar and the coast.[2]

In the lower valley, a mass of waving holcus, we met a multitude of Galla peasants coming from the city market with new potlids and the empty gourds which had contained their butter, ghi, and milk; all wondered aloud at the Turk, concerning whom they had heard many horrors. As we commenced another ascent, appeared a Harar Grandee mounted upon a handsomely caparisoned mule and attended by seven servants who carried gourds and skins of grain. He was a pale-faced senior with a white beard, dressed in a fine Tobe and a snowy turban, with scarlet edges: he carried no shield, but an Abyssinian broadsword was slung over his left shoulder. We exchanged courteous salutations, and as I was thirsty he ordered a footman to fill a cup with water. Half way up the hill appeared the 200 Girhi cows, but those traitors, the Habr Awal, had hurried onwards. Upon the summit was pointed out to me the village of Elaoda: in former times it was a wealthy place belonging to the Gerad Adan.

At 2 p.m. we fell into a narrow fenced land, and halted for a few minutes near a spreading tree, under which sat women selling ghi and unspun cotton. About two miles distant on the crest of a hill, stood the city—the end of my present travel—a long sombre line strikingly contrasting with the whitewashed towns of the East. The spectacle, materially speaking, was a disappointment: nothing conspicuous appeared but two grey minarets of rude shape: many would have grudged exposing three lives to win so paltry a prize. But of all that have attempted, none ever succeeded in entering that pile of stones: the thorough-bred traveller, dear L., will understand my exultation, although my two companions exchanged glances of wonder.

* The Shebelli or Shebayli river.

Drawing of Harar by Burton: 'the spectacle, materially speaking, was a disappointment . . . but of all that have attempted, none ever succeeded in entering that pile of stones: the thorough-bred traveller will understand my exultation'.

Spurring our mules, we advanced at a long trot, when Mad Sa'id stopped us to recite a Fatihah in honour of Ao Umar Siyad and Ao Rahmah, two great saints who repose under a clump of trees near the road. The soil on both sides of the path is rich and red: masses of plantains, limes, and pomegranates denote the gardens, which are defended by a bleached cow's skull, stuck upon a short stick and between them are plantations of coffee, bastard saffron, and the graceful Kat. About half a mile eastward of the town appears a burn called Jalah or the Coffee Water: the crowd crossing it did not prevent my companions bathing, and whilst they donned clean Tobes I retired to the wayside, and sketched the town.

These operations over, we resumed our way up a rough *tranchée* ridged with stone and hedged with tall cactus. This ascends to an open plain. On the right lie the holcus fields, which reach to the town wall: the left is a heap of rude cemetery, and in front are the dark defences of Harar, with groups of citizens loitering about the large gateway, and sitting in chat near the ruined tomb of Ao Abdal. We arrived at 3 p.m., after riding about five hours, which were required to accomplish twenty direct miles.[3]

Advancing to the gate, Mad Sa'id accosted a warder, known by his long wand of office, and sent our salaams to the Amir, saying that we came from Aden, and requested the honour of audience. Whilst he sped upon his errand, we sat at the foot of a round bastion, and were scrutinized, derided, and catechized by the curious of both sexes, especially by that conventionally termed the fair. The three Habr Awal presently approached and scowlingly inquired why we had not apprised them of our intention to enter the city. It was now 'war to the knife'—we did not deign a reply.

The Amir of Harar. Drawing by Burton.

VIII

Ten Days at Harar

AFTER WAITING HALF AN HOUR at the gate, we were told by the returned warder to pass the threshold, and remounting guided our mules along the main street, a narrow up-hill lane, with rocks cropping out from a surface more irregular than a Perote pavement. Long Gulad had given his animal into the hands of our two Bedouin: they did not appear till after our audience, when they informed us that the people at the entrance had advised them to escape with the beasts, an evil fate having been prepared for the proprietors.

Arrived within a hundred yards of the gate of holcus stalks, which opens into the courtyard of this African St. James's, our guide, a blear-eyed, surly-faced, angry-voiced fellow, made signs—none of us understanding his Harari—to dismount. We did so. He then began to trot, and roared out apparently that we must do the same. We looked at one another, the Hammal swore that he would perish foully rather than obey, and—conceive, dear L., the idea of a petticoated pilgrim venerable as to beard and turban breaking into a long 'double!'—I expressed much the same sentiment. Leading our mules leisurely, in spite of the guide's wrath, we entered the gate, strode down the yard, and were placed under a tree in its left corner, close to a low building of rough stone, which the clanking of frequent fetters argued to be a state prison.

This part of the court was crowded with Gallas, some lounging about, others squatting in the shade under the palace walls. The chiefs were known by their zinc armlets, composed of thin spiral circlets, closely joined, and extending in mass from the wrist almost to the elbow: all appeared to enjoy peculiar privileges—they carried their long spears, wore their sandals, and walked leisurely about the royal precincts. A delay of half an hour, during which state affairs were being transacted within, gave me time to inspect a place of which so many and such different accounts are current. The palace itself is, as Clapperton* describes the Fellatah Sultan's state hall, a mere shed, a long, single storied, windowless barn of rough stone and reddish clay, with no other insignia but a thin coat of whitewash over the door. This is the royal and wazirial distinction at Harar, where no lesser man may stucco the walls of his house. The courtyard was about eighty yards long by thirty in breadth, irregularly shaped, and surrounded by low buildings: in the centre, opposite the outer entrance, was a circle of masonry against which were propped divers doors.†

Presently the blear-eyed guide with the angry voice returned from within, released us from the importunities of certain forward and inquisitive youths, and motioned us to doff our slippers at a stone step, or rather line, about twelve feet distant from the palace wall. We grumbled that we were not entering a mosque, but in vain. Then ensued a long dispute, in tongues mutually unintelligible, about giving up our weapons: by dint of obstinacy we retained our daggers and my revolver. The guide raised a door curtain, suggested a bow, and I stood in the presence of the dreaded chief.‡

* Hugh Clapperton, 1788–1827 'From Kano to Sackatoo' [Sokato], in *Narrative Travels and Discoveries in Northern and Central Africa 1822–4*, by D. Denham, H. Clapperton, and W. Oudney, 1826.—Ed.

† I afterwards learned that when a man neglects a summons his door is removed to the royal court-yard on the first day; on the second, it is confiscated. The door is a valuable and venerable article in this part of Africa. According to Bruce, Ptolemy Euergetes engraved it upon the Axum Obelisk for the benefit of his newly conquered Æthiopian subjects, to whom it had been unknown.

‡ In the *Life* (p. 207, vol. 1) there is an additional paragraph: 'I walked into a vast hall, a hundred feet long, between two long rows of Galla spearmen, between whose lines I had to pass. They were large half-naked savages, standing like statues, with fierce movable eyes, each one holding . . . a huge spear, with a head the size of a shovel. I purposely sauntered down them coolly with a swagger, with my eyes fixed upon their dangerous-

The Amir, or, as he styles himself, the Sultan Ahmad bin Sultan Abibakr, sat in a dark room with whitewashed walls, to which hung— significant decorations—rusty matchlocks and polished fetters. His appearance was that of a little Indian Rajah, an etiolated youth twenty-four or twenty-five years old, plain and thin-bearded, with a yellow complexion, wrinkled brows and protruding eyes. His dress was a flowing robe of crimson cloth, edged with snowy fur, and a narrow white turban tightly twisted round a tall conical cap of red velvet, like the old Turkish headgear of our painters. His throne was a common Indian Kursi, or raised cot, about five feet long, with back and sides supported by a dwarf railing: being an invalid he rested his elbow upon a pillow, under which appeared the hilt of a Cutch sabre. Ranged in double line, perpendicular to the Amir, stood the 'court,' his cousins and nearest relations with right arms bared after fashion of Abyssinia.

I entered the room with a loud 'Peace be upon ye!' to which H. H. replying graciously, and extending a hand, bony and yellow as a kite's claw, snapped his thumb and middle finger. Two chamberlains stepping forward, held my forearms, and assisted me to bend low over the fingers, which however I did not kiss, being naturally averse to performing that operation upon any but a woman's hand. My two servants then took their turn: in this case, after the back was saluted, the palm was presented for a repetition. These preliminaries concluded, we were led to and seated upon a mat in front of the Amir, who directed towards us a frowning brow and inquisitive eye.

Some inquiries were made about the chief's health: he shook his head captiously, and inquired our errand. I drew from my pocket my own letter: it was carried by a chamberlain, with hands veiled in his Tobe, to the Amir, who after a brief glance laid it upon the couch, and demanded further explanation. I then represented in Arabic that we had come from Aden, bearing the compliments of our Daulah or governor, and that we had entered Harar to see the light of H. H.'s countenance: this information concluded with a little speech, describing the changes of Political Agents in Arabia, and alluding to the friendship formerly existing between the English and the deceased chief Abibakr.

The Amir smiled graciously.

This smile I must own, dear L., was a relief. We had been prepared

looking faces. I had a six-shooter concealed in my waist-belt, and determined, at the first show of excitement, to run up to the Amir, and put it to his head, if it were necessary, to save my own life.'—Ed.

for the worst, and the aspect of affairs in the palace was by no means reassuring.

Whispering to his Treasurer, a little ugly man with a badly shaven head, coarse features, pug nose, angry eyes, and stubby beard, the Amir made a sign for us to retire. The *baise main* was repeated, and we backed out of the audience-shed in high favour. According to grandiloquent Bruce,'the Court of London and that of Abyssinia are, in their principles, one': the loiterers in the Harar palace yards who had before regarded us with cut-throat looks, now smiled as though they loved us. Marshalled by the guard, we issued from the precincts, and after walking a hundred yards entered the Amir's second palace, which we were told to consider our home. There we found the Bedouin, who, scarcely believing that we had escaped alive, grinned in the joy of their hearts, and we were at once provided from the chief's kitchen with a dish of Shabta, holcus cakes soaked in sour milk, and thickly powdered with red pepper, the salt of this inland region.[1]

When we had eaten, the treasurer reappeared, bearing the Amir's command, that we should call upon his Wazir, the Gerad Mohammed. Resuming our peregrinations, we entered an abode distinguished by its external streak of chunam,* and in a small room on the ground floor, cleanly whitewashed and adorned, like an old English kitchen, with varnished wooden porringers of various sizes, we found a venerable old man whose benevolent countenance belied the reports current about him in Somaliland.† Half rising, although his wrinkled brow showed suffering, he seated me by his side upon the carpeted masonry-bench, where lay the implements of his craft, reeds, inkstands and

---

* Plaster made of shell-lime and sand.—Ed.

† About seven years ago the Hajj Sharmakay of Zayla chose as his agent at Harar, one of the Amir's officers, a certain Hajj Janitay. When this man died Sharmakay demanded an account from his sons; at Berbera they promised to give it, but returning to Harar they were persuaded, it is believed, by the Gerad Mohammed, to forget their word. Upon this Sharmakay's friends and relations, incited by one Husayn, a Somali who had lived many years at Harar in the Amir's favour, wrote an insulting letter to the Gerad, beginning with, 'No peace be upon thee, and no blessings of Allah, thou butcher! son of a butcher, etc., etc.!' and concluding with a threat to pinion him in the market-place as a warning to men. Husayn carried the letter, which at first excited general terror; when, however, the attack did not take place, the Amir Abibakr imprisoned the imprudent Somali till he died. Sharmakay by way of reprisals, persuaded Alu, son of Sahlah Salaseh, king of Shoa, to seize about three hundred Harari citizens living in his dominions and to keep them two years in durance.

The Amir Abibakr is said on his deathbed to have warned his son against the Gerad. When Ahmad reported his father's decease to Zayla, the Hajj Sharmakay ordered a grand Maulid or Mass in honour of the departed. Since that time, however, there has been little intercourse and no cordiality between them.

whitewashed boards for paper, politely welcomed me, and gravely stroking his cotton-coloured beard, in good Arabic desired my object.

I replied almost in the words used to the Amir, adding however some details how in the old days one Madar Farih had been charged by the late Sultan Abibakr with a present to the governor of Aden, and that it was the wish of our people to re-establish friendly relations and commercial intercourse with Harar.

'Khayr Inshallah!—it is well if Allah please!' ejaculated the Gerad: I then bent over his hand, and took leave.

Returning, we inquired anxiously of the treasurer about my servants' arms which had not been returned, and were assured that they had been placed in the safest of store-houses, the palace. I then sent a common six-barrelled revolver as a present to the Amir, explaining its use to the bearer, and we prepared to make ourselves as comfortable as possible. The interior of our new house was a clean room, with plain walls, and a floor of tamped earth; opposite the entrance were two broad steps of masonry, raised about two feet, and a yard above the ground, and covered with hard matting. I contrived to make upon the higher ledge a bed with the cushions which my companions used as shabracques, and, after seeing the mules fed and tethered, lay down to rest worn out by fatigue and profoundly impressed with the *poésie* of our position. I was under the roof of a bigoted prince whose least word was death; amongst a people who detest foreigners; the only European that had ever passed over their inhospitable threshold, and the fated instrument of their future downfall.

I now proceed to a description of unknown Harar.

The ancient capital of Hadiyah, called by the citizens 'Harar Gay', by the Somal 'Adari', by the Gallas 'Adaray', and by the Arabs and ourselves 'Harar', lies, according to my dead reckoning, 220° S.W. of, and 175 statute miles from, Zayla—257° W. of, and 219 miles distant from, Berbera. This would place it in 9° 20' N. lat., and 42° 7' E. long. The thermometer showed an altitude of about 5,500 feet above the level of the sea.* Its site is the slope of a hill which falls gently from west to east. On the eastern side are cultivated fields; westwards a terraced ridge is laid out in orchards; northwards is a detached eminence covered with tombs; and to the south, the city declines into a low

* I say *about*: we were compelled to boil our thermometers at Wilensi, not venturing upon such operation within the city. [The location of Harar is 9° 20' N.; 42° 10' E., so that Burton's location is very nearly correct; the height is given in Lippincott's Gazetteer as 6,000 feet; the distance from Harar to Zayla is 165 miles and to Berbera 209 miles.—Ed.]

valley bisected by a mountain burn. This irregular position is well sheltered from high winds, especially on the northern side, by the range of which Kondura is the lofty apex; hence, as the Persian poet sings of a heaven-favoured city—'its heat is not hot, nor its cold, cold.'

During my short residence the air reminded me of Tuscany. On the afternoon of the 11th January there was thunder accompanied by rain: frequent showers fell on the 12th, and the morning of the 13th was clear; but as we crossed the mountains, black clouds obscured the heavens. The monsun is heavy during one summer month; before it begins the crops are planted, and they are reaped in December and January. At other seasons the air is dry, mild, and equable.

The province of Hadiyah* is mentioned by Makrizi as one of the seven members of the Zayla Empire,† founded by Arab invaders, who in the seventh century of our era conquered and colonized the low tract between the Red Sea and the Highlands. Moslem Harar exercised a pernicious influence upon the fortunes of Christian Abyssinia.

The allegiance claimed by the Æthiopian Emperors from the Adel— the Dankali and ancient Somal—was evaded at a remote period, and the intractable Moslems were propitiated with rich presents, when they thought proper to visit the Christian court. The Abyssinians supplied the Adel with slaves, the latter returned the value in rock-salt, commercial intercourse united their interests, and from war resulted injury to both people. Nevertheless the fanatic lowlanders, propense to pillage and proselytizing, burned the Christian churches, massacred the infidels, and tortured the priests, until they provoked a blood feud of uncommon asperity.

In the fourteenth century (A.D. 1312–42) Amda Sion, Emperor of Æthiopia, taunted by Amano, King of Hadiyah, as a monarch fit only to take care of women, overran and plundered the Lowlands from Tegulet to the Red Sea. The Amharas were commanded to spare nothing that drew the breath of life: to fulfil a prophecy which foretold the fall of al-Islam, they perpetrated every kind of enormity.

Peace followed the death of Amda Sion. In the reign of Zara Yakub‡ (A.D. 1434–68), the flame of war was again fanned in Hadiyah by a Zayla princess who was slighted by the Æthiopian monarch on account

* The province is eight days by nine in extent, with a large army, and money derived from the trade in eunuchs. I have chiefly borrowed from Taki al-Din Ahmad bin Ali al-Makrizi. [Part of note added by Burton to his own copy.—Ed.]

† The other six were Efat, Arabini, Duaro, Sharkha, Báli, and Darah.

‡ This prince built 'Debra Berhan', the 'Hill of Glory', a church dedicated to the Virgin Mary at Gondar.

of the length of her foreteeth: the hostilities which ensued were not, however, of an important nature. Bœda Mariam, the next occupant of the throne, passed his life in a constant struggle for supremacy over the Adel: on his deathbed he caused himself to be so placed that his faced looked towards those lowlands, upon whose subjugation the energies of ten years had been vainly expended.

At the close of the fifteenth century, Mahfuz, a bigoted Moslem, inflicted a deadly blow upon Abyssinia. Vowing that he would annually spend the forty days of Lent amongst his infidel neighbours, when, weakened by rigorous fasts, they were less capable of bearing arms, for thirty successive years he burned churches and monasteries, slew without mercy every male that fell in his way, and driving off the women and children, he sold some to strange slavers, and presented others to the Sherifs of Mecca. He bought over Za Salasah, commander-in-chief of the Emperor's bodyguard, and caused the assassination of Alexander (A.D. 1478–95) at the ancient capital Tegulet. Naud, the successor, obtained some transient advantages over the Moslems. During the earlier reign of the next emperor, David III, son of Na'ud, who being but eleven years old when called to the throne, was placed under the guardianship of his mother the Iteghe Helena, new combatants and new instruments of warfare appeared on both sides of the field.

After the conquest of Egypt and Arabia by Selim I (A.D. 1516) the caravans of Abyssinian pilgrims travelling to Jerusalem were attacked, the old were butchered and the young were swept into slavery. Many Arabian merchants fled from Turkish violence and injustice to the opposite coast of Africa, whereupon the Ottomans took possession from Aden of Zayla, and not only laid the Indian trade under heavy contributions by means of their war-galleys, but threatened the total destruction of Abyssinia. They aided and encouraged Mahfuz to continue his depredations, whilst the Sherif of Mecca gave him command of Zayla, the key of the upper country, and presented him with the green banner of a Crusader.

On the other hand, the great Alburquerque at the same time (A.D. 1508–15) was viceroy of India, and to him the Iteghe Helena applied for aid. Her ambassador arrived at Goa, 'bearing a fragment of wood belonging to the true cross on which Christ died,' which relic had been sent as a token of friendship to her brother Emanuel by the Empress of Æthiopia. The overture was followed by the arrival at Masawwah of an embassy from the King of Portugal. Too proud, however, to await foreign aid, David at the age of sixteen took the field in person against the Moslems.

During the battle that ensued, Mahfuz, the Goliath of the Unbelievers, was slain in single combat by Gabriel Andreas, a soldier of tried valour, who had assumed the monastic life in consequence of having lost the tip of his tongue for treasonable freedom of speech: the green standard was captured, and 12,000 Moslems fell. David followed up his success by invading the lowlands, and, in defiance, struck his spear through the door of the King of Adel.

Harar was a mere mass of Bedouin villages during the reign of Mohammed Gragne, the 'left-handed' Attila of Adel.* Supplied with Arab mercenaries from Mocha, and by the Turks of al-Yemen with a body of Janissaries and a train of artillery, he burst into Efat and Fatigar. In A.D. 1528 he took possession of Shoa, overran Amhara, burned the churches, and carried away an immense booty. The next campaign enabled him to winter at Begmeder: in the following year he hunted the Emperor David through Tigre to the borders of Sana'ar, gave battle to the Christians on the banks of the Nile, and with his own hand killed the monk Gabriel, then an old man. Reinforced by Gideon and Judith, king and queen of the Saman Jews, and aided by a violent famine which prostrated what had escaped the spear, he perpetrated every manner of atrocity, captured and burned Axum, destroyed the princes of the royal blood on the mountain of Amba Gêshê, and slew in A.D. 1540, David, third of his name and last emperor of Æthiopia who displayed the magnificence of 'King of Kings'.

Claudius, the successor to the tottering throne, sent as his ambassador to Europe, one John Bermudez, a Portuguese who had been detained in Abyssinia, and promised, it is said, submission to the Pontiff of Rome, and the cession of a third of his dominions in return for reinforcements. By order of John III, Don Stephen and Don Christopher, sons of Don Vasco da Gama, cruised up the Red Sea with a powerful flotilla, and the younger brother, landing at Masawwah with 400 musqueteers, slew Nur the Governor, and sent his head to Gondar, where the Iteghe Savel Wenghel received it as an omen of good fortune. Thence the Portuguese general imprudently marched in the monsun season, and was soon confronted upon the plain of Ballut by Mohammed Gragne at the head of 10,000 spearmen and a host of cavalry. On the other side stood a rabble rout of Abyssinians, and a little band of

---

* 'Gragne', or in the Somali dialect 'Guray', means a left-handed man; Father Lobo errs in translating it 'the Lame'.

350 Portuguese heroes headed by the most chivalrous soldier of a chivalrous age.

According to Father Jerome Lobo,* who heard the events from an eye-witness, a conference took place between the two captains. Mohammed encamped in a commanding position, sent a message to Don Christopher informing him that the treacherous Abyssinians had imposed upon the King of Portugal, and that in compassion of his opponent's youth, he would give him and his men free passage and supplies to their own country. The Christian presented the Moslem ambassador with a rich robe, and returned this gallant answer, 'that he and his fellow-soldiers were come with an intention to drive Mohammed out of these countries which he had wrongfully usurped; that his present design was, instead of returning back the way he came, as Mohammed advised, to open himself a passage through the country of his enemies; that Mohammed should rather think of determining whether he would fight or yield up his ill-gotten territories than of prescribing measures to him; that he put his whole confidence in the omnipotence of God, and the justice of his cause; and that to show how full a sense he had of Mohammed's kindness, he took the liberty of presenting him with a looking-glass and a pair of pincers'.

The answer and the present so provoked the Adel Monarch that he rose from table to attack the little troop of Portuguese, posted upon the declivity of a hill near a wood. Above them stood the Abyssinians, who resolved to remain quiet spectators of the battle, and to declare themselves on the side favoured by victory.

Mohammed began the assault with only ten horsemen, against whom an equal number of Portuguese were detached: these fired with so much exactness that nine of the Moors fell and the king was wounded in the leg by Peter de Sa. In the mêlée which ensued, the Moslems,

* This reverend Jesuit was commissioned in A.D. 1622 by the Count de Vidigueira, Viceroy of the Indies, to discover where his relative Don Christopher was buried, and to procure some of the relics. Assisted by the son-in-law of the Abyssinian Emperor, Lobo marched with an army through the Gallas, found the martyr's teeth and lower jaw, his arms, and a picture of the Holy Virgin which he always carried about with him. The precious remains were forwarded to Goa.

I love the style of this old father, so unjustly depreciated by our writers, and called ignorant peasant and liar by Bruce, because he claimed for his fellow countrymen the honour of having discovered the Coy Fountains. [The source of the Blue Nile.] The Nemesis who never sleeps punished Bruce by the justest of retributions. His pompous and inflated style, his uncommon arrogance, and over-weening vanity, his affectation of pedantry, his many errors and misrepresentations, aroused against him a spirit which embittered the last years of his life. It is now the fashion to laud Bruce, and to pity his misfortunes. I cannot but think that he deserved them.

dismayed by their first failure, were soon broken by the Portuguese muskets and artillery. Mohammed preserved his life with difficulty, he however rallied his men, and entrenched himself at a strong place called Membret (Mamrat), intending to winter there and await succour.

The Portuguese more desirous of glory than wealth, pursued their enemies, hoping to cut them entirely off: finding, however, the camp impregnable, they entrenched themselves on a hill over against it. Their little host diminished day by day, their friends at Masawwah could not reinforce them, they knew not how to procure provisions, and could not depend on their Abyssinian allies. Yet memorious of their countrymen's great deeds, and depending upon divine protection, they made no doubt of surmounting all difficulties.

Mohammed on his part was not idle. He solicited the assistance of the Moslem princes, and by inflaming their religious zeal, obtained a reinforcement of 2,000 musqueteers from the Arabs, and a train of artillery from the Turks of al-Yemen. Animated by these succours, he marched out of his trenches to enter those of the Portuguese, who received him with the utmost bravery, destroyed many of his men, and made frequent sallies, not, however, without sustaining considerable losses.

Don Christopher had already one arm broken and a knee shattered by a musket shot. Valour was at length oppressed by superiority of numbers: the enemy entered the camp, and put the Christians to the spear. The Portuguese general escaped the slaughter with ten men, and retreated to a wood, where they were discovered by a detachment of the enemy. Mohammed, overjoyed to see his most formidable enemy in his power, ordered Don Christopher to take care of a wounded uncle and nephew, telling him that he should answer for their lives, and upon their death, taxed him with having hastened it. The Portuguese roundly replied that he was come to destroy Moslems, not to save them. Enraged at this language, Mohammed placed a stone upon his captive's head, and exposed him to the insults of the soldiery, who inflicted upon him various tortures which he bore with the resolution of a martyr. At length, when offered a return to India as the price of apostacy, the hero's spirit took fire. He answered with the highest indignation, that nothing could make him forsake his Heavenly Master to follow an 'imposter', and continued in the severest terms to vilify the 'false Prophet', till Mohammed struck off his head. The body was divided into quarters and sent to different places, but the Catholics gathered their martyr's remains and interred them. Every Moor who passed by threw a stone upon the grave, and raised in time such a heap that Father Lobo found difficulty in removing it to exhume the relics. He concludes with a pardonable superstition: 'There is a tradition in the country, that in the place where Don Christopher's head fell, a fountain sprang up of wonderful virtue, which cured many diseases, otherwise past remedy.'

Mohammed Gragne improved his victory by chasing the young Claudius over Abyssinia, where nothing opposed the progress of his arms. At last the few Portuguese survivors repaired to the Christian Emperor, who was persuaded to march an army against the King of Adel. Resolved to revenge their general, the harquebusiers demanded the post opposite Mohammed, and directed all their efforts against the part where the Moslem Attila stood. His fellow religionists still relate that when Gragne fell in action, his wife Talwambara, the heroic daughter of Mahfuz, to prevent the destruction and dispersion of the host of al-Islam, buried the corpse privately, and caused a slave to personate the prince until a retreat to safe lands enabled her to discover the stratagem to the nobles.

Father Lobo tells a different tale. According to him, Peter Leon, a marksman of low stature, but passing valiant, who had been servant to Don Christopher, singled the Adel king out of the crowd, and shot him in the head as he was encouraging his men. Mohammed was followed by his enemy till he fell down dead: the Portuguese then alighting from his horse, cut off one of his ears and rejoined his fellow-countrymen. The Moslems were defeated with great slaughter, and an Abyssinian chief finding the Gragne's corpse upon the ground, presented the head to the Negush or Emperor, claiming the honour of having slain his country's deadliest foe. Having witnessed in silence this impudence, Peter asked whether the king had but one ear, and produced the other from his pocket to the confusion of the Abyssinian.

Thus perished, after fourteen years' uninterrupted fighting, the African hero, who dashed to pieces the structure of 2,500 years. Like the 'Kardillan' of the Holy Land, Mohammed Gragne is still the subject of many a wild and grisly legend. And to the present day the people of Shoa retain an inherited dread of the lowland Moslems.

Mohammed was succeeded on the throne of Adel by the Amir Nur, son of Majid, and, according to some, brother to the 'Left-handed'. He proposed marriage to Talwambara, who accepted him on condition that he should lay the head of the Emperor Claudius at her feet. In A.D. 1559, he sent a message of defiance to the Negush, who, having saved Abyssinia almost by a miracle, was rebuilding on Debra Work, the

'Golden Mount', a celebrated shrine which had been burned by the Moslems. Claudius, despising the eclipses, evil prophecies, and portents which accompanied his enemy's progress, accepted the challenge. On the 22nd March 1559, the armies were upon the point of engaging, when the high priest of Debra Libanos, hastening into the presence of the Negush, declared that in a vision, Gabriel had ordered him to dissuade the Emperor of Æthiopia from needlessly risking life. The superstitious Abyssinians fled, leaving Claudius supported by a handful of Portuguese, who were soon slain around him, and he fell covered with wounds. The Amir Nur cut off his head, and laid it at the feet of Talwambara, who, in observance of her pledge, became his wife. This Amazon suspended the trophy by its hair to the branch of a tree opposite her abode, that her eyes might be gladdened by the sight: after hanging two years, it was purchased by an Armenian merchant, who interred it in the Sepulchre of St. Claudius at Antioch. The name of the Christian hero who won every action save that in which he perished, has been enrolled in the voluminous catalogue of Abyssinian saints, where it occupies a conspicuous place as the destroyer of Mohammed the Left-handed.

The Amir Nur has also been canonized by his countrymen, who have buried their favourite 'Wali' under a little dome near the Jami Mosque at Harar. Shortly after his decisive victory over the Christians, he surrounded the city with its present wall—a circumstance now invested with the garb of Moslem fable. The warrior used to hold frequent conversations with Al-Khizr: on one occasion, when sitting upon a rock, still called Gay Humburti—Harar's Navel—he begged that some Sherif might be brought from Meccah, to aid him in building a permanent city. By the use of the 'Great Name' the vagrant prophet instantly summoned from Arabia the Sherif Yunis, his son Fakr al-Din, and a descendant from the Ansar or Auxiliaries of the Prophet: they settled at Harar, which throve by the blessing of their presence. From this tradition we may gather that the city was restored, as it was first founded and colonized, by hungry Arabs.

The Sherifs continued to rule with some interruptions until but a few generations ago, when the present family rose to power. According to Bruce, they are Jabartis, who, having intermarried with Sayyid women, claim a noble origin. They derive themselves from the Caliph Abibakr, or from Akil, son of Abu Talib, and brother of Ali. The Ulema, although lacking boldness to make the assertion, evidently believe them to be of Galla or pagan extraction.

Costumes of Harar. Drawing by Burton.

The present city of Harar is about one mile long by half that breadth. An irregular wall, lately repaired, but ignorant of cannon, is pierced with five large gates, and supported by oval towers of artless construction. The material of the houses and defences is rough stones, the granites and sandstones of the hills, cemented, like the ancient Galla cities, with clay. The only large building is the Jami or Cathedral, a long barn of poverty-stricken appearance, with broken-down gates, and two white-washed minarets of truncated conoid shape. They were built by Turkish architects from Mocha and Hoday-dah: one of them lately fell, and has been replaced by an inferior effort of Harari art. There are a few trees in the city, but it contains none of

185

those gardens which give to Eastern settlements that pleasant view of town and country combined. The streets are narrow lanes, up hill and down dale, strewed with gigantic rubbish heaps, upon which repose packs of mangy or one-eyed dogs, and even the best are encumbered with rocks and stones. The habitations are mostly long, flat-roofed sheds, double storied, with doors composed of a single plank, and holes for windows pierced high above the ground, and decorated with miserable wood-work: the principal houses have separate apartments for the women, and stand at the bottom of large court-yards closed by gates of Holcus stalks. The poorest classes inhabit 'Gambisa', the thatched cottages of the hill-cultivators. The city abounds in mosques, plain buildings without minarets, and in graveyards stuffed with tombs—oblong troughs formed by long slabs planted edgeways in the ground. I need scarcely say that Harar is proud of her learning, sanctity, and holy dead. The principal saint buried in the city is Shaykh Umar Abadir al-Bakri, originally from Jeddah, and now the patron of Harar: he lies under a little dome in the southern quarter of the city, near the Bisidimo Gate.

The ancient capital of Hadiyah shares with Zabid in al Yemen, the reputation of being an Alma Mater, and inundates the surrounding districts with poor scholars and crazy 'Widads'. Where knowledge leads to nothing, says philosophic Volney, nothing is done to acquire it, and the mind remains in a state of barbarism. There are no establishments for learning, no endowments, as generally in the East, and apparently no encouragement to students: books also are rare and costly. None but the religious sciences are cultivated. The chief Ulema are the Kabir Khalil, the Kabir Yunis, and the Shaykh Jami: the two former scarcely ever quit their houses, devoting all their time to study and tuition: the latter is a Somali who takes an active part in politics.

These professors teach Moslem literature through the medium of Harari, a peculiar dialect confined within the walls. Like the Somali and other tongues in this part of Eastern Africa, it appears to be partly Arabic in etymology and grammar: the Semitic scion being grafted upon an indigenous root: the frequent recurrence of the guttural *kh* renders it harsh and unpleasant, and it contains no literature except songs and tales, which are written in the modern Naskhi character. I would willingly have studied it deeply, but circumstances prevented: the explorer too frequently must rest satisfied with descrying from his Pisgah the Promised Land of Knowledge, which another more fortunate is destined to conquer. At Zayla, the Hajj sent to me an Abyssinian slave who was cunning in languages: but he, to use the popular phrase, 'showed his right ear with his left hand'. Inside Harar, we were so closely watched that it was found impossible to put pen to paper. Escaped, however, to Wilensi, I hastily collected the grammatical forms and a vocabulary, which will correct the popular assertion that 'the language is Arabic: it has an affinity with the Amharic'.*

Harar has not only its own tongue, unintelligible to any save the citizens; even its little population of about 8,000 souls is a distinct race. The Somal say of the city that it is a Paradise inhabited by asses: certainly the exterior of the people is highly unprepossessing. Amongst the men, I did not see a handsome face: their features are coarse and debauched; many of them squint, others have lost an eye by small-pox, and they are disfigured by scrofula and other diseases: the bad expression of their countenances justifies the proverb, 'Hard as the heart of Harar.' Generally the complexion is a yellowish brown, the beard short, stubby and untractable as the hair, and the hands and wrists, feet and ankles, are large and ill-made. The stature is moderate-sized, some of the elders show the 'pudding sides' and the pulpy stomachs of Banyans, whilst others are lank and bony as Arabs or Jews. Their voices are loud and rude. The dress is a mixture of Arab and Abyssinian. They shave the head, and clip the mustachioes and imperial close, like the Shafe'i of al Yemen. Many are bareheaded, some wear a cap, generally the embroidered Indian work, or the common cotton Takiyah of Egypt: a few affect white turbans of the fine Harar work, loosely twisted over the ears. The body-garment is the Tobe, worn flowing as in the Somali country or girt with the dagger-strap round the waist: the richer classes bind under it a Futah or loin-cloth, and the dignitaries have wide Arab drawers of white calico. Coarse leathern sandals, a rosary and a tooth-stick rendered perpetually necessary by the habit of chewing tobacco, complete the costume: and arms being forbidden in the streets, the citizens carry wands five or six feet long.

The women, who, owing probably to the number of female slaves, are much the more numerous, appear beautiful by contrast with their lords. They have small heads, regular profiles, straight noses, large eyes, mouths approaching the Caucasian type, and light yellow complexions. Dress, however, here is a disguise to charms. A long, wide, cotton shirt, with short arms as in the Arab's Aba, indigo-dyed or chocolate-coloured, and ornamented with a triangle of scarlet before

* This is equivalent to saying that the language of the Basque provinces is French with an affinity to English.

and behind—the base on the shoulder and the apex at the waist—is girt round the middle with a sash of white cotton crimson-edged. Women of the upper class, when leaving the house, throw a blue sheet over the head, which, however, is rarely veiled. The front and back hair parted in the centre is gathered into two large bunches below the ears, and covered with dark blue muslin or network, whose ends meet under the chin. This coiffure is bound round the head at the junction of scalp and skin by a black satin ribbon which varies in breadth according to the wearer's means: some adorn the gear with large gilt pins, others twine in it a Taj or thin wreath of sweet-smelling creeper. The virgins collect their locks, which are generally wavy not wiry, and grow long as well as thick into a knot tied à la Diane behind the head: a curtain of short close plaits escaping from the bunch, falls upon the shoulders, not ungracefully. Silver ornaments are worn only by persons of rank. The ear is decorated with Somali rings or red coral beads, the neck with necklaces of the same material, and the fore-arms with six or seven of the broad circles of buffalo and other dark horns prepared in Western India. Finally, stars are tattoed upon the bosom, the eyebrows are lengthened with dyes, the eyes fringed with Kohl, and the hands and feet stained with henna.

The female voice is harsh and screaming, especially when heard after the delicate organs of the Somal. The fair sex is occupied at home spinning cotton thread for weaving Tobes, sashes, and turbans; carrying their progeny perched upon their backs they bring water from the wells in large gourds borne on the head; work in the gardens, and the men—considering, like the Abyssinians, such work a disgrace —sit and sell in the long street which here represents the Eastern bazaar. Chewing tobacco enables them to pass much of their time, and the rich diligently anoint themselves with ghi, whilst the poorer classes use remnants of fat from the lamps. Their freedom of manners renders a public flogging occasionally indispensable. Before the operation begins, a few gourds full of cold water are poured over their heads and shoulders, after which a single-thonged whip is applied with vigour.

Both sexes are celebrated for laxity of morals. High and low indulge freely in intoxicating drinks, beer, and mead. The Amir has established strict patrols, who unmercifully bastinado those caught in the streets after a certain hour. They are extremely bigoted, especially against Christians, the effect of their Abyssinian wars, and are fond of 'Jihading' with the Gallas, over whom they boast many a victory. I have seen a letter addressed by the late Amir to the Hajj Sharmakay, in which he boasts of having slain a thousand infidels, and, by way of bathos, begs for a few pounds of English gunpowder. The Harari hold foreigners in especial hate and contempt, and divide them into two orders, Arabs and Somal.* The latter, though nearly one-third of the population, or 2,500 souls, are, to use their own phrase, cheap as dust: their natural timidity is increased by the show of pomp and power, whilst the word 'prison' gives them the horrors.

The other inhabitants are about 3,000 Bedouin, who 'come and go'. Up to the city gates the country is peopled by the Gallas. This unruly race requires to be propitiated by presents of cloth; as many as 600 Tobes are annually distributed amongst them by the Amir. Lately, when the small-pox, spreading from the city, destroyed many of their number, the relations of the deceased demanded and received blood-money; they might easily capture the place, but they preserve it for their own convenience. These Gallas are tolerably brave, avoid match-lock balls by throwing themselves upon the ground when they see the flash, ride well, use the spear skilfully, and although of proverbially bad breed, are favourably spoken of by the citizens. The Somal find no difficulty in travelling amongst them. I repeatedly heard at Zayla and at Harar that traders had visited the far West, traversing for seven months a country of pagans wearing golden bracelets, till they reached the Salt Sea, upon which Franks sail in ships.† At Wilensi, one Moham-med, a Shaykhash, gave me his itinerary of fifteen stages to the sources

* The hate dates from old times. Abd al-Karim, uncle to the late Amir Abibakr, sent for sixty or seventy Arab mercenaries under Haydar Assal the Auliki, to save him against the Gallas. The matchlock men failing in ammunition, lost twenty of their number in battle and retired to the town, where the Gallas, after capturing Abd al-Karim, and his brother Abd al-Rahman, seized the throne, and, aided by the citizens, attempted to massacre the strangers. These, however, defended themselves gallantly, and would have crowned the son of Abd al-Rahman, had he not in fear declined the dignity; they then drew their pay, and marched with all the honours of war to Zayla. Shortly before our arrival, the dozen of petty Arab pedlars at Harar, treacherous intriguers, like all their dangerous race, had been plotting against the Amir. One morning when they least expected it, their chief was thrown into a prison which proved his grave, and the rest were informed that any stranger found in the city should lose his head. After wandering some months amongst the neigh-bouring villages, they were allowed to return and live under the surveillance. No one at Harar dared to speak of this event, and we were cautioned not to indulge our curiosity.

† M. Krapf relates a tale current in Abyssinia; namely, that there is a remnant of the slave trade between Guineh (the Guinea coast) and Shoa. Connection between the east and west formerly existed: in the time of John the Second, the Portuguese on the river Zaire in Congo learned the existence of the Abyssinian church. Travellers in Western Africa assert that Fakihs or priests, when performing the pilgrimage pass from the Fellatah country through Abyssinia to the coast of the Red Sea. And it has lately been proved that a caravan line is open from the Zanzibar coast to Benguela.

189

of the Abbay or Blue Nile: he confirmed the vulgar Somali report that the Hawash and the Webbe Shebayli both take rise in the same range of well wooded mountains which gives birth to the river of Egypt.

The government of Harar is the Amir. These petty princes have a habit of killing and imprisoning all those who are suspected of aspiring to the throne. Ahmad's greatgrandfather died in jail, and his father narrowly escaped the same fate. When the present Amir ascended the throne he was ordered, it is said, by the Makad or chief of the Nole Gallas, to release his prisoners, or to mount his horse and leave the city. Three of his cousins, however, were, when I visited Harar, in confinement: one of them since that time died, and has been buried in his fetters. The Somal declare that the state-dungeon of Harar is beneath the palace, and that he who once enters it, lives with unkempt beard and untrimmed nails until the day when death sets him free.

The Amir Ahmad's health is infirm. Some attribute his weakness to a fall from a horse, others declare him to have been poisoned by one of his wives. I judged him consumptive. Shortly after my departure he was upon the point of death, and he afterwards sent for a physician to Aden. He has four wives. No. 1 is the daughter of the Gerad Hirsi; No. 2, a Sayyid woman of Harar; No. 3, an emancipated slave girl; and No. 4, a daughter of Gerad Abd al-Majid, one of his nobles. He has two sons, who will probably never ascend the throne; one is an infant, the other is a boy now about five years old.

The Amir Ahmad succeeded his father about three years ago. His rule is severe if not just, and it has all the *prestige* of secrecy. As the Amharas say, the 'belly of the Master is not known': even the Gerad Mohammed, though summoned to council at all times, in sickness as in health, dares not offer uncalled-for advice, and the queen dowager, the Gisit Fatimah, was threatened with fetters if she persisted in interference. Ahmad's principal occupations are spying his many stalwart cousins, indulging in vain fears of the English, the Turks and the Hajj Sharmakay, and amassing treasure by commerce and escheats. He judges civil and religious causes in person, but he allows them with little interference to be settled by the Kazi, Abd al-Rahman bin Umar al-Harari: the latter, though a highly respectable person, is seldom troubled; rapid decision being the general predilection. The punishments, when money forms no part of them, are mostly according to Koranic code. The murderer is placed in the market street, blindfolded, and bound hand and foot; the nearest of kin to the deceased then strikes his neck with a sharp and heavy butcher's knife, and the corpse is given over to the relations for Moslem burial. If the blow prove ineffectual a pardon is generally granted. When a citizen draws dagger upon another or commits any petty offence, he is bastinadoed in a peculiar manner: two men ply their horsewhips upon his back and breast, and the prince, in whose presence the punishment is carried out, gives the order to stop. Theft is visited with amputation of the hand. The prison is the award of state offenders: it is terrible, because the captive is heavily ironed, lies in a filthy dungeon, and receives no food but what he can obtain from his own family—seldom liberal under such circumstances—or buy or beg from his guards. Fines and confiscations, as usual in the East, are favourite punishments with the ruler. I met at Wilensi an old Harari, whose gardens and property had all been escheated, because his son fled from justice, after slaying a man. The Amir is said to have large hoards of silver, coffee, and ivory: my attendant the Hammal was once admitted into the inner palace, where he saw huge boxes of ancient fashion supposed to contain dollars. The only specie current in Harar is a diminutive brass piece called Mahallak —hand-worked and almost as artless a medium as a modern Italian coin. It bears on one side the words: Zaribet al-Harat, the coinage of Harar. On the reverse is the date, A.H. 1248. The Amir pitilessly punishes all those who pass in the city any other coin.

The Amir Ahmad is alive to the fact that some state should hedge in a prince. Neither weapons nor rosaries are allowed in his presence; a chamberlain's robe acts as spittoon; whenever anything is given to or taken from him, his hand must be kissed; even on horseback two attendants fan him with the hems of their garments. Except when engaged on the Haronic visits which he, like his father,* pays to the streets and byways at night, he is always surrounded by a strong bodyguard. He rides to mosque escorted by a dozen horsemen, and a score of footmen with guns and whips precede him: by his side walks an officer shading him with a huge and heavily fringed red satin umbrella—from India to Abyssinia the sign of princely dignity. Even at his prayers two or three chosen matchlock-men stand over him with lighted fusees. When he rides forth in public, he is escorted by a party of fifty men: the running footmen crack their whips and shout 'Let! Let!' (Go! Go!) and

* An old story is told of the Amir Abibakr, that during one of his nocturnal excursions, he heard three of his subjects talking treason, and coveting his food, his wife, and his throne. He sent for them next morning, filled the first with good things, and bastinadoed him for not eating more, flogged the second severely for being unable to describe the difference between his own wife and the princess, and put the third to death.

the citizens avoid stripes by retreating into the nearest house, or running into another street.

The army of Harar is not imposing. There are between forty and fifty matchlock-men of Arab origin, long settled in the place, and commanded by a veteran Maghrabi. They receive for pay one dollar's worth of holcus per annum, a quantity sufficient to afford five or six loaves a day: the luxuries of life must be provided by the exercise of some peaceful craft. Including slaves, the total of armed men may be two hundred: of these one carries a Somali or Galla spear, another a dagger, and a third a sword, which is generally the old German cavalry blade. Cannon of small calibre is supposed to be concealed in the palace, but none probably knows their use. The city may contain thirty horses, of which a dozen are royal property: they are miserable ponies, but well trained to the rocks and hills. The Galla Bedouin would oppose an invader with a strong force of spearmen, the approaches to the city are difficult and dangerous, but it is commanded from the north and west, and the walls would crumble at the touch of a six-pounder. Three hundred Arabs and two gallopper guns would take Harar in an hour.

Harar is essentially a commercial town: its citizens live, like those of Zayla, by systematically defrauding the Galla Bedouin, and the Amir has made it a penal offence to buy by weight and scale. He receives, as octroi, from eight to fifteen cubits of Cutch canvas for every donkey-load passing the gates, consequently the beast is so burdened that it must be supported by the drivers. Cultivators are taxed ten per cent., the general and easy rate of this part of Africa, but they pay in kind, which considerably increases the Government share. The greatest merchant may bring to Harar £50 worth of goods, and he who has £20 of capital is considered a wealthy man. The citizens seem to have a more than Asiatic apathy, even in pursuit of gain. When we entered, a caravan was to set out for Zayla on the morrow; after ten days, hardly one half of its number had mustered. The four marches from the city eastward are rarely made under a fortnight, and the average rate of their Kafilahs is not so high even as that of the Somal.

The principal exports from Harar are slaves, ivory, coffee, tobacco, Wars (safflower or bastard saffron), Tobes and woven cottons, mules, holcus, wheat, 'Karanji', a kind of bread used by travellers, ghi, honey, gums (principally mastic and myrrh), and finally sheep's fat and tallows of all sorts. The imports are American sheeting, and other cottons, white and dyed, muslins, red shawls, silks, brass, sheet copper, cutlery (generally the cheap German), Birmingham trinkets, beads and coral, dates, rice, and loaf sugar, gunpowder, paper, and the various other wants of a city in the wild.

Harar is still, as of old,* the great 'half way house' for slaves from Zangaro, Gurague, and the Galla tribes, Alo and others:† Abyssinians and Amharas, the most valued,‡ have become rare since the King of Shoa prohibited the exportation. Women vary in value from 100 to 400 Ashrafis, boys from 9 to 150: the worst are kept for domestic purposes, the best are driven and exported by the Western Arabs§ or by the subjects of H. H. the Imam of Maskat, in exchange for rice and dates. I need scarcely say that commerce would thrive on the decline of slavery: whilst the Felateas or manrazzias are allowed to continue, it is vain to expect industry in the land.

Ivory at Harar amongst the Kafirs is a royal monopoly, and the Amir carries on the one-sided system of trade, common to African monarchs. Elephants abound in Jarjar, the Erar forest, and in the Harirah and other valleys, where they resort during the hot season, in cold descending to the lower regions. The Gallas hunt the animals and receive for the spoils a little cloth: the Amir sends his ivory to Berbera, and sells it by means of a Wakil or agent. The smallest kind is called 'Ruba Aj' (Quarter Ivory), the better description 'Nuss Aj' (Half Ivory), whilst 'Aj', the best kind, fetches from thirty-two to forty dollars per Farasilah of 27 Arab pounds.

The coffee of Harar is too well known in the markets of Europe to

---

* Al Makrizi informs us that in his day Hadiyah supplied the East with black Eunuchs, although the infamous trade was expressly forbidden by the Emperor of Abyssinia.

† The Arusi Gallas are generally driven direct from Ogadayn to Berbera.

‡ 'If you want a brother (in arms),' says the Eastern proverb, 'buy a Nubian, if you would be rich, an Abyssinian, and if you require an ass, a Sawahili (negroid).' Formerly a small load of salt bought a boy in Southern Abyssinia; many of them however, died on their way to the coast.

§ The Firman lately issued by the Sultan [forbidding slavery] and forwarded to the Pasha of Jeddah for the Kaimakan and the Kazi of Meccah, has lately caused a kind of revolution in Western Arabia. The Olema and the inhabitants denounced the rescript as opposed to the Koran, and forced the magistrate to take sanctuary. The Kaimakan came to his assistance with Turkish troops; the latter, however, were soon pressed back into their fort. At this time, the Sherif Abd al-Muttalib arrived at Meccah, from Taif, and almost simultaneously Rashid Pasha came from Constantinople with orders to seize him, send him to the capital, and appoint the Sherif Nazir to act until the nomination of a successor, the state prisoner Mohammed bin Aun. The tumult redoubled. The people attributing the rescript to the English and French Consuls of Jeddah, insisted upon pulling down their flags. The Pasha took them under his protection, and on the 14th January, 1856, the 'Queen' steamer was dispatched from Bombay, with orders to assist the government and to suppress the contest.

require description: it grows in the gardens about the town, in greater quantities amongst the Western Gallas, and in perfection at Jarjar, a district of about seven days' journey from Harar on the Ífat road. It is said that the Amir witholds this valuable article, fearing to glut the Berbera market: he has also forbidden the Harash, or coffee cultivators, to travel lest the art of tending the tree be lost. When I visited Harar, the price per parcel of twenty-seven pounds was a quarter of a dollar, and the hire of a camel carrying twelve parcels to Berbera was five dollars: the profit did not repay labour and risk.

The tobacco of Harar is of a light yellow colour, with good flavour, and might be advantageously mixed with Syrian and other growths. The Alo, or Western Gallas, the principal cultivators, plant it with the holcus, and reap it about five months afterwards. It is cooked for a fortnight, the woody part is removed, and the leaf is packed in sacks for transportation to Berbera. At Harar, men prefer it for chewing as well as smoking; women generally use Surat tobacco. It is bought, like all similar articles, by the eye, and about seventy pounds are to be had for a dollar.

The Wars or Safflower is cultivated in considerable quantities around the city: an abundance is grown in the lands of the Gallas. It is sown when the heavy rains have ceased, and is gathered about two months afterwards. This article, together with slaves, forms the staple commerce between Berbera and Maskat. In Arabia, men dye with it their cotton shirts, women and children use it to stain the skin a bright yellow; besides the purpose of a cosmetic, it also serves as a preservative against cold. When Wars is cheap at Harar, a pound may be bought for a quarter of a dollar.

The Tobes and sashes of Harar are considered equal to the celebrated cloths of Shoa: hand-woven, they as far surpass, in beauty and durability, the vapid produce of European manufactories, as the perfect hand of man excels the finest machinery. On the windward coast, one of these garments is considered a handsome present for a chief. The Harari Tobe consists of a double length of eleven cubits by two in breadth, with a border of bright scarlet, and the average value of a good article, even in the city, is eight dollars. They are made of the fine long-stapled cotton, which grows plentifully upon these hills, and are soft as silk, whilst their warmth admirably adapts them for winter wear. The thread is spun by women with two wooden pins; the loom is worked by both sexes.

Three caravans leave Harar every year for the Berbera market. The first starts early in January, laden with coffee, Tobes, Wars, ghi, gums, and other articles to be bartered for cottons, silks, shawls, and Surat tobacco. The second sets out in February. The principal caravan, conveying slaves, mules, and other valuable articles, enters Berbera a few days before the close of the season: it numbers about 3,000 souls, and is commanded by one of the Amir's principal officers, who enjoys the title of Ebi or leader. Any or all of these kafilahs might be stopped by spending four or five hundred dollars amongst the Jibril Abokr tribe, or even by a sloop of war at the emporium. 'He who commands at Berbera, holds the beard of Harar in his hand', is a saying which I heard even within the city walls.[2]

The furniture of a house at Harar is simple—a few skins, and in rare cases a Persian rug, stools, coarse mats, and Somali pillows, wooden spoons, and porringers shaped with a hatchet, finished with a knife, stained red, and brightly polished. The gourd is a conspicuous article; smoked inside and fitted with a cover of the same material, it serves as cup, bottle, pipe, and water-skin: a coarse and heavy kind of pottery, of black or brown clay, is used by some of the citizens.

The inhabitants of Harar live well. The best meat, as in Abyssinia, is beef: it rather resembled, however, in the dry season when I ate it, the lean and stringy sirloins of Old England in Hogarth's days. A hundred and twenty chickens, or sixty-six full-grown fowls, may be purchased for a dollar, and the citizens do not, like the Somal, consider them carrion. Goat's flesh is good, and the black-faced Berbera sheep, after the rains, is, here as elsewhere, delicious. The staff of life is holcus. Fruit grows almost wild, but it is not prized as an article of food: the plantains are coarse and bad, grapes seldom come to maturity; although the brab flourishes in every ravine, and the palm becomes a lofty tree, it has not been taught to fructify, and the citizens do not know how to dress, preserve or pickle their limes and citrons. No vegetables but gourds are known. From the cane, which thrives upon these hills, a little sugar is made: the honey of which, as the Abyssinians say, 'the land stinks', is the general sweetener. The condiment of East Africa is red pepper.

.   .   .

To resume, dear L., the thread of our adventures at Harar.

Immediately after arrival, we were called upon by the Arabs, a strange mixture. One, the Haji Mukhtar, was a Maghrebi from Fez: an expatriation of forty years had changed his hissing Arabic as little as his 'rocky face'. This worthy had a coffee-garden assigned to him, as commander of the Amir's bodyguard: he introduced himself to us, however, as a merchant, which led us to look upon him as a spy. Another, Haji Hasan, was a thorough-bred Persian: he seemed to know everybody, and was on terms of bosom friendship with half the world from Cairo to Calcutta, Moslem, Christian, and Pagan. Amongst the rest was a boy from Meccah, a Maskat man, a native of Suez, and a citizen of Damascus: the others were Arabs from al Yemen. All were most civil to us at first; but, afterwards, when our interviews with the Amir ceased, they took alarm, and prudently cut us.

The Arabs were succeeded by the Somal, amongst whom the Hammal and Long Gulad found relatives, friends, and acquaintances, who readily recognized them as government servants at Aden. These visitors at first came in fear and trembling with visions of the Harar jail: they desired my men to return the visit by night, and made frequent excuses for apparent want of hospitality. Their apprehensions, however, soon vanished: presently they began to prepare entertainments, and, as we were without money, they willingly supplied us with certain comforts of life. Our three Habr Awal enemies, seeing the tide of fortune settling in our favour, changed their tactics: they threw the past upon their two Harari companions, and proposed themselves as Abbans on our return to Berbera. This offer was politely staved off; in the first place we were already provided with protectors, and secondly these men belonged to the Ayyal Shirdon, a clan most hostile to the Habr Girhajis. They did not fail to do us all the harm in their power, but again my good star triumphed.

After a day's repose, we were summoned by the Treasurer, early in the forenoon, to wait upon the Gerad Mohammed. Sword in hand, and followed by the Hammal and Long Gulad, I walked to the 'palace', and entering a little ground-floor room on the right of and close to the audience-hall, found the minister sitting upon a large dais covered with Persian carpets. He was surrounded by six of his brother Gerads or councillors, two of them in turbans, the rest with bare and shaven heads: their Tobes, as is customary on such occasions of ceremony, were allowed to fall beneath the waist. The lower part of the hovel was covered with dependents, amongst whom my Somal took their seats: it seemed to be customs' time, for names were being registered, and money changed hands. The Grandees were eating Kat, or as it is here called 'Ját'. One of the party prepared for the Prime Minister the tenderest twigs of the tree, plucking off the points of even the softest leaves. Another pounded the plant with a little water in a wooden mortar: of this paste, called 'Al-Madkuk', a bit was handed to each person, who, rolling it into a ball, dropped it into his mouth. All at times, as is the custom, drank cold water from a smoked gourd, and seemed to dwell upon the sweet and pleasant draught. I could not but remark the fine flavour of the plant after the coarser quality grown in al Yemen. Europeans perceive but little effect from it—friend S. and I once tried in vain a strong infusion—the Arabs, however, unaccustomed to stimulants and narcotics, declare that, like opium eaters, they cannot live without the excitement. It seems to produce in them a manner of dreamy enjoyment, which, exaggerated by time and distance, may have given rise to that splendid myth the Lotos, and the Lotophagi. It is held by the Ulema here as in Arabia, 'Akl al-Salikin', or the Food of the Pious, and literati remark that it has the singular properties of enlivening the imagination, clearing the ideas, cheering the heart, diminishing sleep, and taking the place of food. The people of Harar eat it every day from 9 a.m. till near noon, when they dine and afterwards indulge in something stronger—millet-beer and mead.

The Gerad, after polite inquiries, seated me by his right hand upon the Dais, where I ate Kat and fingered my rosary, whilst he transacted the business of the day. Then one of the elders took from a little recess in the wall a large book, and uncovering it, began to recite a long Dua or Blessing upon the Prophet: at the end of each period all present in toned the response, 'Allah bless our Lord Mohammed with his Progeny and his Companions, one and all!' This exercise lasting half an hour afforded me the opportunity—much desired—of making an impression. The reader, misled by a marginal reference, happened to say, 'Angels, Men, and Jinnis': the Gerad took the book and found written, 'Men, Angels, and Jinnis.' Opinions were divided as to the order of beings, when I explained that human nature, which amongst Moslems is *not* a little lower than the angelic, ranked highest, because of it were created prophets, apostles, and saints, whereas the other is but a 'Wasitah' or connection between the Creator and his creatures. My theology won general approbation and a few kinder glances from the elders.

Prayer concluded, a chamberlain whispered the Gerad, who arose, deposited his black coral rosary, took up an inkstand, donned a white 'Badan' or sleeveless Arab cloak over his cotton shirt, shuffled off the Dais into his slippers, and disappeared. Presently we were summoned to an interview with the Amir: this time I was allowed to approach the outer door with covered feet. Entering ceremoniously as before, I was motioned by the Prince to sit near the Gerad, who occupied a Persian rug on the ground to the right of the throne: my two attendants squatted upon the humbler mats in front and at a greater distance. After sundry inquiries about the changes that had taken place at Aden, the letter was suddenly produced by the Amir, who looked upon it suspiciously and bade me explain its contents. I was then asked by the Gerad whether it was my intention to buy and sell at Harar: the reply was, 'We are no buyers nor sellers; we have become your guests to pay our respects to the Amir—whom may Allah preserve!—and that the friendship between the two powers may endure.' This appearing satisfactory, I added, in lively remembrance of the proverbial delays of Africa, where two or three months may elapse before a letter is answered or a verbal message, delivered, that perhaps the Prince would be pleased to dismiss us soon, as the air of Harar was too dry for me, and my attendants were in danger of the small-pox, then raging in the town. The Amir, who was chary of words, bent towards the Gerad, who briefly ejaculated, 'The reply will be vouchsafed': with this un-satisfactory answer the interview ended.

Shortly after arrival, I sent my Salaam to one of the Ulema, Shaykh Jami of the Berteri Somal: he accepted the excuse of ill health, and at once came to see me. This personage appeared in the form of a little black man aged about forty, deeply pitted by small-pox, with a pro-truding brow, a tufty beard and rather delicate features: his hands and feet were remarkably small. Married to a descendant of the Sherif Yunis, he had acquired great reputation as an Alim or Savan, a peace-policy-man, and an ardent Moslem. Though an imperfect Arabic scholar, he proved remarkably well read in the religious sciences, and even the Meccans had, it was said, paid him the respect of kissing his hand during his pilgrimage. In his second character, his success was not remarkable, the principal results being a spear-thrust in the head, and being generally told to read his books and leave men alone. Yet he is always doing good 'lillah', that is to say, gratis and for Allah's sake: his pugnacity and bluntness—the prerogatives of the 'peaceful'—gave him some authority over the Amir, and he has often been employed on political missions amongst the different chiefs. Nor has his ardour for propagandism been thoroughly gratified. He commenced his travels with an intention of winning the crown of glory without delay, by murdering the British resident at Aden:* struck, however, with the

* The Shaykh himself gave me this information. As a rule it is most imprudent for Europeans holding high official positions in these barbarous regions, to live as they do,

order and justice of our rule, he changed his intentions and offered
al-Islam to the officer, who received it so urbanely, that the simple
Eastern repenting having intended to cut the Kafir's throat, began to
pray fervently for his conversion. Since that time he has made it a
point of duty to attempt every infidel: I never heard, however, that he
succeeded with a soul.

The Shaykh's first visit did not end well. He informed me that the
old Osmanlis conquered Stambul in the days of Omar. I imprudently
objected to the date, and he revenged himself for the injury done to
his fame by the favourite ecclesiastical process of privily damning me
for a heretic, and a worse than heathen. Moreover he had sent me a
kind of ritual which I had perused in an hour and returned to him: this
prepossessed the Shaykh strongly against me, lightly 'skimming'
books being a form of idleness as yet unknown to the ponderous East.

Our days at Harar were monotonous enough. In the morning we
looked to the mules, drove out the cats—as great a nuisance here as at
Aden—and ate for breakfast lumps of boiled beef with peppered
holcus-scones. We were kindly looked upon by one Sultan, a sick and
decrepid Eunuch, who having served five Amirs, was allowed to remain in the palace. To appearance he was mad: he wore upon his poll a
scratch wig, half white and half black, like Day and Night in mas-
querades. But his conduct was sane. At dawn he sent us bad plantains,
wheaten crusts, and cups of unpalatable coffee-tea,* and, assisted by a
crone more decrepid than himself, prepared for me his water-pipe, a
gourd fitted with two reeds and a tile of baked clay by way of bowl:
now he 'nagged' at the slave-girls, who were slow to work, then
burst into a fury because some visitor ate Kat without offering it to
him, or crossed the royal threshold in sandal or slipper. The other inmates of the house were Galla slave-girls, a great nuisance, especially
one Berille, an unlovely maid, whose shrill voice and shameless manners were a sad scandal to pilgrims and pious Moslems.

* In the best coffee countries, Harar and al-Yemen, the berry is reserved for exportation. The Southern Arabs use for economy and health—the bean being considered heating
—Kishr or follicle. This in Harar is a woman's drink. The men considering the berry too
dry and heating for their arid atmosphere, toast the leaf on a girdle, pound it, and prepare
an infusion which they declare to be most wholesome, but which certainly suggests weak
senna. The boiled coffee-leaf has been tried and approved of in England; we omit, however, to toast it.

---

unarmed and unattended. The appearance of utter security may impose, where strong
motives for assassination are wanting. At the same time the practice has occasioned many
losses which singly, to use an Indian statesman's phrase, would have 'dimmed a victory'.

About 8 a.m. the Somal sent us gifts of citrons, plantains, sugar cane, limes, wheaten bread, and stewed fowls. At the same time the house became full of visitors, Harari and others, most of them pretexting inquiries after old Sultan's health. Noon was generally followed by a little solitude, the people retiring to dinner and siesta: we were then again provided with bread and beef from the Amir's kitchen. In the afternoon the house again filled, and the visitors dispersed only for supper. Before sunset we were careful to visit the mules tethered in the court-yard; being half starved they often attempted to desert.

It was harvest home at Harar, a circumstance which worked us much annoy. In the mornings the Amir, attended by forty or fifty guards, rode to a hill north of the city, where he inspected his Galla reapers and threshers, and these men were feasted every evening at our quarters with flesh, beer, and mead.* The strong drinks caused many a wordy war, and we made a point of exhorting the pagans, with poor success I own, to purer lives.

We spent our *soirée* alternately bepreaching the Gallas, 'chaffing' Mad Sa'id, who despite his seventy years was a hale old Bedouin with a salt and sullen repartee, and quarrelling with the slave-girls. Berille the loud-lunged, or Aminah the pert, would insist upon extinguishing the fat-fed lamp long ere bed-time, or would enter the room singing, laughing, dancing, and clapping a measure with their palms, when, stoutly aided by old Sultan, who shrieked like a hyena on these occasions, we ejected her in extreme indignation. All then was silence without: not so—alas!—within. Mad Sa'id snored fearfully, and Abtidon chatted half the night with some Bedouin friend, who had dropped in to supper. On our hard couches we did not enjoy either the *noctes* or the *cœnæ deorum*.

The even tenour of such days was varied by a perpetual reference to the rosary, consulting sooth-sayers, and listening to reports and rumours brought to us by the Somal in such profusion that we all sighed for a discontinuance. The Gerad Mohammed, excited by the Habr Awal, was curious in his inquiries concerning me: the astute Senior had heard of our leaving the End of Time with the Gerad Adan,

---

* This is the Abyssinian 'Tej', a word so strange to European organs, that some authors write it 'Zatsh'. At Harar it is made of honey dissolved in about fifteen parts of hot water, strained and fermented for seven days with the bark of a tree called Kudidah; when the operation is to be hurried, the vessel is placed near the fire. Ignorant Africa can ferment, not distil, yet it must be owned she is skilful in her rude art. Every traveller has praised the honey-wine of the Highlands, and some have not scrupled to prefer it to champagne. It exhilarates, excites and acts as an aphrodisiac; the consequence is, that at Harar all men, pagans and sages, priests and rulers, drink it.

and his mind fell into the fancy that we were transacting some business for the Hajj Sharmakay, the popular bugbear of Harar. Our fate was probably decided by the arrival of a youth of the Ayyal Gedid clan, who reported that three brothers had landed in the Somali country, that two of them were anxiously awaiting at Berbera the return of the third from Harar, and that, though dressed like Moslems, they were really Englishmen in government employ. Visions of cutting off caravans began to assume a hard and palpable form: the Habr Awal ceased intriguing, and the Gerad Mohammed resolved to adopt the *suaviter in modo* whilst dealing with his dangerous guest.

Some days after his first visit, the Shaykh Jami, sending for the Hammal, informed him of an intended trip from Harar: my follower suggested that we might well escort him. The good Shaykh at once offered to apply for leave from the Gerad Mohammed; not, however, finding the minister at home, he asked us to meet him at the palace on the morrow, about the time of Kat-eating.

We had so often been disappointed in our hopes of a final 'lay-public', that on this occasion much was not expected. However, about 6 a.m., we were all summoned and entering the Gerad's levee-room were, as usual, courteously received. I had distinguished his complaint—chronic bronchitis—and resolving to make a final impression, related to him all its symptoms, and promised, on reaching Aden, to send the different remedies employed by ourselves. He clung to the hope of escaping his sufferings, whilst the attendant courtiers looked on approvingly, and begged me to lose no time. Presently the Gerad was sent for by the Amir, and after a few minutes I followed him, on this occasion alone. Ensued a long conversation about the state of Aden, of Zayla, of Berbera, and of Stambul. The chief put a variety of questions about Arabia, and every object there: the answer was that the necessity of commerce confined us to the gloomy rock. He used some obliging expressions about desiring our friendship, and having considerable respect for a people who built, he understood, large ships. I took the opportunity of praising Harar in cautious phrase, and especially of regretting that its coffee was not better known amongst the Franks. The small wizen-faced man smiled, as Moslems say, the smile of Omar:* seeing his brow relax for the first time, I told him that

---

* The Caliph Omar is said to have smiled once and wept once. The smile was caused by the recollection of his having eaten his paste-gods in the days of ignorance. The tear was shed in remembrance of having buried alive, as was customary amongst the Pagan Arabs, his infant daughter, who, whilst he placed her in the grave, with her little hands beat the dust off his beard and garment.

being now restored to health, we requested his commands for Aden. He signified consent with a nod, and the Gerad, with many compliments, gave me a letter addressed to the Political Resident, and requested me to take charge of a mule as a present. I then arose, recited a short prayer, the gist of which was that the Amir's days and reign might be long in the land, and that the faces of his foes might be blackened here and hereafter, bent over his hand, and retired. Returning to the Gerad's levee-hut, I saw by the countenances of my two attendants that they were not a little anxious about the interview, and comforted them with the whispered word 'Achha'—'all right!'

Presently appeared the Gerad, accompanied by two men, who brought my servants' arms, and the revolver which I had sent to the prince. This was a *contretemps*. It was clearly impossible to take back the present, besides which, I suspected some finesse to discover my feelings towards him: the other course would ensure delay. I told the Gerad that the weapon was intended especially to preserve the Amir's life, and for further effect, snapped caps in rapid succession to the infinite terror of the august company. The minister returned to his master, and soon brought back the information that after a day or two another mule should be given to me. With suitable acknowledgements we arose, blessed the Gerad, bade adieu to the assembly, and departed joyful, the Hammal in his glee speaking broken English, even in the Amir's courtyard.

Returning home, we found the good Shaykh Jami, to whom we communicated the news with many thanks for his friendly aid. I did my best to smooth his temper about Turkish history, and succeeded. Becoming communicative, he informed me that the original object of his visit was the offer of good offices, he having been informed that in the town was a man who brought down the birds from heaven, and the citizens having been thrown into great excitement by the probable intentions of such a personage. Whilst he sat with us, Kabir Khalil, one of the principal Ulema, and one Haji Abdullah, a Shaykh of distinguished fame who had been dreaming dreams in our favour, sent their salaams. This is one of the many occasions in which, during a long residence in the East, I have had reason to be grateful to the learned, whose influence over the people when unbiassed by bigotry is decidedly for good. That evening there was great joy amongst the Somal, who had been alarmed for the safety of my companions; they brought them presents of Harari Tobes, and a feast of fowls, limes, and wheaten bread for the stranger.

On the 11th of January I was sent for by the Gerad and received the second mule. At noon we were visited by the Shaykh Jami, who, after a long discourse upon the subject of Sufiism,* invited me to inspect his books. When midday prayer was concluded we walked to his house, which occupies the very centre of the city: in its courtyard is 'Gay Humburti', the historic rock upon which Saint Nur held converse with the Prophet Khizr. The Shaykh, after seating us in a room about ten feet square, and lined with scholars and dusty tomes, began reading out a treatise upon the genealogies of the Grand Masters, and showed me in half a dozen tracts the tenets of the different schools. The only valuable MS. in the place was a fine old copy of the Koran; the Kamus and the Sihah were there,† but by no means remarkable for beauty or correctness. Books at Harar are mostly antiques, copyists being exceedingly rare, and the square massive character is more like Cufic with diacritical points, than the graceful modern Naskhi. I could not, however, but admire the bindings: no Eastern country save Persia surpasses them in strength and appearance. After some desultory conversation the Shaykh ushered us into an inner room, or rather a dark closet partitioned off from the study, and ranged us around the usual dish of boiled beef, holcus bread, and red pepper. After returning to the study we sat for a few minutes—Easterns rarely remain long after dinner and took leave, saying that we must call upon the Gerad Mohammed.

Nothing worthy of mention occurred during our final visit to the minister. He begged me not to forget his remedies when we reached Aden: I told him that without further loss of time we would start on the morrow, Friday, after prayers, and he simply ejaculated, 'It is well, if Allah please!' Scarcely had we returned home, when the clouds, which had been gathering since noon, began to discharge heavy showers, and a few loud thunder-claps to reverberate amongst the hills. We passed that evening surrounded by the Somal, who charged us with letters and many messages to Berbera. Our intention was to mount early on Friday morning. When we awoke, however, a mule had strayed and was not brought back for some hours. Before noon Shaykh Jami called upon us, informed us that he would travel on the most auspicious day—Monday—and exhorted us to patience, deprecating departure upon Friday, the Sabbath. Then he arose to take leave, blessed us at some length, prayed that we might be borne upon

---

* The Eastern parent of Free-Masonry.
† Two celebrated Arabic dictionaries.

the wings of safety, again advised Monday, and promised at all events to meet us at Wilensi.

I fear that the Shaykh's counsel was on this occasion likely to be disregarded. We had been absent from our goods and chattels a whole fortnight: the people of Harar are famously fickle; we knew not what the morrow might bring forth from the Amir's mind—in fact, all these African cities are prisons on a large scale, into which you enter by your own will, and, as the significant proverb says, you leave by another's. However, when the mosque prayers ended, a heavy shower and the stormy aspect of the sky preached patience more effectually than did the divine: we carefully tethered our mules, and unwillingly deferred our departure till next morning.[3]

A herd of Aoul, or Sæmmering's Gazelle.

IX

A Ride to Berbera

LONG BEFORE DAWN ON Saturday, 13th January, the mules were saddled, bridled, and charged with our scanty luggage. After a hasty breakfast we shook hands with old Sultan the Eunuch, mounted and pricked through the desert streets. Suddenly my weakness and sickness left me—so potent a drug is joy!—and, as we passed the gates loudly salaaming to the warders, who were crouching over the fire inside, a weight of care and anxiety fell from me like a cloak of lead.

Yet, dear L., I had time, on the top of my mule for musing upon how melancholy a thing is success. Whilst failure inspirits a man, attainment reads the sad prosy lesson that all our glories 'are shadows, not substantial things'. Truly said the sayer, 'disappointment is the salt of life'—a salutary bitter which strengths the mind for fresh exertion, and gives a double value to the prize.

This shade of melancholy soon passed away. The morning was beautiful. A cloudless sky, then untarnished by sun, tinged with reflected blue the mist-crowns of the distant peaks and the smoke wreaths hanging round the sleeping villages, and the air was a cordial after the rank atmosphere of the town. The dew hung in large diamonds from the coffee trees, the spur-fowl crew blithely in the bushes by the wayside: briefly, never did the face of Nature appear to me so truly lovely.

We hurried forward, unwilling to lose time and fearing the sun of the Erar valley. With arms cocked, a precaution against the possibility of Galla spears in ambuscade, we crossed the river, entered the yawning chasm and ascended the steep path. My companions were in the highest spirits, nothing interfered with the general joy but the villain Abtidon, who loudly boasted in a road crowded with market people, that the mule which he was riding had been given to us by the Amir as a Jizyah or tribute. The Hammal, direfully wrath, threatened to shoot him upon the spot, and it was not without difficulty that I calmed the storm.

Passing Gafra we ascertained from the Midgans that the Gerad Adan had sent for my books and stored them in his own cottage. We made in a direct line for Kondura. At 1 p.m. we safely threaded the Galla's pass, and about an hour afterwards we exclaimed 'Alhamdulillah' at the sight of Sagharrah and the distant Marar Prairie. Entering the village we discharged our fire-arms: the women received us with the Masharrad or joy-cry, and as I passed the enclosure the Geradah Khayrah performed the 'Fola' by throwing over me some handfuls of toasted grain. The men gave cordial *poignées de mains*, some danced with joy to see us return alive; they had heard of our being imprisoned, bastinadoed, slaughtered; they swore that the Gerad was raising an army to rescue or revenge us—in fact, had we been their kinsmen more excitement could not have been displayed. Lastly, in true humility, crept forward the End of Time, who, as he kissed my hand, was upon the point of tears: he had been half-starved, despite his dignity as Sharmakay's Mercury, and had spent his weary nights and days reciting the chapter Y.S. and fumbling the rosary for omens. The Gerad, he declared, would have given him a sheep and one of his daughters to wife, temporarily, but Shirwa had interfered, he had hindered the course of his sire's generosity: 'Cursed be he,' exclaimed the End of Time, 'who with dirty feet defiles the pure water of the stream!'

We entered the smoky cottage. The Gerad and his sons were at Wilensi settling the weighty matter of a caravan which had been plundered by the Usbayhan tribe—in their absence the good Khayrah and her daughters did the duties of hospitality by cooking rice and a couple of fowls. A pleasant evening was spent in recounting our perils as travellers will do, and complimenting one another upon the power of our star.

At eight the next morning we rode to Wilensi. As we approached it all the wayfarers and villagers inquired Hibernically if we were the

party that had been put to death by the Amir of Harar. Loud congratu-
lations and shouts of joy awaited our arrival. The Kalendar was in a
paroxysm of delight: both Shehrazade and Deenarzade were affected
with giggling and what might be blushing. We reviewed our property
and found that the One-eyed had been a faithful steward, so faithful
indeed, that he had well nigh starved the two women. Presently
appeared the Gerad and his sons bringing with them my books; the
former was at once invested with a gaudy Abyssinian Tobe of many
colours, in which he sallied forth from the cottage the admired of all
admirers. The pretty wife Sudiyah and the good Khayrah were made
happy by sundry gifts of huge Birmingham ear-rings, brooches and
bracelets, scissors, needles, and thread. The evening as usual ended in a
feast.

We halted a week at Wilensi to feed—in truth my companions had
been faring lentenly at Harar—and to lay in stock and strength for the
long desert march before us. A Somali was dispatched to the city under
orders to load an ass with onions, tobacco, spices, wooden platters, and
Karanji, which our penniless condition had prevented our purchasing.
I spent the time collecting a vocabulary of the Harari tongue under the
auspices of Mad Sa'id and Ali the poet, a Somali educated at the Alma
Mater. He was a small black man, long-headed, and long-backed, with
remarkably prominent eyes, a bulging brow, nose pertly turned up,
and lean jaws almost unconscious of beard. He knew the Arabic, Somali,
Galla, and Harari languages, and his acuteness was such, that I found
no difficulty in what usually proves the hardest task—extracting the
grammatical forms. 'A poet, the son of a Poet', to use his own phrase, he
evinced a Horatian respect for the beverage which bards love, and his
discourse, whenever it strayed from the line of grammar, savoured of
over reverence for the goddess whom Pagans associated with Bacchus
and Ceres. He was also a patriot and a Tyrtæus. No clan ever attacked
his Girhis without smarting under terrible sarcasms, and his sneers at
the young warriors for want of ardour in resisting Gudabirsi encroach-
ments were quoted as models of the 'withering'. Stimulated by the
present of a Tobe, he composed a song in honour of the pilgrim: I will
offer a literal translation of the exordium, though sentient of the fact
that modesty shrinks from such quotations.

> Formerly, my sire and self held ourselves songsters:
> Only today, however, I really begin to sing.
> At the order of Abdullah, Allah sent, my tongue is loosed,
> The son of the Kuraysh by a thousand generations,

He hath visited Audal, and Sahil and Adari;*
A hundred of his ships float on the sea;
His intellect, etc., etc., etc.

When not engaged with Ali the Poet I amused myself by consoling
Mad Sa'id, who was deeply afflicted, his son having received an ugly
stab in the shoulder. Thinking, perhaps, that the Senior anticipated
some evil results from the wound, I attempted to remove the impression. 'Alas, O Hajj!' groaned the old man, 'it is not that!—how can the
boy be *my* boy, I who have ever given instead of receiving stabs?' nor
would he be comforted, on account of the youth's progeniture. At
other times we summoned the heads of the clans and proceeded to
write down their genealogies. This always led to a scene beginning
with piano, but rapidly rising to the strepitoso. Each tribe and clan
wished to rank first, none would be even second—what was to be
done? When excitement was at its height, the paper and pencil were
torn out of my hand, stubbly beards were pitilessly pulled, and daggers
half started from their sheaths. These quarrels were, however, easily
composed, and always passed off in storms of abuse, laughter, and
derision.

With the end of the week's repose came Shaykh Jami, the Berteri,
equipped as a traveller with sword, praying-skin, and water-bottle.
This bustling little divine, whose hobby it was to make every man's
business his own, was accompanied by his brother, in nowise so prayerful a person, and by four burly, black-looking Widads, of whose birth,
learning, piety, and virtues he spoke in terms eloquent. I gave them a
supper of rice, ghi, and dates in my hut, and with much difficulty excused myself on plea of ill health from a Samrah or night's entertain-
ment—the chanting some serious book from evening even to the small
hours. The Shaykh informed me that his peaceful errand on that
occasion was to determine a claim of blood-money amongst the neighbouring Bedouin. The case was rich in Somali manners. One man gave
medicine to another who happened to die about a month afterwards:
the father of the deceased at once charged the mediciner with poisoning, and demanded the customary fine. Mad Sa'id grumbled certain
disrespectful expressions about the propriety of divines confining
themselves to prayers and Koran, whilst the Gerad Adan, after listening to the Shaykh's violent denunciation of the Somali doctrine, 'Fire,

* The Somal invariably call Berbera the 'Sahil' (meaning in Arabic the sea-shore), as
Zayla with them is 'Audal', and Harar 'Adari'.

but not shame!'* conducted his head-scratcher, and with sly sarcasm declared that he had been Islamized afresh that day.

On Sunday, the 21st of January, our messenger returned from Harar, bringing with him supplies for the road: my vocabulary was finished,† and as nothing delayed us at Wilensi, I determined to set out the next day. When the rumour went abroad every inhabitant of the village flocked to our hut, with the view of seeing what he could beg or borrow: we were soon obliged to close it, with peremptory orders that none be admitted but the Shaykh Jami. The divine appeared in the afternoon accompanied by all the incurables of the country-side: after hearing the tale of the blood-money, I determined that talismans were the best and safest medicines in those mountains. The Shaykh at first doubted their efficacy. But when my diploma as a master Sufi was exhibited, a new light broke upon him and his attendant Widads. 'Verily he hath declared himself this day!' whispered each to his neighbour, still sorely mystified. Shaykh Jami carefully inspected the document, raised it reverently to his forehead, and muttered some prayers: he then in humble phrase begged a copy, and required from me 'Ijazah' or permission to act as master. The former request was granted without hesitation, about the latter I preferred to temporize: he then owned himself my pupil, and received, as a well-merited acknowledgment of his services, a pencil and a silk turban.

The morning fixed for our departure came; no one, however, seemed ready to move. The Hammal, who but the night before had been full of ardour and activity, now hung back; we had no coffee, no water-bags, and Deenarzade had gone to buy gourds in some distant village. This was truly African: twenty-six days had not sufficed to do the work of a single watch! No servants had been procured for us by the Gerad, although he had promised a hundred whenever required. Long Gulad had imprudently lent his dagger to the smooth-tongued Yusuf Dira, who hearing of the departure, naturally absconded. And, at the last moment, one Abdi Aman, who had engaged himself at Harar as guide to Berbera for the sum of ten dollars, asked a score.

A display of energy was clearly necessary. I sent the Gerad with directions to bring the camels at once, and ordered the Hammal to pull down the huts. Abdi Aman was told to go to Harar—or the other place—Long Gulad was promised another dagger at Berbera; a

---

* 'Al-Nár wa lá al-Ar', an Arabic maxim, somewhat more forcible than our 'death rather than dishonour'= 'Hell with Honour'.

† See Appendix 3.

message was left directing Deenarzade to follow, and the word was given to load.

By dint of shouting and rough language, the caravan was ready at 9 a.m. The Gerad Adan and his ragged tail leading, we skirted the eastern side of Wilensi, and our heavily laden camels descended with pain the rough and stony slope of the wide Kloof dividing it from the Marar Prairie. At 1 p.m. the chief summoned us to halt: we pushed on, however, without regarding him. Presently, Long Gulad and the End of Time were missing; contrary to express orders they had returned to seek the dagger. To ensure discipline, on this occasion I must have blown out the long youth's brains, which were, he declared, addled by the loss of his weapon: the remedy appeared worse than the disease.

Attended only by the Hammal, I entered with pleasure the Marar Prairie. In vain the Gerad entreated us not to venture upon a place swarming with lions; vainly he promised to kill sheep and oxen for a feast; we took abrupt leave of him, and drove away the camels.

Journeying slowly over the skirt of the plain, when rejoined by the truants, we met a party of travellers, who, as usual, stopped to inquire the news. Their chief, mounted upon an old mule, proved to be Madar Farih, a Somali well known at Aden. He consented to accompany us as far as the halting place, expressed astonishment at our escaping Harar, and gave us intelligence which my companions judged grave. The Gerad Hirsi of the Berteri, amongst whom Madar had been living, was incensed with us for leaving the direct road. Report informed him, moreover, that we had given 600 dollars and various valuables to the Gerad Adan—Why then had he been neglected? Madar sensibly advised us to push forward that night, and to 'ware the bush, whence Midgans might use their poisoned arrows.

We alighted at the village formerly beneath Gurays, now shifted to a short distance from those hills. Presently appeared Deenarzade, hung round with gourds and swelling with hurt feelings: she was accompanied by Dahabo, sister of the valiant Beuh, who, having for ever parted from her graceless husband, the Gerad, was returning under our escort to the Gurgi of her family. Then came Yusuf Dira with a smiling countenance and smooth manners, bringing the stolen dagger and many excuses for the mistake; he was accompanied by a knot of kinsmen deputed by the Gerad as usual for no good purpose. That worthy had been informed that his Berteri rival offered a hundred cows for our persons, dead or alive: he pathetically asked my attendants 'Do you love your pilgrim?' and suggested that if they did so, they might as well send him a little more cloth, upon the receipt of which he would escort us with fifty horsemen.

My Somal lent a willing ear to a speech which smelt of falsehood a mile off: they sat down to debate; the subject was important, and for three mortal hours did that palaver endure. I proposed proceeding at once. They declared that the camels could not walk, and that the cold of the prairie was death to man. Pointing to a caravan of grain-carriers that awaited our escort, I then spoke of starting next morning. Still they hesitated. At length darkness came on, and knowing it to be a mere waste of time to debate over night about dangers to be faced next day, I ate my dates and drank my milk, and lay down to enjoy tranquil sleep in the deep silence of the desert.

The morning of the 23rd of January found my companions as usual in a state of faint-heartedness. The Hammal was deputed to obtain permission for fetching the Gerad and all the Gerad's men. This was positively refused. I could not, however, object to sending sundry Tobes to the cunning idiot, in order to back up a verbal request for the escort. Thereupon Yusuf Dira, Madar Farih, and the other worthies took leave, promising to dispatch the troop before noon: I saw them depart with pleasure, feeling that we had bidden adieu to the Girhis. The greatest danger we had run was from the Gerad Adan, a fact of which I was not aware till some time after my return to Berbera: he had always been plotting an *avanie** which, if attempted, would have cost him dear, but at the same time would certainly have proved fatal to us.

Noon arrived, but no cavalry. My companions had promised that if disappointed they would start before nightfall and march till morning. But when the camels were sent for, one, as usual if delay was judged advisable, had strayed: they went in search of him, so as to give time for preparation to the caravan. I then had a sharp explanation with my men, and told them in conclusion that it was my determination to cross the Prairie alone, if necessary, on the morrow.

That night heavy clouds rolled down from the Gurays Hills, and veiled the sky with a deeper gloom. Presently came a thin streak of blue lightning and a roar of thunder, which dispersed like flies the mob of gazers from around my Gurgi; then rain streamed through our hut as though we had been dwelling under a system of cullenders. Deenarzade declared herself too ill to move; Shehrazade swore that she would not work: briefly, that night was by no means pleasantly spent.

At dawn, on the 24th, we started across the Marar Prairie with a

* Extortionate exaction.—Ed.

caravan of about twenty men and thirty women, driving camels, carry-ing grain, asses, and a few sheep. The long straggling line gave a 'wide berth' to the doughty Hirsi and his Berteris, whose camp-fires were clearly visible in the morning grey. The air was raw; piles of purple cloud settled upon the hills, whence cold and damp gusts swept the plain; sometimes we had a shower, at others a Scotch mist, which did not fail to penetrate our thin raiment. My people trembled, and their teeth chattered as though they were walking upon ice. In our slow course we passed herds of quagga and gazelles, but the animals were wild, and both men and mules were unequal to the task of stalking them. About midday we closed up, for our path wound through the valley wooded with Acacia—fittest place for an ambuscade of archers. We dined in the saddle on huge lumps of sun-dried beef, and bits of gum gathered from the trees.

Having at length crossed the prairie without accident, the caravan people shook our hands, congratulated one another, and declared that they owed their lives to us. About an hour after sunset we arrived at Abtidon's home, a large kraal at the foot of the Konti cone: fear of lions drove my people into the enclosure, where we passed a night of scratching. I was now haunted by the dread of a certain complaint for which sulphur is said to be a specific. This is the pest of the inner parts of Somaliland; the people declare it to arise from flies and fleas: the European would derive it from the deficiency or rather the impos-sibility, of ablutions.

'Allah help the Goer, but the Return is Rolling': this adage was ever upon the End of Time's tongue, yet my fate was apparently an excep-tion to the general rule. On the 25th January, we were delayed by the weakness of the camels, which had been half starved in the Girhi mountains. And as we were about to enter the lands of the Habr Awal,*

* This is the second great division of the Somal people, the father of the tribe being Awal, the cadet of Ishak al-Hazrami.

The Habr Awal occupy the coast from Zayla and Siyaro to the lands bordering upon the Berteri tribe. They own the rule of a Gerad, who exercises merely a nominal authority. The late chief's name was 'Bon,' he died about four years ago, but his children have not yet received the turban. The royal race is the Ayyal Abdillah, a powerful clan extending from the Dabasanis Hills to near Jigjiga, skirting the Marar Prairie.

The Habr Awal are divided into a multitude of clans: of these I shall specify only the principal, the subject of the maritime Somal being already familiar to our countrymen. The Esa Musa inhabit part of the mountains south of Berbera. The Mikahil tenant the lowlands on the coast from Berbera to Siyaro. Two large clans, the Ayyal Yunis and the Ayyal Ahmad, have established themselves in Berbera and at Bulhar. Besides these are the Ayyal Abdillah Sa'ad, the Ayyal Jira'ato, who live amongst the Ayyal Yunis—the Bahgobo and the Ayyal Hamid.

then at blood feud with my men, all Habr Girhajis, probably a week would elapse before we could provide ourselves with a fit and proper protector. Already I had been delayed ten days after the appointed time, my comrades at Berbera would be apprehensive of accidents, and although starting from Wilensi we had resolved to reach the coast within the fortnight, a month's march was in clear prospect.

Whilst thus chewing the cud of bitter thought where thought was of scant avail, suddenly appeared the valiant Beuh, sent to visit us by Dahabo his gay sister. He informed us that a guide was in the neighbourhood, and the news gave me an idea. I proposed that he should escort the women, camels, and baggage under the command of the Kalendar to Zayla, whilst we, mounting our mules and carrying only our arms and provisions for four days, might push through the lands of the Habr Awal. After some demur all consented.

It was not without apprehension that I pocketed all my remaining provisions, five biscuits, a few limes, and sundry lumps of sugar. Any delay of accident to our mules would starve us; in the first place, we were about to traverse a desert, and, secondly, where Habr Awal were, they would not sell meat or milk to Habr Girhajis. My attendants provided themselves with a small provision of sun-dried beef, grain, and sweetmeats: only one waterbottle, however, was found amongst the whole party. We arose at dawn after a wet night on the 26th January, but we did not start till 7 a.m., the reason being that all the party, the Kalendar, Shehrazade, and Deenarzade, claimed and would have his or her several and distinct palaver.

Having taken leave of our friends and property,* we spurred our mules, and guided by Beuh, rode through cloud and mist towards Koralay the Saddle-back hill. After an hour's trot over rugged ground falling into the Harawwah valley, we came to a Gudabirsi village, where my companions halted to inquire the news, also to distend their stomachs with milk. Thence we advanced slowly, as the broken path required, through thickets of wild henna to the kraal occupied by Beuh's family. At a distance we were descried by an old acquaintance, Fahi, who straightways began to dance like a little Polyphemus, his shock-wig waving in the air: plentiful potations of milk again delayed my companions, who were now laying in a four days' stock.

* My property arrived safe at Aden after about two months. The mule left under the Kalendar's charge never appeared, and the camels are, I believe, still grazing amongst the Eesa. The fair Shehrazade, having amassed a little fortune, lost no time in changing her condition, an example followed in due time by Deenarzade. And the Kalendar after a visit to Aden, returned to electrify his Zayla friends with long and terrible tales of travel.

Remounting, we resumed our journey over a mass of rock and thicket, watered our mules at holes in a Fiumara, and made our way to a village belonging to the Ugaz or chief of the Gudabirsi tribe. He was a middle-aged man of ordinary presence, and he did not neglect to hold out his hand for a gift which we could not but refuse. Halting for about an hour, we persuaded a guide, by the offer of five dollars and a pair of cloths, to accompany us. 'Dubayr'—the Donkey—who belonged to the Bahgobo clan of the Habr Awal, was a 'long Lankin', unable like all these Bedouin, to endure fatigue. He could not ride, the saddle cut him, and he found his mule restive; lately married, he was incapacitated for walking, and he sadly suffered from thirst. The Donkey little knew, when he promised to show Berbera on the third day what he had bound himself to perform: after the second march he was induced, only by the promise of a large present, and one continual talk of food, to proceed, and often he threw his lengthy form upon the ground, groaning that his supreme hour was at hand. In the land which we were to traverse every man's spear would be against us. By way of precaution, we ordered our protector to choose desert roads and carefully to avoid all kraals. At first, not understanding our reasons, and ever hankering after milk, he could not pass a thorn fence without eyeing it wistfully. On the next day, however, he became more tractable, and before reaching Berbera he showed himself, in consequence of some old blood feud, more anxious even than ourselves to avoid villages.

Remounting, under the guidance of the Donkey, we resumed our eastward course. He was communicative even for a Somali, and began by pointing out, on the right of the road, the ruins of a stone-building, called, as customary in these countries, a fort. Beyond it we came to a kraal, whence all the inhabitants issued with shouts and cries for tobacco. Three o'clock p.m. brought us to a broad Fiumara choked with the thickest and most tangled vegetation: we were shown some curious old Galla wells, deep holes about twenty feet in diameter, excavated in the rock; some were dry, others overgrown with huge creepers, and one only supplied us with tolerable water. The Gudabirsi tribe received them from the Girhi in lieu of blood-money: beyond this watercourse, the ground belongs to the Rer Yunis Jibril, a powerful clan of the Habr Awal, and the hills are thickly studded with thorn-fence and kraal.

Without returning the salutations of the Bedouin, who loudly summoned us to stop and give them the news, we trotted forwards in search of a deserted sheep-fold. At sunset we passed, upon an eminence on our left, the ruins of an ancient settlement, called after its patron Saint, Ao Barhi: and both sides of the mountain road were flanked by tracts of prairie-land, beautifully purpling in the evening air. After a ride of thirty-five miles, we arrived at a large fold, where, by removing the inner thorn-fences, we found fresh grass for our starving beasts. The night was raw and windy, and thick mists deepened into a drizzle, which did not quench our thirst, but easily drenched the saddle cloths, our only bedding. In one sense, however, the foul weather was propitious to us. Our track might easily have been followed by some enterprising son of Yunis Jibril; these tracts of thorny bush are favourite places for cattle lifting; moreover the fire was kept blazing all night, yet our mules were not stolen.

We shook off our slumbers before dawn on the 27th. I remarked near our resting-place, one of those detached heaps of rock, common enough in the Somali country: at one extremity a huge block projects upwards, and suggests the idea of a gigantic canine tooth. The Donkey declared that the summit still bears traces of building and related the legend connected with Moga Madir. There, in times of old, dwelt a Galla maiden whose eye could distinguish a plundering party at a distance of five days' march. The enemies of her tribe, after sustaining heavy losses, hit upon the expedient of an attack, not en chemise, but with their heads muffled in bundles of hay. When Moga, the maiden, informed her sire and clan that a prairie was on its way towards the hill, they deemed her mad; the manœuvre succeeded, and the unhappy seer lost her life. The legend interested me by its wide diffusion. The history of Zarka, the blue-eyed witch of the Jadis tribe, who seized Yamamah by her gramarye, and our Scotch tale of Birnam wood's march, are Asiatic and European facsimiles of African 'Moga's Tooth'.

At 7 a.m. we started through the mist, and trotted eastwards in search of a well. The guide had deceived us: the day before he had promised water at every half mile; he afterwards owned with groans that we should not drink before nightfall. These people seem to lie involuntarily: the habit of untruth with them becomes a second nature. They deceive without object for deceit, and the only way of obtaining from them correct information is to inquire, receive the answer, and determine it to be diametrically opposed to fact.

I will not trouble you, dear L., with descriptions of the uniform and uninteresting scenery through which we rode—horrid hills upon which withered aloes brandished their spears, plains apparently rained upon by a shower of stones, and rolling ground abounding only with thorns like the 'wait-a-bits' of Kafir land, created to tear man's skin or clothes. Our toil was rendered doubly toilsome by the Eastern travellers' dread —the demon of Thirst rode like Care behind us. For twenty-four hours we did not taste water, the sun parched our brains, the mirage mocked us at every turn, and the effect was a species of monomania. As I jogged along with eyes closed against the fiery air, no image unconnected with the want suggested itself. Water ever lay before me— water lying deep in the shady well—water in streams bubbling icy from the rock—water in pellucid lakes inviting me to plunge and revel in their treasures. Now an Indian cloud was showering upon me fluid more precious than molten pearl, then an invisible hand offered a bowl for which the mortal part would gladly have bartered years of life. Then—drear contrast!—I opened my eyes to a heat-reeking plain, and a sky of that eternal metallic blue so lovely to painter and poet, so blank and death-like to us, whose χαλον was tempest, rain-storm, and the huge purple nimbus. I tried to talk—it was in vain, to sing in vain, vainly to think; every idea was bound up in one subject, water.*

As the sun sank into the East we descended the wide Gogaysa valley. With unspeakable delight we saw in the distance a patch of lively green: our animals scented the blessing from afar, they raised their drooping ears, and started with us at a canter, till, turning a corner, we suddenly sighted sundry little wells. To spring from the saddle, to race with our mules, who now feared not the crumbling sides of the pits, to throw ourselves into the muddy pools, to drink a long slow draught, and to dash the water over our burning faces, took less time to do than to recount. A calmer inspection showed a necessity for caution—the surface was alive with tadpoles and insects: prudence, however, had little power at that time, we drank, and drank, and then drank again. As our mules had fallen with avidity upon the grass, I proposed to pass a few hours near the well. My companions, however, pleading the old fear of lions, led the way to a deserted kraal upon a neighbouring hill. We had marched about thirty miles eastward, and had entered a safe country belonging to the Bahgoba, our guide's clan.

At sunrise on the 28th of January, the Donkey, whose limbs refused to work, was lifted into the saddle, declaring that the white man must have been sent from heaven, as a special curse upon the children of Ishak. We started, after filling the water-bottle, down the

* As a rule, twelve hours without water in the desert during hot weather, kills a man. I never suffered severely from thirst but on this occasion; probably it was in consequence of being at the time but in weak health.

Gogaysa valley. Our mules were becoming foot-sore, and the saddles had already galled their backs; we were therefore compelled to the additional mortification of travelling at snail's pace over the dreary hills, and through the uninteresting bush.

About noon we entered Wady Danan, or 'The Sour', a deep chasm in the rocks; the centre is a winding sandy water-course, here and there grassy with tall rushes, and affording at every half mile a plentiful supply of sweet water. The walls of the ravine are steep and rugged, and the thorny jungle clustering at the sides gives a wild appearance to the scene. Traces of animals, quagga and gazelle, everywhere abounded: not being however, in 'Dianic humour', and unwilling to apprise Bedouin of our vicinity, I did not fire a shot. As we advanced, large trees freshly barked and more tender plants torn up by the roots, showed the late passage of a herd of elephants: my mule, though the bravest of our beasts, was in a state of terror all the way. The little grey honey bird* tempted us to wander with all his art: now he sat upon the nearest tree chirping his invitation to a feast, then he preceded us with short jerking flights to point out the path. My people, however, despite the fondness for honey inherent in the Somali palate, would not follow him, deciding that on this occasion his motives for inviting us were not of the purest.

Emerging from the valley, we urged on our animals over comparatively level ground, in the fallacious hope of seeing the sea that night. The trees became rarer as we advanced and the surface metallic. In spots the path led over ironstone that resembled slag. In other places the soil was ochre-coloured: the cattle lick it, probably on account of the aluminous matter with which it is mixed. Everywhere the surface was burnt up by the sun, and withered from want of rain. Towards evening we entered a broad slope called by the Somal Dihh Murodi, or Murodilay, the Elephants' Valley. Crossing its breadth from west to east, we traversed two Fiumaras, the nearer 'Hamar', the further 'Las

---

* Buffon has repeated what a traveller had related, namely, that the honey-bird is a little traitor who conducts men into ambuscades prepared by wild beasts. The Lion-Slayer in S. Africa asserts it to be the belief of Hottentots and the interior tribes, that the bird often lures the unwary pursuer to danger, sometimes guiding him to the midday retreat of a grizzly lion, or bringing him suddenly upon the den of the crouching panther. M. Delegorgue observes that the feeble bird probably seeks aid in removing carrion for the purpose of picking up flies and worms; he acquits him of malice prepense, believing that where the prey is, there carnivorous beasts may be met. The Somal, however, carry their superstition still further. The honey-bird is never trusted by them; he leads, they say, either to the lion's den or the snakes' hiding-place, and often guides his victim into the jaws of the Kaum or plundering party.

Dorhhay', or the Tamarisk water-holes. They were similar in appearance, the usual Wady about 100 yards wide, pearly sand lined with borders of leek green, pitted with dry wells around which lay heaps of withered thorns and a herd of gazelles tripping gracefully over the quartz carpet.

After spanning the valley we began to descend the lower slopes of a high range, whose folds formed like a curtain the bold background of the view. This is the landward face of the Ghauts, over which we were to pass before sighting the sea. Masses of cold grey cloud rolled from the table-formed summit, we were presently shrouded in mist, and as we advanced, rain began to fall. The light of day vanishing, we again descended into a Fiumara with a tortuous and rocky bed, the main drain of the landward mountain side. My companions, now half-starved—they had lived through three days on a handful of dates and sweetmeats—devoured with avidity the wild Jujube berries that strewed the stones. The guide had preceded us: when we came up with him, he was found seated upon a grassy bank on the edge of the rugged torrent bed. We sprang in pleased astonishment from the saddle, dire had been the anticipations that our mules—one of them already required driving with the spear—would, after another night of starvation, leave us to carry their loads upon our own backs. The cause of the phenomenon soon revealed itself. In the rock was a hole about two feet wide, whence a crystal sheet welled over the Fiumara bank, forming a paradise for frog and tadpole. This 'Ga'angal' is considered by the Somal a 'fairies' well': all, however, that the Donkey could inform me was, that when the Nomads settle in the valley, the water sinks deep below the earth—a knot which methinks might be unravelled without the interposition of a god. The same authority declared it to be the work of the 'old ancient' Arabs.

The mules fell hungrily upon the succulent grass, and we, with the most frugal of suppers prepared to pass the rainy night. Presently, however, the doves and Katas,* the only birds here requiring water, approached in flights, and fearing to drink, fluttered around us with shrill cries. They suggested to my companions the possibility of being visited by more formidable beasts, and even man: after a short halt, an advance was proposed; and this was an offer which, on principle, I never refused. We remounted our mules, now refreshed and in good spirits, and began to ascend the stony face of the Eastern hill through a

* The sand-grouse of Egypt and Arabia, the rock-pigeon of Sind and the surrounding countries.

thick mist, deepening the darkness. As we reached the bleak summit, a heavy shower gave my companions a pretext to stop: they readily found a deserted thorn fence, in which we passed a wet night. That day we had travelled at fewest thirty-five miles without seeing the face of man: the country was parched to a cinder for want of water, and all the Nomads had migrated to the plains.

The morning of the 29th January was unusually fine: the last night's rain hung in masses of mist about the hill-sides, and the rapid evaporation clothed the clear background with deep blue. We began the day by ascending a steep goat-track: it led to a sandy Fiumara, overgrown with Jujubes and other thorns, abounding in water, and showing in the rocky sides, caverns fit for a race of Troglodytes. Pursuing the path over a stony valley lying between parallel ranges of hill, we halted at about 10 a.m. in a large patch of grass-land, the produce of the rain, which for some days past had been fertilizing the hill-tops. Whilst our beasts grazed greedily, we sat under a bush, and saw far beneath us the low country which separates the Ghauts from the sea. Through an avenue in the rolling nimbus, we could trace the long courses of Fiumaras, and below, where mist did not obstruct the sight, the tawny plains, cut with water-courses glistening white, shone in their eternal summer.

Shortly after 10 a.m., we resumed our march, and began the descent of the Ghauts by a ravine to which the guide gave the name of 'Kadar.' No sandy water-course, the 'Pass' of this barbarous land, here facilitates the travellers' advance: the rapid slope of the hill presents a succession of blocks and boulders piled one upon the other in rugged steps, apparently impossible to a laden camel. This ravine, the Splugen of Somaliland, led us, after an hour's ride, to the Wady Duntu, a gigantic mountain-cleft formed by the violent action of torrents. The chasm winds abruptly between lofty walls of syenite and pink granite, glittering with flaky mica, and streaked with dykes and veins of snowy quartz: the strata of the sandstones that here and there projected into the bed were wonderfully twisted around a central nucleus, as green boughs might be bent about a tree. Above, the hill-tops towered in the air, here denuded of vegetable soil by the heavy monsun, there clothed from base to brow with gum trees, whose verdure was delicious to behold. The channel was now sandy, then flagged with limestone in slippery sheets, or horrid with rough boulders: at times the path was clear and easy; at others, a precipice of twenty or thirty feet, which must be a little cataract after rain, forced us to fight our way through the obstinate thorns that defended some spur of ragged hill. As the noontide heat, concentrated in this funnel, began to affect man and beast, we found a granite block, under whose shady brow clear water, oozing from the sand, formed a natural bath, and sat there for a while to enjoy the spectacle and the atmosphere, perfumed, as in part of Persia and Northern Arabia, by the aromatic shrubs of the desert.

After a short half-hour, we remounted and pursued our way down the Duntu chasm. As we advanced, the hills shrank in size, the bed became more level, and the walls of rock, gradually widening out, sank into the plain. Brisk and elastic above, the air, here soft, damp, and tepid, and the sun burning with a more malignant heat, convinced us that we stood once more below the Ghauts. For two hours we urged our mules in a south-east direction down the broad and winding Fiumara, taking care to inspect every well, but finding them all full of dry sand. Then turning eastwards, we crossed a plain called by the Donkey 'Battaladayti Taranay'—the Flat of Taranay—an exact representation of the maritime regions about Zayla. Herds of camels and flocks of milky sheep browsing amongst thorny Acacia and the tufted Kulan, suggested pleasing visions to starving travellers, and for the first time after three days of hard riding, we saw the face of man. The shepherds, Mikahil of the Habr Awal tribe, all fled as we approached: at last one was bold enough to stand and deliver the news. My companions were refreshed by good reports: there had been few murders, and the sea-board was tolerably clear of our doughty enemies, the Ayyal Ahmad. We pricked over the undulating growth of parched grass, shaping our course for Jabal Almis, to sailors the chief landmark of this coast, and for a certain thin blue stripe on the far horizon, upon which we gazed with gladdened eyes.

Our road lay between low brown hills of lime and sandstone, the Sub-Ghauts forming a scattered line between the maritime mountains and the sea. Presently the path was choked by dense scrub of the Arman Acacia: its yellow blossoms scented the air, but hardly made amends for the injuries of a thorn nearly two inches long, and tipped with a wooden point sharp as a needle. Emerging, towards evening, from this bush, we saw large herds of camels, and called their guardians to come and meet us. For all reply they ran like ostriches to the nearest rocks, uttering the cry of alarm, and when we drew near, each man implored us to harry his neighbour's cattle. Throughout our wanderings in Somaliland this had never occurred: it impressed me strongly with the disturbed state of the regions inhabited by the Habr Awal. After some time we persuaded a Bedouin who, with frantic gestures, was screaming and flogging his camels, to listen: reassured by our oaths, he declared himself to be a Bahgoba, and promised to show us a village of the Ayyal Gadid. The Hammal, who had married a daughter of this clan, and had constituted his father-in law my protector at Berbera, made sure of a hospitable reception: 'Tonight we shall sleep under cover and drink milk,' quoth one hungry man to another, who straightways rejoined, 'And we shall eat mutton!'

After dark we arrived at a kraal, we unsaddled our mules and sat down near it, indulging in Epicurean anticipations. Opposite us, by the door of a hut, was a group of men who observed our arrival, but did not advance or salute us. Impatient, I fired a pistol, when a gruff voice asked why we disturbed the camels that were being milked. 'We have fallen upon the Ayyal Shirdon'—our bitterest enemies—whispered the End of Time. The same voice then demanded in angrier accents, 'Of what tribe be ye?' We boldly answered, 'Of the Habr Girhajis.' Thereupon ensued a war of words. The Ayyal Shirdon inquired what we wanted, where we had been, and how we dared, seeing that peace had not been concluded between the tribes, to enter their lands. We replied civilly as our disappointment would permit, but apparently gained little by soft words. The inhospitable Bedouin declared our arrival to be in the seventeenth house of Geomancy—an advent probable as the Greek Kalends—and rudely insisted upon knowing what had taken us to Harar. At last a warrior, armed with two spears, came to meet us, and bending down recognized the End of Time: after a few short sentences he turned on his heel and retired. I then directed Long Gulad to approach the group, and say that a traveller was at their doors ready and willing to give tobacco in exchange for a draught of milk. They refused point-blank, and spoke of fighting: we at once made ready with our weapons, and showing the plain, bade them come on and receive a 'belly full'. During the lull which followed this obliging proposal we saddled our mules and rode off, in the grimmest of humours, loudly cursing the craven churls who knew not the value of a guest.

We visited successively three villages of the Ayyal Gadid: the Hammal failed to obtain even a drop of water from his connections, and was taunted accordingly. He explained their inhospitality by the fact that all the warriors being at Berbera, the villages contained nothing but women, children, servants, and flocks. The Donkey when strictly questioned declared that no well nearer than Bulhar was to be found: as men and mules were faint with thirst, I determined to push forward to water that night. Many times the animals were stopped, a mute hint that they could go no further: I spurred onwards, and the rest, as on such occasions they had now learned to do, followed without a word. Our path lay across a plain called Banka Hadla, intersected in many places by deep water-courses, and thinly strewed with Kulan clumps. The moon arose, but cast a cloud-veiled and uncertain light: our path, moreover, was not clear, as the guide, worn out by fatigue, tottered on far in the rear.

About midnight we heard—delightful sound!—the murmur of the distant sea. Revived by the music, we pushed on more cheerily. At last the Donkey preceded us, and about 3 a.m. we found, in a Fiumara, some holes which supplied us with bitter water, truly delicious after fifteen hours of thirst. Repeated draughts of the element, which the late rains had rendered potable, relieved our pain, and hard by we found a place where coarse stubbly grass saved our mules from starvation. Then rain coming on, we coiled ourselves under the saddle cloths, and, reckless alike of Ayyal Ahmad and Ayyal Shirdon, slept like the dead.

At dawn on the 30th January, I arose and inspected the site of Bulhar. It was then deserted, a huge heap of bleached bones being the only object suggestive of a settlement. This, at different times, has been a thriving place, owing to its roadstead, and the feuds of Berbera: it was generally a village of Gurgis, with some stone-houses built by Arabs. The coast however is open and havenless, and the Shimal wind, feared even at the Great Port, here rages with resistless violence. Yet the place revives when plundering parties render the plain unsafe: the timid merchants here embark their goods and persons, whilst their camels are marched round the bay.

Mounting at 6 a.m. we started slowly along the sea coast, and frequently halted on the bushy Fiumara-cut plain. About noon we bathed in the sea, and sat on the sands for a while, my people praying for permission to pass the kraals of their enemies, the Ayyal Ahmad, by night. This, their last request, was graciously granted: to say sooth rapid travelling was now impossible; the spear failed to urge on one mule, and the Hammal was obliged to flog before him another wretched animal. We then traversed an alluvial plain, lately flooded, where slippery mud doubled the fatigue of our cattle; and, at 3 p.m., again halted on a patch of grass below the rocky spur of Dabasenis, a hill half way between Bulhar and Berbera. On the summit I was shown an object that makes travellers shudder, a thorn-tree, under which the Habr Girhajis[1] and their friends of the Eesa Musa sit, vulture-like, on the look-out for plunder and murder. Advancing another mile, we came to some wells, where we were obliged to rest our animals. Having there finished our last mouthful of food, we remounted, and following the plain eastward, prepared for a long night-march.

As the light of day waned we passed on the right hand a table-formed hill, apparently a detached fragment of the sub-Ghauts or coast range. This spot is celebrated in local legends as 'Auliya Kumbo', the Mount of Saints, where the forty-four Arab Santons sat in solemn conclave before dispersing over the Somali country to preach al-Islam. It lies about six hours of hard walking from Berbera.

At midnight we skirted Bulho Faranji, the Franks' Watering-place,* a strip of ground thickly covered with trees. Abounding in grass and water, it has been the site of a village: when we passed it, however, all was desert. By the moon's light we descried, as we silently skirted the sea, the kraals and folds of our foe the Ayyal Ahmad, and at times we could distinguish the lowing of their cattle: my companions chuckled hugely at the success of their manœuvre, and perhaps not without reason. At Berbera we were afterwards informed that a shepherd in the bush had witnessed and reported our having passed, when the Ayyal Ahmad cursed the star that had enabled us to slip unhurt through their hands.

Our mules could scarcely walk: after every bow-shot they rolled upon the ground and were raised only by the whip. A last halt was called when arrived within four miles of Berbera: the End of Time and Long Gulad, completely worn out, fell fast asleep upon the stones. Of all the party the Hammal alone retained strength and spirits: the sturdy fellow talked, sang, and shouted, and, whilst the others could scarcely sit their mules, he danced his war-dance and brandished his spear. I was delighted with his 'pluck'.

Now a long dark line appears upon the sandy horizon—it grows more distinct in the shades of night—the silhouettes of shipping appear against sea and sky. A cry of joy bursts from every mouth: cheer, boys, cheer, our toils here touch their end!

The End of Time first listened to the small still voice of Caution. He whispered anxiously to make no noise lest enemies might arise, that my other attendants had protectors at Berbera, but that he, the hated and feared, as the *locum tenens* of Sharmakay—the great *bête*

* So called from the *Mary Anne* brig, here plundered in 1825.

noire—depended wholly upon my defence. The Donkey led us slowly and cautiously round the southern quarter of the sleeping town, through bone heaps and jackals tearing their unsavoury prey: at last he marched straight into the quarter appropriated to the Ayyal Gadid our protectors. Anxiously I inquired if my comrades had left Berbera, and heard with delight that they awaited me there.

It was then 2 a.m. and we had marched at least forty miles. The Somal, when in fear of forays, drive laden camels over this distance in about ten hours.

I dismounted at the huts where my comrades were living. A glad welcome, a dish of rice, and a glass of strong waters—pardon, dear L., these details—made amends for past privations and fatigue. The servants and the wretched mules were duly provided for, and I fell asleep, conscious of having performed a feat which, like a certain ride to York, will live in local annals for many and many a year.

The Gerenúk, or Waller's Gazelle.

Berbera.

X

Berbera and its Environs

IT IS INTERESTING TO COMPARE the earliest with the latest account of the great emporium of Eastern Africa.*

Bartema, writing in the sixteenth century 'of Barbara and the Island of Ethiope', offers the following brief description: 'After that the tempests were appeased, we gave wind to our sails, and in short time arrived at an island named Barbara, the prince whereof is a Mahometan.† The island is not great but fruitful and well peopled: it hath abundance of flesh. The inhabitants are of colour inclining to black. All their riches is in herds of cattle.'

Lieut. Cruttenden of the I.N., writing in 1848, thus describes the place: 'The annual fair is one of the most interesting sights on the coast, if only from the fact of many different and distant tribes being drawn together for a short time, to be again scattered in all directions. Before the towers of Berbera were built,‡ the place from April to the early part of October was utterly deserted, not even a fisherman being found

---

* In 1567 (the year after Zayla's fall) Lopez Suarez took without resistance—the inhabitants having fled—and burned the City 'Barbora near to Zayla, a place not unlike to it, but much less'.

† I cannot guess why Bartema decided 'Barbara' to be an island, except that he used 'insula' in the sense of 'peninsula'. The town is at very high tides flooded round, but the old traveller manifestly speaks of the country.

‡ These are the four martello towers erected, upon the spot where the town of huts generally stands, by the Hajj Sharmakay, who garrisoned them with thirty Arab and Negro matchlockmen. They are now in ruins, having been dismantled by orders from Aden.

there; but no sooner did the season change, than the inland tribes commenced moving down towards the coast, and preparing their huts for their expected visitors. Small craft from the ports of Yemen, anxious to have an opportunity of purchasing before vessels from the gulf could arrive, hastened across, followed about a fortnight to three weeks later by their larger brethren from Muscat, Soor, and Ras el Khyma, and the valuably freighted Bagalas from Bahrein, Bussorah, and Graen. Lastly, the fat and wealthy Banian traders from Porebunder, Mandavie, and Bombay, rolled across in their clumsy Kotias,* and with a formidable row of empty ghee jars slung over the quarters of their vessels, elbowed themselves into a permanent position in the front tier of craft in the harbour, and by their superior capital, cunning, and influence, soon distanced all competitors.

'During the height of the fair, Berbera is a perfect Babel, in confusion as in languages: no chief is acknowledged, and the customs of bygone days are the laws of the place. Disputes between the inland tribes daily arise, and are settled by the spear and dagger, the combatants retiring to the beach at a short distance from the town, in order that they may not disturb the trade. Long strings of camels are arriving and departing day and night, escorted generally by women alone, until at a distance from the town; and an occasional group of dusky and travel-worn children marks the arrival of the slave Cafila from Hurrur and Efat.

'At Berbera, the Gurague and Hurrur slave merchant meets his correspondent from Bussorah, Bagdad, or Bunder Abbas: and the savage Gidrbeersi (Gudabirsi), with his head tastefully ornamented with a scarlet sheepskin in lieu of a wig, is seen peacefully bartering his ostrich feathers and gums with the smooth-spoken Banian from Porebunder, who prudently living on board his ark, and locking up his puggree, which would infallibly be knocked off the instant he was seen wearing it, exhibits but a small portion of his wares at a time, under a miserable mat spread on the beach.

'By the end of March the fair is nearly at a close, and craft of all kinds, deeply laden, and sailing generally in parties of three and four, commence their homeward journey. The Soori boats are generally the last to leave, and by the first week in April, Berbera is again deserted, nothing being left to mark the site of a town lately containing 20,000 inhabitants, beyond bones of slaughtered camels and sheep, and the

* The Bagala is an Arab craft, the Kotia belongs to the Northern Coasts of Western India.

framework of a few huts, which is carefully piled on the beach in readiness for the ensuing year. Beasts of prey now take the opportunity to approach the sea: lions are commonly seen at the town well during the hot weather; and in April last year, but a week after the fair had ended, I observed three ostriches quietly walking on the beach'.*

Of the origin of Berbera little is known. Al-Firuzabadi derives it, with great probability, from two Himyar chiefs of Southern Arabia. About A.D. 522 the troops of Anushirwan expelled the Abyssinians from al Yemen, and re-established there a Himyari prince under vassalage of the Persian Monarch. Tradition asserts the port to have been occupied in turns by the Furs, the Arabs, the Turks, the Gallas, and the Somal. And its future fortunes are likely to be as varied as the past.

The present decadence of Berbera is caused by petty internal feuds. Girhajis the eldest son of Ishak al-Hazrami, seized the mountain ranges of Gulays and Wagar lying about forty miles behind the coast, whilst Awal, the cadet, established himself and his descendants upon the lowlands from Berbera to Zayla. Both these powerful tribes assert a claim to the customs and profits of the port on the grounds that they jointly conquered it from the Gallas. The Habr Awal, however, being in possession, would monopolize the right: a blood feud rages, and the commerce of the place suffers from the dissensions of the owners.

Moreover the Habr Awal tribe is not without internal feuds. Two kindred septs, the Ayyal Yunis Nuh and the Ayyal Ahmad Nuh,[1] established themselves originally at Berbera. The former, though the more numerous, admitted the latter for some years to a participation of profits, but when Aden, occupied by the British, rendered the trade valuable, they drove out the weaker sept, and declared themselves sole 'Abbans' to strangers during the fair. A war ensued. The sons of Yunis obtained aid of the Mijjarthayn tribe. The sons of Ahmad called in the Habr Girhajis, especially the Musa Arrah clan, to which the Hajj Sharmakay belongs, and, with his assistance, defeated and drove out the Ayyal Yunis. These, flying from Berbera, settled at the haven of Bulhar, and by their old connection with the Indian and other foreign traders, succeeded in drawing off a considerable amount of traffic. But the roadstead was insecure: many vessels were lost, and in 1847 the Eesa Somal slaughtered the women and children of the new-comers,

---

* The wild animals have now almost entirely disappeared. As will afterwards be shown, the fair since 1848 has diminished to one third its former dimensions. [The quotation is from p. 53, *Journal of the R.G.S.*, vol. xix, 1849, by Lient. C. J. Cruttenden—Ed.]

compelling them to sue the Ayyal Ahmad for peace. Though the feud thus ended, the fact of its having had existence ensures bad blood: amongst these savages treaties are of no avail, and the slightest provocation on either side becomes a signal for renewed hostilities.

. . .

After this dry disquisition we will return, dear L., to my doings at Berbera.

Great fatigue is seldom followed by long sleep. Soon after sunrise I awoke, hearing loud voices proceeding from a mass of black face and tawny wig, that blocked up the doorway, pressing forward to see their new stranger. The Berbera people had been informed by the Donkey of our having ridden from the Girhi hills in five days: they swore that not only the thing was impossible, but moreover that we had never sighted Harar. Having undergone the usual catechizing with credit, I left the thatched hut in which my comrades were living, and proceeded to inspect my attendants and cattle. The former smiled blandly: they had acquitted themselves of their trust, they had outwitted the Ayyal Ahmad, who would be furious thereat, they had filled themselves with dates, rice, and sugared tea—another potent element of moral satisfaction—and they trusted that a few days would show them their wives and families. The End of Time's brow, however, betrayed an *arrière pensée;* once more his cowardice crept forth, and he anxiously whispered that his existence depended upon my protection. The poor mules were by no means so easily restored. Their backs, cut to the bone by the saddles, stood up like those of angry cats, their heads drooped sadly, and their hams showed red marks of the spear-point. Directing them to be washed in the sea, dressed with cold-water bandages, and copiously fed, I proceeded to inspect the Berbera Plain.

The 'Mother of the Poor', as the Arabs call the place, in position resembles Zayla. The town—if such name can be given to what is now a wretched clump of dirty mat-huts—is situated on the northern edge of alluvial ground, sloping almost imperceptibly from the base of the Southern hills. The rapacity of these short-sighted savages has contracted its dimensions to about one-sixth of its former extent: for nearly a mile around, the now desert land is strewed with bits of glass and broken pottery. Their ignorance has chosen the worst position: *Mos Majorum* is the Somali code, where father built there son builds, and there shall grandson build. To the S. and E. lies a saline sand-flat, partially over-flowered by high tides: here are the wells of bitter water, and the filth and garbage make the spot truly offensive. Northwards the sea-strand has become a huge cemetery, crowded with graves whose dimensions explain the Somali legend that once there were giants in the land: tradition assigns to it the name of Bunder Abbas. Westward, close up to the town, runs the creek, which forms the wealth of Berbera. A long strip of sand and limestone—the general formation of the coast—defends its length from the northern gales, the breadth is about three quarters of a mile, and the depth varies from six to fifteen fathoms near the Ras or Spit at which ships anchor before putting out to sea.

Behind the town, and distant about seven miles, lie the Sub-Ghauts, a bold background of lime and sandstone. Through a broad gap called Duss Malablay appear in fine weather the granite walls of Wagar and Gulays, whose altitude by aneroid was found to be 5,700 feet above the level of the sea.* On the eastward the Berbera plain is bounded by the hills of Siyaro, and westwards the heights of Dabasenis limit the prospect.[2]

It was with astonishment that I reflected upon the impolicy of having preferred Aden to this place.

The Emporium of Eastern Africa has a salubrious climate,† abundance of sweet water—a luxury to be 'fully appreciated only after a residence at Aden'—a mild monsun, a fine open country, an excellent harbour, and a soil highly productive. It is the meeting-place of commerce, has few rivals, and with half the sums lavished in Arabia upon engineer follies of stone and lime, the environs might at this time have been covered with houses, gardens, and trees.

The Eye of al Yemen, to quote Carlyle, is a 'mountain of misery towering sheer up like a bleak Pisgah, with outlooks only into desolation, sand, salt water, and despair'. The camp is in a 'Devil's Punchbowl', stifling hot during nine months of the year, and subject to alternations of sandstorm and Samun, 'without either seed, water, or trees', as Ibn Batutah described it 500 years ago, unproductive for want

---

* It was measured by Lt. Herne, who remarks of this range that 'cold in winter, as the presence of the pine-tree proves, and cooled in summer by the Monsoon, abounding in game from a spur fowl to an elephant; this hill would make an admirable Sanitarium'. Unfortunately Gulays is tenanted by the Habr Girhajis, and Wagar by the Eesa Musa, treacherous races.

† The climate of Berbera is cool during the winter, and though the sun is at all times burning, the atmosphere, as in Somaliland generally, is healthy. In the dry season the plain is subject to great heats, but lying open to the north, the sea-breeze is strong and regular. In the monsun the air is cloudy, light showers frequently fall, and occasionally heavy storms come up from the southern hills.

of rain—not a sparrow can exist there, nor will a crow thrive*—and essentially unhealthy. Our loss in operatives is only equalled by our waste of rupees; and the general wish of Western India, is that the extinct sea of fire would, Vesuvius-like, once more convert this dismal cape into a living crater.

After a day's rest—physical not spiritual, for the Somal were as usual disputing violently about the Abbanship³—I went with my comrades to visit an interesting ruin near the town. On the way we were shown pits of coarse sulphur and alum mixed with sand; in the low lands senna and colocynth were growing wild. After walking a mile south-south-east, from present Berbera to a rise in the plain, we found the remains of a small building about eight yards square divided into two compartments. It is apparently a Mosque: one portion, the sole of which is raised, shows traces of the prayer niche; the other might have contained the tomb of some saint now obsolete, or might have been a fort to protect a neighbouring tank. The walls are of rubble masonry and mud, revetted with a coating of cement hard as stone, and mixed with small round pebbles.† Near it is a shallow reservoir of stone and lime, about five yards by ten, proved by the aqueduct, part of which still remains, to be a tank of supply. Removing the upper slabs, we found the interior lined with a deposit of sulphate of lime and choked with fine drift sand; the breadth is about fifteen inches and the depth nine. After following it fifty yards towards the hills, we lost the trace; the loose stones had probably been removed for graves, and the soil may have buried the firmer portion.

Mounting our mules we then rode in a south-south-east direction towards the Dubar Hills. The surface of the ground, apparently level, rises about 100 feet per mile. In most parts a soft sand overlying hard loam, like work *en pisé*, limestone and coralline; it shows evidences of inundation: water-worn stones of a lime almost as compact as marble, pieces of quartz, selenite, basalt, granite, and syenite in nodules are everywhere sprinkled over the surface. Here and there torrents from the hills had cut channels five or six feet below the level, and a thicker vegetation denoted the lines of bed. The growth of wild plants, scanty near the coast, became more luxuriant as we approached the hills; the

---

* The experiment was tried by an officer who brought from Bombay a batch of sparrows and crows. The former died, scorbutic I presume; the latter lingered through an unhappy life, and to judge from the absence of young, refused to entail their miseries upon posterity.

† The similarity between the Persian 'Gach' and this cement, which is found in many ruins about Berbera, has been remarked by other travellers.

Arman Acacia flourished, the Kulan tree grew in clumps, and the Tamarisk formed here and there a dense thicket. Except a few shy antelopes, we saw no game.

A ride of seven or eight miles led us to the dry bed of a water-course overgrown with bright green rushes, and known to the people as Dubar Wena, or Great Dubar. The strip of ground, about half a mile long, collects the drainage of the hills above it: numerous Las or Pits, in the centre of the bed, four or five feet deep, abundantly supply the flocks and herds. Although the surface of the ground, where dry, was white with impure nitre, the water tasted tolerably sweet. Advancing half a mile over the southern shoulder of a coarse and shelly mass of limestone, we found the other rushy swamp, called Dubar Yir or Little Dubar. A spring of warm and bitter water flowed from the hill over the surface to a distance of 400 or 500 yards, where it was absorbed by the soil. The temperature of the sources immediately under the hill was 106° Fahr., the thermometer standing at 80° in the air, and the aneroid gave an altitude of 728 feet above the sea.

The rocks behind these springs were covered with ruins of mosques and houses. We revisited a little tower commanding the source: it was built in steps, the hill being cut away to form the two lower rooms, and the second story showed three compartments. The material was rubble and the form resembled Galla buildings; we found, however, fine mortar mixed with coarse gravel, bits of glass bottles and blue glazed pottery, articles now unknown to this part of Africa. On the summit of the highest peak our guides pointed out remains of another fort similar to the old Turkish watch-towers at Aden.

About three quarters of a mile from the Little Dubar, we found the head of the Berbera Aqueduct. Thrown across a water-course apparently of low level, it is here more substantially built than near the beach, and probably served as a force pipe until the water found a fall. We traced the line to a distance of ten yards, where it disappeared beneath the soil, and saw nothing resembling a supply-tank except an irregularly shaped natural pool.*

* Lieut. Cruttenden in considering what nation could have constructed, and at what period the commerce of Berbera warranted, so costly an undertaking, is disposed to attribute it to the Persian conquerors of Aden in the days of Anushirwan. He remarks that the trade carried on in the Red Sea was then great, the ancient emporia of Hisn Ghorab and Aden prosperous and wealthy, and Berbera doubtless exported, as it does now, ivory, gums, and ostrich feathers. But though all the maritime Somali country abounds in traditions of the Furs or ancient Persians, none of the buildings near Berbera justifies our

A few days afterwards, accompanied by Lieut. Herne, I rode out to inspect the Biyu Gora or Night-running Water. After advancing about ten miles in a south-east direction from Berbera, we entered rough and broken ground, and suddenly came upon a Fiumara, about 250 yards broad. The banks were fringed with Brab and Tamarisk, the Daum palm and green rushes: a clear sparkling and shallow stream bisected the sandy bed, and smaller branches wandered over the surface. This river, the main drain of the Ghauts and Sub-Ghauts, derives its name from the increased volume of the waters during night: evaporation by day causes the absorption of about a hundred yards. We found its temperature 73° Fahr. (in the air 78°), and our people dug holes in the sand instead of drinking from the stream, a proof that they feared leeches. The taste of the water was bitter and nauseous.

Following the course of the Biyu Gora through two low parallel ranges of conglomerate, we entered a narrow gorge, in which lime and sandstone abound. The dip of the strata is about 45° west, the strike north and south. Water springs from under every stone, drops copiously from the shelves of rock, oozes out of the sand, and bubbles up from the mould. The temperature is exceedingly variable: in some places the water is icy cold, in others, the thermometer shows 68° Fahr., in others, 101°—the maximum, when we visited it, being 126°. The colours are equally diverse. Here, the polished surface of the sandstone is covered with a hoar of salt and nitre. There, where the stream does not flow, are pools dyed greenish-black or rust-red by iron sediment. The gorge's sides are a vivid red: a peculiar creeper hangs from the rocks, and water trickles down its metallic leaves. The upper cliffs are crowned with tufts of the dragon's-blood tree.

Leaving our mules with an attendant, we began to climb the rough and rocky gorge, which, as the breadth diminishes, becomes exceedingly picturesque. In one part, the side of a limestone hill hundreds of feet in height, has slipped into the chasm, half filling it with gigantic

---

assigning to them, in a country of monsun rain and high winds, an antiquity of 1,300 years ago.

The Somal assert that ten generations ago their ancestors drove out the Gallas from Berbera, and attribute these works to the ancient Pagans. That nation of savages, however, was never capable of constructing a scientific aqueduct. I therefore prefer attributing these remains at Berbera to the Ottomans, who after the conquest of Aden by Sulayman Pasha in A.D. 1538, held al Yemen for about 100 years, and as auxiliaries of the King of Adel, penetrated as far as Abyssinia. Traces of their architecture are found at Zayla and Harar, and according to tradition, they possessed at Berbera a settlement called, after its founder, Bunder Abbas.

boulders: through these the noisy stream whirls, now falling in small cascades, then gliding over slabs of sheet rock: here it cuts grooved channels and deep basins clean and sharp as artificial baths in the sandstone, there it flows quietly down a bed of pure sparkling sand. The high hills above are of a tawny yellow: the huge boulders, grisly white, bear upon their summits the drift wood of the last year's inundation. During the monsun, when a furious torrent sweeps down from the Wagar Hills, this chasm must afford a curiously wild spectacle.

Returning from a toilsome climb, we found some of the Ayyal Ahmad building near the spot where Biyu Gora is absorbed, the usual small stone tower. The fact had excited attention at Berbera; the erection was intended to store grain, but the suspicious savages, the Eesa Musa, and Mikahil, who hold the land, saw in it an attempt to threaten their liberties. On our way home we passed through some extensive cemeteries: the tombs were in good preservation; there was nothing peculiar in their construction, yet the Somal were positive that they belonged to a race preceding their own. Near them were some ruins of kilns—comparatively modern, for bits of charcoal were mixed with broken pieces of pottery—and the oblong tracery of a dwelling-house divided into several compartments: its material was the sun-dried brick of Central Asia, here a rarity.

After visiting these ruins there was little to detain me at Berbera. The town had become intolerable, the heat under a mat hut was extreme, the wind and dust were almost as bad as Aden, and the dirt perhaps even worse. As usual we had not a moment's privacy, Arabs as well as the Somal assuming the right of walking in, sitting down, looking hard, chatting with one another, and departing. Before the voyage, however, I was called upon to compose a difficulty upon the subject of Abbanship. The Hammal had naturally constituted his father-in-law, one Burhali Nuh, of the Ayyal Gadid, protector to Lieut. Herne and myself. Burhali had proved himself a rascal: he had been insolent as well as dishonest, and had thrown frequent obstacles in his employer's way; yet custom does not permit the Abban to be put away like a wife, and the Hammal's services entitled him to the fullest consideration. On the other hand Jami Hasan, a chief and a doughty man of the Ayyal Ahmad, had met me at Aden early in 1854, and had received from me a ring in token of Abbanship. During my absence at Harar, he had taken charge of Lieut. Stroyan. On the very morning of my arrival he came to the hut, sat down spear in hand, produced the ring and claimed my promise. In vain I objected that the token had been given when a previous trip was intended, and that the Hammal must not be disappointed: Jami replied that once an Abban always an Abban, that he hated the Hammal and all his tribe, and that he would enter into no partnership with Burhali Nuh:—to complicate matters, Lieut. Stroyan spoke highly of his courage and conduct. Presently he insisted rudely upon removing his *protégé* to another part of the town: this passed the limits of our patience, and decided the case against him.

For some days discord raged between the rivals. At last it was settled that I should choose my own Abban in presence of a general council of the Elders. The chiefs took their places upon the shore each with his followers forming a distinct semicircle, and all squatting with shield and spear planted upright in the ground. When sent for, I entered the circle sword in hand, and sat down awaiting their pleasure. After much murmuring had subsided, Jami asked in a loud voice, 'Who is thy protector?' The reply was, 'Burhali Nuh!' Knowing, however, how little laconism is prized by an East African audience, I did not fail to follow up this answer with an Arabic speech of the dimensions of an average sermon, and then shouldering my blade left the circle abruptly. The effect was success. Our wild friends sat from afternoon till sunset: as we finished supper one of them came in with the glad tidings of a 'peace conference'. Jami had asked Burhali to swear that he intended no personal offence in taking away a *protégé* pledged to himself: Burhali had sworn, and once more the olive waved over the braves of Berbera.

On the 5th February, 1855, taking leave of my comrades, I went on board *Al-Kasab* or the *Reed*—such was the ill-omened name of our cranky craft—to the undisguised satisfaction of the Hammal, Long Gulad, and the End of Time, who could scarcely believe in their departure from Berbera with sound skins.* Coasting with a light breeze, early after noon on the next day we arrived at Siyaro, a noted wateringplace for shipping, about nineteen miles east of the emporium. The roadstead is open to the north, but a bluff buttress of limestone rock defends it from the north-east gales. Upon a barren strip of sand lies the material of the town; two houses of stone and mud, one yet unfinished, the other completed about thirty years ago by Farih Binni, a Mikahil chief.

* They had been in some danger: a treacherous murder perpetrated a few days before our arrival had caused all the Habr Girhajis to fly from the town and assemble 5,000 men at Bulhar for battle and murder. This proceeding irritated the Habr Awal, and certainly, but for our presence, the strangers would have been scurvily treated by their 'cousins'.

Some dozen Bedouin spearmen, Mikahil of a neighbouring kraal, squatted like a line of crows upon the shore to receive us as we waded from the vessel. They demanded money in too authoritative a tone before allowing us to visit the wells, which form their principal wealth. Resolved not to risk a quarrel so near Berbera, I was returning to moralize upon the fate of Burckhardt—after a successful pilgrimage refused admittance to Aaron's tomb at Sinai—when a Bedouin ran to tell us that we might wander where we pleased. He excused himself and his companions by pleading necessity, and his leanness lent conviction to the plea.

The larger well lies close to the eastern wall of the dwelling-house: it is about eighteen feet deep, one third sunk through ground, the other two thirds through lime-stone, and at the bottom is a small supply of sweet clear water. Near it I observed some ruined tanks, built with fine mortar like that of the Berbera ruins. The other well lies about half a mile to the westward of the former: it is also dug in the limestone rock. A few yards to the north-east of the building is the Furzah or custom-house, whose pristine simplicity tempts me to describe it: a square of ground surrounded by a dwarf rubble enclosure, and provided with a proportional mosque, a tabular block of coralline niched in the direction of Meccah. On a little eminence of rock to the westward, rise ruined walls, said by my companions to have been built by a Frank, who bought land from the Mikahil and settled on this dismal strand.

Taking leave of the Bedouin, whose hearts were gladdened by a few small presents, we resumed our voyage eastwards along the coast. Next morning we passed two broken pyramids of dark rock called Dubada Gumbar Madu—the Two Black Hills. After a tedious day's sail, twenty miles in twenty-four hours, the Captain of *Al-Kasab* landed us in a creek west of Aynterad. A few sheep boats lay at anchor in this 'back-bay', as usual when the sea is heavy at the roadstead, and the crews informed us that a body of Bedouin was marching to attack the village. Abdi Mohammed Diban, proprietor of the Aynterad Fort, having constituted me his protector, and remained at Berbera, I armed my men, and ordering the captain of the *Reed* to bring his vessel round at early dawn, walked hurriedly over the three miles that separated us from the place. Arrived at the fort, we found that Abdi's slaves knew nothing of the reported attack. They received me, however, hospitably, and brought a supper of their only provision, vile dates and dried meat. Unwilling to diminish the scanty store, the Hammal and I but dipped our hands in the dish: Long Gulad and the End of Time, however, soon cleared the platters, while abusing roundly the unpalatable food. After supper, a dispute arose between the Hammal and one of the Habr Tul Jailuh, the tribe to whom the land belongs. The Bedouin, not liking my looks, proposed to put a spear into me. The Hammal objected that if the measure were carried out, he would return the compliment in kind. Ensued a long dispute, and the listeners laughed heartily at the utter indifference with which I gave ear. When it concluded, amicably as may be expected, the slaves spread a carpet upon a coarse Berbera couch, and having again vented their hilarity in a roar of laughter, left me to sleep.

We had eaten at least one sheep per diem, and mutton baked in the ship's oven is delicious to the Somali mouth. Remained on board another dinner, a circumstance which possibly influenced the weak mind of the Captain of the *Reed*. Awaking at dawn, I went out, expecting to find the vessel within stone's throw: it was nowhere visible. About 8 a.m., it appeared in sight, a mere speck upon the sea-horizon, and whilst it approached, I inspected the settlement.

Aynterad, an inconsiderable place lying east-north-east of, and about forty miles from, Berbera, is a favourite roadstead principally on account of its water, which rivals that of Siyaro. The anchorage is bad: the Shimal or north wind sweeps long lines of heavy wave into the open bay, and the bottom is a mass of rock and sand-reef. The fifty sunburnt and windsoiled huts which compose the settlement, are built upon a bank of sand overlying the normal limestone: at the time when I visited it, the male population had emigrated *en masse* to Berbera. It is principally supported by the slave trade, the Arabs preferring to ship their purchases at some distance from the chief emporium.* Lieut. Herne, when he visited it, found a considerable amount of 'black bullion' in the market.

The fort of Aynterad, erected thirty years ago by Mohammed Diban, is a stone and mud house square and flat-roofed, with high windows, an attempt at crenelles, and, for some reason intelligible only to its own Vitruvius, but a single bastion at the northern angle. There

---

* Of all the slave-dealers on this coast, the Arabs are the most unscrupulous. In 1855, one Mohammed of Maskat, a ship-owner, who, moreover, constantly visits Aden, bought within sight of our flag a free-born Arab girl of the Yafa'i tribe, from the Akarib of Bir Hamid, and sold her at Berbera to a compatriot. Such a crime merits severe punishment; even the Abyssinians visit with hanging the Christian convicted of selling a fellow religionist. The Arab slaver generally marries his property as a ruse, and arrived at Maskat or Bushiri, divorces and sells them. Free Somali women have not unfrequently met with this fate.

is no well, and the mass of huts cluster close to the walls. The five guns here deposited by Sharmakay when expelled from Berbera, stand on the ground outside the fort, which is scarcely calculated to bear heavy carronades: they are unprovided with balls, but that is a trifle where pebbles abound. Moreover, Abdi's slaves are well armed with matchlock and pistol, and the Bedouin Tul Jailah[4] find the spear ineffectual against stone walls. The garrison has frequently been blockaded by its troublesome neighbours, whose prowess, however, never extended beyond preliminaries.

To allay my impatience, that morning I was invited into several huts for the purpose of drinking sour milk. A malicious joy filled my soul, as about noon, the Machiavellian Captain of the *Reed* managed to cast anchor, after driving his crazy craft through a sea which the violent Shimal was flinging in hollow curves foam-fringed upon the strand. I stood on the shore making signs for a canoe. My desires were disregarded, as long as decency admitted. At last, about 1 p.m., I found myself upon the quarter-deck.

'Dawwir al-farman'—shift the yard!—I shouted with a voice of thunder.

The answer was a general hubbub. 'He surely will not sail in a sea like this?' asked the trembling Captain of my companions.

'He will!' sententiously quoth the Hammal, with a Burleigh nod

'It blows wind——' remonstrated the Rais.

'And if it blew fire?' asked the Hammal with the air *goguenard*, meaning that from the calamity of Frankish obstinacy there was no refuge.

A kind of death-wail arose, during which, to hide untimely laughter, I retreated to a large drawer, in the stern of the vessel, called a cabin. There my ears could distinguish the loud entreaties of the crew vainly urging my attendants to propose a day's delay. Then one of the garrison, accompanied by the Captain who shook as with fever, resolved to act forlorn hope, and bring a *feu d'enfer* of phrases to bear upon the Frank's hard brain. Scarcely, however, had the head of the sentence been delivered, before he was playfully upraised by his bushy hair and a handle somewhat more substantial, carried out of the cabin, and thrown, like a bag of biscuit, on the deck.

The case was hopeless. All strangers plunged into the sea—the popular way of landing in East Africa—the anchor was weighed, the ton of sail shaken out, and the *Reed* began to dip and rise in the yeasty sea laboriously as an alderman dancing a polka.

For the first time in my life I had the satisfaction of seeing the Somal unable to eat—unable to eat mutton. In sea-sickness and needless terror, the captain, crew, and passengers abandoned to us all the baked sheep, which we three, not being believers in the Evil Eye, ate from head to trotters with especial pleasure. That night the waves broke over us. The End of Time occupied himself in roaring certain orisons, which are reputed to calm stormy seas: he desisted only when Long Gulad pointed out that a wilder gust seemed to follow as in derision each more emphatic period. The Captain, a noted reprobate, renowned onshore for his knowledge of erotic verse and admiration of the fair sex, prayed with fervour: he was joined by several of the crew, who apparently found the charm of novelty in the edifying exercise. About midnight a Sultan al-Bahror Sea-king—a species of whale—appeared close to our counter: and as these animals are infamous for upsetting vessels in waggishness, the sight elicited a yell of terror and a chorus of religious exclamations.

On the morning of Friday, the 9th February, 1855, we hove in sight of Jabal Shamsan, the loftiest peak of the Aden Crater. And ere evening fell, I had the pleasure of seeing the faces of friends and comrades once more.

The chapter which follows covers the period of nearly a month while Burton was in Aden, and is based largely on his unpublished official report to the Bombay Governor.—Ed.

Drawing by Burton of Zanzibar harbour.

XI

Planning the Expedition to Zanzibar*

RICHARD BURTON'S OFFICIAL REPORT of his journey to Harar was
sent from Aden to Bombay through Coghlan, now Brigadier, on
February 22, 1855:

> I hope that his Lordship in Council [Burton wrote] will approve of
> my forwarding notes to the Royal Geographical Societies of London
> and Paris and of preparing at some future time my diary for publication.
> In these pages all political allusions shall carefully be avoided; the
> former shall be purely geographical and the latter, which shall also
> contain a grammatical outline and vocabulary of the Harar dialect, is
> intended to be a mere narrative of adventure.[1]

The previous pages show that it was a good deal more than a mere
narrative of adventure. In a country such as Somaliland personal likes
and dislikes have significant political implications and Burton was
always definite in his views. The preface of his *First Footsteps in East
Africa* and many of his notes were highly critical of decisions taken by
the Court of Directors of the East India Company and of the Governor
General of India or anyone else who had a different viewpoint.

* Chapter inserted by Editor, based on official reports and other sources.

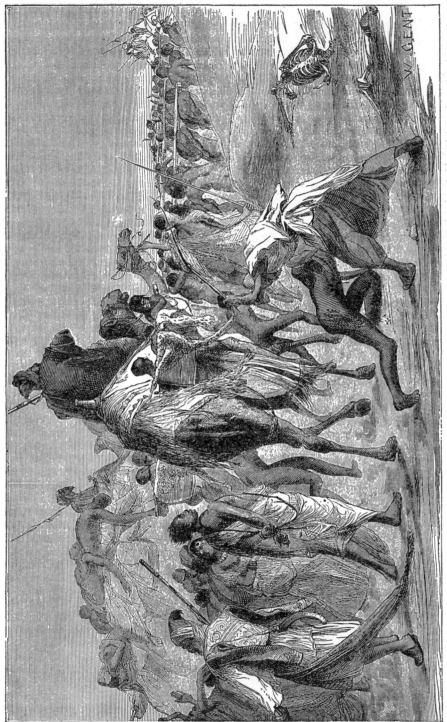

The slave trade: 'men whose spirits must be tamed by diabolical tortures.'

His report to Government contained some interesting passages which were not published in the book, such as the following on slavery.

Tajjurah, Zayla, and Berbera are now the only ports for the export of slaves from the vast region included under Efat, Guragur and the Galla country. It is no Quixotic theory against slavery which urges me to recommend its extinction. But where slavery flourishes commerce declines. It is far more satisfactory for a barbarous people to fire a kraal and sell the fugitives than to sow cotton and grow coffee. I have ever spoken favourably of domestic thraldom among the Moslems; but the practice of slave-driving must ever be abominable to a philanthropic people. My report might be adorned with pictures of horror—children left to be destroyed by wild beasts, women whose persons are subject to the extreme of brutality and men whose spirits must be tamed by diabolical tortures.

Three plans could be proposed [he wrote] for settling the Somali coast and abolishing the slave-trade. A Consul or Vice-Consul might be established at Berbera or the Port could be abandoned to the Hajj Sharmakay of Zayla, or finally there might be a Commercial Agency directed by an Assistant to the Political Resident at Aden.

He argued that it would be unwise to send a Consul since other Powers might do the same; there were complications about Hajj Sharmakay since he was a Turkish Official and could not fly the star at Zayla and the British flag at Berbera, nor did he consider that the Somali at Berbera would be prepared to see Hajj Sharmakay fortify himself in their country; 'he is, after all, a Somali'. Burton considered, however, that it was possible for the British to establish themselves in Berbera without advancing one mile into the interior.

An Empire confined within an unbroken frontier is an army without light infantry. Every great nation has acted upon the principle that outposts secure its safety and increase its power. For by establishing posts where trade meets, an inlet to commerce is secured and there arise friendly relations which would be broken by change to the detriment of both parties.

It has been asserted by Lt. Cruttenden, I. N., that the Somal have offered their port to us and that, provided their rights as Abbans be respected they would make no objection to our occupying it for the protection of trade. Under all circumstances they would prefer us to the other alternative—the Turks. They admire our rule, respect our power, comprehend our forbearance, not attributing it to fear as the Arabs do, and they evince a gentleness of disposition and a docility which offer fair hopes to civilization in this region of barbarism. Their ardour for commerce is such that when the blood-feuds deter men from accompanying their caravans, the camels are escorted by women and children; this is a feature in the national character which time will strengthen.

Viewed in connection with Aden, the establishment of an Agency at Berbera is highly desirable. During the last fourteen years our Arabian settlement has risen from the extreme of depression with a rapidity which at the same time will soon restore it to its old position—that of the great Emporium of the Peninsula. In 1842 its population was 16,454; in 1854 it had increased to at least 25,000. But we have difficulties to contend with which the Abyssinians, the Persians and the Turks—formerly masters of Aden—had not.

The Bedouin of al Yemen, the most fanatical and least respected of their race, are incensed at the presence of the Infidel, and a knowledge of their character teaches us to despair of taming within centuries this race of robbers. Perhaps the most effectual step would be to draw from Berbera and the other African ports those supplies for which, since our occupation of Aden, we have been wholly dependent upon inner Arabia. The dollars and rupees which now find their way into the Fuzli and the Audali's lands to be converted into ornaments for women and weapons, in the Somali country would lead to the re-establishment of those cities and marts which poverty and misrule have laid waste.

It is the opinion of every traveller that an Agency in Berbera would be the nucleus of a large permanent town. Caravans would arrive regularly and not confine themselves, as they do now, to a few months in the cold season when the Bedouin migrate to the coast. From Lieut. Herne's geological observations at Berbera I am persuaded that by digging as at Siyaro and Aynterad fifteen or twenty feet below the surface of the plain into the subjacent soft limestone pure potable water is everywhere procurable. Water for the purpose of cultivation is found in the Fiumaras and, from the wild vegetation which abounds even in the dry season, it is evident that with irrigation the soil is fitted for the growth of vegetables and fruit trees. The cocoa and the date would flourish along the coast. South of the Berbera plains, and one day's journey from the sea, lies a mountainous region of which 'gulays' is the apex—the height by aneroid is 5,700 feet—the pine tree clothes its upper peaks; it enjoys a delightful climate even in the hottest months, abounds in perennial springs and is tenanted by a comparatively civilized people.

A drawing is given of the building he proposed for the Berbera Agency and, in flattering terms which were unusual to him, he suggests that it should be called Elphinstone.

Might the Agency at Berbera be permitted to bear the name of that nobleman under whose auspices the exploration of the country and the resolution of its commercial difficulties were undertaken! May the name of Elphinstone be as propitious to Eastern Africa as it has been to Western India.

It might be expected, he said, that he would himself volunteer to take on the job of Agent, but, 'in the first place I hope for permission to extend our geographical and commercial survey of the country, and, secondly, being better known as a soldier than as a civilian, they would distrust the traveller . . . who reappears among them as a government agent.' He recommended Lieut. Dansey, 1st Fusiliers:

> To him I beg leave to refer for the mode of treating with the Somal, the erection of the Agency, the settlement of the Abban duties, the formation of a Somali guard and other details of execution . . .
> With Consuls at Suez, Massowah, and Jeddah, an Agent at Berbera, a missionary establishment at Mombasa, and a Consul at Zanzibar, we provide at a small expense and efficiently enough against any danger of a rival occupying a commanding position in East Africa. By means of a small steamer at Aden we should connect this chain of outposts, be instantly prepared for any emergency which might arise from the shock of events in the West, and in the common destiny of things regulate the supplies required at our Arabian settlement.

Richard Burton then turned to the practical problems of the Expedition, which he discussed with Speke whom he regarded as second in command; Herne and Stroyan were waiting for them in Berbera. Burton used ingenious arguments to obtain extended leave so that he could settle the question of the 'eternal snows', which meant also looking for the source of the Nile.

> In concert with Lieut. Speke I propose adhering to our original plan of entering the country via Berbera. We have now visited sundry triangles based upon Zayla and Berbera with Harar for their apex . . . Remains the southern portion which must be the object of our future endeavours. Should we start about the end of the Berbera season, April, before the monsoon we may hope to reach the Webbe Shebelli (Haines river)[2] in the Ogadyn country. Contrary to what I supposed the monsoon is the favourite travelling season of the Somal; the wells are full, grass for cattle abounds and the land flows with milk.
> Throughout Africa it is vain to expect any important results to be obtained in a short time. The style of travelling forbids it. He is an

energetic man who induces the Somal to march once in three days. When on a journey their progress suggests the old simile of cattle browsing through the thickets. It is every man's interest to detain you because he and his friends are devouring your rice and dates. It is every man's interest to mislead you because in some distant village he has an uncle or a cousin who wants your cloth. These impositions must be endured with patience. Nothing increases the perils of sickness and the fatigue of man and the elements so much as haste; in time the most dangerous district may be traversed, but the traveller who would hurry through the country places himself in a predicament of peculiar danger; again, it is mortifying to be obliged to return at the moment perhaps when, after waiting for months, a most favourable opportunity for advance presents itself.

I venture to hope that if His Lordship in Council honor with his approval our last season's work that he will obtain for us leave for a second year. The Honble Court of Directors (Despatch, 28th August, 1854) grant us but twelve months leave, which period dates from the beginning of October 1854. I am positively enjoined in that document not to incur any immoderate risk in carrying out the object in view, carefully to feel my way and not to proceed onwards without reasonable ground for believing that my own life and that of my associates will not be seriously endangered; an additional leave for the same period would I believe enable us to explore the Eastern Horn of Africa ... I fear little from the Somal beyond our being gradually stripped in the most friendly way of all our goods—excepting our arms.

He hoped that the expedition 'may extend to the Æthiopic Olympus (Kilimanjaro) and settle the question of its eternal snows'. He asked for local rank of Major in East Africa:

In the first place I am now in charge of an expedition composed of officers considerably my seniors in the service; also the higher any military rank is, the more weight, political as well as scientific, will my reports and publications bear with the learned societies of England and France ... It is erroneous to suppose that the Somal savages ignore our habits and attach no importance to rank. From Zayla to Harar I met with men who had returned to their jungles after wandering through Arabia, India and Egypt; many speak with fluency three and four languages and are perfectly acquainted with English manners and customs. We now no longer travel detached and in disguise; we are Englishmen, for convenience wearing Asiatic garments and names. The Somal not only understand rank but also act upon the principle of meting out their deference according to the authority which they see exercised and the regard with which Government honors the exertions of its servants.*

Burton argued that there was need for more time to carry out his plans in a letter to Dr. Norton Shaw, Secretary of the Royal Geographical Society, which he sent on February 25, 1855, three days after he had sent his report to Bombay.

> My success at Harar has emboldened me and I have applied for a second years' leave. The Court of Directors will not, I think, refuse it, especially if it be at all backed by the Royal Geographical Society.
>
> My plans (public) are now to march southward to the Webbi Shebayli and Gorrana; privately and *entre nous* I want to settle the question of Krapf and 'eternal snows'. There is little doubt of the White Nile being thereabouts. And you will hear with pleasure that there is an open route through Africa to the Atlantic. I heard of it at Harar and will give the whole account . . .
>
> Dr. Beke passed through Aden a second time and kindly left for me some Galla works much wanted. Our difficulties will be principally amongst that penis-cutting people. Altogether the prospects of the 'Somali Expedition' are bright enough; there are difficulties however. This time we march as masters with 20 guns and horses etc. so that by day we need not fear a host.

The letter is edged with black as Burton was in mourning for his mother who had died on December 18, and to whom he was very devoted.

John Speke had arrived in Aden from his three months' expedition. He had failed to reach the Wadi Nogal, and Speke hated failure. He blamed Burton for having selected a dishonest 'Abban' or Protector called Sumunter and this had ruined the expedition; not only that, Burton had also chosen Ahmed as an interpreter, who knew some Hindustani (Speke's only language), and he belonged to the same tribe as Sumunter, the Warsangali; 'by having both men of the same tribe for my entire dependence', wrote Speke, 'they invariably acted in concert against me like two brothers.'[3] Sumunter had returned with Speke, although he knew that there would be trouble for him in Aden, but his wife and family were there, and he also had a thriving business as a merchant. Speke did not wish to punish him, but Burton insisted in

---

* 'Moreover, paradoxical as it may appear in relation to his own egalitarian system, the Somali pastoralist is keenly sensitive to differences in others, especially among Government officials. With Europeans he displays a snobbish regard for status and rank' (Introduction, p. 30, *A Pastoral Democracy* by I. M. Lewis, O.U.P., 1961).—Ed.

order to set a good example. 'Against my inclination,' wrote Speke, 'I was appointed to be Sumunter's prosecutor and, with my servants as witnesses, a verdict of guilty was speedily effected in the Aden Police Court.' Sumunter was sentenced to two months in prison and a fine of two hundred rupees and to be banished from Aden.

Speke had kept notes of his journey which he handed over to Burton and his collection of stuffed animals were sent to the museum in Calcutta; it included a new species of rat which was named after Speke.*

There were other grievances which were only revealed five years later when Speke fell ill and was nursed by Burton during their expedition to Lake Tanganyika.

> During Jack's delirium [wrote Burton] he let out all his little grievances of fancied wrongs, of which I had not even the remotest idea. He was vexed that his diary (which I had edited so carefully and put into the Appendix of *First Footsteps in Eastern Africa*) had not been printed *as he wrote it*—geographical blunders and all; also because he had not been paid for it; I have lost money over the book myself. He asked me to send his collections to the Calcutta Museum of Natural History; now he was hurt because I had done so.⁴†

Speke had found his dairy cut down from over twenty-four thousand words to a little over thirteen thousand; Burton had interposed remarks of his own and in one case at least had misquoted Speke. The last paragraphs added by Burton in an appendix to *First Footsteps in East Africa* were certainly unnecessarily patronizing.

> It is evident from the perusal of these pages [wrote Burton], that though the traveller suffered from the system of blackmail to which the inhospitable Somal of Makhar subject all strangers, though he was delayed, persecuted by his 'protector', and threatened with war, danger, and destruction, his life was never in real peril. Some allowance must also be made for the people of the country. Lieut. Speke was, of course, recognized as a servant of Government; and savages cannot believe that a man wastes his rice and cloth to collect dead beasts and to ascertain the direction of streams. He was known to be a Christian; he is ignorant

---

* There was also a rat named after Burton in West Africa during his travels there.

† The full diary was not published until 1864 in Speke's *What Led to the Discovery of the Source of the Nile*.
Speke wrote to Rigby, October 6, 1860: 'Burton thought I never would write [for publication] because I had been soft enough to give him up my Somali diaries, or he never would have asked me to go with him [on the expedition to Lake Tanganyika]. *Burton* by Byron Farwell, Longmans, 1963, p. 178.

of the Moslem faith; and, most fatal to his enterprise, he was limited in time. Not knowing either the Arabic or the Somali tongue, he was forced to communicate with the people through the medium of his dishonest interpreter and Abban.[5]

This passage was dated Camp Aden, March 1855. Did Burton himself during the days before his camp was attacked at Berbera give sufficient allowance for the people of the country? It was clear from Speke's report that members of the tribes through which he passed— the Warsingali, the Dulbahanta, and the Habr Girhajis—were all suspicious that his journey meant that the British Government had some designs on the country. The continued presence of Lieutenants Stroyan and Herne in Berbera had also aroused suspicions. Stroyan had made some short expeditions inland shooting and had killed three elephants; wells had been dug to find drinking water and notes were made about the extent of the trade in Berbera.

When Speke crossed to the Somali coast again on March 20 to collect more camels from Kurrum he obtained further information of Somali suspicions. This time he had an excellent Somali guide and interpreter recommended by Lieut. Dansey, Assistant Political Agent at Aden. This was Mahmoud Gooled, nicknamed 'al Balyuz', or Ambassador, because he had carried out a successful mission in Somaliland for the Aden Government.

Balyuz [wrote Speke] was a clever Hindustani scholar, and, as I ultimately found, possessed such honesty of purpose and straightforwardness of character, as rendered him a perfect *rara avis* among all Somali. He was of the Mijjertaine tribe. Travelling in his company, after my experiences with Sumunter and Ahmed, was verily a luxury.[6]

In Kurrum Speke found that the Somalis were upset by stories that the English intended to stop the slave-trade which, they considered, would be unjust since slavery was in accordance with the teaching of the Koran; another rumour was that the English intended to take possession of Berbera or to give it to Burton's friend Sharmakay of Zayla, and there were reports that the English wished to suppress the system of Abbans, which would be a great loss of money to them. After buying camels in Kurrum, Speke started along the coast towards Berbera and reached Aynterad where he found a group of old men arguing that the British expedition would never reach the Webbe Shebelli river or even the Ogaden country; they said that the Somali would stop them before they got half way. The Balyuz then said: 'But the English are strong, and can do anything they like.' They laughed and replied:

If the Somali came down to fight, and then ran away back into the fastnesses of their hills, what would the English do then, who cannot live a day without drinking beer and eating meat? Whereas the Somali can do very well without anything, seldom requiring even water, and not more than one morsel of meat, for a whole week together.

If Outram had allowed the Somali expedition to start in one body the previous October there would have been no occasion for such rumours, but during the six months' delay reports had spread from one tribe to another with fatal consequences. 'Had we gone straight from Aden without any preliminary fuss,' wrote Speke, 'and joined the Ogaden caravan at Berbera just as it was starting, I feel convinced that we would have succeeded.'

Speke arrived in Berbera on April 3 and was given a warm welcome by Herne and Stroyan. They watched the approach of the annual Harar caravan and the arrival of Richard Burton, commanding the expedition, who described what happened in Berbera in the following 'Postscript'.

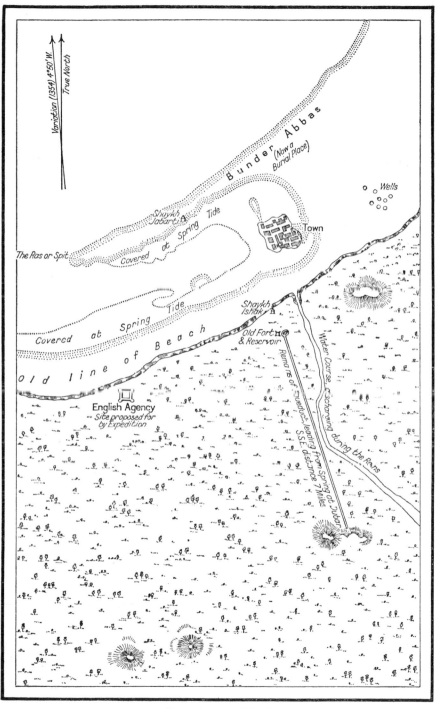

Variation (1354) 4°50' W.
True North

Bunder Abbas
(Now a Burial Place)

Wells

Shaykh Jabarti
Covered at Spring Tide
Town

The Ras or Spit
Covered at Spring Tide

Covered at Spring Tide
Shaykh Ishak

Old line of Beach
Old Fort & Reservoir

Water Course discharging during the Rains

Remains of Aqueduct, leading from Spring at Dubar S.S.E. distance 7 Miles

English Agency
— Site proposed for
by Expedition

Burton's map of Berbera.

Postscript

ON SATURDAY, the 7th April 1855, the H.E.I. Company's Schooner *Mahi*, Lieut. King, I.N., commanding, entered the harbour of Berbera, where her guns roared forth a parting salute to the 'Somali Expedition'. The Emporium of East Africa was at the time of my landing, in a state of confusion. But a day before, the great Harar caravan, numbering 3,000 souls, and as many cattle, had entered for the purpose of laying in the usual eight months' supplies, and purchase, barter, and exchange were transacted in most hurried and unbusiness-like manner. All day, and during the greater part of night, the town rang with the voices of buyer and seller: to specify no other articles of traffic, 500 slaves of both sexes were in the market.* Long lines of laden and un-laden camels were to be seen pacing the glaring yellow shore; rumours of plundering parties at times brought swarms of spear-men, bounding and yelling like wild beasts, from the town: already small parties of

* The Fair-season of 1854–5 began on the 15th November, and may be said to have broken up on the 15th April.

The principal caravans which visit Berbera are from Harar the Western, and Ogadayn, the Southern region: they collect the produce of the numerous intermediate tribes of the Somal. The former has been described in the preceding pages. The following remarks upon the subject of the Ogadayn caravan are the result of Lieuts. Stroyan and Herne's observations at Berbera.

'Large caravans from Ogadayn descend to the coast at the beginning and the end of the Fair-season. They bring slaves from the Arusa country, cattle in great quantities, gums of sorts, clarified butter, ivory, ostrich feathers, and rhinoceros horns to be made into handles for weapons. These are bartered for coarse cotton cloth of three kinds, for English and American sheeting in pieces of seventy-five, sixty-six, sixty-two, and forty-eight yards, black and indigo-dyed calicos in lengths of sixteen yards, nets or fillets worn by the married women, iron and steel in small bars, lead and zinc, beads of various kinds, especially white porcelain and speckled glass, dates and rice.'

The Ayyal Ahmad and Ayyal Yunis classes of the Habr Awal Somal have constituted themselves Abbans or brokers to the Ogadayn Caravans, and the rapacity of the patron has produced a due development of roguery in the client. The principal trader of this coast is the Banyan from Aden and Cutch, facetiously termed by the Somal their 'Milch-cows'. The African cheats by mis-measuring the bad cotton cloth, and the Indian by falsely weighing the coffee, ivory, ostrich feathers, and other valuable articles which he receives in return. Dollars and even rupees are now preferred to the double breadth of eight cubits which constitutes the well known 'Tobe'.

travellers had broken ground for their return journey; and the foul heap of mat hovels, to which this celebrated mart had been reduced, was steadily shrinking in dimensions.

Our little party consisted of forty-two souls. At Aden I had applied officially for some well-trained Somali policemen, but as an increase of that establishment had been urged upon the home authorities, my request was refused. We were fain to content ourselves with a dozen recruits of various races, Egyptian, Nubian, Arab and Negro, whom we armed with sabres and flint muskets. The other members of the expedition were our private servants, and about a score of Somal under our rival protectors Jami Hasan and Burhali Nuh. The Ras or Captain of the Kafilah was one Mahmud of the Mijjarthayn, better known at Aden as al Balyuz or the Envoy: he had the reputation of being a shrewd manager, thoroughly acquainted with the habits and customs, as well as the geography, of Somaliland.

Our camp was pitched near the site of the proposed Agency, upon a rocky ridge within musket-shot of the southern extremity of the creek, and about three quarters of a mile distant from the town. This position had been selected for the benefit of the *Mahi*'s guns. Political exigencies required the *Mahi* to relieve the *Elphinstone*, then blockading the seaboard of our old Arab foe, the Fazli chief; she was unable to remain upon the coast, and superintend our departure, a measure which I had strongly urged. Our tents were pitched in one line: Lieut. Stroyan's was on the extreme right, about a dozen paces distant was the 'Rowtie'* occupied by Lieut. Herne and myself, and at a similar distance on the left of the camp was that in which Lieut. Speke slept. The baggage was placed between the two latter, the camels were tethered in front upon a sandy bed beneath the ridge [of] our camping-ground, and in rear stood the horses and mules. During day-time all were on the alert: at night two sentries were posted, regularly relieved, and visited at times by the Ras and ourselves.

I had little reason to complain of my reception at Berbera. The chiefs appeared dissatisfied with the confinement of one Mohammed Sammattar [or Sumunter], the Abban who accompanied Lieut. Speke to the Eastern country: they listened, however, with respectful attention to a letter in which the Political Resident at Aden enjoined them to treat us with consideration and hospitality.

There had been petty disputes with Burhali Nuh,[1] and the elders of

* A Sepoy's tent, pent-house shaped, supported by a single transverse and two upright poles and open at one of the long ends.

the Eesa Musa tribe, touching the hire of horse-keepers and camel-drivers: such events, however, are not worthy to excite attention in Africa. My friend at Harar, the Shaykh Jami, had repeatedly called upon us, eaten bread and salt, recommended us to his fellow country-men, and used my intervention in persuading avaricious ship-owners to transport, gratis, pauper pilgrims to Arabia. The people, after seeing the deaths of a few elephants, gradually lowered their loud boasts and brawling claims: they assisted us in digging a well, offered their ser-vices as guides and camel-drivers, and in some cases insisted upon en-camping near us for protection. Briefly, we saw no grounds of appre-hension. During thirty years, not an Englishman of the many that had visited it had been molested at Berbera, and apparently there was as little to fear in it as within the fortifications of Aden.*

Under these favourable circumstances we might have set out at once towards the interior. Our camels, fifty-six in number, had been purchased, and the Ogadayn Caravan was desirous of our escort. But we wished to witness the close of the Berbera fair, and we expected instruments and other necessaries by the mid-April mail from Europe.

About 3 p.m., on the 9th April, a shower, accompanied by thunder and lightning, came up from the southern hills, where rain had been falling for some days, and gave notice that the Gugi or Somali monsun had begun. This was the signal for the Bedouin to migrate to the plateau above the hills. Throughout the town the mats were stripped from the frameworks of stick and pole, the camels were laden, and thousands of travellers lined the roads. The next day Berbera was almost deserted except by the pilgrims who intended to take ship, and by merchants, who, fearful of plundering parties, awaited the first favourable hour for setting sail. Our protectors, Jami and Burhali, re-ceiving permission to accompany their families and flocks, left us in charge of their sons and relations. On the 15th April the last vessel sailed out of the creek, and our little party remained in undisputed possession of the place.

Three days afterwards, about noon, an Aynterad craft en route from Aden entered the solitary harbour freighted with about a dozen Somal

---

* Since returning I have been informed, however, by the celebrated Abyssinian traveller M. Antoine d'Abbadie, that in no part of the wild countries which he visited was his life so much perilled as at Berbera.

[Antoine d'Abbadie, 1810–97, explored Ethiopia and the Galla country, wrote *Géodesie de la haute Ethiopie*, 1837; his brother Arnaud Michel, 1815 to 1893, accompanied him and wrote *Douze ans de séjour dans la haute Ethiopie*, 1867.—Ed.]

desirous of accompanying us towards Ogadayn, the southern region. She would have sailed that evening; fortunately, however, I had ordered our people to feast her commander and crew with rice and the irresistible dates.

At sunset on the same day we were startled by a discharge of musketry behind the tents: the cause proved to be three horsemen, over whose heads our guard had fired in case they might be a foraging party. I reprimanded our people sharply for this act of folly, ordering them in future to reserve their fire, and when necessary to shoot into, not above, a crowd. After this we proceeded to catechize the strangers, suspecting them to be scouts, the usual forerunners of a Somali raid: the reply was so plausible that even the Balyuz, with all his acuteness, was deceived.* The Bedouin had forged a report that their ancient enemy the Hajj Sharmakay was awaiting with four ships at the neighbouring port, Siyaro, the opportunity of seizing Berbera whilst deserted, and re-erecting his forts there for the third time. Our visitors swore by the divorce-oath, the most solemn which the religious know, that [seeing] a vessel entering the creek at such unusual season, they had been sent to ascertain whether it had been freighted with materials for building, and concluded by laughingly asking if we feared danger from the tribe of our own protectors. Believing them, we posted as usual two sentries for the night, and retired to rest in our wonted security.

Between 2 and 3 a.m. of the 19th April I was suddenly aroused by the Balyuz, who cried aloud that the enemy was upon us.† Hearing a rush of men like a stormy wind, I sprang up, called for my sabre, and sent Lieut. Herne to ascertain the force of the foray. Armed with a 'Colt', he went to the rear and left of the camp, the direction of danger, collected some of the guard—others having already disappeared—and fired two shots into the assailants. Then finding himself alone, he turned hastily towards the tent; in so doing he was tripped up by the ropes, and as he arose, a Somali appeared in the act of striking at him with a club. Lieut. Herne fired, floored the man, and rejoining me, declared that the enemy was in great force and the guard nowhere. Meanwhile, I had aroused Lieuts. Stroyan and Speke, who were sleeping in the extreme right and left tents. The former, it is presumed, arose to defend

---

* The Balyuz's own account is different (see p. 277).—Ed.

† The attacking party, it appears, was 350 strong; 12 of the Mikahil, 15 of the Habr Girhajis, and the rest Eesa Musa. One Ao Ali wore, it is said, the ostrich feather for the murder of Lieut. Stroyan.

himself, but, as the sequel shows, we never saw him alive.* Lieut. Speke, awakened by the report of fire-arms, but supposing it the normal false alarm—a warning to plunderers—he remained where he was: presently hearing clubs rattling upon his tent, and feet shuffling around, he ran to my Rowtie, which we prepared to defend as long as possible.

The enemy swarmed like hornets with shouts and screams intending to terrify, and proving that overwhelming odds were against us: it was by no means easy to avoid in the shades of night the jobbing of javelins, and the long heavy daggers thrown at our legs from under and through the opening of the tent. We three remained together: Lieut. Herne knelt by my right, on my left was Lieut. Speke guarding the entrance, I stood in the centre, having nothing but a sabre.† The revolvers were used by my companions with deadly effect: unfortunately there was but one pair. When the fire was exhausted, Lieut. Herne went to search for his powder-horn, and that failing, to find some spears usually tied to the tent-pole. Whilst thus engaged, he saw a man breaking into the rear of our Rowtie, and came back to inform me of the circumstance.

At this time, about five minutes after the beginning of the affray, the tent had been almost beaten down, an Arab custom with which we were all familiar, and had we been entangled in its folds we should have been speared with unpleasant facility. I gave the word for escape, and sallied out, closely followed by Lieut. Herne, with Lieut. Speke in the rear.‡ The prospect was not agreeable. About twenty men were kneeling and crouching at the tent entrance, whilst many dusky figures stood further off, or ran about shouting the war-cry, or with shouts and blows drove away our camels. Among the enemy were many of our friends and attendants: the coast being open to them, they naturally ran away, firing a few useless shots and receiving a modicum of flesh wounds.

After breaking through the mob at the tent entrance, imagining that I saw the form of Lieut. Stroyan lying upon the sand, I cut my way to-

* Mohammed, his Indian servant, stated that rising at my summons he had rushed to his tent, armed himself with a revolver, and fired six times upon his assassins. Unhappily, however, Mohammed did not see his master fall, and as he was foremost amongst the fugitives, scant importance attaches to his evidence. [See p.281—Ed.]

† The Balyuz stated that he gave Lieut. Burton a gun which he found in the tent, but it was not loaded (see p. 280).—Ed.

‡ According to Speke: 'Lieut. Burton now said, "Don't step back, or they will think we are retiring." Chagrined by this rebuke at my management at fighting, and imagining by the remark I was expected to defend the camp, I stepped boldly to the front . . .' (p. 132). *What Led to the Discovery of the Source of the Nile*, by John Hanning Speke, William Blackwood & Sons, 1864.—Ed.

wards it amongst a dozen Somal, whose war-clubs worked without mercy, whilst the Balyuz, who was violently pushing me out of the fray, rendered the strokes of my sabre uncertain. This individual was cool and collected: though incapacitated by a sore right-thumb from using the spear, he did not shun danger, and passed unhurt through the midst of the enemy: his efforts, however, only illustrated the venerable adage, 'defend me from my friends'. I turned to cut him down: he cried out in alarm; the well-known voice caused an instant's hesitation: at that moment a spearman stepped forward, left his javelin in my mouth, and retired before he could be punished. Escaping as by a miracle, I sought some support: many of our Somal and servants lurking in the darkness offered to advance, but 'tailed off' to a man as we approached the foe. Presently the Balyuz reappeared, and led me towards the place where he believed my three comrades had taken refuge. I followed him, sending the only man that showed presence of mind, one Golab of the Yusuf tribe, to bring back the Aynterad craft from the Spit into the centre of the harbour.*

Again losing the Balyuz in the darkness, I spent the interval before dawn wandering in search of my comrades, and lying down when over-powered with faintness and pain: as the day broke, with my remaining strength I reached the head of the creek, was carried into the vessel, and persuaded the crew to arm themselves and visit the scene of our disasters.†

Meanwhile, Lieut. Herne, who had closely followed me, fell back, using the butt-end of his discharged six-shooter upon the hard heads around him: in so doing he came upon a dozen men, who though they loudly vociferated, 'Kill the Franks who are killing the Somal!' allowed him to pass uninjured.

He then sought his comrades in the empty huts of the town, and at early dawn was joined by the Balyuz, who was similarly employed. When day broke he sent a Negro to stop the native craft, which was apparently sailing out of the harbour, and in due time came on board. With the exception of sundry stiff blows with the war-club, Lieut. Herne had the fortune to escape unhurt.

On the other hand, Lieut. Speke's escape was in every way wonder-

---

* At this season native craft quitting Berbera make for the Spit late in the evening, cast anchor there, and set sail with the land breeze before dawn. Our lives hung upon a thread. Had the vessel departed, as she intended, the night before the attack, nothing could have saved us from destruction.

† It was only after Burton had been taken on board that it was possible to extract the javelin from his jaw.—Ed.

ful. Sallying from the tent he levelled his 'Dean and Adams' close to his assailant's breast. The pistol refused to revolve. A sharp blow of a war-club upon the chest felled our comrade, who was in the rear and unseen. When he fell, two or three men sprang upon him, pinioned his hands behind, felt him for concealed weapons—an operation to which he submitted in some alarm*—and led him towards the rear, as he supposed to be slaughtered. There, Lieut. Speke, who could scarcely breathe from the pain of the blow, asked a captor to tie his hands before, instead of behind, and begged a drop of water to relieve his excruciating thirst. The savage defended him against a number of the Somal who came up threatening and brandishing their spears, he brought a cloth for the wounded man to lie upon, and lost no time in procuring a draught of water.

Lieut. Speke remained upon the ground till dawn. During the interval he witnessed the war-dance of the savages—a scene striking in the extreme. The tallest and largest warriors marched in a ring round the tents and booty, singing, with the deepest and most solemn tones, the song of thanksgiving. At a little distance the grey uncertain light disclosed four or five men, lying desperately hurt, whilst their kinsmen kneaded their limbs, poured water upon their wounds, and placed lumps of dates in their stiffening hands.† As day broke, the division of plunder caused angry passions to rise. The dead and dying were abandoned. One party made a rush upon the cattle, and with shouts and yells drove them off towards the wild, some loaded themselves with goods, others fought over pieces of cloth, which they tore with hand and dagger, whilst the disappointed, vociferating with rage, struck at one another and brandished their spears. More than once during these scenes, a panic seized them; they moved off in a body to some distance; and there is little doubt that had our guard struck one blow, we might still have won the day.

Lieut. Speke's captor went to seek his own portion of the spoil, when a Somali came up and asked in Hindustani, what business the

* In his official report Speke stated: 'whilst I was being pinioned they felt my private parts'; in his book he added: 'I felt as if my hair stood on end; and, not knowing who my opponents were, I feared that they belonged to a tribe called Eesa, who are notorious, not only for their ferocity in fighting, but for the unmanly mutilations they delight in. Indescribable was my relief when I found that my most dreaded fears were without foundation. The men were in reality feeling whether, after an Arab fashion, I was carrying a dagger between my legs, to rip up a foe after his victim was supposed to be powerless', (p. 133), *What Led to the Discovery of the Source of the Nile.*—Ed.

† The Somal places dates in the hands of the fallen to ascertain the extent of injury: he who cannot eat that delicacy is justly decided to be *in articulo.*

Frank had in their country, and added that he would kill him if a Christian, but spare the life of a brother Moslem. The wounded man replied that he was going to Zanzibar, that he was still a Nazarene, and therefore that the work had better be done at once: the savage laughed and passed on. He was succeeded by a second, who, equally compassionate, whirled a sword round his head, twice pretended to strike, but returned to the plunder without doing damage. Presently came another manner of assailant. Lieut. Speke, who had extricated his hands, caught the spear levelled at his breast, but received at the same moment a blow from a club which, paralysing his arm, caused him to lose his hold. In defending his heart from a succession of thrusts, he received severe wounds on the back of his hand, his right shoulder, and his left thigh. Pausing a little, the wretch crossed to the other side, and suddenly passed his spear clean through the right leg of the wounded man: the latter 'smelling death', then leapt up, and taking advantage of his assailant's terror, rushed headlong towards the sea. Looking behind, he avoided the javelin hurled at his back, and had the good fortune to run, without further accident, the gauntlet of a score of missiles. When pursuit was discontinued, he sat down faint from loss of blood upon a sandhill. Recovering strength by a few minutes' rest, he staggered on to the town, where some old women directed him to us. Then, pursuing his way, he fell in with the party sent to seek him,* and by their aid reached the craft, having walked and run at least three miles, after receiving eleven wounds, two of which had pierced his thighs. A touching lesson how difficult it is to kill a man in sound health!

When the three survivors had reached the craft, Yusuf, the captain, armed his men with muskets and spears, landed them near the camp, and ascertained that the enemy expecting a fresh attack, had fled, carrying away our cloth, tobacco, swords, and other weapons.† The corpse of Lieut. Stroyan was then brought on board. Our lamented comrade was already stark and cold. A spear had traversed his heart, another had pierced his abdomen, and a frightful gash, apparently of a sword,

* This party included the Balyuz who stated, according to Speke, that 'Lieutenants Burton and Herne had *run away* with him immediately after I left the central tent to *fight*'. Editor's italics.

† They had despised the heavy sacks of grain, the books, broken boxes, injured instruments, and a variety of articles which they did not understand. We spent that day at Berbera, bringing off our property, and firing guns to recall six servants who were missing. They did not appear, having lost no time in starting for Karam and Aynterad, whence they made their way in safety to Aden. On the evening of the 19th of April, unable to remove the heavier effects, and anxious to return with the least possible delay, I ordered them to be set on fire.

Speke's miraculous escape from the Somali.

had opened the upper part of his forehead: the body had been bruised with war-clubs, and the thighs showed marks of violence after death. This was the severest affliction that befell us. We had lived together like brothers: Lieut. Stroyan was a universal favourite, and his sterling qualities of manly courage, physical endurance, and steady perseverance had augured for him a bright career, thus prematurely cut off. Truly melancholy to us was the contrast between the evening when he sat with us full of life and spirits, and the morning when we saw amongst us a livid corpse.

We had hoped to preserve the remains of our friend for interment at Aden. But so rapid were the effects of exposure, that we were compelled most reluctantly, on the morning of the 20th April, to commit them to the deep, Lieut. Herne reading the funeral service.

Then with heavy hearts we set sail for the near Arabian shore, and, after a tedious two days, carried to our friends the news of unexpected disaster.

This is the end of Richard Burton's story, but it was not the end for the Government of India, and another chapter has been added giving some of the official reactions to the Berbera disaster.

Somali horseman.

XII

Burton Attacked in Official Reports*

THE ACTING CIVIL SURGEON in Aden visited Burton and Speke in an hotel at Steamer Point and made his official report on April 22, 1855. He said that the spear had entered the left side of Burton's face and had come out on the right, removing two molar teeth and dividing the roof of the palate. The doctor said that it was a serious wound 'and as he [Burton] has recently suffered from secondary syphilis [he] must immediately proceed to Europe as it would not be proper to allow him to remain in Aden during the approaching hot weather'.

Speke's wounds were so severe that it was surprising that he lived; his arms and legs were 'contracted into indescribable positions', and he began to suffer from partial blindness. Lieut. Dansey gave him room in his house and nursed him tenderly and Colonel Coghlan sat at the end of his bed 'with tears in his eyes'; when he could be moved he was sent

* New chapter based on unpublished official reports and other sources.

to England. 'Thus ended my first expedition,' wrote Speke, 'a signal of failure from inexperience, and with a loss of £510 worth of my own private property, which I never recovered.'[1]

The population of Aden, European and Arab, had not had such a momentous story about which to gossip for at least five years—not since a ship's boat from the steamer *Auckland* had been attacked at the northern shore of the harbour of Aden and a member of the crew killed, nor since the murder of Captain Milne at Wahat in March 1851, and the attempt to assassinate the Political Resident, Captain Haines, by an armed man from Bir Ahmed. The Chaplain of the Aden garrison reminded his parishioners that he had always said that such an expedition would fail and there were many others who boasted that they had known what would happen. People argued that insufficient precautions had been taken; others criticized the authorities in Aden for not giving sufficient help, and some said that the Somalis were savages and it was unwise to advance into their territory.

> We have been condemned [wrote Speke] for not putting on more sentries to watch; but had the whole camp been in a state of ordinary preparation for war, with such cowardly hearts as our men had, we should have been signally defeated.
>
> Had any of the guard, or Somali, stood [wrote Lieut. Herne], we should have resisted the attack, but under such overpowering numbers we had no chance.
>
> The officers under my charge [wrote Burton in his official report] fought cooly and with energy, but of our twelve men armed with swords and muskets, Saad, a black slave, only is severely wounded; there are also three slightly hurt—Abdel Mahmoun, an Egyptian, Abdullah and Zarhan, two other Negroes—the others behaved with the vilest cowardice . . . they threw down their weapons and ran after firing only three shots high in the air.

Questions were asked as to why Burton had delayed in Berbera and not accompanied the Ogaden caravan under the protection of the Somali chiefs, and there were stories that he had been warned of an impending attack. Burton's official report of April 22, 1855, was sent to the Government in Bombay through the Political Agent in Aden, Brigadier Coghlan.

> On the 15th instant [wrote Burton] the Berbera Fair concluded and the last vessel left the Port; our party remained behind awaiting the mid-April mail. In their utter security, the Abbans or Protectors accompanied their families and property to the Highlands, leaving with us

their sons and other representatives. Beyond the rumour of raids and forays, which daily abound in the Somali country, we heard of no hostile intention and, as a body, the people were decidedly friendly to us. The Melancholy occurrence was the act of a troop of Bedouin brigands, and it will be reprobated as severely in Africa as in Europe. It is in every way opposed to the customs of the country and a flagrant infraction of the people's code of honour; true, the brigands did not appear at the first flush of the affair to be determined on bloodshed. This is proved by the fact of their using bludgeons at the beginning, but the passions of the Somal are easily aroused, and when they saw their kinsmen—four or five in number, it is stated by Lieut. Speke—laid out and unable to eat the plundered dates, they proceeded to the cold-blooded and dastardly act. As a proof that their primary object was plunder, they even carried off the camels and a little merchandise belonging to some Ogadayn travellers who had stayed behind to accompany us . . .

In conclusion [wrote Burton] I cannot refrain from remarking, that as I took upon myself the responsibility of the expedition, so I have discharged it to the utmost of my ability. Our arrangements were hurriedly made; we could not draw from Aden the number of well-trained Somali policemen, upon which I originally calculated, and had to depend upon raw recruits who fled at the first charge. But we had been ever led by all to believe that the coast about Berbera was safe as Bombay itself, and calculated that by the time of our reaching the interior the new party would have fallen into good order. Political events at Aden also prevented our detaining the H.E.I. Co's Schooner *Mahi*, whose presence would have rendered the start safe, and once in the interior we were secure from the Bedouins who have a horror of fire-arms. Had our letters, sent from Aden, arrived within a moderate time, we should have been enabled to leave Berbera with the Ogadayn Caffilah. Such, and a multitude of similar little combinations have given rise to our late disaster.

Brigadier Coghlan reacted to this criticism in his official report of April 23 with which Burton's report was sent.

The reasons adduced by Lieut. Burton for the failure of the expedition are inconsistent; the surprise obviously occurred, less by the fault of his own raw recruits, than by the false security in which the Expedition indulged. To use Lieut. Burton's own words to me 'they felt no more need of watchfulness than if they had been living at Aden'. Had the surprise occurred farther inland it is probable that not a single member of the expedition would have returned to tell the tale, and it is beyond belief that if plunder were the only object, that motive would not have operated as forcibly inland as on the coast.

It may seem harsh to criticize the conduct of these officers who, to the grief of their wounds and the loss of their property, must add the total failure of their long-cherished scheme; but I cannot refrain from observing that their whole proceeding is marked by a want of that caution and vigilance, which the character of the people amongst whom they dwell, ought to have suggested. These four active young officers occupied three separate tents; they kept no watch among themselves; it appears that only two of them had their fire-arms ready; they defended themselves bravely as might be expected, but combination and previous arrangement for such a contingency had not been made, and a treacherous assault, which common prudence and forethought might have prevented, unhappily prevailed to the total ruin of the expedition and the serious embarrassment of our already complicated relations with the political range (?) of this Residency.

Although Lieut. Burton is persuaded that the only object of this attack was the hope of plunder and that blood was only shed in consequence of resistance, I am by no means satisfied that such was the case.

Coghlan believed that the tribes were suspicious that Sharmakay intended to establish himself again in Berbera through his friendship with Lieut. Burton.

From inquiries I have instituted elsewhere, I am fully convinced that Lieut. Burton's favourite theory—of the willingness of the Habr Awal to receive a British Agent—as far at least as the lower and wilder classes are concerned, is a fallacy, and that they were urged on to the attack . . . by jealousy of our interference in their country; ignorance of our real designs, and fearing my determination (which Lieut. Burton communicated to them) to put a stop to the slave trade, one of their principal sources of revenue.

But whatever the cause, we have now to deal with the fact, that a barbarous outrage has been committed on our countrymen who were travelling in their proper character, under the auspices of Government and duly introduced and accredited to the Chiefs of the tribe with whom we are on terms of professed friendship and who profit largely by the trade with this settlement . . .

Berbera is already desolate, and neither man nor animal exists there and the tribes have dispersed. With the means at my disposal it would be madness to attempt to follow these robbers to the interior, and though doubtless I could march from one end of their country to the other I could inflict no punishment upon them. Happily, such a course is not necessary and, unlike the Arab tribes who have so often laughed us to scorn, these offenders are completely in our power . . . I would suggest that early in the approaching season, a strict blockade of their coast should be instituted; for this purpose I would detach from this Garrison one company of European soldiers and a small detachment of artillery, to occupy a position at Berbera, this force to be covered for a short time by a small armed steamer, which would cruize along the Somali coast touching every two or three days at Berbera . . . The efficacy of the measure is beyond doubt: the Somalis cannot exist without Berbera . . . and they will certainly comply with our demands . . .

If this be not done the insolence of the Somali tribes will rise with their impunity and our connection with that coast will be severed greatly to our inconvenience, while the slave trade, which it is our endeavour to extinguish, will gain a new impetus when no longer watched by our Agents and informants on shore.[2]

Coghlan also sent on to Bombay a report which Burton had written in Berbera in April while waiting to proceed inland:

I have communicated to the Chiefs of Berbera [wrote Burton] that English gentlemen visiting their countries will not hereafter consider themselves obliged to travel like Arabs and Banyans under the charge of Abbans or Protectors. They will engage, if you approve of this arrangement, an efficient Somali servant at Aden and pay him for his services after return a price settled by mutual agreement. The people have offered no objection to my proposal and they freely recognize the impropriety of a British officer placing himself under the protection of a Somali, who, according to the custom of the country, becomes lord of the property and director of the proceedings of his *protégé*.[3]

When these reports reached Bombay very careful consideration was given to them by the Governor and President of the Council, Lord Elphinstone, and by Mr. Lumsden and Mr. Malet, members of the Council. Lord Elphinstone agreed with Coghlan that Lieut. Burton and his companions 'did not take all the precautions which they ought to have done against surprise', and he was critical of Burton's statement to the Chiefs of Berbera that travellers would in future dispense with the services of Abbans or Protectors.

Acting in this spirit of what I must call overweening confidence, Lieut. Burton allowed his Abbans to accompany their families to their own homes after the conclusion of the Fair at Berbera, leaving only their sons or representatives with his party. I fear that this must have had something to do with what followed.

Lord Elphinstone favoured Coghlan's arguments for the reason of the attack adding: 'If it is difficult to appreciate the motives of savages, it is certainly not less difficult to know how to deal with them. One rule, however, may be, I believe, laid down as an invariable one—

never ask what you are not prepared and determined to enforce.' He regretted that Coghlan had demanded a sum of money, and that it should have been such a large one, for he doubted whether the Chiefs of the Habr Awal would be able to collect it, nor was he sure that the blockade of the coast and even the landing of the troops would be sufficient to compel compliance with the demands. He did not think that the establishment of an Agency at Berbera was a good plan: 'After the proofs we have just had of the disposition of the tribes in that part of the country, I fear that this would be attended with much greater risk and expense than I was led to expect when, in a former minute, I expressed myself somewhat in favour of this project.'

Burton's friend, Lumsden, tried to soften the impact of these reports. 'My impression is that a certain degree of self-security on the part of the Mission had been created by all antecedent experience, whether of officers who had previously visited Berbera or of the members of the Mission themselves, which induced them to consider themselves in perfect safety.' He agreed with Burton that the motive was probably cupidity and that they could ruin the Berbera annual fair by a strict blockade, but he did not think it was necessary to land troops; the Somalis would miss their profits from the Aden markets, which would be closed to them and transferred to others. Lumsden argued that there would still be advantages in eventually having an Agency at Berbera. Mr. Malet, another member of the Bombay Council, also was in favour of keeping in mind the Agency, but on other points he agreed with the Governor's minute.[4]

On May 7 Brigadier Coghlan sent another letter to Bombay, and forwarded statements taken in Aden from Somali and other members of the expedition. He said that the testimony of Balyuz, the Chief of the caravan, and of Sheikh Ahmed, Burton's servant, which had been corroborated by others, gave conclusive proof that these men distrusted 'the spies'—the three men who arrived on horseback at the camp on the evening before the attack—and that they

> duly communicated their suspicions to Lieut. Burton with a recommendation that he should exercise increased vigilance that night. Lieut. Burton, however, entertained too great contempt for Somali courage to contemplate the possibility of an attack, and all his proceedings (such as his neglecting to assure himself that his followers were properly armed and supplied with ammunition) mark the perfect security in which he imagined himself.[5] *

* See Appendix I for depositions of Somalis and others.

While these critical reports were being made the Royal Geographical Society appeared unaffected by the Berbera disaster. The Earl of Ellesmere, in his Presidential address to the Society in May, referred to Lieut. Burton's 'bold journey from Zayla to Harar', and said that the importance of the achievement was not be measured by the time that it occupied. A letter had been received from him 'in a spirit of dauntless joviality, which marks the character of the writer'; Ellesmere also referred to the attack on the camp at Berbera which he said had been prompted by a desire for plunder.[6]

The official dossier on the Somali Expedition was by now becoming large, and was sent to The Most Noble the Governor-General of India, Lord Dalhousie, who considered that condemnation of the manner in which the expedition was conducted by Lieut. Burton and those who were associated with him should have been expressed in stronger terms. 'In such a country, and among such a people, their negligence and disregard of all common prudence and ordinary precaution cannot be extenuated far less excused.' He regretted that Brigadier Coghlan should have demanded so large a sum of money as 15,000 rupees, 'or any money at all'. He did not think that the officers had any just claim on the Government for compensation 'having regard to the conduct of the expedition'.*

Lord Dalhousie considered that Brigadier Coghlan should be authorized to take the measure he had suggested.

> If they fail to pay the money, from inability to do so, but deliver the offenders His Lordship would be content with that reparation. One at least of the murderers should, in His Lordship's opinion, be put to death, if convicted of the offence, and the rest should be banished. And the tribe should be informed that, as the British Government sets no store by the loss of money, but is deeply solicitous for the lives and safety of its subjects and will never suffer these to be destroyed with impunity, it is satisfied with the punishment of the guilty actors in the outrage, and will remit the payment of the money demanded.[7]

* The following claim was made by Lieut. Burton in his official report.

Loss of Government cloth, camels, horses, etc.		Rupees	5,500
Speke private property			4,100
Herne ,, ,,			500
Stroyan ,, ,,			1,750
Burton ,, ,,			1,950
		Rupees	13,800

[The rupee was then worth two shillings so that the total was £1,380.—Ed.]

These were fine words but ineffective, for the Habr Awal had no power, even if they had the inclination, to deliver up a member or members of a sub-tribe. Burton was correct in saying that a large fine was an effective way of dealing with them, for the Somalis were by no means as poor as the authorities in India seemed to think.* The blockade of the Somali coast from Seyarrah to Jebel Elmas was instituted on September 4, 1855, and the trade of the Habr Awal was cut off since the tribes to the east and west would not allow them to make use of other ports in Somaliland.

In October 1855, when Burton was in the Crimea, Brigadier Coghlan did a tour of the Somali coast in the schooner *Mahi*. He had not previously been favourably disposed to Burton's proposal of setting up an Agency at Berbera, but changed his mind after seeing conditions there and being suspicious of French ambitions; he reported to Bombay that they should 'secure for British interests this port which is not only the Emporium of the trade of North Eastern Africa, but it may yet be worth while to prevent others from settling in such inconvenient proximity to Aden'. He found that the blockade was acting 'with great severity' on the Habr Awal tribe which inspired hope of ultimate success. He had been told the name of the murderer of Lieut. Stroyan, a man of the Eesa Moosa by name Aw Ali, who was with his tribe one day's journey from Berbera and had boasted of the deed.[8]

While Brigadier Coghlan was visiting the Somali coast a letter in Arabic arrived from the Somali Elders of the Ayyal Nuh, a sub-tribe of the Habr Awal; it was in reply to a letter he had sent to the Elders of the tribe, warning them that the British Government was taking severe measures to deal with the culprits responsible for the attack on the expedition.

> Your letters have arrived and we have understood their contents. Firstly, Oh Sahib! The outrage came from the English party who came to Berbera . . . We went to them and said: 'Oh Sahib! (Lt. Burton) You must not stay now in this country, and if you wish to go to Ogadayn proceed with us. He said he would not; (therefore) the fault is with the English, not the Ayal Noh, not upon the Habr Awal but upon those who covet the country . . .
>
> Regarding the (attacking) party which you have mentioned in the

---

* When he learned that the Governor-General had objected to the fine, Burton commented in a footnote to his Preface: 'The reason of the objection is not apparent. A savage people is imperfectly punished by a few deaths: the fine is the only true way to produce a lasting impression upon their heads and hearts. Moreover, it is the custom of India and the East generally, and is in reality the only safeguard of a traveller's property.'

letter, the report is known. But when the party went against the English gentlemen, a man named Wabahalie went to them and said: 'Oh Sahibs! I give notice of the (attacking) party; take your things and get into a boat.' They did not consent and said: 'Oh boy! the danger will not eat you, but if there is a body of men we are not afraid' . . .

We have sent a candid answer to your letter. No good comes from tumult and we do not desire it. We have told you the truth and if you doubt these words, God is our witness . . . Do not blockade the sea Oh Sahib as we have no rule upon the Bedouin when we leave the town. Everyone becomes an independent Sultan; but we are not to blame, all the blame is with the English gentlemen.'

This letter when it reached Aden was dealt with by Lieut. R. L. Playfair, who was in charge during the absence of Brigadier Coghlan. He also was critical of Burton and in sending the Somali statement to Bombay he commented:

Brigadier Coghlan's original opinions relative to the atrocity are fully borne out by it [the Somali document]. The attack was not, as represented by Lieut. Burton, the work of mere casual plunderers, but was an organized scheme to rid the country of officers who were supposed to have a design on the country. This idea of theirs was fostered by Lieut. Burton's having imprudently remained in Berbera after the breaking up of the Fair.[9]

On the 15th October ten Elders of the Habr Awal arrived in Aden to see the Political Resident on his return from Somaliland to persuade him to lift the blockade. As anyone knows who has had anything to do with Somalis they have intelligence, charm, and a considerable ability in arguing a case which concerns their interest. Brigadier Coghlan, who had not previously to this tour met Somalis in their own country, was clearly attracted and impressed by them. The arguments they put forward that they had clearly and repeatedly warned Lieut. Burton of the danger of remaining in Berbera, may have been sincere or they may have been ingenious arguments to influence the Brigadier. The Somalis took the offensive and made an impression on the Aden authorities with the argument that travellers should only be sent to Somaliland with the consent of the Elders and that if the travellers disregarded their advice the authorities in Aden should arrange the recall of the travellers.*

* The Somalis are shrewd disputants. During the last war I did a four-day canoe journey from Alula to Gardafui and back with two Somalis during the monsun, achieved against the strong opposition of the Somali Elders of Alula. They did not use the arguments I expected—that Somalis could do many things better than I could, though this was always put in elaborately courteous terms—but stated, pungently enough, that the sharks noticed a white skin more easily than a black one.—Ed.

'The Elders of the Habr Awal,' wrote Burton ... 'falsely asserted that they repeatedly urged us, with warnings of danger, to leave Berbera at the end of the Fair, but that we positively refused compliance, for other reasons. The facts of the case are those stated in the text.'— i.e in his 'Postscript'. Lieut. Playfair had already written to Bombay in such a way as to show that he believed the arguments of the Ayyal Nuh Elders rather than the statements of Lieut. Burton and Brigadier Coghlan also shewed that he believed the Somalis' story in a report dated November 26, 1855.

> It is only within the last few days that I have learnt the full extent of the negligence evinced by Lieut. Burton in his management of this ill-fated expedition: no opportunity has offered till now of acquiring complete information although I have endeavoured to procure it ever since the event.
>
> Heedless of advice, and confident in his own powers, Lieut. Burton neglected the usual precautions and defied danger when it was pointed out to him—I was this day informed by one of the Somali Chiefs that he [Burton] disregarded a solemn and special warning which the Elders gave him on the breaking up of the Fair at Berbera.
>
> It is stated that they went to him and implored him to leave the country, and took with them some merchants to witness their words, but the only reply given was a reference to his revolver.
>
> These circumstances in their full extent are known to me now for the first time; they are elicited by my recent visit to the African coast and my interview with the Elders here, and I confess I have much sympathy with those of the Habr Awal who, though themselves guiltless, are suffering the consequences of Lieut. Burton's obstinate neglect, and a treachery of a branch of their tribe with whom they are at variance ...
>
> They declared their inability to comply with my demands, stating that the Eesa Moosa were their enemies though a branch of their tribe, and that though they could make war upon them they could not, with the strongest desire to do so, make sure of apprehending the offenders— that Africa was wide and there were many quarters accessible to the culprits, where they could not be followed.[10]

Coghlan's dispatch was forwarded to the Governor-General for instructions with regard to the blockade; there were passages in it which were not well received at the Bombay Council and the following reprimand was sent to Aden:

> He [Brigadier Coghlan] should be informed that he would seem to have received all that the Elders of the Habr Awal advanced to the prejudice of Lieut. Burton as undoubted fact, but it might be as well that

he should confine himself to stating what was told him, until after communication with Lieut. Burton or his party should either prove or disprove the truth of the Habr Awal's assertions. The extreme carelessness evinced in the utter disregard of a solemn warning, as stated, appears highly improbable, and the silence maintained by the surviving members of the Mission on the subject, subsequent to the catastrophe, is a strong reason for entertaining doubts if it were ever given as alleged. (*Signed by J. G. Lumsden and A. Malet, Members of the Bombay Council.*)[11]

Coghlan regretted that Government should imagine that he accepted all that the Somali Elders said as undoubted facts.

But I thought their assertions worthy of considerable weight confirming, as they do, to a certain extent the statements of the subordinates of the expedition. I beg to draw attention of Government to the deposition of Sheikh Ahmed, taken immediately after the termination of the expedition, and which formed one of the accompaniments of my letter No. 65 dated 7th May, 1855, . . . and the deposition of Mahomed Gooled, al Balyuz—the Ras Kafilah of the expedition.

Having quoted two effective passages he concluded:

Their depositions were taken by my assistant, in presence of Lieut. Herne, while Lieut. Burton was yet in Aden; they were never questioned or contradicted as far as I am aware. I therefore considered myself justified in accepting them as an authentic data by which to compare the statements of the Elders themselves . . . I have no desire to damage Lieut. Burton in the estimation of Government, but it is impossible for me . . .[12]

I am well aware [wrote Burton] that after my departure from Aden in 1855, an inquiry was instituted during my absence, and without my knowledge, into the facts of the disaster which occurred at Berbera. The 'privileged' communication was, I believe, in due course, privily forwarded to the Bombay Government, and the only rebuke which this shuffling procedure received was from a gentleman [Lumsden] holding a high and honourable position, who could not reconcile himself to seeing a man's character stabbed in the back.[13]

Burton was particularly annoyed by a statement in a book written by Captain Lambert Playfair and printed for Government in Bombay in 1859, which was called *A History of Arabia Felix* but also gave an account of the attack on Burton's camp at Berbera. It was stated:

During the afternoon of the same day (April 18, 1855), three men visited the camp, *probably as spies*, and, as such, *the officers of the ex-*

pedition were warned against them by their native attendants. Heedless of this warning, they retired to rest at night, in the fullest confidence of security, and without taking any extra *or even ordinary measures* to guard against surprise. About 2. a.m. on the following morning, the expedition was attacked by a body of from 150 to 200 well-armed Somalis.

The italics are my own [wrote Burton]; they designate mistatements unpardonable in an individual whose official position enabled him to ascertain and record the truth. The three men were represented to me as spies, who came to ascertain whether I was preparing to take the country for the Chief Sharmakay, then hostile to their tribe, not as spies to spy out the weakness of my party. I received no warning of personal danger. The 'ordinary measures', that is to say, the posting of two sentinels in front and rear of the camp during the night were taken, and I cannot blame myself because they ran away.*[14]

The East India Company officials in Aden were quite clear in their minds that no blame was attached to them and that Burton alone was responsible. Burton certainly knew that there were dangers; the account of his journey to and from Harar is full of stories of unrest among the Habr Awal, blood-feuds between tribes in the vicinity of Berbera and trouble between two powerful Abbans attached to his own expedition. His statement that he thought Berbera would be safe since he had been told in Aden that it would be, is a little too naïve to be accepted.

Burton, however, also knew that a display of caution was not always the best course to follow in a wild country, if it revealed fear and anxiety. He had so far been successful on his expeditions because of the careful preparations he made beforehand, but also, in part, because of his calculated display of bravado. On his journey to Mecca he had won respect among the Bedouin by calling for his dinner while the caravan was being attacked, though he had made sure first that the marauders were being effectively beaten off; in Harar, if he had given any hint of fear he would have been in even greater danger; the favourite sport of the Somali Bedouin was, he knew, to feign an attack and, if the traveller turned and fled, the feint was apt to turn into a reality. Burton had great faith in the Bedouin code of honour towards their guests and felt a close kinship with nomads, but at times he held too romanticized a view of them. When the Bedouin of Sinai murdered in cold blood his friend Professor Palmer, he protested that the act was against the Bedouin tradition and the murderers must have been influenced by others.[15] A traveller of much the same period, Henry Layard, escaped

* See letters from Speke, pp. 282-4.

death on several occasions by a display of bravado, but was nearly killed in the Mountains of Moab by putting too much faith in the chivalry of the Bedouin; he wrote of the double character of the Arab: 'The same man who at one moment would be grasping, deceitful, treacherous, and cruel, would show himself at another, generous, faithful, trustworthy, and humane.'[16] 'Soft, merry, and affectionate souls,' Burton wrote of the Somali, 'they pass without any apparent transition into a state of fury, when they are capable of terrible atrocities.'

Later investigation suggested that Burton had been right in stating that the Somalis who attacked the camp at Berbera had wished only to plunder—'an act of a troop of Bedouin brigands and it will be reprobrated in Africa as in Europe'. But he certainly put too much trust in the Bedouin code of honour when he allowed the Abbans to accompany their families home, and failed to make sure that the camp guards were properly armed; nor did he take into consideration that the suspicions of the Somalis had been aroused by the various expeditions undertaken by the British officers, which had certainly led some of them to think that either the British, or Sharmakay with the help of the British, intended to take Berbera. As a result, there may have been some connivance on the part of the Somali Elders.

If they had, in fact, come to Burton at Berbera and told him emphatically that an attack had been planned, as they argued later that they had done, it is difficult to believe that Burton and the other officers would not have taken more effective precautions. Burton stated in his official report that they had heard of no hostile intention against the expedition and that there were only the usual rumours of raids and forays; nor did the other officers make reference to any specific warning. They would not all have been lying.

It is very probable that the Somali Elders talked in general terms about the dangers of remaining in Berbera after the conclusion of the fair, and these general warnings became, for their own defence, more specific when they came to make their formal depositions. Jami Hasan, for instance, was reputed to be an Abban of high character; would he have gone away with his family and left Lieut. Stroyan, who was under his protection, if he had known definitely that an attack had been planned? It is possible that the plans were not known, for the attacking party came with horses, which they left some distance away on the night of the attack; this suggests that they had come from the interior and that their movements and intentions were not known to the Somalis encamped at Berbera.

The other alternative cannot be excluded. Some of the Somali Elders may have known that an attack had been planned and considered that by giving a general warning they had salved their consciences. They may have been confused in their own minds as to where their loyalties lay, since they must have heard rumours that the British officers had come to take Berbera, and some of them may have believed it.

There is certainly confusion about the intentions of the 'spies', and Burton does not help to clarify matters in his comments on Playfair's remarks. Burton is probably right, however, in saying that the Chief of the Caravan (al Balyuz) believed at the time that the visitors had been reassured when Burton had told them that there was no question of handing over Berbera to Sharmakay. It would be natural for al Balyuz, who felt responsible for the Englishmen under his charge, to improve on his story later, as the other Somalis may have done.

It was unlikely that Burton, who was then in great pain, bothered to find out what statements were being taken down from the Somalis and others. If he had known he would have protested at the time.*

In a letter of January 15, 1856, to Brigadier Coghlan, the Secretary to Government in Bombay, Mr. Anderson, stated:

> His Lordship in Council [Lord Elphinstone] is satisfied that you could have had no wish to prejudice Lieutenant Burton or to do more than state your impression after due inquiry but ... you certainly accuse Lieutenant Burton in very positive terms of culpable carelessness.
>
> While you do this on the authority of the Elders of the Habr Awal you do not appear to have required any officer of the expedition to reply to their statements and your present references to the depositions do not show that, before you went to Berbera, it was even understood, either by the members of the expedition or by anyone else, that a solemn caution had, in reality, been received or given.

By that time Burton had volunteered for service in the Crimea, had joined General Beatson's irregular force of Bashi-bazouks, and was back in London finishing his *First Footsteps in East Africa*. The last paragraph of his Preface, dated February 10, 1856, from 14 St. James's Square, suggests that he was still unaware of the many criticisms that had been levelled at him:

> The writer has had the satisfaction of receiving from his comrades assurances that they are willing to accompany him once more in the task of African exploration. The plans of the Frank are now publicly known

* See Speke's reactions, p. 282.

to the Somali. Should the loss of life, however valuable, be an obstacle to prosecuting them, he must fall in the esteem of the races around him. On the contrary should he, after duly chastizing the offender, carry out the original plan, he will command the respect of the people, and wipe out the memory of a temporary reverse. At no distant period the project will, it is hoped, be revived. Nothing is required but permission to renew the attempt—an indulgence which will not be refused by a Government raised by energy, enterprise, and perserverance from the ranks of a Company of merchants to national wealth and imperial grandeur.

This was nearly a year after the Berbera disaster and it could be argued that Burton had been writing with his tongue in his cheek. The Court of Directors of the East India Company had written to Bombay in August of the previous year (1855): 'The disaster to the Somali Expedition renders it, in our opinion, inexpedient to entertain any application for its further prosecution.'[17] It is possible, however, that, owing to the great delays in the London–Bombay communications and to Burton's absence in the Crimea, Burton had not received the communication.

It was not, for instance, until Burton reached Aden in November, 1856, on his way to Zanzibar for his expedition with Speke to central Africa, that he was told, unofficially, that the claim for compensation by the officers of the Somali Expedition had been refused. He protested strongly when he learned that it had been decided to raise the blockade of the African Coast without exacting compensation from the Somalis, and he was incensed to find that the Aden officials believed the Somali story that he had been warned that there was to be an attack on the Berbera camp, rather than his own denials.

Lieut. Playfair had recently returned after settling the terms of the Treaty with the Habr Awal and representatives of other tribes. He had reported to Brigadier Coghlan, the Political Resident:

> Regarding the right of British subjects to travel in their country (article 3) and to enjoy perfect security there, they [the Habr Awal Elders] replied that such a guarantee was simply impossible as they could not always guarantee their own safety, but they begged that officers who refused their counsel should not again be sent. On this point they were excessively earnest. It would be for our part to prevent travellers from visiting their country save with their consent, and should any disregard their reasonable warnings, they had but to inform us thereof and we would take means to recall them'.[18]

On his way to Zanzibar Burton wrote a long letter to the Royal Geographical Society on December 16, 1856, in which he stated that the raising of the blockade without obtaining compensation was a mistake politically. When the *Mary Ann* brig had been plundered near Berbera in 1825 compensation had been obtained, and in India officers who were robbed in states not under British control were compensated; 'semi-barbarians and savages part with money less willingly than with life'.[19] He also wrote from Zanzibar in April 1857 asking for official confirmation or otherwise as to whether the officers were to receive compensation, and he wrote again from central Africa in June 1858. He finally received a letter from the Government of Bombay, written just after the outbreak of the Indian Mutiny, on June 13, 1857, making it clear that the Government was not feeling friendly disposed: 'Having regard to the conduct of the Expedition, his Lordship [Lord Elphinstone] cannot think that the officers who composed it have any just claims on the Government for their personal losses.'[20]

The Government of India was annoyed that Burton should have criticized in his letter of December 16, 1856, the lack of protection given to trade, and to British protégées in the Red Sea ports owing to the insufficiency of the naval force at Aden, and that these criticisms should have been sent to the Royal Geographical Society for it to pass to the Court of Directors or to the Foreign Office. Burton was informed in a letter from Bombay of July 1857: 'Your want of discretion, and due respect for the authorities to whom you are subordinate, has been regarded with displeasure by the Government.'

It was typical of Burton that he should not understand what the Government was making such a fuss about, as his intention had been to give them a friendly warning, which he considered fully justified. Owing to the fact that he was on his expedition with Speke in central Africa he received, at much the same time as the reprimand of July 1857, a newspaper cutting from the *Telegraph Courier* of Bombay stating that on June 30, 1858, there had been a massacre of nearly all the Christians of Jedda on the Red Sea; the British and French Consuls and about twenty-three others had been killed. The Government of India was particularly sensitive to Burton's criticisms, for it knew very well how weak the naval position was and had been trying for sometime to increase it, but the Crimean War had been followed by the Indian Mutiny and it had been difficult to find the money.

The main difference of opinion between Burton and his superiors was that he was in favour of extending British influence by such acts as the occupation of Berbera, while the Government was forced to pursue a passive role. When Brigadier Coghlan had eventually been persuaded to Burton's view that Berbera should be occupied, at any rate during the season of the fair, since there was danger that the French or the Turks might take over the port, the official reply was: 'The Governor-General ... deprecates a counter-policy on the part of India which shall hinder its government with the obligation to defend—a nook of Africa at a distance of 1,600 miles from its resources.'[21]

The Story told by Somalis and Others*

APRIL 18. THE DAY OF THE ATTACK ON THE CAMP AT BERBERA

Statement by the Chief of the caravan, Mahmoud Gooled, known as the Balyuz or representative:

About sunset of the day when the affray took place, namely before the fight, we being quite alone in Berbera, three men came to our camp on horseback. One was Dublay of the Ail Ahmed, the second Mahomed of the Sahil branch of the Eesa Moosa; the name of the third I do not know—he was about sixteen years of age. I asked them why they had come; they replied that their Akils were about a day's ride from the coast and had sent them to see if the report which they had heard was true—namely that Sharmakay, with the assistance of the English, was about to build a fort there; that the English did not intend to go to Ogaden but intended remaining on the coast. We replied that they were liars and had come as spies; they denied this and swore the Oath of divorce that this was not the case.

I narrated all this to Lieut. Burton and told him that I did not believe their assertion [story] and recommended that eight or nine additional men should be set to watch that night. Mr. Burton spoke to Sheikh Ahmed, his head servant in Persian and in consequence I do not know the result. I did not repeat my caution.

The Akils of the Habr Awal told us before they departed that we ought not to remain behind nor delay in Berbera; that it would be much better for us to go inland with them, as they said that if we waited for our letters they could not wait for us. They said that they did not fear for us, but they should fear for themselves. Regarding Dublay; I saw him in the afternoon before we were attacked and I swear that I recognized him in the fray. I also saw him riding his horse the morning after the fray . . . The greater portion of the attacking party were Eesa Moosa; this I found out by the shouts in seizing the booty.

Every day before the Fair broke up, the Habr Awal used to ask me if the English really intended to remain in Berbera or go to Ogaden. I replied that the English did not want this country—if they did they would not come as they had done but in two or three large ships.

Statement of Sheikh Ahmed, who was Burton's personal servant and in charge of the stores of the expedition.

On the 18th April Balyuz had told Mr. Burton that the Somalis of the party

* From official reports in the India Office Library and from private papers, previously unpublished.

had had recourse to necromancy and it had been revealed that a body of men would attack the camp; Mr. Burton called them 'liars'. After describing the visit of the three horsemen he said:

Balyuz told Mr. Burton that he thought it would be better to place extra guards on that night. I told Mr. Burton, in Persian, that he had better put four of the guards as sentries and that the rest should remain ready and vigilant. He replied that the Somalis who said that a party would come to attack us were a set of cowards—that no one would come to attack us; that two (guards) were enough and that I might go to sleep. I did so. Before going to sleep Balyuz came and asked me to load a pistol for him. The ammunition which I had was finished, so I asked Mergool, a Cabauli, for some and loaded the pistol. I also got some for my own rifle from the same man, put it below my head and went to sleep.

Said was one of the guard. I did not give him any ammunition—one of the officers always did so. I did not serve out ammunition to anyone. The men had 3, 4, 5, 6, and 7 rounds each; the first day 5 rounds were given to each. I am not sure how much ammunition each had that night; they had been shooting all day . . . I did not hear anyone ask for ammunition that night.

Said, the guard referred to, stated:

I had a gun but the Sirkars did not give me either powder or lead. They gave me five rounds about eight days before. I fired three shots at a mark; one I fired when the three horsemen came and the fifth when the assailants came upon us. The evening before the attack I asked Mr. Burton for some ammunition. He asked where was the ammunition which had been served out to me; I replied that 2 rounds only remained. Mr. Burton told me never to mind as there was no fear.

Jami Hasan, the Abban or Protector of the late Lieut. Stroyan, stated:

At the end of last season all the inhabitants of Berbera left for the interior and the expedition remained encamped by the sea-side. I, in company with several Elders of the tribe, went to the officers, who were sitting in the tent of Lieut. Herne and told them that we (as Abbans) had authority in Berbera for five months but that we ourselves were afraid to remain there alone, and recommended them either to come inland with us, or to embark in a boat, which was in harbour, and return to Aden. This was about eight days before the attack. Mr. Burton replied that he feared no one and bid me go to where my tribe were and to return to him after nine days . . .

I had told Mr. Burton on at least three distinct occasions that he would be attacked as the tribe had left and plunderers were always about at the termination of the fair. Mr. Burton said that if a thousand attacked him he had no fear. He said, 'Solitude will not eat you.'

Jami Hasan said that he left and went into the interior. He set out on his return journey so as to be in Berbera on the ninth day and when half way he met one of the expedition's servants, who described the attack.

Goolab, one of the guard, stated that on April 18 he had gone westwards with the camels to find pasture and saw a horseman 'hovering'. Furban (presumably another of the guard who was with him) fired at the horseman without asking him any question, whereupon he rode away. 'The Somalis who were with me were of the opinion that this man was a spy and preceded a large party who intended to attack us.' Goolab returned to Berbera with the camels and in the evening three horsemen arrived:

> As soon as we saw them we fired over their heads. Mr. Burton forbade our doing so, and the Somalis themselves said that they were not enemies . . . The night before the assault I only had four cartridges remaining out of the ten which were supplied to me about ten days previously.

Goolab stated that one of the men who had arrived in the evening was Dublay of the Ail Ahmed whom he had seen the morning after the attack 'riding a white horse'.

Abd-a-Rahman, one of the guard, described the arrival of the three horsemen: Several of the guards fired over their heads when they arrived. Mr. Burton reprimanded them and ordered them not to waste their powder thus.

APRIL 19/20 THE NIGHT OF THE ATTACK

Mahmud Gooled, al Balyuz, Chief of the Caravan stated:

> On the night of 18th April I was sleeping between the tents occupied by Lieuts. Burton and Herne on the west and Lieut. Stroyan on the east; I was alone and no-one else was between the tents. I was lying on the ground with my arms (two spears and a shield) under me. About midnight I heard the sentries—one of whom was posted on either flank (named Salim, an Arab, on the east and Saad, an African, on the west) call out 'Get up! Get up!' They did not come towards me but remained in the position in which they formerly were. As soon as I heard the shout I immediately jumped on my feet and seized my arms and looked about. I saw a crowd approaching; they were about thirty yards off, and appeared to have come from the south, skirting the west . . . I should say about ninety or a hundred men; they were then all on foot.
> As soon as I saw them coming I called out to the Somalis and rushed towards Mr. Burton's tent. I awoke him and he awoke Lieut. Herne. Immediately I entered the tent I gave a gun, which I found tied to a table, into Mr. Burton's hands. I then went off to look for another gun, but not finding one immediately I ran out to see if the soldiers were awake or no. When I got out I saw the attacking party very little in advance of their former position and moving very slowly as if restrained by fear. I saw some of our soldiers then rising up—some had already risen. I called out sometimes in Arabic, sometimes in Somali and sometimes in Hindoostani 'Fire! Fire!' Three of the soldiers accordingly fired; one was Goolab but I did not see who

the other two were. The party had by this time come upon us. I threw my spear amongst them, but I do not know if it took effect. I saw, however, the mass break, as if it had done so. I could not get anyone else to fire. They then rushed in a body upon us, whereupon all the soldiers fled and ran between Mr. Speke's and Mr. Burton's tents. I followed them and saw Mr. Burton and Mr. Herne coming towards us. Here the soldiers tripped up among the tent ropes and one after another tumbled down, and as they rose up each ran away his own way. There remained only six. Mr. Burton, Mr. Herne, a slave called Said, another called Saad, a Somali called Awadth, and one called Yussuf of the Awal Jedeed; I made the seventh. Mr. Herne had a pistol in his hand, Mr. Burton a sword (he told me next morning that the gun I had given him was not loaded). Mr. Burton and Mr. Herne began fighting and I remained with them. Mr. Herne's first shot took effect on a Somali who fell down. Mr. Burton also struck a man in the neck with his sword and I thrust a second. Mr. Herne then fired again but apparently without effect. These are all the shots and blows which I saw.

The party then cried out 'Kill the Sahibs, they have killed us!' Whereupon about forty rushed upon us. I told Mr. Herne to effect his escape; he pushed a man on each side out of the way with his pistol and cleared a road for himself and escaped. I then told Awadth to assist Mr. Burton to escape. He cleared a way for Mr. Burton with his spear and I pushed him away. Mr. Burton, myself and Awadth then escaped together. This we were enabled to do, as the Somalis fell upon the property lying on the ground and began to plunder it.

I saw Mr. Stroyan only once during the fray—he was standing at the door of his tent; he had something in his hand with which he was beating some of the Somalis round about him, but I did not see properly what he was doing . . .

In my opinion the reason for the attack was, not only desire of plunder, but fear that the party was not going inland, but intended staying at Berbera to assist Sharmakay. The Habr Awal do not, in my opinion, wish anyone to live in Berbera, but if they must have someone, they would much rather have the English than Sharmakay.

Statement by Sheikh Ahmed, Burton's personal servant.

All of a sudden about 12.30 a.m. Salem awoke me by calling out that a party was upon us. I told him several times, rubbing my eyes, to awake the gentlemen. I then saw the Somalis, so I knelt down and fired off my rifle. I then looked round and saw none of our party, so I took up my rifle and deliberately walked through the midst of the Somalis; an old man, a camelier, told me that Balyuz and the gentlemen had gone towards Kurrem, so I also went that way and escaped.

After giving an account of how he had been roused by Balyuz between two and three in the morning of April 19, Burton reported:

My first impulse was to request Lieut. Herne to go out with his revolver in the direction of the danger; secondly I answered Lieuts. Speke and Stroyan, who both asked if any shooting were going on, that they must arm and get ready, and then with no particular hurry (such incidents are but too com-mon in the countries thro' which I have travelled) drew my sabre and pre-pared for work.

Meanwhile Lieut. Herne arrived hurriedly from the back of the Rowtie, pistol in hand and declared our servants had run and that the enemy was in great force. We three—Lieuts. Herne, Speke, and I—defended the entrance to the Rowtie during which I saw both these officers pistol their man with revolvers.

Presently their fire being exhausted and the enemy pressing on, I perceived that our position was untenable; the Rowtie was nearly knocked down by clubs and had we been entangled in its folds, we should have been speared like rats . . .

Statement by Lieut. J. H. Speke, 46th Regiment Bengal, N.I.:

I was awoke about 3 a.m. on the morning of the 10th inst. by hearing Lieut. Burton crying out to Lieut. Stroyan 'Get up old fellow'—almost at the same instant I heard the report of three discharges from fire-arms as if fired in a volley; the sound proceeded from the rear of my tent; conceiving it to be nothing but firing to keep off persons supposed to be prowling about the camp, or in other words a false alarm, I remained in my tent.

Immediately after I heard, as it were, the beating of clubs on my tent (a Sepoys No. 1 Routine) and a shuffling of feet outside. On this I ran across to Lieut. Burton's tent and asked him if there was 'any shooting'—(meaning 'were we attacked?') He replied, 'I rather think that there is.' I then took my revolver and went outside the tent, receiving a smart blow on the knee from a stone but could see nothing.

I put myself in a position to watch whoever might approach and soon saw two heads peeping over our ammunition boxes about seven or eight yards to my left, but I did not fire at them not being certain of my shot . . .

The rest of the account of what happened to him is fully covered by Burton and in Speke's own published account.

Lieut. B. S. Herne, Fusiliers; report to Lieut. Burton April 22, 1855.

The first notice I had of the attack was from you; you awoke me and told me that we were about to be attacked . . .

In conclusion I beg to remark that the attack which occurred was an accident not to be avoided by any of the ordinary methods of prudence. Two sentries had been duly placed, one in front and the other in the rear; and the men had been especially ordered not to fire over the heads of their enemies (in other words to fire at them). Had any of the guard or Somalis stood, we should have resisted the attack, but under such overpowering numbers we had no chance.

Mahomed, Lieut. Stroyan's Indian servant, stated:

I was Lieut. Stroyan's butler. On the night of the attack Lieut. Stroyan was sleeping in front of his tent on a *charpoy* and I was sleeping at the door of the tent. Lieut. Stroyan had no arms of any kind at his bed-side or near him; neither had I. There were two guns and two pistols in the tent; one barrel of one gun was loaded and so were both pistols; the guns were in a corner of the tent; the pistols below a bed on which he used to sleep during the day.

When the attack took place both Lieut. Stroyan and myself awoke at the same time. He came to look for me and I went to look for him; we met each other at the door of the tent. I saw that he had no pistol or any arms, so I went in and got one and put it into his hand. I took the gun, one barrel of which was loaded. As soon as I had done so we were surrounded by Somalis. One Somali called out something about a 'Feringhi' and made as if to spear my master; he bent down and the spear missed him. I then went off towards the cook-room.

The pistol which I gave my master was a revolver. When he was down he fired it three times but I do not think he struck anyone. I never saw my master again. As I was standing by the cook-room the Somalis came up to me and asked me where the money was. I replied that it was in the tent. I then went to look for my master but could not find him. I met a Somali riding on a white horse; he asked me in Somali 'Who goes there?' I replied by the same question. There were many horses some distance from the fight but none entered. I did not touch anyone. I never saw my master again till he was brought a corpse on board the *buggalow*.

Abd-a-Rahman, a guard, stated:

In the morning when the assault took place I did not notice the attacking party until they were actually upon us . . . I fired my gun: I had a single-barrelled gun with me. I had expended all my ammunition in shooting birds by order of Lieut. Burton, and when the fight took place I had none save what was in the gun—namely, powder and shot. I did not ask for more ammunition when I returned as it was late . . . I was slightly wounded in the neck.

Yusuf Deria, servant to Lieut. Herne:

At night when the attack took place my rifle was in the tent, but I had the sword of the rifle with me. When the cry was received that the assailants were upon us, I got up, took my rifle, loaded it and fired once. I was about to load the second time when the Arabs and Somalis of the expedition ran away and I ran with them.

Speke's later comments:

The following comments were made four and a half years after the Berbera disaster by J. H. Speke in letters to Captain Lambert Playfair (later Sir Lambert Playfair). On October 24, 1859, Speke wrote from Somerset:

I think that everybody concerned in the expedition should have been fully heard, as to what they did at the time of the attack before the Government came to any decision of inculpation, whether individually or collectively applied. I am a great loser by reputation as well as by pocket in consequence of the failure and feel very sour about it as you may suppose, indeed I feel I ought not to keep silent . . . I think it very hard on us that the Somalis were not allowed to refund anything for our losses when they (according to Captain [name unreadable]) offered to do so;* but that the Government, taking advantage of the disruption, turned everything to their own advantage: by making the robbery of our kit by the Somal a penalty on them to stop their slave trade, and so the Government enhanced their own requirements to the detriment of us, the prime losers. Nothing would have appeared more just to the Somal, or would have had better effect on them in keeping down their rebellious spirits for the future than treating them in accordance with their own laws, of taking like for like—blood or money—and they owed us both and should have paid us both . . . I do not believe that if all things were properly investigated and understood that the Government would allow its servants to be losers in this way. When I have done my next journey and I have time to set about it, I shall move for an appeal to Government for an investigation into the matter in a more general way.

Nothing, however, was investigated; no Somalis were tried and no compensations were paid. In a previous letter of September 3, 1859, Speke had written to Playfair objecting to his statement in his book, *A History of Arabia Felix*, that all the members of the Somali expedition were taken by surprise:

I cannot answer for Burton, all I saw about him in that respect was that from the outset until I last saw him, he was engaged in loading his pistol *within* his tent. I never for one moment saw him out of it, but, that Herne was ready, is proved by his having advanced, at Burton's order I believe, to check the advance of the plunderers. I was ready, having placed my pistol and sword handily by me in case of an emergency. Stroyan, I imagine, was killed whilst lying in his bed.

To this letter Playfair sent a long reply in which he quoted various official documents including Burton's report to Government after the attack at Berbera. Speke referred to Burton's statement: 'briefly these spies not only deceived us but deceived even their own countrymen, accordingly the two usual sentries were posted for the night and the usual orders were issued', and commented:

Burton, as I have said before, was the only person who spoke with the intruders and from him we heard that the men were visiting us on the plea which he has stated in his letter. I then told Herne that I did not like the cool manner in which the men walked in under fire, but he decided that nothing could be done more than we usually did in keeping guard and *I* placed the sentries and arranged the sleeping place for the guard, every man to have his gun beside him. I think in my former letter that I said I had placed four sentries on that occasion; this may be an error for if the usual number was only two, then I placed only two, because I felt it would only have distressed the guard and have made them discontented without producing any benefit had I

* Burton in his Preface stated that the Somalis had offered an indemnity of fifteen thousand dollars.

put more on. Of this I told Burton, Herne, and Stroyan, and all agreed. I still maintain that the guard could not have been better disposed of than it was that night and so far I did my duty. If there was any error at all, except Burton's own confessed unpreparedness,* it was that no officer was on watch. This we did considerately and with the full belief that we had better reserve ourselves for the interior, for we knew that we should have enough wear and tear when we left the coast in keeping watch, for these Somalis might, were we not really careful, have had it in their power to polish us off with impunity. We never believed that the Somalis would be such fools as to touch us on the coast, knowing as they must have done, how easily the Government could have punished them did it feel inclined. . . . If *all* the guard had been on sentry that night and, if we had *all* been awake, I am certain that we could not have resisted the attack effectually.

Speke, therefore, did not consider fair an official statement 'that had ordinary prudence governed arrangements the tragedy would not have occurred'.

I cannot comprehend [continued Speke in his letter to Playfair] how you could have discovered that not one of the Somalis were killed and that only two were wounded. Herne says that he saw two fall back from his fire. One of our Seedi guardsman, it was generally understood, gave an awful slice to a Somali hitting him on the shoulder and I fired at close quarters into three men, but the night was very dark so I cannot say positively with what effect. Burton *said* he cut one man with his sword and one of our Seedis *was* wounded by a sword. Then I certainly saw from four to six men stretched on the ground with bloody garments on them and not more than thirty yards or so from me.

Speke then criticized, as had the Government of Bombay, the excessive attention paid by Coghlan and Playfair to the Somali statements quoting Burton's replies to their alleged warnings about the danger of remaining in Berbera:

Burton's defying danger and bragging, as well as all the Somalis intimidating speeches (although so much remarked upon), I regard as only so much clap-trap and not deserving of any notice. If a man is to be frightened by men who live by lying and tricking everybody they can, travelling amongst them should cease. The matter rests on this: either we were equal to penetrating the country or we were not, for we could not always have been dependent on any support-ing caravans. Again if we were not to hazard anything, we could not expect to gain anything and, therefore, if the Government were not prepared to risk on this occasion as they would have done in any case of war, they should not have promoted the project at all . . .†

* Speke is probably referring to the following slightly arrogant passage in Burton's official report: 'My first impulse was to request Lieut. Herne to go out with his revolver in the direction of the danger; secondly I answered Lieuts. Speke and Stroyan, who both asked if any shooting were going on that they "must arm and get ready", and then with no particular hurry (such incidents are but too common in the countries thro' which I have travelled) drew my sabre and prepared for work.'

† Unpublished letters obtained through the kindness of Sir Edward Playfair, grandson of Sir Lambert Playfair, and of Mr. Alexander Maitland, who is writing on Speke.

Excision and Infibulation

IN HIS FIRST EDITION OF *First Footsteps in East Africa* Burton had intended to publish an appendix (4) entitled 'A brief description of certain peculiar customs noticed in Nubia by Browne and Werne under the name of fibulation', but publication was stopped and it disappeared. Recently, however, a first edition was discovered which had two pages of Burton's 'censored' appendix included by mistake. This, possibly unique, copy belongs to Mrs. Fawn Brodie of California, who is writing a biography of Richard Burton and has very generously allowed these two pages to be published for the first time in this edition; they arrived when the book was already in page-proof, but were too interesting a discovery to leave out. Burton wrote in Latin, except for the title, presumably to try to avoid 'censorship'. Following is the translation:

A BRIEF DESCRIPTION OF CERTAIN PECULIAR CUSTOMS

There is a most remarkable method regularly practised by the Somalis, as it is also among the Abyssinians, Nubians and Galla, of preserving the chastity of their women. They sew up the lips of the girl's private parts either with a leather lace or, more often, with one of horse-hair. A female slave, whom the Arabs call *Khadimah* and the Somali *Midgan*, cuts out the girl's clitoris and nymphae with a large knife; when the excision has been made she takes a needle and sews up the lips with a continuous series of large stitches. A small passage for passing water is left in the lower part, and the pudendum thus loses its natural shape and becomes circular. They heal the girl's wound by fumigating it with myrrh, bandaging her thighs and placing her over a fire which gives off the fumes; the cure takes ten or eleven days. All the upper classes among the Somalis use the sewing-up method. In the towns quite young girls are so treated; in the country districts it is not done until they are fifteen.

This barbarous guarantee of virginity and chastity is preserved until marriage. If a man wishes to fornicate with a girl, and she is shameless enough to permit it, he unpicks the stitches; a husband, on the other hand, will take great pains to increase and amplify his physical strength by a meat diet, and at night when he goes to bed with his newly-wed bride will strain to break through the blockage with his sword of love. Generally he is unsuccessful; then he will attack this artificial hymenal membrane with his finger. If he cannot overcome its defences by this method, he opens the pudendum from the lower end with a knife and immediately thrusts his penis up through the bloody opening. The pain is so intense as to cause the woman to shriek; to counteract this, male and female musicians drown the cries of the bride by singing; older girls, however, restrain their cries for shame. Some in their lust for pleasure summon a slave girl who enlarges the wife's pudendum to suit the size of the husband's penis. For about a week husband and wife stay in the same hut and devote themselves night and day to the act of love. Those who suspect their wife's fidelity, when they go on a journey will sew up again the aperture of the pudendum; but a woman who is so minded will break the suture with the greatest ease and sew it up again when her desires are satisfied. They say that in a single year twelve bastards were born in Zayla.

There are no harlots in Somaliland; but there are plenty of wives who, because of the inactivity of their husbands, prostitute their bodies without scruple. The man makes his intentions clear by nods, smiles and shameless finger gestures. If the woman smiles Venus rejoices. Then the fornicator indicates with his fingers the sum he is prepared to pay; the woman replies by a gesture, and both happily look forward to a suitable occasion. The adulterer always makes for the woman's house; to chat at the cross-roads is awkward in daylight, and dangerous at night.

The Somalis have only one method of making love. Both parties lie on their sides, never, as is our custom, the man on the woman. The woman lies on her left side, the man on his right . . .

There it ends in the middle of a sentence and it is not known how much more Burton wrote.

A paper was read on this same subject before the Anthropological Society of Bombay on January 23, 1889, by Major J. S. King who wrote: 'Burton's description being, unfortunately, lost to the world, I shall endeavour in a few words to supply the omission.' He gave very similar information, but there was the following account of pre-marital relations:

It might be thought that infibulation would effectually compel a girl to chastity; but such is not invariably the case. When the preliminaries of a match are being arranged, the proposer is given an opportunity of testing the virginity of the object of his choice by ocular demonstration. The ceremony —as described to me by Somalis who had gone through it themselves is as follows:

The man, having his face concealed by a corner of his tobe drawn over it, is seated in a hut, when the maiden enters, and saying in a playful way—'Am I disagreeable to the sight or smell, that you cover up your face?'—removes the end of his tobe. He then bids her strip, and proceeds to critically examine the whole of her nude form.

After the amount of the marriage portion has been fixed, and at least a portion of it paid to the father or nearest male relative, the man is allowed private interviews with his fiancée, but has to pay (generally 12 dollars) for each. At these interviews modesty as well as raiment is discarded, and the loving couple indulge in much amorous dalliance; but the girl takes care that her *velum virginale* shall not be ruptured. Although without that, actual penetration is a physical impossibility, still, a want of due caution sometimes leads to her impregnation, which places her in an awkward position if the marriage does not come off... One instance in which what I have described above actually took place, came prominently to my notice and I can vouch for the facts.

Somalis themselves admit that infibulation is a relic of paganism, but they are so thoroughly conservative, in the worse sense of the word, that they dare not relinquish the custom.

(*The Journal of the Anthropological Society of Bombay*, vol. II, No. I, 1890.)

W. G. Browne, the author referred to by Burton, states that excision is practised by the Christians of Abyssinia and by the Mohammedans of Egypt. (Chapter XX, *Travels in Africa, Egypt and Syria from the year 1792 to 1798*, London, 1806, 2nd edition.)

James Bruce adds a list of a number of races who practise it besides the Abyssinians and the Egyptians. He wrote that the Roman Catholic priests in Egypt at first forbade the excision of Coptic girls who had become Roman Catholics, but found that they were losing converts as a result and therefore allowed the practice to be resumed. 'The man found,' wrote James Bruce, 'that by chusing a wife among Catholic Copts, he subjected himself to a very disagreeable inconvenience, to which he had conceived an unconquerable aversion, and therefore he married a heretical wife, free from this objection, and with her he relapsed into heresy.' (*The Source of the Nile, 1768 to 1773*, Chapter XII, Kinnaird, London, 1790.)

The second book referred to by Burton in the title was by Ferdinand Werne, who accompanied expeditions up the White Nile sent by Mohamed Ali, Pasha of Egypt, between 1839 and 1842. Werne published *Reise durch Senaar nach Mandera, Noesub, Cheli, im Lande zwischen dem blauen Nile and dem Atbara;* female excision and infibulation are described on pp. 25–7.

Dr. I. M. Lewis in his *A Pastoral Democracy*, 1961, states: 'An exceedingly high value is placed on virginity in women at marriage, which the Somali practice of infibulation is designed to ensure'; see his *Marriage and the Family in Northern Somaliland*, East African Studies, No. 18, Kampala and London, Kegan Paul and Trench, 1962. In a letter to the Editor of April 27, 1965, Dr. Lewis states: 'There is considerable pressure amongst young educated Somalis to end infibulation. Excision would, I think, probably continue even if infibulation were stopped.'

The Harari Language

[RICHARD BURTON'S APPENDIX II, 'Grammatical Outline and Vocabulary of the Harari Language', consists of seventy-one pages and is of interest only to the specialist, but his 'Preliminary Remarks' are of general interest and show his intense eagerness to study, even under the most adverse circumstances.]

'The caution necessary for the stranger who would avoid exciting the suspicions of an African despot and Moslem bigots prevented my making any progress, during my short residence at the capital, in the Harari language. But once more safe among the Girhi mountains, circumspection was no longer necessary. The literati who assisted in my studies were a banished citizen of Harar: Said Wal, an old Bedouin; and Ali Shar, "the Poet", a Girhi Somali celebrated for his wit, his poetry, and his eloquence. I found the last most useful, and his linguistic sagacity enabled me to perform a feat of no ordinary difficulty, that of drawing out a grammatical sketch of the language. But time pressed, and few days remained for work. Our hours were spent in unremitting toil: we began at sunrise, the hut was ever crowded with Bedouin critics, and it was late at night before the manuscript was laid by. On the evening of the third day my literati started upon their feet, and shook my hand, declaring that I knew as much as they themselves did.

'Returning to Aden I was fortunate to find there a friend, Lieutenant Dansey, 1st. Bombay European Regiment, who, seeing me embarrassed by preparations for an expedition, kindly volunteered to write out, and, with the assistance of one Farih Dibani, a Somali of the Habr Jul Jailah clan, to revise my notes . . .

'Afterwards at Berbera I met the Harar caravan; and here my difficulty of procuring an instructor was truly characteristic. The timid merchants feared to lose their heads, and I should have failed but for the presence of a Sayyid, Aydrus bin Mohammed el Barr el Madani, who, with the real Sherif spirit, aided me, in the hope that one day I might revenge his wrongs upon the Amir of Harar.

'The people of Harar ignore the origin of their language. It probably dates from our mediæval times, when the Hadiyah Empire flourished upon the ruins of the Christian states. In the present day it is absolutely confined within the walls of the city, which is surrounded on all sides by Gallas. Through the medium of Harari the Arabic language and the religious sciences are explained to the inhabitants: almost all the women and not a few of the citizens can speak no other tongue. The numerous Somal who visit and temporarily settle at Harar usually learn some sentences. But few penetrate deep into the language: at this moment, in Aden, amongst about 2,000, one only is found capable of revising the vocabulary.

'2. The Harari appears, like the Galla, the Dankali, and the Somali, its sisters, to be a Semitic graft into an indigenous stock. The pronouns, for instance, and many of the numerals are clearly Arabic, whilst the form of the verbs are African, and not unlike the vulgar tongues of modern India. Again, many of the popular expressions, without which conversation could not be carried on (e.g. *Labbay*, "here I am," in answer to a call), are pure Arabic. We are justified then in determining this dialect to be, like the Galla, the Dankali, and the Somali, a semi-Semite.*

'3. The Harari is not a written language, and the Arabic character imperfectly expresses its sound. It excites our wonder to see tongues so elaborate, with rules of eloquence and a poetry cultivated after the canons of rhythm and rhyme, destitute of an alphabet. In Sindh and India, on the contrary, every local variety of dialect has its own syllabarium modified from the Arabic or the Sanscrit. To account for the phenomenon, we must take refuge in some psychical cause hitherto unexplained. The Harari, when writing their songs and translations, use the Koranic character.

'4. The pronunciation of the Harari dialect, unlike the soft Galla and Somali, is harsh and guttural; a fact which causes astonishment, as it is spoken in a warm climate and within walls, where men generally soften sound.'

The following note was given to the Editor by Edward Ullendorff, Professor of Ethiopian Studies at the University of London:

'Burton had some predecessors in the study of Harari, such as Salt (1814) and Beke (1845), but his essay was the most substantial. It was a considerable achievement at his time in the conditions then prevailing. Within the history of the study of Harari Burton's name has an honoured place, but since his time there have been detailed and exhaustive studies, such as the monumental work on the Amharic language by F. Praetorius (Halle, 1879), and by others including E. Cerulli's *La Lingua e la storia di Harar*, Rome 1936.']

* Lieutenant (now Captain) Rigby, 16th Regiment Bom., N.I., in an excellent paper published by the Bombay Asiatic Society, under the modest title of an 'Outline of the Somauli Language, with Vocabulary', asserts that the dialect of which he is writing 'has not the slightest similarity to Arabic in construction'. Burton then proceeds to argue the opposite.

Notes

A great many of the references are to documents in the Library of the former India Office in London and consist of reports sent by East India Company officials between the Political Resident in Aden, the Governor in Council in Bombay, the Governor-General of India, and the Honourable East India Company in London. The hierarchy was as follows:

The Honourable East India Company in London
|
India Board, Secret Board, and other Boards in London
|
Government of India under the Governor-General
|
Bombay Presidency under a Governor-in-Council
|

| Indian Navy | Aden, Political Resident and Commandant. | Persian Gulf, Political Agent | Baghdad, Political Agent |

The East India Trading Company appointed its own agents and diplomatic representatives and had gradually built up a government of its own following the defeat of its French rivals in India during the Seven Years War of 1756 to 1763. It was not until 1858, after the Indian Mutiny, that the British Government's India Office took over control. 'The main change in procedure which occurred after the abolition of the East India Company and the establishment of the India Office was the sending of duplicate copies of all reports direct to London, thus cutting down on the interminable delay in the Aden Bombay London system of communication and on the power often exercised by the Bombay Government in Company days, of suppressing documents until the bound volumes of the Consultations [reports of proceedings] arrived in London, probably a year after the documents had been acted on in Bombay. . . . After 1821 the Foreign Office inherited the appointment of diplomatic and consular officials in the Levant Company's trading area . . . [Egypt, Hedjaz, Lebanon, Syria, Asia Minor, and the Ottoman Empire in Europe]. Thus the division of interest in the nineteenth century between the Foreign Office and the East India Company and its successor, the India Office, was dictated by this early trading agreement' (Introduction to *Britain's Imperial Role in the Red Sea Area, 1800–1878*, by Thomas E. Marston, The Shoe String Press Inc. Connecticut, 1961).

The currencies used in the early nineteenth century in the Red Sea area and in North-East Africa were the crown, the Maria Theresa thaler and the ryal each worth about five shillings; they were often referred to as dollars; there was also the Indian rupee, worth about two shillings.

The Life of Captain Sir Richard F. Burton, K.C.M.G., F.R.G.S., by his wife, Isabel Burton, in two volumes, Chapman and Hall Ltd, 1893, will be referred to as *The Life*.

All the letters from Richard Burton to Dr. Norton Shaw, Secretary of the Royal Geographical Society, referred to in the text, are MS. letters with the Burton papers at the Royal Geographical Society, London, and will not have reference notes.

INTRODUCTION

1 *Journal of the Royal Geographical Society*, vol. 25, 1855, pp. 136–50; Richard Burton's report of his journey to Harar and of the attack on the camp at Berbera. The report is

also published in *Selected Papers on Anthropology, Travel and Exploration*, by Sir Richard Burton, K.C.M.G., edited by N. M. Penzer, A. M. Philpot Ltd., 1924.

[2] Sidgwick and Jackson Ltd, 1961.

[3] *Monckton Milnes, The Flight of Youth*, by James Pope-Hennessy, pp. 123–4, Constable, 1951.

[4] *The Life*, vol. 1, p. 402, and see p. viii of Introduction by Fawn M. Brodie to new edition of *The City of the Saints*, by Richard Burton, Eyre and Spottiswoode, 1964.

[5] *The Life*, vol. I, pp. 166–7.

[6] The explorer V. Lovett Cameron on Burton quoted by N. M. Penzer in *An Annotated Bibliography of Sir Richard Francis Burton*, London, 1923.

[7] *The True Life of Sir Richard F. Burton*, written by his niece Georgiana M. Stisted, H. S. Nichols, 1896. Burton's sister married General Sir William Stisted.

[8] *The Life*, vol. 1., p. 32.

[9] *The Autobiography of Sir Henry Morton Stanley*, G.C.B., p. 424, London, 1909.

[10] *The Life*, vol. 1., pp. 1 and 2.

[11] Ibid. pp. 51 and 52.

[12] *The Life*, vol. 1, p. 103. Subsequent autobiographical quotes with regard to life in India are from Chapters 5, 6 and 7; Burton sometimes refers to himself in the third person.

[13] *Athenaeum*, July 24, 1852, pp. 802, 803. On July 17 the *Athenaeum* had published a critical review of *Falconry in the Valley of the Indus* to which he replied.

[14] *Goa and the Blue Mountains; or Six Months of Sick Leave*, and *Scinde or the Unhappy Valley*, Richard Bentley, 1851; *Sindh and the Races that Inhabit the Valley of the Indus*, William H. Allen, London, 1851; *Falconry in the Valley of the Indus*, J. van Voorst, London, 1852; *A Complete System of Bayonet Exercise*, William Clowes & Sons, London, 1853. There was no training for using the bayonet in close combat and the book earned Burton an official reprimand at the time, but later became a textbook during the Crimean War and was purchased by a number of foreign governments.

[15] *Personal Narrative of a Pilgrimage to el-Medinah and Meccah* by Richard F. Burton Lieutenant, Bombay Army, Ch. I, vol. I, London, 1855.

[16] *The Life*, vol. 1., pp. 172, 3, vol. I.

[17] All letters quoted from Burton to Shaw are MS.letters with the Burton papers at the Royal Geographical Society.

[18] Among the books published were *Ananga Ranga*, 1873, *The Kama Sutra of Vatsyayana*, 1883, *The Perfumed Garden of Shaikh Nefzaoui*, 1886, *The Beharistan*, 1887, and *The Gulistan*, 1888; some of these have recently been republished.

[19] Burton's view of the two men is endorsed by Charles Rathbone Low in his *History of the Indian Navy* (1613–1863), vol. 2, pp. 64–7, 206, etc., London, 1877.

[20] Bombay Letter of May 10, No. 34 of 1854 in 'Bombay Political Letters Received'. Burton's letter to the Government of Bombay was dated May 6.

[21] 'Notes on Aden', by Brigadier W. M. Coghlan, Aden, September 12, 1855; 'Bombay Secret Consultations', October to December 1855, vol. 4. There are also some interesting accounts of the slave trade, enclosure No. 444.

[22] *Allen's Indian Mail* of August 6, 1860, stated: 'A mere debtor—if, indeed, he were that—has been for nearly six years confined in jail in a deadly climate, at the suit of the Government he served with pre-eminent zeal and ability'. The article is quoted in *History of the Indian Navy*, by C. R. Low, vol. 2, p. 527.

[23] Captain J. D. Milne was killed at Wahut in March 1851 by Sayed Mohamed Husain; Baghi was not responsible for this murder but for that of a British sailor on May 25, 1850. The facts are given by Brigadier Coghlan in his 'Notes on Aden' referred to above, and in *Britain's Imperial Role in the Red Sea, 1800–1878*, by Thomas E. Marston, p. 154, The Shoe String Press Inc., Connecticut, 1961.

[24] 'Letters to Bombay', 1854, vol. 16, August 23, 1854, Political Department to Governor-in-Council at Bombay, No. 24.

25 *The Life*, by Isabel Burton, vol. I, pp. 118, 119.

26 *What Led to the Discovery of the Source of the Nile*, by J. H. Speke, pp. 6 and 7, William Blackwood & Sons, 1864.

27 *Journal of the Royal Geographical Society*, p. xcv, vol. 24, 1854.

28 *The Lake Regions of Central Africa*, London, 1860, vol. I, pp. 67–8.

29 A British expedition to the province of Shoa in Abyssinia had left Aden on May 15, 1841, under the command of Captain W. C. Harris; only about half the stores had reached Shoa and there had been several deaths. The Court of Directors of the East India Company in their letter from London of August 23, 1854, agreeing to Burton's Somali Expedition stated: 'The error committed in the case of the Shoa expedition . . . of creating suspicion and distrust, by the display of magnificence and extravagant expenditure will be avoided by the manner in which this exploration is to be performed.'

Lieut. William Barker was a member of the Shoa Mission and was instructed by Captain Harris to return to the Somali coast via Harar, but he did not succeed in reaching it. Burton published a summary of Lieut. Barker's account of the journey as Appendix V to *First Footsteps in East Africa* because it showed, 'what obstacles the suspicious characters and the vain terrors of the Bedouin have thrown in the way of energy and enterprise'. *The Journal of the Royal Geographical Society*, vol. 12, 1842, p. 238, contained 'Extract Report on the probable Geographical Position of Harrar', by Lieut. W. C. Barker, I. N. His estimate of its position was not accurate, as was shown by Burton, who gave a correct map-reading.

30 *What Led to the Discovery of the Source of the Nile*, p. 23; the quote which follows is p. 4.

31 Letter from Speke to Rigby, British Consul in Zanzibar, October 6, 1860, quoted in *Burton* by Byron Farwell, p. 178, Longmans, 1963.

32 *The Life*, vol. I, p. 315.

33 C. E. X. Rochet d'Hericourt, page 263, *Second Voyage sur les deux rives de la Mer Rouge dans le pays des Adels et le Royaume de Choa*, Paris, 1846. The author visited Abyssinia in 1839 and 1840; in 1842–3 he signed a political and commercial treaty on behalf of France with the King of Shoa.

34 With the Burton correspondence at the Dulwich Library, Camberwell, London.

35 Burton's official report of February 22, 1855; Enclosures to Secret Letters from Bombay, January to April 1855.

36 *First Footsteps*, Appendix I, pp. 503–4.

37 *A Pastoral Democracy*, by I. M. Lewis, p. 2., O.U.P., 1961.

38 Ali Sharmakay, the Somali, seized Zayla in the summer of 1843 and imprisoned the garrison of the Turkish Pasha of Mocha; he came to Aden with an offer to place Zayla under British protection, to suppress slavery, and open the caravan road to Harar. The offer was refused by the Government, which replied to Captain Haines, the Political Resident in Aden: 'The British Government only retains Aden for the purpose of protecting our depot of coal, not for that of promoting intervention in the affairs of the neighbouring Chiefs of Africa and Arabia and of generally extending its possessions in that quarter . . . The Governor-General in Council deeply regrets the enormous cost at which a mere depot of coals is now protected' (*Britain's Imperial Role in the Red Sea Area, 1800–1878*, Thomas E. Marston, p. 108, The Shoe String Press Inc., Connecticut, 1961).

39 Fifth Burton Memorial Lecture, Royal Asiatic Society, May 27, 1937.

40 'Bombay Secret Consultations', April 7 to June 27, 1855, vol. 2; minute by the Rt. Hon. the Governor, dated May 12, 1855.

41 E. L. James and his brothers left Aden on December 8, 1884, for the Webbe Shebelli river, which was described in 'A Journey through the Somali country to the Webbe Shebeyli', by E. L. James Esq., *Proceedings of the Royal Geographical Society*, vol. 7, 1885. In this report James stated: 'Captain Burton was the first explorer, but his explorations were far to the west of our intended route. We found his book *First Footsteps in Eastern*

Africa, however, a useful guide and a capital account of one of the most successful and plucky journeys ever accomplished in Africa.'
The expedition to the Nogal Valley was accomplished in January 1891 by Lieut. E. J. E. Swayne and his brother Capt. Swayne. Since Speke's journey no further efforts had been made to reach the district.

42 *Burton* by Byron Farwell, Longmans, 1963, p. 174

43 Ibid., p. 177. The exchange of letters between Captain (later General) C. P. Rigby and John Speke about Burton make unattractive reading. 'It is difficult to escape the conclusion,' writes Mr. Farwell (p. 178), 'that the discoverer of the major source of the Nile and the largest lake in Africa was a cad.' In *The Life*, vol. 2, pp. 567–77, 'Letters bearing on Speke and Rigby Cabal'.

44 *Journal of the Discovery of the Source of the Nile*, by John Hanning Speke, chapter I, William Blackwood & Sons, 1863.

45 *The Life*, vol. 1, p. 328.

46 Ibid., vol. 1, p. 327.

47 Ibid., vol. 2, p. 426.

48 *Dramatis Personae* by Arthur Symons, 'A neglected Genius: Sir Richard Burton', pp. 250–1, Faber and Faber, 1925.

49 *Journal of the Royal Asiatic Society*, July 1923; quoted p. 10, Introduction to *Selected Papers on Anthropology, Travel and Exploration*, by Sir Richard Burton, edited by N. M. Penzer, London, 1924.

I. DEPARTURE FROM ADEN

1 With the departure of Colonel James Outram, Lieut.-Col. W. M. Coghlan had become Acting Political Resident in Aden and reported to Bombay on November 6, 1854: 'Lieutenant Burton, Commanding the Somali Expedition, left Aden en route to Hurrur [Harar] on the 29th ultimo. Lieutenant Speke left for Las Ghorain on the 18th ultimo purposing to proceed among the Wara Sungali Hills and thence to Berbera. Lieutenant Herne purposes proceeding direct to Berbera about the 15th inst. there to await the arrival of his companions ('Letters from Aden,' 1854, vol. 33).—Ed.

2 Adel, according to M. Krapf, derived its name from the Ad Ali, a tribe of the Afar or Danakil nation, erroneously used by Arab synecdoche for the whole race. Mr. Johnston (*Travels in Southern Abyssinia*, ch. 1) more correctly derives it from Adule, a city which, as proved by the monument which bears its name, existed in the days of Ptolemy Euergetes (247–222 B.C.), had its own dynasty, and boasted of a conqueror who overcame the Troglodytes, Sabaeans, Homerites, etc., and pushed his conquests as far as the frontier of Egypt. Mr. Johnston, however, incorrectly translates Barr al-'Ajam 'land of fire', and seems to confound Avalites and Adulis.

3 The following genealogical table was given to me by Mohammed Sharmakay:

1. Ishak (ibn Ahmaid ibn Abdillah).
2. Girhajis (his eldest son).
3. Sa'id (the eldest son: Da'ud being the second).
4. Arrah (also the eldest; Ili, i.e. Ali, being the second).
5. Musa (the third son: the eldest was Ismail; then, in succession, Ishak, Misa, Mikahil Gambah, Dandan. etc.).

6. Ibrahim.	12. Ali.
7. Fikih (i.e. Fakih).	13. Awaz.
8. Adan (i.e. Adam).	14. Salih.
9. Mohammed.	15. Ali.
10. Hamid.	16. Sharmarkay
11. Jibril (i.e. Jibrail).	

The last is a peculiarly Somali name, meaning 'one who sees no harm'—Shar-ma-akay. [In the official reports the spelling became Sharmakay and this has been followed in the text.—Ed.]

4 [In 1840 Sharmakay had acted as interpreter to Captain Robert Moresby of the Indian Navy when he visited the Sultan of Tajjura to conclude a treaty by which two small islands were ceded to Britain. Three years later Sharmakay seized Zayla and the Turkish Government decided that it was simpler to appoint this determined Somali as Governor of Zayla.]

Burton stated in his official report, after the journey to Harar, that Sharmakay in 1848 paid as rent to the Turkish Government 500 dollars, which had risen to 1,000 dollars when Burton was in Zayla 'not including what may politely be called presents'. He added that the friendship of Hajj Sharmakay Ali Sahib and his son with so great a power as England had produced notable results. 'Whilst all the county about Berbera is in anarchy and confusion, around Zayla the Bedouins have learned to fear and to obey Sharmakay,' (Burton's report of February 22, 1855; enclosures to Secret Letters from Bombay, January to April 1855).

In July 1855 the Hajj Sharmakay was deposed by the Turkish Pasha of Hodaydah, ostensibly for failing to keep some road open, or, according to others, for assisting to plunder a caravan belonging to the Dankali tribe. It was reported that he had been made a prisoner, and the Political Resident at Aden saw the propriety of politely asking the Turkish authorities to 'be easy' upon the old man. In consequence of this representation, he was afterwards allowed, on paying a fine of 3,000 dollars, to retire to Aden.

I deeply regret that the Hajj should have lost his government. He has ever clung to the English party, even in sore temptation. A few year ago, the late M. Rochet (soi-disant d'Héricourt), French agent at Jeddah, paying treble its value, bought from Mohammed Sharmakay, in the absence of the Hajj, a large stone house, in order to secure a footing at Zayla. The old man broke off the bargain on his return, knowing how easily an Agency becomes a Fort, and preferring a considerable loss to the presence of dangerous friends.

5 Zayla, called Audal or Auzal by the Somal, is a town about the size of Suez, built for 3,000 or 4,000 inhabitants, and containing a dozen large whitewashed stone houses, and upwards of 200 Arish or thatched huts, each surrounded by a fence of wattle and matting. The situation is a low and level spit of sand, which high tides make almost an island. There is no harbour: a vessel of 250 tons cannot approach within a mile of the landing-place; the open roadstead is exposed to the terrible north wind, and when gales blow from the west and south, it is almost unapproachable. Every ebb leaves a sandy flat, extending half a mile seaward from the town; the reefy anchorage is difficult of entrance after sunset, and the coralline bottom renders wading painful.

The shape of this once celebrated town is a tolerably regular parallelogram, of which the long sides run from east to west. The walls, without guns or embrasures, are built, like the houses, of coralline rubble and mud, in places dilapidated. There are five gates. The Bab al-Sahil and the Bab al-Jadd (a new postern) open upon the sea from the northern wall. At the Ashurbara, in the southern part of the enceinte, the Bedouin encamp, and above it the governor holds his Durbar. The Bab Abd al-Kadir derives its name from a saint buried outside and eastward of the city, and the Bab al-Saghir is pierced in the western wall.

The public edifices are six mosques, including the Jami, or cathedral, for Friday prayer: these buildings have queer little crenelles on whitewashed walls, and a kind of elevated summer-house to represent the minaret. Near one of them are remains of a circular Turkish Munar, manifestly of modern construction. There is no Mahkamah or Kazi's court: that dignitary transacts business at his own house, and the Festival prayers are recited near the Saint's Tomb outside the eastern gate. The north-east angle of the town is occupied by a large graveyard with the usual deleterious consequences.

The climate of Zayla is cooler than that of Aden, and the site being open all around, it is not so unhealthy. Much spare room is enclosed by the town walls: evaporation and Nature's scavengers act succedanea for sewerage.

Zayla commands the adjacent harbour of Tajjurrah, and is by position the northern port of Aussa (the ancient capital of Adel), of Harar, and of southern Abyssinia: the feuds of the rulers have, however, transferred the main trade to Berbera. It sends caravans north-wards to Dankali, and south-westwards, through the Eesa and Gudabirsi tribes as far as Efat and Gurague. It is visited by Cafilas [caravans] from Abyssinia, and by the different races of Bedouin, extending from the hills to the seaboard. The exports are valuable—slaves, ivory, hides, honey, antelope horns, clarified butter, and gums: the coast abounds in sponge, coral, and small pearls, which Arab divers collect in the fair season. In the harbour I found about twenty native craft, large and small: of these, ten belonged to the governor. They trade with Berbera, Arabia, and Western India, and are navigated by 'Rajput' or Hindu pilots.

Provisions at Zayla are cheap; a family of six persons live well for about 30*l.* per annum. The general food is mutton: a large sheep costs one dollar, a small one half the price; camels' meat, beef, and in winter kid, abound. Fish is rare, and fowls are not commonly eaten. Holcus, when dear, sells at forty pounds per dollar, at seventy pounds when cheap. It is usually levigated with slab and roller, and made into sour cakes. Some, however, prefer the Arab form 'balilah', boiled and mixed with ghí. Wheat and rice are imported: the price varies from forty to sixty pounds the Riyal or dollar. Of the former grain the people make a sweet cake called Sabaya, resembling the Fatirah of Egypt: a favourite dish also is 'harisah'—flesh, rice flour, and boiled wheat, all finely pounded and mixed together. Milk is not procurable during the hot weather; after rain every house is full of it; the Bedouin bring it in skins and sell it for a nominal sum.

Besides a large floating population, Zayla contains about 1,500 souls. They are com-paratively a fine race of people, and suffer from little but fever and an occasional ophthal-mia. Their greatest hardship is the want of the pure element; the Hissi or well, is about four miles distant from the town, and all the pits within the walls supply brackish or bitter water, fit only for external use. This is probably the reason why vegetables are unknown, and why a horse, a mule, or even a dog, is not to be found in the place.

II. LIFE IN ZAYLA

1 The Tobe, or Abyssinian 'Quarry', is the general garment of Africa from Zayla to Bornou. In the Somali country it is a cotton sheet eight cubits long, and two breadths sewn together. An article of various uses, like the Highland plaid, it is worn in many ways; sometimes the right arm is bared; in cold weather the whole person is muffled up, and in summer it is allowed to fall below the waist. Generally it is passed behind the back, rests upon the left shoulder, is carried forward over the breast, surrounds the body, and ends hanging on the left shoulder, where it displays a gaudy silk fringe of red and yellow. This is the man's Tobe. The woman's dress is of similar material, but differently worn: the edges are knotted generally over the right, sometimes over the left shoulder; it is girdled round the waist, below which hangs a lappet, which in cold weather can be brought like a hood over the head. Though highly becoming, and picturesque as the Roman toga, the Somali Tobe is by no means the most decorous of dresses: women in the towns often prefer the Arab costume—a short-sleeved robe extending to the knee, and a Futah or loin-cloth underneath.

2 The system of caste, which prevails in al Yemen, though not in the northern parts of Arabia, is general throughout the Somali country. The principal families of outcasts are the following:

The Yabir correspond with the Dushan of Southern Arabia: the males are usually jesters to the chiefs, and both sexes take certain parts at festivals, marriages, and cir-cumcisions. The number is said to be small, amounting to about 100 families in the northern Somali country.

The Tomal or Handad, the blacksmiths, originally of Aydur race, have become vile by intermarriage with serviles. They must now wed maidens of their own class, and live apart from the community: their magical practices are feared by the people—the connec-tion of wits and witchcraft is obvious—and all private quarrels are traced to them. It has been observed that the blacksmith has ever been looked upon with awe by barbarians on the same principle that made Vulcan a deity. In Abyssinia all artisans are Budah, sorcerers, especially the blacksmith, and he is a social outcast as amongst the Somal; even in Al-Hijaz, a land, unlike El-Yemen, opposed to distinctions amongst Moslems, the Khala-wiyah, who work in metal, are considered vile. Throughout the rest of al-Islam, the blacksmith is respected as treading in the path of David, the father of the craft.

The word 'Tomal', opposed to Somal, is indigenous. 'Handad' is palpably a corruption of the Arabic 'Haddad', ironworker.

The Midgan, 'one-hand', corresponds with Khadim of al Yemen: he is called Rami or 'archer', by the Arabs. There are three distinct tribes of this people, who are numerous in the Somali country: the best genealogists cannot trace their origin, though some are silly enough to derive them, like the Akhdam, from Shimr. All, however, agree in expelling the Midgan from the gentle blood of Somaliland, and his position has been compared to that of Freedman amongst the Romans. These people take service under the different chiefs, who sometimes entertained great numbers to aid in forays and frays; they do not, however, confine themselves to one craft. Many Midgans employ themselves in hunting and agriculture. Instead of spear and shield, they carry bows and a quiver full of diminutive arrows, barbed and poisoned with the Waba—a weapon used from Faizoghli to the Cape of Good Hope. Like the Veddah of Ceylon, the Midgan is a poor shot, and scarcely strong enough to draw his stiff bow. He is accused of maliciousness; and the twanging of his string will put to flight a whole village. The poison is greatly feared: it causes, say the people, the hair and nails to drop off, and kills a man in half an hour. The only treatment known is instant excision of the part; and this is done the more frequently, because here, as in other parts of Africa, such *stigmates* are deemed ornamental.

In appearance the Midgan is dark and somewhat stunted; he is known to the people by peculiarities of countenance and accent.

3 'The Porter and the Three Ladies of Baghdad' is one of the better known stories, and Burton in his telling did not omit the bawdy words. These were left out in E. W. Lane's edition of 1865, but were included in Burton's famous 'plain and literal translation of the *Arabian Nights' Entertainments*', published in sixteen volumes in 1885 (see p. 82, vol. I, *The Book of a Thousand Nights and a Night*, by Richard F. Burton, printed in Benares by the Kamashastra Society (for private subscribers only), 1885). In the Foreword (p. ix) Burton wrote: 'Nor was it only in Arabia that the immortal Nights did me such notable service: I found the wildlings of Somaliland equally amenable to its discipline; no one was deaf to the charm and the two women cooks of my caravan, on its way to Harar, were incontinently dubbed by my men "Shehrazade" and "Deenarzade".' The Somalis also called one of their companions the 'Kalendar' because he had only one eye; Burton had followed up the Porter's tale with that of the three Kalandars (or Kalenders), the three royal mendicants who had each lost an eye; the Police Sergeant was 'the porter'.—Ed.

4 The Moslem rosary consists of ninety-nine beads divided into sets of thirty-three each by some peculiar sign, as a bit of red coral. The consulter, beginning at a chance place, counts up to the mark: if the number of beads be odd, he sets down a single dot, if even, two. This is done four times, when a figure is produced as in the margin. Of these there are sixteen, each having its peculiar name and properties. The art is merely Geomancy in its rudest shape; a mode of vaticination [prophecy] which, from its wide diffusion, must be of high antiquity. The Arabs call it Al-Ramel, and ascribe its present form to the Imam Ja'afar al-Sadik; amongst them it is a ponderous study, connected as usual with astrology. Napoleon's *Book of Fate* is a specimen of the old Eastern superstition presented to Europe in a modern and simple form.

o o

o

o

o o

5 Dr. I. M. Lewis considers that witchcraft is more Arab than Somali in origin: 'Where tensions are resolved as freely by fighting as they are in Somaliland, there is little need of witchcraft. . . . Accordingly the sociologist who constantly looks for this or that custom

in some non-Islamic system of supernatural belief is likely to be disappointed. He found Somalis eminently practical; when he asked why they abstained from sexual relations on the eve of a battle or raiding party he was told 'that sexual intercourse was exhausting, and that tired men who were not fully alert could hardly be expected to give a good account of themselves' (*A Pastoral Democracy*, O.U.P., 1961).—Ed.

III. EXCURSIONS NEAR ZAYLA

1 The Arabs were probably the earliest colonists of this coast. Even the Sawahil people retain a tradition that their forefathers originated in the south of Arabia.

To the present day the district of Gozi is peopled by Mohammedans called Arablet, 'whose progenitors', according to Harris, 'are said by tradition to have been left there prior to the reign of Nagasi, first king of Shoa. Hossain, Wahabit, and Abdool Kurreem, generals probably detached from the victorious army of Graan (Mohammed Gragne), are represented to have come from Meccah, and to have taken possession of the country— the legend assigning to the first of these warriors as his capital, the populous village of Medina, which is conspicuous on a cone among the mountains, shortly after entering the valley of Robi.'

2 The Turks, under a show of protecting commerce, established these posts in their different ports. But they soon made it appear that the end proposed was only to ascertain who were the subjects from whom they could levy the most enormous extortions. Jeddah, Zabid, and Mocha, the places of consequence nearest to Abyssinia on the Arabian coast, Suakin, a seaport town on the very barriers of Abyssinia, in the immediate way of their caravan to Cairo on the African side, were each under the command of a Turkish Pasha, and garrisoned by Turkish troops sent thither from Constantinople by the Emperors Salim and Sulayman.

3 Bartema's account of its productions is as follows: 'The soil beareth wheat and hath abundance of flesh and divers other commodious things. It hath also oil, not of olives, but of some other thing, I know not what. There is also plenty of honey and wax; there are likewise certain sheep having their tails of the weight of sixteen pounds, and exceeding fat; the head and neck are black, and all the rest white. There are also sheep altogether white, and having tails of a cubit long, and hanging down like a great cluster of grapes, and have also great laps of skin hanging down from their throats, as have bulls and oxen, hanging down almost to the ground. There are also certain kind with horns like unto harts' horns; these are wild, and when they be taken are given to the Sultan of that city as a kingly present. I saw there also certain kind having only one horn in the midst of the forehead, as hath the unicorn, and about a span of length, but the horn bendeth backward: they are of bright shining red colour. But they that have harts' horns are inclining black colour. Living is there good and cheap.'

[As Burton wrote in his appendix II of Vol. 2, of his pilgrimage to Mecca and Medina, Ludovicus Vertomannus or Ludovico Bartema, was the first of the pilgrims to Mecca and Medina who has left an account of the Holy Cities, published in Rome in 1510.—Ed.]

4 Occasionally at Zayla—where all animals are expensive—Dankali camels may be bought: though small, they resist hardship and fatigue better than the other kinds. A fair price would be about ten dollars. The Somal divide their animals into two kinds, Gel Ad and Ayyun. The former is of white colour, loose and weak, but valuable, I was told by Lieut. Speke, in districts where little water is found: the Ayyun is darker and stronger; its price averages about a quarter more than the Gel Ad.

To the Arabian traveller nothing can be more annoying than these Somali camels. They must be fed four hours during the day, otherwise they cannot march. They die from change of food or sudden removal to another country. Their backs are ever being galled, and, with all precautions, a month's march lays them up for three times that period. They are never used for riding except in cases of sickness or accidents.

5 The following is an extract from the Pharmaceutical Journal, vol. xii, No. v, Nov. 1,

1852. Notes upon the drugs observed at Aden, Arabia, by James Vaughan, Esq., M.R.C.S.E., Assist. Surg., B.A., Civil and Port. Surg., Aden, Arabia.

'Kât, the name of the drug which is brought into Aden from the interior, and largely used, especially by the Arabs, as a pleasurable excitant. It is generally imported in small camel-loads, consisting of a number of parcels, each containing about forty slender twigs with the leaves attached, and carefully wrapped so as to prevent as much as possible exposure to the atmosphere. The leaves form the edible part, and these, when chewed, are said to produce great hilarity of spirits and an agreeable state of wakefulness. Some estimate may be formed of the strong predilection which the Arabs have for this from the quantity used in Aden alone, which averages about 280 camel-loads annually. The market price is one and a quarter rupees per parcel, and the exclusive privilege of selling it is farmed by the government for 1,500 rupees per year.' [Burton gives a great deal more information from publications.—Ed.]

⁶ The price of blood in the Somali country is the highest sanctioned by al-Islam. It must be remembered that amongst the pagan Arabs, the Koraysh 'diyat', was twenty she-camels. Abd al-Muttalib, grandfather of Mohammed, sacrificed 100 animals to ransom the life of his son, forfeited by a rash vow, and from that time the greater became the legal number. The Somal usually demand 100 she-camels, or 300 sheep and a few cows; here, as in Arabia, the sum is made up by all the near relations of the slayer; 30 of the animals may be aged, and 30 under age, but the rest must be sound and good. Many tribes take less—from strangers 100 sheep, a cow, and a camel; but after the equivalent is paid, the murderer or one of his clan, contrary to the spirit of al-Islam, is generally killed by the kindred or tribe of the slain. When blood is shed in the same tribe, the full reparation, if accepted by the relatives, is always exacted; this serves the purpose of preventing fratricidal strife, for in such a nation of murderers, only the Diyat prevents the taking of life.

Blood money, however is seldom accepted unless the murdered man has been slain with a lawful weapon. Those who kill with the Dankalah, a poisonous juice rubbed upon meat, are always put to death by the members of their own tribe.

IV. THE SOMAL, THEIR ORIGIN AND PECULIARITIES

¹ The Aden stone has been supposed to name the 'Berbers', who must have been Gallas from the vicinity of Berbera. A certain amount of doubt still hangs on the interpretation: the Rev. Mr. Forster and Dr. Bird being the principal contrasts.

Rev. Mr. Forster.	Dr. Bird.
'We assailed with cries of hatred and rage the Abyssinians and Berbers. 'We rode forth wrathfully against this refuse of mankind.'	'He, the Syrian philosopher in Abadan, Bishop of Cape Aden, who inscribed this in the desert, blesses the institution of the faith.'

[The 'stone' was the first to be discovered in Aden with an Hymiaritic inscription; it was found in 1842 twenty feet below the surface and described as 'a circular slab of pure and very compact white marble, with a raised rim round it and apparently forming part of an altar'. It was sent to the Government of Bombay with a report dated September 29, 1842, by Captain S. B. Haines, Political Resident in Aden.

Burton referred to it because it was thought that the inscription had a reference to 'Berbers', but it was not deciphered correctly. According to Mr. T. L. Fenton of the British Museum the inscription is to the following effect: 'Našakarib son of Rabib. Evil and stripes(?) upon whoever steals it'. Captain Haines certainly did suffer evil, being imprisoned by the Government of the East India Company.—Ed.]

² Excision was and is practised by a number of races (see Appendix 2) and is not very conclusive proof that they were the progenitors of the Somali. 'Whether the Somali are simply Arabized Galla, or whether they are a separate Cushitic group who reached Somaliland after the Galla, remain undetermined,' states Dr. I. M. Lewis in *A Pastoral*

Democracy, p. 23. He considers it more likely that they belong to an independent Hamitic ethnic group subjected to Arab influence. They 'delight in vaunting those traditions which proclaim their descent from noble Arab lineages and from the family of the Prophet. These claims, dismissed by Somali nationalists today as fanciful, are nevertheless part and parcel of the traditional and profound Somali attachment to Islam' (see pp. 4, 5, *The Modern History of Somaliland*, by Dr. I. M. Lewis, Weidenfeld and Nicolson, 1965).—Ed.

3 'Burton left us a very poor opinion of the Somali', wrote Ralph Drake-Brockman, 'but it must be remembered that his knowledge of him was not only small, but was almost entirely limited to the northern tribes, which, most travellers seem agreed, do not compare favourably with the Ishaak and Darod tribes'; these tribes did not, as did the Eesa, murder men in cold blood in order to obtain the right to marry (*British Somaliland*, by Ralph E. Drake-Brockman, Hurst and Blackett, 1912).—Ed.

4 The fact that there is no written language often leads to a high development of eloquence and of poetry. Burton may have found this strange because 'in Sindh and India, on the contrary, every local variety of dialect has its own syllabarium modified from the Arabic or the Sanscrit'; (see Appendix 3 on the Harari language which was also unwritten).

In *Somali Poetry an Introduction*, by B. W. Andrzejewski and I. M. Lewis (Clarendon Press, 1964), it is stated: 'Poetry is frequently employed to publicize events and as propaganda for or against some person, group, or matter of concern . . . Truly memorable verse persists for generations . . . and in many cases is known throughout the length and breadth of the Somali Peninsula—from the Gulf of Aden to the Northern Province of Kenya.'—Ed.

5 The artificial causes (those referred to in Appendix 2), were disapproved of by Burton: 'The moral effect of female circumcision is peculiar. While it diminishes the heat of passion it increases licentiousness, and breeds a debauchery of mind far worse than bodily unchastity, because accompanied by a peculiar cold cruelty and a taste for artificial stimulants to "luxury" ' (quoted p. 105, *Burton*, by Byron Farwell, Longmans, 1963). It is surprising that Burton found the women of cold temperament.—Ed.

6 Since defibulation on the wedding night was a painful operation it is unlikely that Burton's story about the bridegroom horse-whipping the bride is correct. 'I can hardly credit its ever having been a common practice,' wrote Drake-Brockman, 'as the unfortunate woman is always suffering for the first few days of her married life from the after-effects of a barbarous operation and is hardly likely to show any propensity to "shrewishness" ' (*British Somaliland*, p. 30).—Ed.

V. FROM ZAYLA TO THE HILLS

1 The following list of my expenses may perhaps be useful to future travellers. It must be observed that, had the whole outfit been purchased at Aden, a considerable saving would have resulted:

	Rupees
Passage money from Aden to Zayla	33
Presents at Zayla	100
Price of four mules with saddles and bridles	225
Price of four camels	88
Provisions (tobacco, rice, dates, etc.) for three months . . .	428
Price of 150 Tobes	357
Nine pieces of indigo-dyed cotton	16
Minor expenses (cowhides for camels, mats for tents, presents to Arabs, a box of beads, three handsome Abyssinian Tobes bought for chiefs)	166
Expenses at Berbera, and passage back to Aden	77

Total Rupees 1,490 = £149

² Snakes are rare in the cities, but abound in the wilds of Eastern Africa, and are dangerous to night travellers, though seldom seen by day. To kill a serpent is considered by the Bedouin almost as meritorious as to slay an Infidel. The Somal have many names for the reptile tribe. The Subhanyo, a kind of whipsnake, and a large yellow rock snake called Got, are little feared. The Abesi (in Arabic Al-Hayyah—the Cobra) is so venomous that it kills the camel; the Mass or Hanash, and a long black snake called Jibis, are considered equally dangerous. Serpents are in Somaliland the subject of many superstitions. One horn of the Cerastes, for instance, contains a deadly poison: the other, pounded and drawn across the eye, makes man a seer and reveals to him the treasures of the earth. There is a flying snake which hoards precious stones, and is attended by a hundred guards: a Somali horseman once, it is said, carried away a jewel; he was pursued by a reptile army, and although he escaped to his tribe, the importunity of the former proprietors was so great that the plunder was eventually restored to them. Centipedes are little feared; their venom leads to inconveniences more ridiculous than dangerous. Scorpions, especially the large yellow variety, are formidable in hot weather: I can speak of the sting from experience. The first symptom is a sensation of nausea, and the pain shoots up after a few minutes to the groin, causing a swelling accompanied by burning and throbbing, which last about twelve hours. The Somal bandage above the wound and wait patiently till the effect subsides

³ Mr. Drake-Brockman has other views: 'I know of no natives that can compare with them [the Somali] for trekking in a dry and waterless country. Their powers of endurance are at times nothing short of marvellous' (*British Somaliland*, p. 96).—Ed.

⁴ The Somali Tol or Tul corresponds with the Arabic Kabilah, a tribe; under it is the Kola or Jilib (Ar. Fakhizah), a clan. 'Gob', is synonymous with the Arabic Kabail, 'men of family', opposed to 'Gum', the caste-less. In the following pages I shall speak of the Somali *nation*, the Eesa tribe, the Rer Musa *clan*, and the Rer Galan *sept*, though by no means sure that such verbal graduation is generally recognized.

The Eesa for instance, are divided into—

1. Rer Wardik (the royal clan).	6. Rer Hurroni.
2. Rer Abdullah.	7. Rer Urwena.
3. Rer Musa.	8. Rer Furlabah.
4. Rer Mummasan.	9. Rer Gada.
5. Rer Gulani.	10. Rer Ali Addah.

These are again subdivided: the Rer Musa (numbering half the Eesa, split up, for instance, into—

1. Rer Galan.	4. Rer Dubbah.
2. Rer Harlah.	5. Rer Kul.
3. Rer Gadishah.	6. Rer Gedi.

⁵ The most dangerous disease is small-pox, which history traces to Eastern Abyssinia, where it still becomes at times a violent epidemic, sweeping off its thousands. The patient, if a man of note, is placed upon the sand, and fed with rice and millet bread till he recovers or dies. The chicken-pox kills many infants; they are treated by bathing in the fresh blood of a sheep, covered with the skin, and exposed to the sun. Smoke and glare, dirt and flies, cold winds and naked extremities, cause ophthalmia, especially in the hills, this disease rarely blinds any save the citizens, and no remedy is known. Dysentery is cured by rice and sour milk, patients also drink clarified cow's butter; and in bad cases the stomach is cauterised, fire and disease, according to the Somal, never co-existing. Hæmorrhoids, when dry, are reduced by a stick used as a bougie and allowed to remain in *loco* all night. Sometimes the part affected is cupped with a horn and knife, or a leech performs excision. The diet is camels' or goats' flesh and milk; clarified butter and Bussorah dates—rice and mutton are carefully avoided. For a certain local disease, they use Senna or colocynth, anoint the body with sulphur boiled in ghi, and expose it to the sun, or they leave the

patient all night in the dew; abstinence and perspiration generally effect a cure. For the minor form, the afflicted drink the melted fat of a sheep's tail. Consumption is a family complaint, and therefore considered incurable; to use the Somali expression, they address the patient with 'Allah have mercy upon thee!' not with 'Allah cure thee!'

There are leeches who have secret simples for curing wounds. Generally the blood is squeezed out, the place is washed with water, the lips are sewn up and a dressing of astringent leaves is applied. They have splints for fractures, and they can reduce dislocations.

VI. FROM THE ZAYLA HILLS TO THE MARAR PRAIRIE

1 It is a round stiff evergreen, not unlike a bay, seldom taller than twenty feet, affecting hill sides and torrent banks, growing in clumps that look black by the side of the Acacias; thornless, with a laurel-coloured leaf, which cattle will not touch, unless forced by famine, pretty bunches of pinkish-white flowers, and edible berries black and ripening to red. The bark is thin, the wood yellow, compact, exceedingly tough and hard, the root somewhat like liquorice; the latter is prepared by trituration and other processes, and the produce is a poison in substance and colour resembling pitch.

Travellers have erroneously supposed the arrow poison of Eastern Africa to be the sap of a Euphorbium.

[Burton gives a long account of experiments carried out with the poison by Dr. F. S. Arnott in Aden on sheep and dogs, which has been omitted.—Ed.]

2 See 'The Ruined Towns of Somaliland', by A. T. Curle in *Antiquity*, pp. 315 to 327 vol. XI, 1937, No. 43. There is a description and photograph of the tomb of Shaykh Au Boba (Burton's Shaykh Aububah), and an account and photograph of the ruined town of Amud, referred to by Burton as Ahammed and which he did not visit. There is also a good map of the area facing page 316 showing the ruined towns.

Mr. Curle writes: 'Although none of the inland sites investigated can be identified for certain with any one mentioned in the histories or chronicles, it seems probable that they formed part of the seven Mohammedan provinces which existed in the fourteenth-century in the east and south of Ethiopia, and two of these, namely, Hadya and Adal, can be recognized as the ancient counterpart of Harar and Zayla. As most of the ruined towns lie between Zayla and Harar it is impossible to say to which of these provinces they belonged, but one can clearly associate them with the trade of Zayla, which served as their port.'

The early graves with their phallic stones are described by Mr. Curle in *Carved Stones, British Somaliland*, pp. 352–5; one of these is in the Department of Ethnology at the British Museum.—Ed.

3 The Abodi devours small deer and birds: the female lays a single egg in a large loose nest on the summit of a tall tree, and she abandons her home when the hand of man has violated it. The Somal have many superstitions connected with this eagle: if it touch a child the latter dies, unless protected by the talismanic virtues of the 'Hajar Abodi', a stone found in the bird's body. As it frequently swoops upon children carrying meat, the belief has doubtlessly frequently fulfilled itself.

4 The Ayyal Yunis, the principal clan, contains four septs, viz.—

1. Jibril Yunis.	3. Ali Yunis.
2. Nur Yunis.	4. Adan Yunis.

The other chief clans are—

1. Mikahil Dera.	7. Basannah.
2. Rer Ugaz.	8. Bahabr Hasan
3. Jibrain.	9. Abdillah Mikahil.
4. Rer Mohammed Asa	10. Hasan Mikahil.
5. Musa Fin.	11. Eyah Mikahil.
6. Rer Abokr	12. Hasan Waraba.

VII. FROM THE MARAR PRAIRIE TO HARAR

1 They are, however, divided into clans, of which the following are the principal: 1. Bahawiyah, the race which supplies the Gerads. 2. Abu Yunis (divided into ten septs). 3. Rer Ibrahim (similarly divided). 4. Jibril. 5. Bakasiyya. 6. Rer Madmud. 7. Musa Dar. 8. Rer Auro. 9. Rer Walembo. 10. Rer Khalid.

2 When the Earl of Ellesmere, in his presidential address to the Royal Geographical Society, reported on the journey it was clear that the position of the upper waters of the Nile continued to be the main interest. 'Lieut. Burton's bold journey from Zayla to Harar,' he stated, 'placed him in that city on an altitude of 5,000 feet, in a delightful climate, on the eastern flank of the mountains, running north and south, which appear to separate the waters of the Nile from those flowing to the Indian Ocean; and which [the mountains] are stated by the missionaries Krapf and Rebmann to ascend above the snow line in the two peaks called by them "Kenia and Kilimanjaro"; the same range farther south forming also the probable basin of the Lake N'yassi.' (Presidential address of May 1855; *Journal of the Royal Geographical Society*, vol. 25.)

3 The following is a table of our stations, directions, and distances:

			Miles
1. From Zayla to Gudingaras	. . . . .	S.E.165^6	19
2. To Kuranyali	. . . .	145^6	8
3. To Adad	, , , , , , , , ,	225^6	25
4. To Damal	. . . .	205^6	11
5. To Al-Armo	. . . .	190^6	11
6. To Jiyaf	. . . .	202^6	10
7. To Halimalah (the Holy Tree, about half way)	. .	192^6	7
			— 91 miles.
8. To Aububah	. . . .	245^6	21
9. To Koralay	. . . .	165^6	25
10. To Harar	. . . .	160^6	65
			111 miles.

Total statute miles 202

VIII. TEN DAYS AT HARAR

1 Other details of interest were contained in Burton's report to the Royal Geographical Society: 'I was called upon by the Wazir or Prime Minister, who sat upon a rug on the right of and below the throne, to answer a variety of questions concerning my name, nation and business at Harar. The replies proving, it is presumed, satisfactory, I was invited to become the prince's guest during my ten days' residence, and received every day three dishes of bread and beef from his own kitchen. At subsequent visits I was admitted to the honour of a seat next to the Wazir, and the Amir did not disdain to be indoctrinated with the principles of free-trade in coffee and cotton. Slavery was a more delicate topic, and not being authorized to treat upon the subject officially I contented myself with observing its operations . . .

'The Government may briefly be described as the Amir. This petty prince, whose signet bears the grandiose title of "Sultan son of Sultan", is by origin a Galla, by pretension a descendant from the Caliph Abibakr . . . The Amir preserves all the dignity of Empire. Those presented to him must kiss the back and palm of his hand. He must not be stared at. When his cough affects him an attendant presents the hem of his robe' ('Narrative of a trip to Harar', by Richard Burton, read June 11, 1855, *Journal of the Royal Geographical Society*, vol. 25, pp. 136-50).—Ed.

2 'The Harar Chief's nightmare', wrote Burton, 'is the idea that Sharmakay may one day occupy Berbera in force. Harar is a purely commercial city which, like Zayla, thrives

by systematically and by order of the Governor cozening and defrauding the ignorant Galla Bedouin. The citizens obtain for a nothing of cotton the rich produce of the wide lands lying westward of Harar. This they export twice or thrice a year to Berbera and sell or barter for "dungaree", indigo-dyed cotton, black satin, surat tobacco, beads, trinkets, and other foreign articles. The trade is capable of great development demanding no conditions but a safe road and a ready market at Berbera' (Burton's official report to Bombay of February 22, 1855, 'Enclosures to Secret Letters from Bombay', January to April 1855).—Ed.

3 'My speedy dismissal,' wrote Burton, 'was perhaps owing to a report that three brothers had been sent by the Government of India to Eastern Africa. Visions of cutting off caravans induced the Amir to get rid of me, he being, it is said, much puzzled how to treat so uncommon a case. Yet I had no reason to complain of him; and as a proof that my modest endeavours to establish friendly relations were not unsuccessful, the Prince wrote, immediately after my departure to Aden, requesting to be furnished with a "Frank physician". ' (Report to the Royal Geographical Society on June 11, 1855, as quoted above.)

Brigadier Coghlan, when he received the letter, was circumspect and wrote to Bombay on March 14, 1855: 'As it is important for the Somali Expedition and for the future opening out of the African trade that this Chief should be conciliated, I have accordingly dispatched a Sayyed, who pretends to some slight medical skill to him. In the event of failing to alleviate his sufferings which, as the Amir's disease is consumption, is a certainty, the Holiness of this man's descent will render it impossible that any suspicion of poisoning the Amir should operate against him.' Coghlan paid the Sayed twenty German crowns and sent presents to the Amir of a gun, a pair of pistols, and some scarlet cloth. The Amir died in September or October of the following year and was succeeded by a relative ('Letters from Aden', vol. 34, March 14, 1855, and 'Letters from Aden', vol. 35, October 10, 1856).—Ed.

IX. A RIDE TO BERBERA

1 The Habr Girhajis, or eldest branch of the sons of Ishak (generally including the children of 'Arab'), inhabit the Ghauts behind Berbera, whence they extend for several days' march towards Ogadayn, the southern region. This tribe is divided into a multitude of clans. The Ismail Arrah supply the Sultan, a nominal chief like the Eesa Ugaz; they extend from Makhar to the south of Gulays, number about 15,000 shields and are subdivided into three septs. The Musa Arrah hold the land between Gulays and the seats of the Mijjarthayn and Warsingali tribes on the windward coast. The Ishak Arrah count 5,000 or 6,000 shields, and inhabit the Gulays Range. The other sons of Arrah (the fourth in descent from Ishak), namely, Mikahil, Gambah, Daudan, and others, also became founders of small clans. The Ayyal Da'ud, facetiously called 'Idagallah' or earth-burrowers, and sprung from the second son of Girhajis, claim the country south of the Habr Awal, reckon about 4,000 shields, and are divided into 11 or 12 septs.

As has been noticed, the Habr Girhajis have a perpetual blood feud with the Habr Awal, and, even at Aden, they have fought out their quarrels with clubs and stones. Yet as cousins they willingly unite against a common enemy, the Eesa for instance, and become the best of friends.

X. BERBERA AND ITS ENVIRONS

1 Yunis and Ahmad were brothers, children of Nuh, the ninth in descent from Ishak al-Hazrami. The former had four sons, Hosh Yunis, Gadid Yunis, Mahmud Yunis, and Shirdon Yunis; their descendants are all known as the Ayyal or progeny of Yunis. The Ayyal Ahmad Nuh hold the land immediately behind the town, and towards the Ghauts, blend with the Eesa Musa. The Mikahil claims the Eastern country from Siyaro to Illanti, a wooded valley affording good water and bad anchorage to wind-bound vessels.

² This part of Somaliland is a sandy plain, thinly covered with thorns and bounded by two ranges, the Ghauts and Sub-Ghauts. The latter or maritime mountains begin at Tajjurah, and extend to Karam (long. 46° E.), where they break into detached groups; the distance from the coast varies from 6 to 15 miles, the height from 2,000 to 3,000 feet, and the surface is barren, the rock being denuded of soil by rain. The Ghauts lie from 8 to 40 miles from the sea, they average from 4,000 to 6,000 feet, are thickly covered with gum-arabic and frankincense trees, the wild fig and the Somali pine, and form the seaward wall of the great table-land of the interior. The Northern or maritime face is precipitous, the summit is tabular and slopes gently southwards. The general direction is E. by N. and W. by S., there are, however, some spurs at the three hills termed 'Ourat', which project to-wards the north. Each portion of the plain between these ranges has some local name, such as the 'Shimberali Valley' extending westwards from the detached hill Dimoli, to Geuli Dinanjir, and Gularkar. Intersected with Fiumaras which roll torrents during the monsoon, they are covered with a scrub of thorns, wild fig, aloe, and different kinds of Cactus.

³ The Abban is now the pest of Berbera. Before vessels have cast anchor, or indeed have rounded the Spit, a crowd of Somal, eager as hotel-touters, may be seen running along the strand. They swim off, and the first who arrives on board inquires the name of the Abban; if there be none he touches the captain or one of the crew and constitutes him-self protector. For merchandise sent forward, the man who conveys it becomes answerable.

The system of dues has become complicated. Formerly, the standard of value at Berbera was two cubits of the blue cotton stuff called Sauda, this is now converted into four pice of specie. Dollars form the principal currency; rupees are taken at a discount. Traders pay according to degree, the lowest being one per cent., taken from Maskat and Suri merchants. The shopkeeper provides food for his Abban, and presents him at the close of the season with a Tobe, a pair of sandals, and half a dozen dollars. Wealthy Banyans and Mehmans give food and raiment, and before departure from 50 to 200 dollars. This class, however, derive large profits: they will lend a few dollars to the Bedouin at the end of the Fair, on condition of receiving cent. per cent., at the opening of the next season. Travellers not transacting business must feed the protector, but cannot properly be forced to pay him. Of course the Somal take every advantage of Europeans. Mr. Angelo, a merchant from Zanzibar, resided two months at Bulhar; his broker of the Ayyal Gadid tribe, and an Arab who accompanied him, extracted, it is said, 3,000 dollars. As a rule the Abban claims one per cent. on sales and purchases, and two dollars per head of slaves. For each bale of cloth, half a dollar in coin is taken; on gums and coffee the duty is one pound in twenty-seven. Cowhides pay half a dollar each, sheep and goat's-skins four pice, and ghi about one per cent.

Lieut. Herne calculates that the total money dues during the Fair-season amount to 2,000 dollars, and that, in the present reduced state of Berbera, not more than 10,000l. worth of merchandise is sold. This estimate the natives of the place declare to be consider-ably under the mark.

⁴ The Habr Tul Jailah (mother of the tribe of Mailah) descendants of Ishak al-Hazrami by a slave girl, inhabit the land eastward of Berbera. Their principal settlements after Aynterad are the three small ports of Karam, Unkor and Hais. The former, according to Lieut. Cruttenden, is 'the most important from its possessing a tolerable harbour, and from its being the nearest point from Aden, the course to which place is N. N. W.—conse-quently the wind is fair, and the boats laden with sheep for the Aden market pass but one night at sea, whilst those from Berbera are generally three. What greatly enhances the value of Kurrum (Karam), however, is its proximity to the country of the Dulbahanteh, who approach within four days of Kurrum, and who therefore naturally have their chief trade through that port. The Ahl Yusuf, a branch of the Habr Tel Jailah, at present hold possession of Kurrum, and between them and the tribes to windward there exists a most bitter and irreconcileable feud, the consequence of sundry murders perpetrated about five years since at Kurrum, and which hitherto have not been avenged. The small ports of

Aynterad, Unkor, Hais, and Rukudah are not worthy of mention, with the exception of the first named place, which has a trade with Aden in sheep.'

XI. PLANNING THE EXPEDITION TO ZANZIBAR

1 Burton's official report on his journey to Harar of February 22, 1855 (No. 28 of 1855), sent by Brigadier Coghlan, Acting Political Resident and Commandant at Aden, to Anderson, Secretary of the Government of Bombay, is contained in 'Secret Department. Enclosures to Secret Letters from Bombay', January to April 1855; India Office Library.

2 It was named the 'Haines river' by Lieut. W. Christoper, I. N., as a tribute to Captain Haines, the first Political Resident in Aden and perhaps lost the name after Captain Haines was arrested and imprisoned by the Bombay Government (see 'Journal by Lieut. W. Christoper, Commanding the H. C. Brig-of-War *Tigris* on the East Coast of Africa', May 8, 1843, *Journal of the Royal Geographical Society* vol. 14, p. 96).

3 *What Led to the Discovery of the Source of the Nile*, p. 21, note, and p. 109.

4 *The Life*, vol. 1, pp. 322, 323.

5 Burton's comment on Lieut. Speke's diary in Appendix I of *First Footsteps*, pp. 502, 503. 1st ed.

6 *What Led to the Discovery of the Source of the Nile*, pp. 111, 112; subsequent quotation pp. 120, 121.

POSTSCRIPT

1 Burton is here, for some reason, very lenient to Burhale Nuh considering what a bad opinion he had of him. A week before the attack on the camp, Burton had written from Camp Berbera, April 12, to Brigadier Coghlan saying that Burhale Nuh should be struck off the list in Aden of capable servants as he had in Lieut. Herne's service 'distinguished himself only by rapacity, insolence and by throwing obstacles in that officer's way' (Coghlan forwarded Burton's letter on April 20, 'Bombay Secret Consultations', April 7 to June 27, vol. 2, 1855).

Before Burton's departure from Aden for Berbera in February, and presumably with his knowledge, a letter was written from Aden to Speke warning him to have nothing to do with Burhale Nuh, as he had proved himself 'an infamous scoundrel'. This letter, which had not been opened, was brought to Lieut. Playfair in November 1856 when he went to make a treaty with the Habr Awal tribe to end the blockade. The letter was one of the relics of the attack on Burton's camp at Berbera. 'I have little doubt,' wrote Playfair, 'that Barallie [Burhale Nuh] was in some manner connected with the attack' (Report from Lieut. R. S. Playfair to Coghlan, November 9, 1856, contained in 'Letters from Aden', vol. 35, Coghlan to Anderson, Bombay, November 9, 1856).—Ed.

XII. BURTON ATTACKED IN OFFICIAL REPORTS

1 *What Led to the Discovery of the Source of the Nile*; these and subsequent quotations, pp. 144 and 145.

2 Coghlan to Anderson, April 23 1855 (No. 55 of 1855) 'Bombay Secret Consultations', April 7 to June 17, 1855, vol. 2, enclosing reports from Burton, Speke and Herne. The earlier report from Burton is dated Camp Berbera, April 12, 1855.

3 This was certainly an unwise move and it must have been galling to Burton to read in *What Led to the Discovery of the Source of the Nile* (p. 112), Speke's comments on the idea of suppressing the Abbanship: 'This perhaps was scarcely the right time to dictate a policy which would be distasteful as well as injurious (in a monetary sense) to the people among whom we were about to travel, and with whom it was highly essential to our interest to be on friendly terms.' Speke asked Playfair for his opinion which was added as a note: 'In this Lieutenant Burton erred; and this was the *termina cause* of all the mishaps which befell the expedition ... A traveller who hopes for success in exploring a new country must accept the institutions he finds in existence; he can hardly hope by his simple *fiat*, to revolutionize the time-honoured and *most profitable* institutions of a people,

amongst whom precedent is a law as unchangeable as that of the Medes and Persians.

[4] The official reports are from 'Bombay Secret Consultations, April 7 to June 27', vol. 2; minute by the Rt. Hon. Governor (Lord Elphinstone), May 12, 1855, No. 316; minute by the Hon. Mr. Lumsden, May 26, 1855, No. 307.

[5] Ibid, Coghlan to Anderson, No. 63 of 1855, May 7, 1855.

[6] *Journal of the Royal Geographical Society*, vol. 25, 1855. Burton's official report to Bombay of April 23 on the Berbera disaster was sent to Lord Ellesmere by the Directors of the East India Company, who also probably sent on the subsequent criticisms from the Governor of Bombay and the Governor-General of India.

[7] 'Bombay Secret Consultations', July 11 to October 1855, vol. 3, No. 296, from G. H. Edmonton, Secretary to the Governor-General of India to H. L. Anderson (Bombay), dated Ootacamund, June 29, 1855.

[8] 'Letters from Aden', vol. 34, Coghlan to Anderson, November 8, 1855.

[9] 'Enclosures to Secret Letters from Bombay,' October to December 1855; Lieut. R. L. Playfair (in charge of Residency in absence of Brigadier Coghlan) to H. L. Anderson, Bombay, October 14, 1855.

[10] Report from Coghlan to Bombay of November 26, 1855, 'Letters from Aden', vol. 34, No. 55, of 1855.

[11] 'Enclosures to Secret Letters from Bombay,' October to December 1855; Resolution of the Bombay Council, December 15, 1855.

[12] 'Letters from Aden', vol. 34, Coghlan to Anderson, December 27, 1855.

[13] *The Lake Regions of Central Africa*, by Richard F. Burton, vol. I, p. 68n, London, 1860.

[14] Ibid.

[15] *The Life*, vol. 2, Appendix H.

[16] *Layard of Nineveh* by Gordon Waterfield, p. 37, John Murray, 1963.

[17] 'Political Letters to Bombay,' 1855, vol. 17, Letter from London dated August 1855.

[18] Lieut. Playfair's report of November 9, 1856, included in Coghlan's report to Anderson (Bombay) of the same date, 'Letters from Aden', vol. 35.

[19] Burton's letter of December 15, 1856, published in Appendix II of vol. 2, *The Lake Regions of Central Africa;* also in *The Life*, vol. 2, Appendix F.

[20] Ibid.

[21] 'Bombay Secret Consultations', Government of India to Bombay, July 28, 1856 (see also *Britain's Imperial Role in the Red Sea Area 1800–1878*, p. 215).

Index

309

INDEX